Sustainable Urbanism and Direct Action

Radical Subjects in International Politics

Series Editor: Ruth Kinna

This series uses the idea of political subjection to promote the discussion and analysis of individual, communal, and civic participation and activism. "Radical subjects" refers both to the character of the topics and issues tacked in the series and to the ethic guiding the research. The series has a radical focus in that it provides a springboard for the discussion of activism that sits outside or on the fringes of institutional politics, yet which, insofar as it reflects a commitment to social change, is far from marginal. It provides a platform for scholarship that interrogates modern political movements; probes the local, regional, and global dimensions of activist networking and the principles that drive them; and develops innovative frames to analyze issues of exclusion and empowerment. The scope of the series is defined by engagement with the concept of the radical in contemporary politics but includes research that is multi- or interdisciplinary, working at the boundaries of art and politics, political utopianism, feminism, sociology, and radical geography.

Titles in Series:

The Crisis of Liberal Democracy and the Path Ahead
Bernd Reiter

Becoming a Movement
Identity and Narratives in the European Global Justice Movement
Priska Daphi

Liminal Subjects
Weaving (Our) Liberation
Sara C. Motta

Autonomy, Refusal and the Black Block
Positioning Class Analysis in Critical and Radical Theory
Robert F. Carley

A Post-Western Account of Critical Cosmopolitan Social Theory
Being and Acting in a Democratic World
Michael Murphy

Sustainable Urbanism and Direct Action
Case Studies in Dialectical Activism
Benjamin Heim Shepard

Sustainable Urbanism and Direct Action

Case Studies in Dialectical Activism

Benjamin Heim Shepard

ROWMAN & LITTLEFIELD
London • New York

Rowman & Littlefield
4501 Forbes Boulevard, Suite 200, Lanham, Maryland 20706, USA
With additional offices in Boulder, New York, Toronto (Canada), and Plymouth (UK)
www.rowman.com

British Library Cataloguing in Publication Data
A catalogue record for this book is available from the British Library

ISBN: HB 978-1-78348-315-0

Library of Congress Cataloging-in-Publication Data
Names: Shepard, Benjamin, 1969– author.
Title: Sustainable urbanism and direct action : case studies in dialectical activism /
   Benjamin Heim Shepard.
Description: Lanham, Maryland : Rowman & Littlefield, [2021] | Series: Radical
   subjects in international politics | Includes bibliographical references and index. |
   Summary: "Connecting urban activism to historical, philosophical and theoretical
   ideas of the dialectic, this book builds a new theoretical framework for reimagining
   the work of anarchist organizing and social movements"—Provided by publisher.
Identifiers: LCCN 2021009826 (print) | LCCN 2021009827 (ebook) | ISBN
   9781783483150 (cloth) | ISBN 9781783483174 (epub) | ISBN 9781783483167 (pbk)
Subjects: LCSH: City dwellers—Political participation. | Cities and
   towns—Social aspects. | Sociology, Urban.
Classification: LCC HT255 .S54 2021 (print) | LCC HT255 (ebook) |
   DDC 307.76—dc23
LC record available at https://lccn.loc.gov/2021009826
LC ebook record available at https://lccn.loc.gov/2021009827

Contents

Figures

Acknowledgments between the Sculptured Air of Midtown

Caroline Shepard used to have a cat named Walter. Then I came along and, for a while there, she had a Walter and a Benjamin in her life. Then Walter died. Increase, reduce, she just had Benjamin Shepard, which was not quite the same, but it would have to suffice. So, we kept on reading and talking, Walter Benjamin's books continuing to inspire our precious coffee moments, chatting about movies, authors as producers, immigrants and refugees stranded, his coming and goings, and historical materialism. Conversations with Caroline about Benjamin and the street clashes of New York City ignited this story; her paintings and photos still inspire.

Countless people took part in this conversation about what the city could be. The Public Space Party, the Center for Popular Democracy, Rise and Resist, ACT UP, San Energy Project, Extinction Rebellion, Monica, Barbara, Catherine, JC, Ken, Andrew, Emily, Wendy, Ziggy, Craig, Erik M., Jay, Fly, Virginia, Jennifer Flynn, Austin, L. A. Kauffman, Brennan, Jerry "The Peddler" Wade, and countless other peeps, activists, squatters, community gardeners, artists, gospel singers, performers, and students participated in actions, or sat for interviews, or experimented with their own recipes for sustainable urbanism. I'm thinking about Judith Kaye, who shared Seder dinner with us and got me out of jail, and Dodi for being the eternal flaneur of the city, and Scarlett, who reminded us all that streets are for sharing. Greg Smithsimon talked with me for hours on the stoop. For years, I used to talk with Spencer Sunshine about Marxism, anarchism, and Aronowitz. We went to shows, chatted, and talked it through. Thanks to Spencer for a content edit that was bar none. He may not have agreed with me, but he was generally willing to talk. And for that I am grateful. Steve Duncombe and Ron Hayduk offered wonderful clarification, suggestions, and encouragement, building on the compelling commentary from anonymous readers. Between an interview and an edit, Bill Weinberg helped in countless ways. Anna Reeves, Dhara Snowden, and the other good folks at Rowman & Littlefield believed in and engaged this story. Ian Landau gave the book a final copy edit. Stanley Aronowitz and Bertell Ollman walked me through a vast history of ideas as we sat trying to make sense of it all. Throughout nearly fifteen years of classes, with topics from Balzac to Faulkner, Marcuse to Marx, this conversation extended from war to peace, critiques of capitalism to Black Lives Matter, from the Graduate Center to Downtown Brooklyn. This history of ideas informed this project in ways they can't imagine.

Much of this manuscript was written in 2015 and 2016. A trial of editing chaos, hiking trails through Spain, a broken arm in Italy, a snorkeling trip in Jamaica, missed deadlines, disappearing editors, missing friends, lost manuscripts, a novel from San Francisco, a lost map in Shinjuku, scheduling miscues, activism, wildfires and plagues followed. As I finish this final round of edits, we are in quarantine in New York as a global pandemic changes everything. Pollution levels are falling around the world. Mother Earth seems to be taking things into her own hands. The result is a book about a current moment and a historical moment simultaneously, as history unfolds into an ever-flowing present, connected and separated with everything around it. Written in the summer of 2020, the afterword considers some of the mutual aid that took shape during this period. It is probably better that way.

I would like to acknowledge the editors of the books and journals where several of the chapters for *Sustainable Urbanism* first saw the light of day, including *Fifth Estate*, *The Brooklyn Rail*, *Contemporary Theater Review*, *Theory and Action*, *Socialism and Democracy*, *New Political Science*, *Sexualities*, *European Journal of Humour Research*, *French Review of American Studies*, *LOGOS: a journal of modern society and culture*, the edited collections *Queering Anarchism: Addressing and Undressing Power and Desire*, *Beyond Zuccotti Park*, *Environmental Social Work*, and *Ecosocial Transition of Societies: Contribution of Social Work and Social Policy*.

For the commons and comrades, the streets melting and gardens rising, Jim Carroll reminds us:

> I have walked these streets so often I could forge the shadows of skyscrapers as they fall to rest between the sculptured air of midtown.

Chapter 1

Cities as DIY Spaces: On Dialectical Activism and the Future of Cities

> This world contradicts itself. . . . Dialectical thought starts with the experi-
> ence that the world is unfree; that is to say, man and nature exist in condi-
> tions of alienation, exist as "other than they are."
>
> —To Herbert Marcuse, "A Note on the Dialectic" in *Reason and
> Revolution: Hegel and the Rise of Social Theory,* 1941/1960, vii

Alienation extends everywhere, but so does connection. This is just part of life in cities. It certainly was the other day. I was with a group of cyclists on a naked bike ride. As we zoomed down Bleecker Street, in the West Village of Manhattan, past the apartment where Bob Dylan wrote "A Hard Rain's A-Gonna Fall," this group of semi-clad and nude cyclists was ringing their bells, dancing, and vamping it up for onlookers, when a police car (disguised as a taxi cab) reeled through the traffic, its horns blaring, forcing the cyclists to pull to the side. Several cyclists were arrested in what felt like a rehash of a clash dating back to the days of the Dionysus cults (Ehrenreich, 2007; Maffe-soli, 1993, 1996). Riders expressing a sense of freedom and liberatory play, clashing with the forces of order, the conflict seemed to pit the linear logic of Apollo against the paradoxical, irrational Eros of Dionysus. It is a conflict that takes place every day here. Our sense of a carnival is their sense of disorderly conduct. A dialectic of freedom and control influences the politics of public space, lending itself to an ever-expanding understanding of our totality. The dialectic process begins with clashes between opposing forces, which merge and clash, creating new spaces for alternate approaches, social relations, con-nections, possibilities, and new categories that split anew ad infinitum. Social movements build on each other, adding new chapters, a "yes and" instead of canceling each other out. While we may want a formula moving from thesis to antithesis to synthesis, this misses the point, placing an undue burden on

Figure 1.1.   Bikes and cars and a city in motion.

Source: Photo by Benjamin Shepard.

a philosophy built around internal relations between objects in capitalism (Ollman, 1976). Rather than reformulate a Marxist and Hegelian schema (which I am not interested in), this elusive concept invites us into a conversation about history and social activism, merging thinking about constellations of ideas about urban community practice through an interplay between theory and practice, direct action, and efforts to prefigure a sustainable model for the future of cities. Such approaches toward sustainability involve a risk reduction approach to limiting harms to the environment, depleting fewer natural resources, and supporting ecological balance. Sustainable urbanism connects this environmental awareness with a theoretical lens that supports making cities livable and interconnected.

A dialectical frame helps us strive to understand questions of sustainability, while coming to grips with a world and environment in flux. "The subject of dialectics is change, all change and interaction, all kinds and degrees of interaction," notes Bertell Ollman (2003, 59). This subject helps us extend old conversations between reform and revolution, use and exchange, with debates about housing and gardens, bikes and cars, streets and sidewalks, race and class, harm reduction and pleasure, apocalypse and utopia, evolving over time. This book builds on the stories of movements, activists, and the contradictions Marcuse describes to offer a means of coping with the changing nature of cities and social movements, building a dialogue between past movements and current activist practices.

Throughout the book, we consider ways cities are formed and sustained through bundles of ideas and practices, movement strategies, and organizational approaches. Tensions between human interactions with nature are anything but new, as Georg Lukács (1968) explores in *History and Class Consciousness*. Today, countless activists wonder: Is there room for a livable merger? Radical historian L. A. Kauffman recalls the ways stories and approaches to activism change over time. In the campaign to save New York's community gardens, she was able to trace a through line of movement ideas and practices extending back five decades. "Obviously, the people who created community gardens were very community minded," explains Kauffman, reflecting back on her organizing work in the late 1990s. "But a lot of them were more than that, they were people with activist histories, who had maybe been in the Panthers or were in the Young Lords. You found a lot of people who were in one way or another tied to older radical traditions, especially the Puerto Rican and Black radical traditions in New York. There was a real sense of reconnecting with these older legacies of struggle," she elaborates. "It's often women who do the work of community survival—maintaining a community garden in an economically diminished neighborhood, that's survival work. The people who had been doing this over the years were fully prepared to step into the fight."

Many of these efforts grew out of the Black Panther survival programs. Others involved in the campaign were the children of activists who'd lived in the neighborhood decades prior or worked in groups such as Up Against the Wall Motherfucker. There was a continuation of the story, not a gap in radical history. Radical history kept moving, building on the contradictions of history to move forward. Kauffman's activism and writing has long taken on this trajectory, "trying to understand these complicated interwoven relationships we have. And how when movements emerge, they always, always are carrying forth traditions of multiple other groups. There's no longer a single left. We have all these different identity-based movements, community-based movements, and issue-based movements. But there are through lines. And they are powerful. Those moments when people come together. So when you look at how the gardens were saved, you can say, 'Oh, Bette Midler came in and saved them,' or you can look at how legacies of the Black Panthers and Young Lords and ACT UP and Earth First! all came together over the course of the campaign."

After all, as movements meander from class-based narratives toward engagements with identity, postmodernism, queer theory, questions of public space, and class-based engagements anew, dialectical thinking helps us review these steps as part and parcel of an ongoing dialogue, with voices added, rather than as a zero-sum game. This is a story about flux, adaption, and continuity, as well as a dialectic of human subjectivity versus objective history.

We all have our stories that connect with larger culture tales. Through ethnography and historical narratives, this book offers an investigation into dialectical activism in thought and practice, expanding on this narrative about the contested nature of the city and its public spaces, bike lanes, and parks, as well as its people, their struggles, the pills they take, the poems they read, and their labor. This reflexive case study builds on multiple data sources, including my voice as an observing participant, discussions with other participants, and historic accounts to highlight the public space movements these efforts support (Butters, 1983; Myerhoff and Ruby, 1982, 1992; Shepard and Smithsimon, 2011; Snow and Trom, 2002). Interview sources without a date are from my research as opposed to other sources. Further, through participant observation, this report makes use of the researcher's experiences, thoughts, and reflections as subject of consideration in and of themselves (Ellis and Bochner, 2000; Juris, 2007; Tedlock, 1991). This form of research is useful for considering urban behavior and political participation, as well as highlighting effective practices in organizing and movement participation, translating knowledge into action as the groups covered here have done to fashion their own distinct brand of sustainable urbanism (Birch, 2012). Through these chapters, we explore models of community and social change activism, considering efforts to find meaning through planning, thinking, talking, theorizing, reflecting, and storytelling as the groups considered here evolve, collectively striving for something of a more livable city in which to ride, grow plants for food, and breathe.

The struggles organizers face often involve stark contrasts. The clash between gardeners and developers that Kauffman describes becomes a contest of visions of urban space, involving conflicts between those who see urban space as a commodity from which to extract profits and those who see this as space for life, liberty, and multiple expressions of happiness (Logan and Molotch, 1987). As New York community gardener Adam Purple[1] (2006) suggests, reflecting on the destruction of the Garden of Eden in 1986:

Well, the Garden was land and you know what happened to that? It was destroyed because it was FREE, we can't have free land, you can't go around growing food for people, come on! You got to buy and sell it. In fact, how many, how much food is produced on the lots of the New York City Housing Authority? How much? Very little, if any. Maybe, maybe, I don't know. I mean I had apple trees, pear trees, nectarine trees, black walnut trees that were all free.

These struggles involve an inherent anti-capitalist sensibility. Listening to Purple, it sounds as if he is paraphrasing Marx's descriptions of primitive accumulation in *Capital* describing the social dynamics of the struggle for the garden.

For all the criticisms, the work of the preeminent social theorist of capitalism, Karl Marx, offers a compelling analysis of these circumstances. But so does the story of L. A. Kauffman and the countless other movements covered here. And, of course, this is the point of dialectical thinking. We can all take part in a dance of the dialectic, if we analyze, historicize, visionize, and organize, to borrow the parlance of Bertell Ollman (2003, 69), one step to the left, one to the right, one backward, and two forward, with a jump into something else, before we repeat to deepen our understandings. Here new categories and thoughts about action bubble up to the surface, contradict themselves, crumble, and rise anew into movements of ideas and actions.

We dance through steps looking at the present, at capitalism, and at the preconditions of problems we see, stepping back into the past with a long abstraction of capitalism into the future, asking more questions. And then we go back from the future to the present, which deepens our insight, from projections of sustainable futures in our capitalist moment. Now we're moving. The sprouts of a better world are everywhere (Ollman, 2016). "System Change, Not Climate Change," activists have declared in recent years. Marx studied this economic and social system in its totality. Questions of sustainability run throughout his work (Foster, 2000). Tensions between environment and economic forces informs this work, especially today as activists have once again set their sights on this economic system itself. "Capitalism = Climate Chaos" read the giant banner activists unfolded during the Flood Wall Street action of September 2014. Throughout his early career in the 1840s, Marx clashed with the Young Hegelians and their advocacy for liberal reform in much the same way movement groups clash with each other over appropriate targets (Lukács, 1975). Activists wonder: Do we tackle basic reforms or take on the system that perpetuates climate change (Klein, 2015)? Marx grappled with similar questions, recognizing that history, as well as humanity, proceeds through constant change, development, conflict, and contradiction.

The story of Marx's work cannot be told without thinking about Hegel (1770–1831) (Lukács, 1975; Marcuse, 1941/1960). His thinking about philosophy, and in particular dialectics, informed the young Marx. Born in 1818, Marx received his PhD in 1841, writing his dissertation on pre-Socratic philosophy; the dialect rooted in the same Greek philosophy Hegel studied. Yet it can also be found in Eastern philosophy. It teaches us to understand the phenomena of constant change. Even when he criticized the other Hegelians, he did so by using Hegelian logic, adhering to the dialectical method, always moving and never static in its approach. Instead of a simple formula,

Marx suggested that dialectical analysis grew out of distinct social relations involving interpretation of opposites, internal relations, contradictions, quantity into quality, and identity and difference (Ollman, 2003, 15). The movement of these contrasts, the negation of the negation, goes on and on, as the system absorbs more and more working-class people into capital, consuming resources faster than the world can cope.

Rosa Luxemburg (1915) suggested the resolution could be socialism or perhaps barbarism. Today, it feels like the latter, with more wars of resources, lines of refugees, floods, droughts, Black men killed by police, kids in cages on the border, and displaced bodies. But is the descent into environmental chaos inevitable? Or could an ecosocial transition toward sustainable urbanism be a point of resolution? Is there a different story out there beyond neoliberal barbarism or socialism? The contradictions and contractions in categories suggest there is a place for thinking about a different kind of city out there, beyond the neoliberal urbanism in which we currently reside. Thinking about this question opens up a conversation about the ways capital flows through cities and states, transforming social ties and interactions, perhaps resolving into socialism?

None of this space is neutral; rather, the state is contested terrain, as are its public spaces (Gramsci, 1971). Over years of conversation in a study group on the dialectics of race and class, environmental catastrophe and climate change I took part in, Stanley Aronowitz would emphasize that the state was a mechanism through which capitalism functions. Liberal reformers have long sought changes in voting access and increases in the minimum wage. But Marx, Georg Lukács (1968), and others have suggested that the problem is much more fundamental and cannot be adjusted through piecemeal changes. Money has transformed human social relations, reducing humans to a means of exchange, with people measuring their own worth by their financial value, reducing human solidarity. The replacement of the human workers with machines was a tendency Marx started to see in 1858, drafting notes on this idea, later published as part of the *Grundrisse*.

Marx's method for grappling with the tensions between humans, cities, and nature began with naming this capitalist system as his subject. He moved from abstract to concrete, considering the categories propelling this system, analyzing how they function and contradict themselves (Ollman, 2003). These categories are constantly evolving through time, production, consumption, and motion, as ideas merge, change, and contradictions follow, often into a splitting of value into use and exchange. This is perhaps the main tension in the stories that follow, as understandings of land, labor, art, bodies, and desires are ever-meandering in a city that commodifies space and lives by the inch (Klein, 2002). Other chapters consider vantage points between subject and object. Still, tensions over value and space propel this story, opening any number of questions. Is there room for a different kind of city that embraces the opposite, a strategy that reveres things that are smaller in scale, that does not consume people-based uses, but degrows? Hegel felt that the law of contradiction resolves itself in thought; Marx saw it in material conditions and generations of social movements. Today, a degrowth movement is linking struggles for community gardens with anti-consumer movements and efforts to occupy space (with degrowth growing contradictions everywhere). This counter-narrative suggests that cities can become do-it-yourself (DIY) spaces where people become active subjects in history capable of impacting lives and transforming urban spaces (Aronowitz, 2003; Duncombe, 1997). Here, street clashes offer striking contrasts of opposites: between despair and promise, work and play, nature and society, yin and yang (Merrifield, 2002b). Cities, like capitalism itself, evolve through crises when the contradictions cannot hold and new movements arise from them.

Dialectical thinking helped Marx consider these changes, just as it can for us, as we navigate the world between abstract and concrete, rising tides and droughts, hydraulic fracking and climate chaos, struggles for reform and revolution. All things are in flux. "We cannot imagine, depict movement without interrupting continuity," notes Lenin (1976); this is the essence of dialectics, moving through a process of unity and identity of opposites. For Marx (1973), it involves a "force of a moving mass"; herein, "the whole is in motion, the totality of it develops." Beneath the fences with "No Trespassing" signs, armed guards, security gates, and open spaces for alternate explorations (Klein, 2002; Nicolaus, 1973, 31). For Hegel, negation became a creative energy, with negations propelling the contradictions, moving forward, as negative dialectics. Just as the outcome of the dialectic is not necessarily positive, as Adorno (1973) argues, it is not necessarily negative. Here, movements take shape, propelling a few of the counter-narratives traced throughout this text.

In "Method in Ecological Marxism: Science and the Struggle for Change," Hannah Holleman (2015) suggests that Marx's method opens a door for ecological research and activism built around a few basic principles including a materialist approach to viewing reality, the use of abstraction, a dialectical lens, awareness of history, and "commitment to Socio-Ecological Change." For the purposes of this story, we consider the fluid nature of intersections between ideas mixing and flowing. While some theoretical schools claim the mantle of dialectical thinking, it is worth noting that no one owns this idea, which is constantly evolving along the contexts of the world.

"Anyone who has ever mixed paint understands how quantity can be transformed into quality," explained Anthony Marcus, the editor of the *Dialectical Anthropology*, at a rally for our union of the Professional Staff Congress of the City University of New York, outside the chancellor's office in

October 2015. He was, of course, referring to Hegel's law. "It is said that there are no sudden changes in nature, and the common view has it that when we speak of a growth or a destruction, we always imagine a gradual growth or disappearance," writes Hegel. "Yet we have seen cases in which the alteration of existence involves not only a transition from one proportion to another, but also a transition, by a sudden leap, into a . . . qualitatively different thing; an interruption of a gradual process, differing qualitatively from the preceding, the former state" (quoted in Carneiro, 2000). Looking at activists putting their bodies in front of bulldozers in order to try to prevent pipelines from being built or gardens destroyed, one has to wonder if we are seeing such a leap in the environmental activism today. "Leave It In the Ground!" activists chant the world over.

The point is that dialectical analysis is open to everyone. In *The Prison Notebooks*, Gramsci (1971) suggests it be used to consider the everyday struggles. This is a continuation of ideas, from before Marx and long afterward. Marx used it as part of a critique of capital, while laying out a framework for a new way of living and thinking about urban space. In recent years, Marxist geographers have extended this framework to ask fundamental questions about space and sustainability, accompanying the influx of people into cities expanding to constitute a sort of "planetary urbanism" (Lefebvre, 1996; Merrifield, 2002a, b). Today, waves of migrants bring both questions about democracy and the impulse toward conflict anew.

"What is the dialectic of movement success and failure?" posits New York activist Jim Fouratt as we talk about his life story, full of successes and struggles working with civil rights movement groups, the Youth International Party and Gay Liberation Front. Thinking about this story of activism, we see narratives of movements shifting from Marx's class-based struggles through Freud's engagement with the unconscious that so influenced the Surrealists, the Situationists, struggles for sexual freedom, reproductive autonomy, and harm reduction explored here (Tatchell, 1989). Over time, movements ebb in thinking from postmodernism, Foucault, and ACT UP, back to anti-capitalism, and through engagements with anarchism, DIY politics, ecology, decolonial struggles, anti-fascism, and a dialectic of race and class (although not necessarily in that order) (Aronowitz, 2003; Singh, 2004). Throughout, questions about alienation never quite went away (Ollman, 1976).

Freud and psychoanalysis used the dialectic to consider interconnections and changes in categories of people as they struggled to find more liberatory ways of living (Tatchell, 1989; Einstein, 2013). In Buddhism, the vehicle for human liberation is through desirelessness. In Marx, it is through class struggle (Ollman, 2016). Through the dialectic, we expand this conversation, tracing connections between seemingly disparate objects and ideas, and their constant flux, with solid becoming melting spaces, housing rising, gardens bulldozed, and so on. All internal relations overlap, connecting us. Activist narratives are rewritten as we reinterpret the world. All phenomena are influenced by conflict; they are transformed, not fixed.

Social critic Walter Benjamin was quick to point out that culture tales such as these images and texts have an existence both in and of themselves, as well as a life that extends beyond their original intentions or purposes. Each gains afterlives through a constant process of "reconfiguration and re-evaluation" (Gilloch, 2002, 2). In "The Dialectics of Intoxication," Benjamin argues that surrealism blurs a line between images of what we see and what they may actually be (Gilloch, 2002, 107). Hence, the appeal of film, pop culture, art, and theater exploring the contradictions of intoxication. Benjamin's thinking ushers these conversations into subsequent movements. Regarding surrealism, Benjamin suggests: "Everything with which it came into contact was integrated. Life only seemed worth living where the threshold between waking and sleeping was worn away in everyone as by the steps of multitudinous images flooding back and forth, language only seemed itself where sound and image, image and sound interpenetrated with automatic precision and such felicity that no chink was left for the penny in the slot called 'meaning'" (Pensky, 2001, 189).

Movements evolve, as do the lives of activists who have watched their worlds altered as subjects and objects ebb and flow, along with targets, and actors find meaning in different forms of engagement. New meanings and approaches are found in these stories of movements as parts of a larger body of ideas. If you had watched the Highlander Center in the 1930s, you would have thought it was a project about labor; in the 1950s and 1960s, you would have thought it was about civil rights; and in the 1970s and 1980s, you would have thought it was about toxic waste and mountaintop removal, explains Bernice Johnson Reagon (Phenix and Selver, 1985) in a film about the Highlander Folk School. "I think the future is . . . well, as somebody said one time, 'it's out there,'" notes Myles Horton, the founder of Highlander, reflecting on his five decades of organizing. "It's not only out there, but it's ready to be changed. It's malleable, and there's nothing fixed that you can't unfix. But to unfix things that appear to be fixed, you have to not only be creative and imaginative, but courageously dedicated to the long haul" (quoted in Phenix and Selver, 1985). This story of the movement's evolution between subjective and objective history can be understood as dialectical movement. An awareness of these changes helps connect these stories, two steps back, one step forward. Recall L. A. Kauffman's story of garden activism evolving to and from in struggles to sustain themselves.

The world is changing in front of us, from quantity to quality, from solid to melting, from ice to water—literally, as the Greenland glaciers melt (Davenport et al., 2015). We are in a crisis now—an ecological crisis, born of an economic system that seems blind in its often-carcinogenic character; the roots of this recalcitrance can be found in a market economy, which rationalizes capital acquisition, and a compulsion to accumulate (Aronowitz, 2003, 175). Such thinking can be found in Cartesian logic, calculated mathematization, and financialization of everything. Facing this, a degrowth movement suggests we need to slow down and find our way out of a dead end. Such thinking compels us to explore new approaches, beyond the orthodoxies of *Capital* or neoliberalism. This extends beyond Marxism into our current constellations of activism, often energized by direct action, not orthodoxy. Hence, the term "dialectical activism." These constellations of ideas move it forward. "For dialectical philosophy nothing is final, absolute, sacred. It reveals the transitory character of everything and in everything; nothing can endure before it except the uninterrupted process of becoming and of passing away, of endless ascendancy from the lower to the higher," explains Friedrich Engels (1886).

The term "dialectic" derives from the Greek word "dia," or splitting into two, across opposing forces (Nicolaus, 1973, 27–28). This separating helps us make sense of a world in constant flux along with our efforts to change it. Referring to Hegel, Georg Lukács (1968, 141) suggests these breaks "be expressed in terms of mind and matter, body and soul, faith and reason, freedom and necessity, etc. . . . transformed as culture advanced into contrasts between reason and the senses, intelligence and nature, and in its most general form, between absolute subjectivity and absolute objectivity." The point of dialectical philosophy is to "transcend such ossified antitheses" (Lukács, 1968, 141). The same point could be made about social activism, helping us find meaning of the world and efforts to have an impact for the better.

Today, an animating principle of organizing involves horizontal notions of self-organization many recognize as a part of anarchism. "What is anarchism?" wonders Scott Crow (2014), who helped found the Common Ground Collective to respond to the ravages of Hurricane Katrina. "Yes, we can debate the minutiae, the labels, the histories, words, influences . . . does it really matter? People often internet-fight like our lives depend on it instead of letting anarchy be the fluid and dynamic ideal that it is. . . . Anarchy offers a crack in history to revisit long forgotten paths. And enables us to forge new ones daring us to take risks for ourselves and those around us. Until we are all free."

There is a certain dialectical quality within Crow's thinking. We are always splitting and churning forward. Here, anarchism functions as an energizing force within a range of social movements. It opens a space for new dialogues between movements. "Fortunately, the acrimony that existed between Marxists and anarchists for so long—starting even before Marx and Bakunin duked it out during the First International—is beginning to dissolve and fade away," notes Bill Koehnlein (2015), reflecting on the death of Murray Bookchin. "Something shifted in the movement when he died in 2006," says Chuck Morse (2015) in a review of a new biography of Bookchin. "Now that he was gone we had to make sense of him," Morse (2015) continues. "Who was he and how had he lived? These are compelling questions for those who had worked with him and for anyone contemporary who wants to understand anarchism." After all, Bookchin was both "anti-Marxist" on paper and deeply influenced by Hegel and Marx and was strongly dialectical in his theory. If anything, Bookchin's lifework laid the groundwork for a combination of Hegelianized-Marxism and anarchism.

"With the recognition of the importance of ecology to both revolutionary thought and revolutionary movements for social change, and the integration of a strong ecological sensibility into radical movements—which has become a crucial imperative—we are now seeing a rapprochement between the two similar ideologies," argues Bill Koehnlein (2015). "Younger radicals are not plagued with the idiotic polemical baggage carried around by my generation, and the generations before me, in discussions or Marxism and anarchism, and I am frequently heartened to see a synthesis of the two. A nice dialectical process. . . . Karl would be proud! So might Murray." This interplay between Marxism and anarchism opens the door for an engaged praxis, merging theory and practice, and hopefully room to disagree. This space is vital for dialogue.

Connecting both a philosophy of praxis and consciousness of the historic nature of social change, dialectical thinking has long been a part of anarchism. But only a few have ever named the process as such. Mikhail Bakunin was very clear about this being a main theoretical plank for him; he was the first person to translate Hegel into Russian, for example. Bakunin immersed himself into Hegelian idealist philosophy in Berlin in the 1840s, where he knew Marx and Engels (McLaughlin, 2002). Murray Bookchin was deeply dialectical as well. For Charles Johnson (2008), this merging offers an invitation to a conversation linking "anarchism with a systematic understanding and critique of the dynamics of social power." This need not assume that anarchism has no theory itself and is just a practice, but rather that left Hegelianism extends into anarchism and activism. Dialectical activism is a way of looking at social activism, connecting past breaks with new openings in a methodological tradition that extends from Bakunin to Bookchin and to today. This is a space where activists are striving to offer an affirmative image of something which we can all create through direct action and dual power, community organization and innovation. This thinking opens up the door for both historical analyses connected with theory and practice that ignites social movements.

Dialectical activism is a way of thinking about history, anarchism, and the transformation of urban spaces. It is a way of reconciling ourselves with the messy contradictions in modern thinking, the pregnant opposites of our world. It suggests that instead of dueling between points of view, we add ideas into an expanding conversation. Rather than embrace an -ism, dialectical thinking opens a space for us to think about social change in relation to the ever-changing nature of cities. It is a way of thinking about the process of organizing for social change.

Dialectical activism acknowledges the merging of contradictions between ideas and art, bodies and movements, and public spaces and cities. Along the way, it helps us explore the interconnections between street activism and social history. "Themes of imagination, creativity and desire run throughout the radical left movements," explains Stevphen Shukaitis in *Imaginal Machines* (13–14). Such thinking ties together projects ranging from the Mujeres Libres of the Spanish Civil War to today's Critical Mass bike rides. "They exist within a secret drift of history that runs from medieval heresies to bohemian dreams of the Big Rock Candy Mountain in the 1930s. It is a drift that connects Surrealism with migrant workers, the IWW with Dadaism, and back again" (14). Often neglected, these ambitions "find channels of influence in collective dreams and a pervasive yearning for freedom" (14). These "imaginal machines" remind us that we are not passive spectators of history. There are other ways of living. It is up to us to set out a path toward different kinds of stories. Like the social movements covered throughout the rest of this text, they remind us where we have been, where we are, and where we are going. Such imaginal thinking helps us think of cites as mutable DIY spaces we can impact through the merging of liberatory gestures and direct action with a closer, more humane model of what cites can and should be, one garden, bike ride, and prank at a time. Through such actions, cites are engaged in a process of becoming.

In *Dance of the Dialectic*, Bertell Ollman (2003) suggests there is a tale of two cities in each urban space, contrasting the free market of goods and services that people are free to buy, yet rarely can afford. And there is the world of people trying to create something else through experiments in collective experience. A close reading of Marx's (1973) *Grundrisse* points to such a situation, with a jobless future for workers, whose livelihood is lost to machines, and questions about just how sustainable the city can be if people can't find work—or clean water. *The German Ideology* (1846/1970) highlights similar themes of fishermen losing their livelihood, "as soon as the river is made to serve industry, as soon as it is polluted by dyes and other waste products and navigated by steamboats, or as soon as its water is diverted into canals where simple drainage can deprive the fish of its medium of existence" (Marx, 1846/1970, 132). Capitalism distorts our form of living in relation to nature. Production is a mode of life, transforming workers into bystanders, translating production into a domination of nature (Kovel, 2007). According to legend, Henry Ford and General Motors bought out the Los Angeles railway system in the early twentieth century so that everyone in the city would need to drive (Davis, 1990). This system seemed to anticipate an image of humans as machines, or cyborgs, who are connected to their phones, cars, screens, and Google glasses, merging with their gadgets (Deleuze and Guattari, 1983; Haraway, 1991). A hundred years later, smog and pollution, rising temperatures, and drought can be found throughout the region. How we produce is how we live. Our relationship to nature and each other is a way of life. We have to understand this to contend with the ecological crisis, extending from means of production to social interactions. Marx's subject was never exclusively capitalism, as much as the relations between people and products, machines and jobs, and labor and the world around us (Ollman, 2003, 1). Today, the question remains: How can cities sustain themselves in the face of competing needs for jobs and a climate flux?

To address this question, theorists have looked to various approaches including Freud and Marx, pop culture, and movies. For Walter Benjamin, Herbert Marcuse, Theodor Adorno, and other Frankfurt School thinkers, dialectical analysis served as a "tool for a critical analysis of society," notes Susan Buck-Morris (1977, ix). "Instead of trying to fit present historical conditions dogmatically into Marxist theory, it applied Marx's method to the present . . . its criticism of the patterns of authoritarian domination within bourgeois society applied to the purposefully 'revolutionary' societies of Russia and Eastern Europe as well" (iv). Within the Frankfurt School, ideas blurred within a dialectical—rather than a rigid—view of Marxism, opening a space for a critical theory and a philosophy of praxis still influencing activism today (Jay, 1973). Stalin had Trotsky exiled and killed some time after Trotsky took to writing about poetry as part of the revolution in 1924. He saw art as part of an interplay between social forces. "Each new rising class places itself on the shoulders of its preceding one. But this continuity is dialectic, that is, it finds itself by means of internal repulsions and breaks," he wrote in 1924, shortly before he was exiled in 1928 (Trotsky, 1924, 77). Soon, he found himself as one of those breaks. Stalin can be equated with the state, bureaucracy, and the death drive in contrast with an affirming engagement between Eros, life, and art. Here, poetry in motion is part the moving of bodies toward something different, a space for connection among ideas, hopes, and movements. The Frankfurt School would help merge Freudian analysis with Marxism to extend this dialogue (Jay, 1973). But so would countless other movements. Anarchists were explicit in their rejection of modes of domination, favoring constellations of bodies as opposed to states, and friendship as means of resistance (Shepard, 2015). As Richard Day (2005, 95) suggests, "The logic of affinity has been always already present in anarchism. . . . It has existed as a counter-pole to the tantalizing revolutionary urge that dominated not only anarchist socialism, but every other political ideology of the modern era as well."

I never was inured to Marxism, anarchism or the left. After attending social work school at University of Chicago, where Marx was never assigned, I moved to New York and saw the ways neoliberalism quietly seeps into countless elements of people's subjectivities. Looking for an apartment in the city, a broker commented that he thought I had made a bad decision studying social work. I wondered why I was being given career advice by a real estate broker. Class struggle was everywhere in this city. The notion was only confirmed in work creating affordable housing in the Bronx, and later as a faculty member at City University of New York, where I saw the legacies of redlining, disinvestment, and structural adjustment programs used to balance the city budget on the backs of the poorest after the fiscal crisis of the mid-1970s (Berman, 1982; Harvey, 2005). I first started reading Marx as a member of the Lower East Side Collective (LESC), where many of my colleagues had studied with Marxist theoreticians such as Marshall Berman, Bertell Ollman, and Stanley Aronowitz. This was the late 1990s in New York, when the global justice movement highlighted some of the "dirty little secrets" about capitalism. Through the group and the movements around us, I saw a merging of queer and critical theories of power and capital, and overlapping movements. Many in the collective were anarchists. The split seemed to be even between Emma Goldman and Karl Marx, and ACT UP and Reclaim the Streets (RTS). But there were overlaps (Shepard, 2009, 2011). The majority of us made fun of the rigidity of the older left groups, such as the International Socialist Organization and the Workers World Party, still out there trying to impose a rigid Marxist-Leninist ideology and peddling their newspapers. Others made fun of the often-humorless or homophobic qualities of the left. Members of Church Ladies for Choice (2005, 12), a New York drag group born of ACT UP, sung "I'm a homophobic lefty" to the tune of "Yankee Doodle" with a boisterous sartorial splendor after watching New York left groups crash and attempt to take over the agenda of ACT UP meetings.

> Oh, I'm a homophobic leftist homophobic through and through.
> A real live nephew of my uncle Karl. He was a homophobe too.
> Oh, I would like to crash your meeting
> Claim your issues as my own. acronym acronym acronym
> I am a homophobic drone.

I didn't know if Marx was homophobic or not. But the old left seemed tired. There were other stories we could tell.

The post-1968 reaction challenged terms such as alienation and dialectics, removing them from the mix. Even so, the problems with capitalism never went away. Autonomous theory reminded us that class struggle still counts, pulling the category from the back burner of history. In between new social movements, Italians started rereading Marx's texts in light of contemporary conditions (Shukaitis and Graeber, 2007). Antonio Negri (1991) led readers through a close reading of *The Grundrisse* at the Ecole Normale Superieure at the invitation of Louis Althusser in 1978. While new movements, autonomous theory, and post-structuralism grew, the logic of the factory, exploitation, extraction of surplus value, and alienation from work, as well as labor power, persisted. The commodity was everywhere, everything co-opted. By the late 1990s, the global justice movement arose along with a critique of global capitalism; people were reading Marx with their own interpretations, in a dialogue with anarchism, liberating lived experience from alienation, within a struggle to inject the imagination into struggles over everyday life (Shukaitis and Graeber, 2007). Within this milieu, we recognized that class counts; a shitty union is better than no union, intersectionality between movements strengthened us all, and there were things we could all do to help organizing. Class mattered, but so did questions about race, sexuality, and pleasure. Queer theory was important but so were other approaches and street activism, as ideas mixed. What was interesting were the mergers, sometimes between anarchism and queer theory, pop culture and critical theory, among others. Negri's partner Michael Hard even came to a few LESC meetings.

Steve Duncombe, one of the organizers of LESC, had a poster of Marx on the wall of his rental across from Tompkins Square Park. His work on punk and DIY politics frequently referred to Marx's books, such as the *Poverty of Philosophy* and the *German Ideology*. "As individuals express their life, so they are," wrote Marx (1846/1970, 114), in one of Duncombe's favorite passages, highlighting a materialist view of history and the need for a lived theory. "What they are coincides with their production, both with what they produce and with how they produce. The nature of individuals thus depends on the material conditions determining their production." We are born in conditions not of our making. What exists are our activities, impacting history. "The production of ideas, of conceptions, of consciousness is at first directly interwoven with the material activity and the material intercourse of men, the language of real life," Marx (1846/1970, 118) follows. "Conceiving, thinking, the mental intercourse of men, appear at this stage as the direct effect of their material behavior. The same applies to mental production as expressed in the language of politics . . . of people" (118). The text offered an optimistic view of human agency and our capacity to have an influence on the world. Such a philosophy of praxis seemed immediately appealing as a basis for activism.

"The philosophy of praxis is a reform and a development of Hegelianism"; it is a philosophy that has been liberated from any fanatical ideological elements, notes Gramsci (1971, 405) in *The Prison Notebooks*. "It is consciousness full of contradictions, in which the philosopher himself, understood both individually and as an entire social group, not only grasps in contradictions, but posits himself as an element of contradiction and elevates this element to a principle of knowledge and therefore of action," Gramsci (1971, 405) continues. "'Man in general,' in whatever form he presents himself, is denied and all dogmatically 'unitary' concepts are spurned and destroyed," Gramsci (1971, 405) elaborates. Rejecting "dogma," this philosophy of praxis offered both a critique and call to act. His point was that power counts, as the expression of a social group. Parties can be useful, but their limitations are many—hence the appeal of a flexible philosophy of praxis, open to multiple points of engagement, including anarchism.

In his *Theses on Feuerbach* in 1845, Marx (1845/1985, 27) famously argues it is one thing to analyze the world and another to improve the conditions of people's lives. Yet how do we do this? Gramsci (1971) would suggest we need a theory and practice of change to get started. Marx argued we need to pay attention to the world around us, looking at what is actually going on and respond from there. Both are probably right. Such thinking considers the application of knowledge to action, or, to speak theoretically, it integrates the concepts of dialogue and praxis (Freire, 1970). Here, theory is thought to be the application of knowledge to action, as a "kind of self-creating action . . . unifying theory and praxis," in Martin Jay's (1973, 4) words. You could borrow the critique without being burdened by past models of action. The world is changing, as are our models of action. We have to believe in autonomy of political groups, offering a countervailing power to push back, to fight the big banks, and create alternatives. Dialectical discourse helps us come to grips and make meaning of this constant process (Ollman, 2003). We move forward, make progress, stumble, before struggling anew.

In *History and Class Consciousness*, Georg Lukács (1968) considers just these sorts of interactions between humans and the world. His is a study of reification and of humans moving further away from nature and becoming like machines. We create new ideas and our efforts become commodified over and over again, even as we resist "the reification of every aspect of life" (Lukács, 1968, 149). His theory takes on the efforts of humankind to achieve a merger with nature.

Under capitalism, good things are linked to bad things; the good life always has its dark underbelly. Thus, Marx contends, "Everything is pregnant with its contrary" (Merrifield 2002a, 5). The pulse of the city thrives in just such a jazz-like urban dialectic. Here, opposites clash, propelling an ongoing conflict between often-paradoxical forces merging and synthesizing. Psychoanalyst Nancy McWilliams (2004) frames this circumstance as a contrast between the tragic and comic elements of life. "'Tragic' denotes a sense that one has to come to terms with inherently flawed and painful realities; 'comic' captures the more pragmatic, problem solving view that changes can be made to bring about a happy ending" (28).

Much of anarchism is born from a similar paradoxical vantage point, with a similar nod toward agency. "The passion for destruction is a creative passion!" Bakunin (1842) famously suggested, demonstrating his dialectical thinking (several decades off from being an anarchist at this point). This negative dialectic is presented by Bakunin as a potentially creative force, opening a space for justice, freedom, and love (McLaughlin, 2002).

These explosions and implosions suggest we can build a new world out of the tragedy of the old, out of the pain and seeming failures of our efforts. After being expelled from the French Communist Party, French social theorist Henri Lefebvre developed an increasingly festive, exuberant, even playful Marxist urbanism, expressed in social spaces created by the actions of regular people. Asked if he had become an anarchist, he is known to have replied, "I'm a Marxist, of course . . . so that one day we can all become anarchists" (Soja, 1996, 33). This playful disposition churns throughout anti-authoritarian organizing circles.

This book offers a framework for a dialogue between street activism, anarchism, and the social forces that push the world forward. The stories that make up this book are situated within the global city of New York (and in chapter 14 Paris) and the clashes that impact both urban activism and space itself. The cases are determined through an interplay between street ethnography and history, grappling with the collision between social forces and the streets to highlight a story of urban public space movements and the ways they shape and are shaped by history. Dialectical activism helps us come to grips with the contradictions that are part of a larger social struggle between parts of a whole. Through such thinking, we grapple with the constant turns and evolutions of urban living; "all that is solid melts into air," as Marx (1848) puts it in the *Communist Manifesto*, offering a distinction between "solid" and "melting" space. A dialectical activism grapples with these clashes between opposing social forces and the collisions between order and chaos, magical and everyday thinking, remembering and forgetting, condos and community gardens, libraries and reification, and cultural history and amnesia and their opposites pulsing through conflicts to reshape the future. This clash takes shape through an interplay between those who see space as a commodity to monetize by the inch and users who see it as a place for ideas and connections between bodies and cultures. Each chapter explores a history of collisions and intersections between work and play, cars and bikes, gardens and condos, order and chaos, repression and expression, poetry and reification, nature and civilization, and health and illness, offering a way forward through an ever-evolving interaction between social forces and the constant flux of urban space. Case narratives on sustainable urbanism and

Figure 1.2.   Walter Benjamin was the most playful and forward thinking of dialectical thinkers.

Source: Illustration by Caroline Shepard.

its components, including reproductive autonomy, health, harm reduction, naked bike rides, housing, gardens, nonpolluting transportation, libraries, and poetry, explore the ways cities are shaped through the intersection between history, clashes between bikes and cars, ideas and forces of order, activism, and the melding of ingredients within an urban gumbo. These intersections are all connected in this city. Here, urban space is reshaped and transformed as cities are remade.

Notions of sustainable urbanism and dialectical activism involve taking urban activism seriously, connecting them to historical models that provide both context and guidance. Thinking about them, my thoughts trail back to Frankfurt School critic Walter Benjamin. Keenly aware of the contradictions of capitalism but still intrigued with the city, Walter Benjamin was drawn to the messiness of life, philosophy, writing, living, criticism, and making sense of the commodity fetish of the everyday (Berman, 1982). Benjamin was the most playful of the dialectical thinkers. He brought countless components of high and low culture into his writings about Marxism, urban space, and the arcades. His essay, "The Author as Producer," suggests historical awareness has to be at the center of conversations about the dialectic. Otherwise, it was frivolous. Combining pop culture and philosophy, Benjamin paved his own way, although the academics punished him for it (Adorno et al., 1977; Buck-Morris, 1977). Theodor Adorno famously criticized references to Bertolt Brecht or other cultural figures such as Baudelaire not to his liking in Benjamin's writings; yet, over time, Benjamin's engaging interplay between Marxism and cultural work gained favor (Gilloch, 2002, 18). Benjamin fought for a point of view, putting together constellations of ideas, images, and montages of words fashioning alternate ways of seeing (Gilloch, 2002). And, time has proven that he was right (Caygil, Coles, and Klimowski, 1998; Eiland and Jennings, 2014).

Many of the pioneers of sustainable urbanism have been doing the same—trying to put together the constellations of a livable urban ecology (Bronfenbrenner 1979). The street clashes and seed bombs traced throughout these stories expand dialectically, like a conflict of ideas. Seed bombs are constellations of ideas that float through the air, taking shape in a zeitgeist, as activists share resources and food in a gesture that deprivatizes food production, pushing back against a neoliberal movement claiming intellectual property rights for everything from water to seeds (DuBrul, 2013). Each piece supports a larger montage of a city as a work of art. They are also part of a growing movement aimed at challenging the exchange value of agribusiness. Seeds in vacant lots help grow gardens, expanding use value while restricting capital. Here, a commodity form—agribusiness—clashes with spaces such as the community gardens and urban farms; these are commons where use is valued over exchange. The dialectics of community gardens take shape in countless forms as green spaces make neighborhoods more livable, which brings in real estate investment, which stimulates development, which creates conflict, which creates new coalitions of old residents and newer "gentrifier" residents who like nature, have political resources, and so on, which create new activists. Here, regular people drop by and say hello, creating a commons of their own making. Gardens are the future of cities, argue proponents of sustainable urbanism, in contrast with advocates of neoliberal urbanism.

The original flaneur, Benjamin was a lover of the city. It's not hard to imagine him thinking of constellations, observing arcades he explored in Paris or the streets of New York he daydreamed about, or contemplating his last days along the Pyrenees before he took his own life. Writing to Adorno in October 1938, he reflected on his life in transit: "Every now and then, I glance at the city plan of New York that Brecht's son Stefan has mounted on his wall and I walk up and down the long street on the Hudson where your house is" (Caygil, Coles, and Appignanesi, 1998, 172).

Reflecting on his life story, we contend with montages of images through history. Benjamin was engaged in an abundant approach to thinking, expanding like seeds in a garden. His work builds on a number of essential themes, including the "afterlife of the object" and the "engineer" (Gilloch, 2002, 4). Navigating a social world of war, anti-Semitism, and violence, themes of "disintegration and disorientation" and "upheavals" churn through his work (Gilloch, 2002, 4). Through it, we grapple with an urban condition contending with a dialectic of dystopia and utopia, of "destruction and (re)construction." Benjamin's ruminations on a "process of disintegration and ruination in which the object emerges from earlier contexts" offer a way out (Gilloch, 2002, 4; Merrifield, 2002b). Facing vast technical change and an erosion of "traditional values, hierarchies and boundaries," he strived to reimagine the efforts of the writer as critic, refugee, and historian (Gilloch, 2002, 5). His own experience as a critic who was never quite viewed as sufficiently dialectical, especially by colleagues, is particularly germane to this investigation. The debates about whether Walter Benjamin is himself a properly "dialectical thinker" inform contemporary understanding that dialectical reasoning is rarely static. Benjamin speaks of the "dialectic at a standstill" in a way that suggests a subversion of this basic tenet of Marxist theory for other purposes (Pensky, 2001). Benjamin himself is highly anarchist and comes near to calling himself one at various times in his life. He extended constellations of ideas into events that were connected as they subverted their contexts. Through his writing, he brought together an eclectic melding of ideas as cinematic montages of thoughts, dreams, snapshots, and images (Gilloch, 2002, 4, 6). Rejecting didactic thinking, he aspired to create a new kind of language, unshackled by past ideologies. Linked to movements from surrealism to Situationism and from Bertolt Brecht to journalism, radio, and movies, his thinking melded into a distinct materialist critique (6). He outlined distinct "dialectical techniques with which to implode the dazzling, dizzying 'dreamworld' of consumerist fantasies formed by spectacular shopping complexes . . . to bring the intoxicated consuming masses to their sober senses," elaborates Graeme Gilloch (2002, 7).

He saw "the rapidly expanding and ever-changing metropolitan environment as the principal site of capitalist domination" (7). He also loved the city, grasping its contradictions within its multitude. For him, the city was not simply "a site of alienation and the diminution of experience"; it was also a place for "cultural innovation and intellectual excitement," as the high clashed with the low in "electrifying encounters and erotic adventures, of intoxication and sophistication." For Benjamin, the city offered both "delights and distractions." He understood the dizzying peaks and descents of urban life as a modern disposition that was both urban and global, inviting us to navigate a mysterious "urban labyrinth" (7–8). Riding my bike across the Manhattan Bridge, looking at the movement of the water below, the light reflecting with the ripples, and smelling the ganja smoke from a couple of people sitting looking out, I wonder what it would be like if Benjamin were riding with us, smoking hash, as we zigzag through the city on our human-powered machines. Thinking and riding, and looking and taking snapshots, we move through the congested streets of the city as active agents, not passive, as moviegoers, flaneurs, videographers, bloggers, activists, photographers, gardeners, squatters, culture jammers, gospel singers, DJs, poets, and pioneers of sustainable urbanism. These efforts to fashion a new city propel this story.

Between praxis and a reflection on activism, the theory traced through these stories is intended to be a bit loose and decentralized, like the anarchism, DIY politics, and street clashes, which inspire this project. We move from a glimpse of the city, through a reading of a theorist critiqued for being insufficiently dialectical, to the stories of activists melding an activism born of postidentitarian organizing. A tension between seemingly opposing forces weaves it way throughout the story, highlighting the point that anarchist practices and activism are always in struggle. The text moves back and forth between models of ethnography and social history, with personal reflection and reaction to events in ways that are perhaps contradictory. Throughout this story, there are constant dialectical tensions, which of course could lead us nowhere, or maybe somewhere beyond the storyline of activism from class- to identity-based movements, through anarchism and queer theory, back to class-based movements, environmentalism, multi-issue activism, linking theory, praxis, and a way out of a dead end.

"Even a philosophy of praxis is an expression of historical contradictions," Gramsci (1971, 405) reminds us. "If, therefore it is demonstrated that contradictions will disappear, it is also demonstrated implicitly that the philosophy of praxis will disappear, or be superseded."

Dialectical thinking helps us understand history as a fluid process. Through it, we are subjects capable of impacting and making sense of history. During his concerts in community gardens and in front of polluted rivers, folk musician and environmental activist Pete Seeger (2001) used to describe hearing people talk about gloom and doom. "This is the last century of the human race," people used to claim to the iconic musician. "I tell em, 'Did you expect to see our great Watergate president leave office the way he did?' And they say 'No I guess I didn't.' I said did you expect the Pentagon to have to leave Viet Nam the way it did? 'Nope I didn't.' I said 'Did you expect to see the Berlin Wall come down so peacefully?' 'No I didn't expect that.' I said 'Did you expect to see Mandela be the head of South Africa?' 'No I really didn't. I thought he'd rot in jail the rest of his life.' Well, I said, 'If you couldn't be confident in predicting those things, don't be confident that you can predict no hope.'" None of us can ever really predict what is really going to happen. History is not static. Still today, people speak of a looming catastrophe with the certainty of savants. What purpose does this serve? Through a dialectical lens, we see history unfolding. "We know only one science," Marx famously wrote in the *German Ideology* (1846, 1870, 113–14). "History can be viewed from two sides: it can be divided into the history of nature and that of man. The two sides however are not to be seen as independent entities. As long as man has existed, nature and man have affected each other." In between, the subject-object dialectic forces the question: What is the nature of subjectivity for understanding the totality of everything (Aronowitz, 2014–2015)? We are all part of this ever-evolving totality (Foster, 2000). It is in all of us, including the art, films, bike rides, sports, the books we read, and the actions we take collectively within a multiplicity of determinations and conversations. If these inquiries are to mean anything, they point to the biggest of dialogues, the grandest narratives there are: the large-scale reproduction in capitalism of contradictions that separate and alienate people. Dialectical thought points to these like no other tool.

In the "Illusion of the Epic" in *The German Ideology*, Marx laid out his theory of history, suggesting it has an interlocutor. There is no independent history of philosophy. All our categories are dependent on social relations and on productive forces that are dialectically linked. Our relation to material conditions and nature is mediated by our relation to each other. These relations propel social change (Aronowitz, 2014–2015). The process by which people gain subjectivity is maintained by their activity, their actions in their own lives and movements. A class is formed when people act together (Aronowitz, 1981, 2003). Today, more and more are engaged in just such a dialectical conversation.

People in the streets from New York to Paris suggest we can move from Climate Change to System Change. "The only solution to violence is dialogue," noted Donna Schaper (2015), of Judson Memorial Church, just days before leaving for the COP21 Climate Conference in Paris. Speaking, she laid out a set of conflicting ideas about sustainability. "The primary goal of the climate movement is sustainability, reducing negative elements of capitalism. But today, this is not good enough. We need better," she argued. "We need a different, more affirmative path." The stories ebbing through these pages speak to a possibility of a counter-narrative. But they also point to the contradictions of our living, eco-activists flying to conferences, increasing their carbon footprint as they rail against climate change. "We drink bottled water created by fossil fuels instead of drinking from a faucet to continue our folly. I'm not sure if we don't need a larger crisis to awaken us," notes Schaper (2015). If history is divided into four categories in the West—primitive communism, slavery and feudalism, capitalism, and communism as Marx would contend—then what comes next? John Bellamy Foster (2015) points out that the world has moved through profound transformations in production, from Agrarian to Industrial Revolutions. Could an eco-friendly, degrowth transition emerge from this crisis or will we see more war or human extinction?

Through the stories of groups and movements, we trace contradictions, steps backward and lurches forward, through factions of a dialectical activism; each offers a picture of various modes of engagement organized around the city and efforts to sustain it. We see environmental activists grappling with a dialectic of human society and nature, as activists strive to navigate from a dead end toward a more sustainable future (Foster, 2000; Klein, 2015). Over the chapters to come, we consider the ways activist narratives navigate between public and ever encroaching private space. Exploring the city and its parts, its gardens, streets, housing, means of transportation, sex workers, stories, and poetry, we navigate from abstract to the concrete, breaking down the pieces of the city in order to see the parts on a meaningful level. Along the way, we trace a line from Hegel to Marx, Marcuse to Bookchin, broadening our understandings of dialectical activism. Admittedly, some chapters are more dialectical than others in this story, with some focusing on questions about reproductive autonomy or queer theory or mutual aid adding to the story. Still, each in part supports a conversation about activism and class struggle against the commodification of water, air, and our bodies in favor of a livable, autonomous, and sustainable urban space. And, in the end, we wonder if questions about sustainability can have a dialectical outcome in a new, positive form.

NOTE

1. For more on the contradictions and abuses of Adam Purple's life, see chapter 3.

Chapter 2

Eco-Activism as Increase/Reduce, Growth/Degrowth: From Seed Bombs to Community Gardens and Bike Lanes to Sustainable Urbanism

I have a vivid memory of a cold bike ride on February 27, 2012, with the Occupy Wall Street Sustainability Committee and several garden and cycling groups. We rode from Zuccotti Park up through some vacant lots, throughout the Lower East Side. Borrowing a page from the Green Guerrillas, we threw seed bombs into vacant lots along the way, spreading seeds (Guerrilla Gardening, 2015). According to Rob Sproule (2015), seed bombing, also known as aerial reforestation, allows guerrilla gardeners to hurl balls of compressed seeds and clay from bikes or cars. He regards seed bombs as a less risky, albeit less accurate, method of planting: "While its modern incarnation traces back to Liz Christy flying balloons full of tomato seeds over New York in 1973, its actual history goes back much farther," explains Sproule (2015). After falling, each seed crashed on the ground, mixing and colliding with the dirt while laying the groundwork for a new community garden, and, by extension, a different way of looking at the city. Each seed offered a new possibility for a spring, which just might sprout something wonderful. Those taking part in the seed-bomb ride were all invited to see urban lots as potential green spaces and the city as a sustainable space capable of regenerating itself. Of course, many of these seeds were dislodged from their roots and the earth the following fall, when the waves of a hurricane, Super Storm Sandy, crashed the shore, flooding many of the coastlines of New York City.

This was partly why so many of us, some 400,000, were inspired to join the People's Climate March of September 2014. Throughout the march, participants rode dinosaurs and swordfish bikes, with theatrical images of flooding bodies and bouncing globes, tumbling trees and screaming people, clashing forces and melting statues, crashing bodies colliding and creating something new. Each person there seemed to be painfully aware that we are in the midst

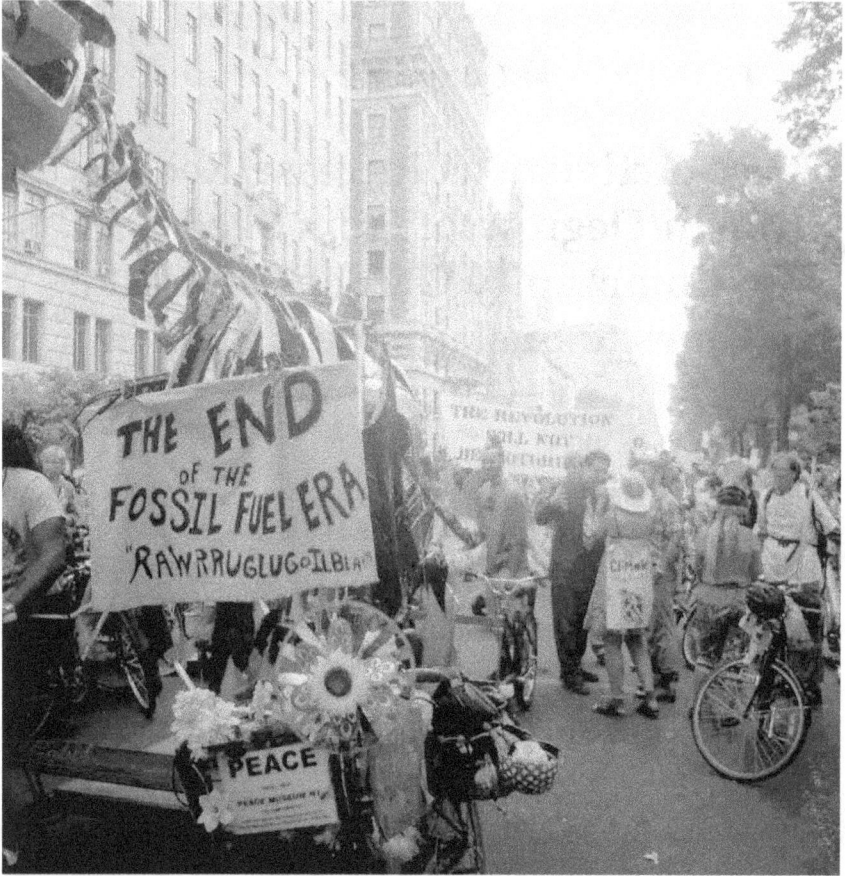

Figure 2.1.   The Bike Bloc of the People's Climate March.

Source: Photo by Smiling Hogshead Ranch.

of an ecological crisis expanding with each day as "human activities exceed nature's capacity to replenish and regenerate" (Coates, 2003).

Using satire and street theater, those taking part highlighted trends pointing to "overpopulation, depletion of energy resources, excessive use of toxic chemicals, likelihood of mass famines and starvation, and dramatic declines in the quality of life" (Zapf, 2009; Zastrow, 2004, 24). Recognizing the interdependence of all living creatures and organisms, the march pointed toward a different kind of city we could all fashion through our own actions to combat this crisis.

Marching through the streets, this cavalcade of bodies served as a critique of capitalist commodity production and its domination of nature. The

Figure 2.2.   Seed bombs flow into a community garden.

Source: Photo by Benjamin Shepard.

contradictions of our modern era create a crisis shaped through conflicts between gardens and neoliberal urbanism, bikes and cars, streets and sidewalks, and apocalypse and utopia.

Interpenetration of these opposites invites us into a process of historical flux leading into what looks like either a descent into chaos or ecosocial transition into a different kind of living (Foster, 2000, 2015). Still, the interconnections between these clashing forces are everywhere, opening and closing spaces (Ollman, 1976). Through their efforts, organizers engage in a long-term project of experimenting with what sorts of sustainable urbanism—livable DIY solutions, such as nonpolluting transportation and urban gardening—really work. Challenging a system of neoliberal economics based on constant growth, these activists ask: Is there room for a different kind of city that embraces the opposite, a degrowth strategy that embraces all that's small? Is there room for a greener, more renewable city that degrows and regrows?

This chapter is an extended case analysis on cycling, gardening, and sustainable urbanism born from social movements in New York City. I have been a volunteer with groups involved with urban social movements for over two decades, engaging in activism in and around my job as a social worker in AIDS housing, in harm reduction settings, and later at City University (Shepard, 1997; Shepard and Hayduk, 2002). Over the years, I connected day-to-day struggles for housing and access to health care with broader questions of urban health and the environment, involving questions about where people access space, on what terms, and how. In between work and teaching, I spend my days cycling and supporting urban community gardens, seeing their viability and the connection between people, streets, and green spaces as intricate parts of a fragile urban ecosystem (Shepard, 2009, 2011, 2012, 2014; Shepard and Smithsimon, 2011).

I became involved in organizing for the People's Climate March only a few days after returning from a summer hike through Spain. Throughout the hike, the Camino de Santiago (a traditional pilgrimage route), participants talked about ways of living in quieter, more sustainable ways. We literally walked hundreds of miles, traversing northern Spain, seeing the ways nonpolluting transportation reveals vital images of the world, allowing us to slow down, talk with neighbors, and become more aware of the environment around us (Frey, 1998).

When I returned to the urban jungle of New York City, I hoped to continue this exploration, organizing with long-term comrades to support the march as part of a group offering a solution to the crisis of fossil fuels: nonpolluting transportation. We formed the Bike Bloc to highlight the role of cyclists in the process of urban change. I attended meeting after meeting, making banner after banner and prop after prop. The Bike Bloc viewed cycling as a form of activism that creates immediate solutions (Furness, 2010; Horton, 2006). Bikes are solutionary vehicles, we argued. A few of us drafted a mission statement for the Bike Bloc (2014).

The MISSION:
"Whenever I see an adult on a bicycle, I no longer despair for the future of the human race."
—H. G. Wells
OUR MISSION—Bike Bloc is an open group dedicated to creating a massive bicycle presence on the march and in the streets during the weeks of action.
We acknowledge that changing one's personal carbon footprint isn't enough to combat climate change, so we use our bicycle mass of people-powered transportation as a physical demonstration of our commitment to fight against the fossil fuel industry and to demand clean renewable energy.
We hope to engage the larger cycling community in a conversation about climate justice and to see biking as a step towards deeper investment in fighting the global crisis with people power.
The Possibility Bike Parade!
Our Possibility Bike Parade will include a wide array of bicycles expressing the ingenuity, creativity and power of grassroots organizing. We invite

cyclists to join the parade chasing down a massive dinosaur skeleton float up in "flames"—representing the toppling of fossil fuel industry. The mass of bicyclists will win the day!

Let's ride together and make everyday cycling a reality for every New Yorker! Human Power is the most sustainable energy, and bicycles are truly a great vehicle for social change. Let's make all streets inviting and welcoming. Our streets, our climate, our future! (Bike Bloc, 2014)

An overarching theme of the Bike Bloc was that social change, particularly cycling more, could be engaging and viable. Early in the organizing, a few of us had a conversation with David Solnit, a San Francisco-based carpenter and activist who played a leading role in the organization of both the Seattle World Trade Organization (WTO) protests and the Direct Action to Stop the War (DASW) actions. These were global justice campaigns that connected joy and justice. That night he suggested that we emphasize a livable, highly engaging model of organizing, creating images of a better world, of what the world we want to see could look like through our Bike Bloc. It is a point Solnit (2004) has been making for years: build the community or world you want into the struggle to achieve it; without doing so, movements will be disappointed in their efforts. "Why Fun and Sustainability?" wrote members of the bloc in our outreach materials:

> Because we must have fun while we are fighting for a carbon free future.
> And bikes are part of that solution.
> Put the fun between your legs and
> ride. Bikes are fun and clean!
> The revolution will not be motorized.
> Bikes—Vehicles for Social Change. (Bike Bloc, 2014)

For cyclists, the approach builds on what is known as the Copenhagen Theory of Change, whereby regular people support small gestures of personal changes, which have a large impact on cities. Rather than waiting for a solution at a policy meeting, regular people find their own solutions in themselves. Five decades ago, the people of Copenhagen were as reliant on cars as those in the most suburban places in the world. But after the oil·crisis and a spike in child deaths by automobiles, a movement was born that stretched from Denmark to Holland, as people made a decision to look to bikes as a means of daily transportation. In Holland, cyclists dubbed their movement "Stop de Kindermoord" (Stop the Child Murder), propelling an initiative to make streets more livable and safer for their kids. Regular people made a commitment to cycle more and drive less, reducing carbon emissions and deaths by automobile (Fried, 2013; Hembrow, 2011; Wagner, 2015). Such practice is very much built on a DIY approach to activism and community engagement, wherein individual people are committed to save the climate by taking multiple small actions. Imagine if every city around the world emulated the Copenhagen approach to nonpolluting transportation? Through the application of this approach, we can trace a lineage of activism, including direct action-based campaigns to create public space, community gardens, and cycling, all pointing us toward a more livable future for cities and the world (Furness, 2010; Horton, 2006).

Many of us in the Bike Bloc had worked together for years. Our experiences with cycling events included Critical Mass bike rides and support for the Occupy Wall Street (OWS) sustainability committee. At OWS we used cargo bikes to transport food waste and compost from the occupation downtown to community gardens throughout New York City. When OWS lost its power generators in October 2011, cyclists brought bike generators to power the occupation in the park. There, Charlie Meyers (2015), and others in the Occupy Sustainability Committee, created bicycles that generate electricity. Meyers explains:

> At first, a generator made enough power to keep a small laptop running, but we've since tripled the output through a couple of clever design tricks. While this was a neat project with a very small use case, it was mostly a learning experience. Everyone who took a minute to ride a bike got a very keen sense of the amount of energy we use in our homes, businesses, and schools. Each became intimately aware that an hour of web-surfing translates to an hour of continuous cycling. Most people spend much more time surfing the net than that every day, and that calculation doesn't include the power that the heater/air-conditioning draws (much, much more), the power of one's phone (small, but not insignificant), or the environmental manufacturing costs of the computer (astronomical). Eventually, those generators ended up in the basement of a building in the Lower East Side.

A year later, these bike generators would prove tremendously helpful in post-Superstorm Sandy organizing efforts. "After Sandy, they were fished out and used to power people's phones and pump water out [of flooded buildings]," noted Meyers. "Other than the Goldman Sachs building, Occupy Wall Street amateur engineers (I among them) were generating the only power south of 42nd Street" (Meyers, 2015). Cyclists would organize relief rides with cargo bikes, bringing supplies and sharing food under the slogan, "Mutual aid, not charity." Cyclists moved thousands of pounds of food to areas in need throughout New York City, charging phones and pointing to the biking as a vital resource for post-disaster cities (Shepard, 2013).

"Everything we knew was not certain," explained Wendy E. Brawer (2015), Green Map System's founder and director, who participated in the relief rides, reflecting on what she saw as a "cascading scenario." For Brawer,

Sandy created the tipping point. Living in a city surrounded by rising waters, we would take part in countless experiments over the next couple of years with our ever-expanding Bike Bloc. We also hoped to bring the floods to their source.

FLOOD WALL STREET

The climate march was grand, but the week after was possibly more important. The Monday after the march, a group of us got together for a direct action at the heart of the financial district. I will never forget that warm September morning when we met for the civil disobedience climax of the climate march. All summer, David Solnit explained Flood Wall Street would be the most simple action we'd ever take part in. We met at Bowling Green, the bottommost tip of Manhattan.

"The time for speeches was yesterday," declared Takaia Blaney. "The time to act is today. Climate change is already causing damages. These criminal acts started a long time ago, from slavery to colonialism, destroying life. Now it's time to take back our power."

"We are all victims of the same global model, in which energy plays a role," proclaimed Elisa Estronioli. "There's no clean energy in the capitalist system."

"The planet is dying. The time has come to act now," explained Miriam Miranda. Speaker after speaker described the impacts on their communities, such as fishing holes drying up, depleted fish, and so on.

"We have a climate crisis causing poverty and immigration," noted Srijana Poudel, describing her experience in Nepal. "We used to have clean water. We cultivate our land but nothing grows, with local farming disappearing. We believe in sustainable development, not destructive development."

"I want to go over a plan," declared Fithian, leading everyone in a review of the action scenario. "When we are down here, we want to flow out and be a river. We are all getting together. There are three groups. Starting with those willing to get arrested."

"We have three code words and signals," noted Monica Hunken. "Surge, forward, and sit." We rehearsed surging, forward, sitting, and flowing like a river with our hands.

"That was perfect," Hunken complimented everyone with the human mic. "We should keep coming down here," Ron Hayduk gushed, standing by me. "So thrilled to be down here taking part."

"We may be seated for a while," explained Fithian. "So move your arms like a storm. Once we take our plan and storm through, we want to link our hearts together. The flood is water in our bodies. The oil they are extracting is the blood of the earth. So when you hear an order to disperse, we flow again. We'd invite you all to stay. We believe we will be facing minor charges. This is a perfect action to join."

"That's a great invitation," Ron chimed in with a smile.

"We are just about to go," Lisa said. Excitement filled the air. "Look at each other. Listen for clues," Fithian instructed us as we got ready for the action on Bowling Green. "Be like water and flood Wall Street," she instructed us. And fill the street. Sit and fill the street. We looked at each other, excited to be doing this, to be standing up together. We met everyone. On the way to Wall Street, walking turned to running. Making our way through the traffic, we sprinted up Broadway, running into friends, zigging and zagging between cars, and making our way past the bull, where we took a U-turn and ran back around. For a second, a memory of that first day of Occupy, from three years prior, flashed across my mind.

> Decolonize the water. Decolonize the land
> We're changing up the system.
> We're changing up the plan.

Someone started to gesture for us to sit. So we sat, occupying the hub of the financial district.

> "There are a lot of us here," I nodded, looking at Ron. "A lot."
> "2,600 of us," one man explained standing behind me. And we sat.
> Some of us were bouncing the large carbon ball making its way
> through the crowd. Others unfurled a large banner over our heads,
> down Broadway, flooding the street with bodies. And sat. And sat
> (some for over eight hours). Filling the space.

We talked about why we were there. We told stories. We conspired. And some left. Others stayed, and over 102 were eventually arrested, but not before hours and hours of waiting to make a point. The world was overheating and we all had to change, they declared, by any means necessary.

At court, on March 11, 2015, those arrested made the novel argument that what they had done was a "necessity." They would put their liveli-hoods on the line that defending the climate was a matter of life and death, and that breaking the law was a necessity to defend the planet, they argued, just as AIDS activists and others had successfully argued over the years, at high risk to themselves. The risk to the planet was just so high they had to risk arrest, noted the defendants. And eventually they were found not guilty.

SOCIAL MOVEMENTS AND GLOBALIZATION

Much of this organizing takes place in response to an ever-expanding economic steamroller. Flood Wall Street was an extension of a movement of local actors—community groups and movements that have come to lament the negative dynamics associated with globalization, such as expanding inequality, pollution, and loss of sovereignty (Harvey, 2013). Simultaneously, community organizers have looked to community practices to address unmet contemporary concerns (Shepard, 2014). Doing so, many of these movements have come to take on the rising tide of neoliberal economic systems (Sites, 2002). Here, community practice supports progressive solutions associated with emerging social movements (Shepard, 2014).

The Saturday after the march, a few members of the Bike Bloc, including members of the Public Space Party, and I rode through New York City to an old vacant lot, a brownfield-turned-community-garden along vacant railroad tracks between Long Island City and Brooklyn, where we planted seed bombs. The urban farm, dubbed Smiling Hogshead Ranch, would later be made into a city park, where cohorts of youth now learn lessons of urban agriculture and environmental science. Throughout the work day at the farm, we dug and experimented, linking the transformation of brownfields into community gardens, seed sharing and agriculture, bike lanes and nonpolluting transportation—all parts of an expanding model of sustainable urbanism framed around remediation of urban space, ecological social work, and community development.

Such efforts are part of a distinct approach to coping with social problems, beginning with community organizing and development and extending through dialogue and deliberation to examine options for meeting the challenges; remediation to fix what is wrong; prevention and development to slow problems while creating alternatives; and social justice-based social action, from direct action to direct services (Shepard, Totten, and Homens, 2012). Models of remediation involve taking what is wrong with the world and fixing it. For example, bioremediation is "a process by which microorganisms, fungi, and plants degrade pollutant chemicals through use or transformation of the substances" (Grindstaff, 1998; Rhodes, 2014). Everyday materials, such as oyster shells and mushrooms, break down oil from spills, reminding us there are simple feasible solutions to countless problems we face in our communities—grow mushrooms, clean the earth (Rhodes, 2014). But remediation extends in countless directions. Members of the Occupy Wall Street Sustainability Committee held various bioremediation balls in community gardens, wherein members played and experimented with natural elements.

"Eat oysters for the shells, make mud balls for waterways," notes the invitation for the 2014 Bioremediation Ball. "Learn the PharmaSeed game for future pharmacy, sow sunflower seeds to pull toxins from soil, crush shells for soil, grow mushrooms, stomp cob for bricks, make egg-carton balls for play," the invitation for the ball continues. The ball, which took place at Smiling Hogshead Ranch, connected countless community development strategies, linking direct action to direct services, mutual aid, dialogue and deliberation, and efforts to create and support spaces. To protect such spaces, activists make use of a wide range of research approaches, including measuring the social rate of return—highlighting the various benefits produced, such as reduced crime and increased oxygen as well as community cohesiveness, compared to resources invested. The social rate of return for community gardens includes increased quality of life, property values, civic participation, food security, green space, and community resiliency. At the same time, such spaces help reduce asthma and global warming and crime, creating the kinds of "eyes on the street" that Jane Jacobs (1961, 1992) long argued were necessary for cities to thrive. Paradoxically, they also support gentrification, as the dialectic of community development fosters counter-narratives and categories that contradict themselves, splitting between good development and bad. These opposing dynamics take multiple expressions supporting community development and displacement. As property values increase, they lure investors. Housing stock around gardens increases, sometimes claiming the garden in the process. New people move in, become active, and propel civil society. In this way, community gardens can also be understood as necessary components of the sustainable future of cities (Nettle, 2014).

Through such organizing, cities are viewed as living mutable systems whose resiliency is worth supporting. Just as people need healthy spaces to grow, cities need gardens for oxygen and functioning streets to thrive. Working in the gardens, those involved participate in an ongoing expanding sustainable urbanism born of a right to organize, ride bikes, plant and share seeds, striving to create a better city for today. This is a right of the city to be celebrated (Harvey, 2013).

ECOSOCIAL WORK

Social workers have long talked about looking at people in their environments (Zapf, 2009); however, the emphasis has tended to focus on the social world. Yet, there is a physical world that impacts the lives of people around the globe, the majority of whom now live in cities riddled with brownfields, pollutants, toxic waste, congestion, and polluted water—vulnerable to tornadoes, hurricanes, conflicts over resources, and increasing temperatures

(Hessle, 2014). (People in rural areas are equally exposed to these climatic events.) A reciprocal view of the physical world, with an interactive dynamic between people, the environment, and biosphere, is more apt (Powers et al., 2013). Such a view involves a far more holistic approach (Pyles and Adam, 2016). Sociologist Henri Lefebvre (1996) suggests such a view be understood as a sort of "planetary urbanism." This involves connecting the self and the world in the context of an ecological crisis, which has been described as something akin to a game of Jenga: if you take out enough pieces, the whole planet crumbles just as in this children's game (Barnosky et al., 2012; Knight, 2006; Nye, 2011). By considering the physical environment, we balance our lives with others, becoming better equipped as change agents. I saw this in our garden in our housing program in the Bronx, where clients watched growing plants mirror their recovering, healing selves. Gardens help heal people with a wide range of wounds, helping them become more whole. There is something profound about planting seeds and watching them grow. For many, creating a garden feels like a second chance at life, offering the possibility of a model for regeneration. This experience is borne out again and again (DuBrul, 2013).

I became involved with environmental social work when I saw the disasters and hazards and social injustices, such as earthquakes experienced in California, superstorms such as Sandy on the East Coast, and skyrocketing asthma rates among low-income populations living in toxic environments with few green spaces, where I provided housing. Along the way, I saw urban gardens as a solution to help us fashion more livable cities. Many involved with urban gardening were also involved with efforts around biking, connecting streets with green spaces with models of sustainability (Hessle, 2014; Kearney, 2014; Nettle, 2014).

DO-IT-YOURSELF AS AN ECOSOCIAL APPROACH

Much of this thinking stems from a view that the problems people face can be addressed through their own actions. "The power to clean up our world lies more in our hands than most of us admit," argues writer Natalie Pace (2015). While she acknowledges that legislation and public policy are necessary, she suggests, "Every day in every corner of the world, there are leaders and everyday folks living more sustainable lives, and leading by example." Through this DIY politics, social change activists consider contradictions between ideas and art, bodies and movements, on streets and in public spaces. Be it community-installed street signs, or occupations, or guerilla gardening, DIY culture opens spaces for people to create solutions to their immediate problems with whatever resources they have (Duncombe, 1997). "Actions such as these—unauthorized, highly local, largely anonymous, simple, impermanent, and often far from slick—may seem rather insignificant when considered individually, or in comparison with the broad strokes of formal planning and public infrastructure," argues Gordon Douglas (2015). "And yet they are bold contributions to the very fabric of the city and quintessential elements of the phenomenon of spontaneous interventions that we are celebrating." These projects, such as guerrilla bike lanes installed by activists themselves to create traffic safety, "have found great popularity among cycling activists, the small-scale, DIY approach can be seen addressing issues throughout the built environment," notes Douglas (ibid.). Such gestures help us explore the interconnections between street activism and social history, tying together projects ranging from Mujeres Libres to Critical Mass to Food Not Bombs free food distribution (Shukaitis, 2009, 13–14). Here small efforts, such as sharing food and cycling together, create livable models for everyone. Often neglected, such thinking and action helps remind us that we are not passive spectators of history. It is up to us to create and set out a path toward different kinds of stories of living in cities (Gordan, 2015).

Taking part, we see cities as mutable spaces formed through competing actions, clashes between liberatory gestures and swinging police batons, practices in sustainable urbanism contrasting with police brutality. Through such moments, cities are engaged in a process of becoming. We can all be part of this. As an organizer and social worker, I have seen countless advocates engaged in such work. Much of it started for me in the Lower East Side of Manhattan, where I lived fifteen years ago. My colleagues and I in the Lower East Side Collective (LESC) connected struggles to save urban gardens with deforestation on the West Coast that Earth First! was contesting. Some came to New York after taking part in the Earth First! tree-sits on the West Coast. And others of us took part in the Seattle World Trade Organization protests in the fall of 1999, connecting various DIY campaigns (Shepard and Hayduk, 2002).

"We met as Earth Firsters," says New York anarchist Warcry, known also as Priya Reddy, recalling her encounter with her best friend Brad Will during a tree-sit in Oregon, to halt the destruction of old-growth forests. "It was starkly clear: direct action was needed to save America's treasures. There was a clear moral objective. Direct action in Earth First! prepared us for Seattle." In Seattle, coalitions of environmentalists, anarchists, and trade unionists helped shut down the World Trade Organization meetings in November 1999. "It was completely transformative being in a forest," Reddy enthused, recalling a "visceral feeling of connection there."

Many of us were motivated by this culturally inspired movement, with roots in anarchism and deep ecology. "Most anarchists were very much environmentalists," notes Spencer Sunshine, who lived in Oregon in the late 1990s, before moving to New York City. "There was not a big gap between ecology and anarchism. We were interested in counterculture and engaged in pragmatic actions." Police accountability, squatting, and bike activism were part of this. "Food Not Bombs fit in well with countercultural stuff," he explains. "We were influenced by Lefebvre's [2014] critique of everyday life. It wasn't just about access to goods, we wanted to live a different way."

Many were particularly drawn to cultural activism, as well as DIY culture. Here, a problem-solving, community-building spirit extended from punk to a DIY ethos, building a community with whatever one had, such as zines, punk, and dance music, and people getting together and creating space together. Such an ambition extends from squatting homes out of abandoned buildings to creating shows for friends and building something of one's own. People want something authentic with which to connect. Hence the appeal of punk shows, dance music, live music, street performance, poetry readings, and rave culture—pulsing ideas and other cultural streams (McKay, 1998). People shared a blurry, bohemian, ambivalent space, where desires reflect the biodiversity of nature and vice versa. And we found life was far more random than any of us could imagine (Ziff, 2012).

In LESC, we organized in an intersectional way, working with local anarchists, squatters, graduate students, and even local elected Democrats—whomever we needed to work with. We had a strike team, a public space group, a community gardening group, and a community labor coalition; we did graffiti and stickering campaigns; our big fundraisers were dance events in squatted buildings, dancing and building a community together. Theory was for outside meetings. Every three weeks we had a general community meeting; everyone had three minutes to say what their project had done and what they wanted, and they were not allowed to talk about ideology. Meetings were short, five affinity groups getting together. We helped undocumented workers get paid back wages, created community gardens, and participated in the workings of a movement that would later be dubbed the global justice movement, helping it link local ambitions—gardens, squats, and AIDS activism—with global activism (Shepard, 2011).

DIY is more than an ideology or political philosophy; rather, it builds on a diverse culture of anarchism, cultural activism, and community organization. Through it, regular people come together to organize, injecting a pulse of freedom into the practice of social change work and connecting autonomy of bodies and freedom to be queer in public space. This is anarchism in self-organization and self-determination. The idea is affinity groups; ten of us in the room can do it ourselves. That's how other successful campaigns, such as AIDS Coalition to Unleash Power (ACT UP), create change. It is born through retail politics—people shaking hands, having a conversation, participating in unpermitted marches—and expanding an awareness of the public commons.

Over time, we came to see the commons we were talking about as the planet, and we didn't want to see it bulldozed. This low-impact activism invites people in, giving those with little else a space to ride, to clean a garden, to participate—seeing their life as connected within a far larger context. In an ideal way, the commons helps us all feel part of something larger.

A popular working group in LESC was Reclaim the Streets, a local branch of the international protest movement. Born in England in the 1990s, the movement was inspired by DIY culture, helping regular people engage (McKay, 1998). The movement helped me rethink what cities were becoming—more polluted and dense—as opposed to what they could be— more integrated and reliant on trains, bikes, walking paths, and green spaces, and so on. Participating in the group, many of us were acutely aware that our city, New York, faced a stark choice: either it would be transformed into a sustainable city or it could be overdeveloped, lost, flooded away. As a global city, like Tokyo, Paris, and London, New York has long been considered a model for the best and worst aspects of urban development, with increasing congestion, expanding inequality, pollution, police brutality; it is also representative of a distinct brand of activism (Sites, 2002). These practices have changed the city. Wendy Brawer (2015) points to ways the city is changing, with less cars and more people on bikes. "So many people see themselves as part of this city. We have to be a mirror of the society's values—seeing things globally, not locally." We can walk, we can use solar energy, ride bikes, and expand our own sustainable agriculture—and hopefully survive this, trying to use common-sense tools, greening public space, and supporting alternative energy. We are already seeing the benefits of this approach. The city has made bike lanes because a lot of people showed they were already riding. Throughout this activism, we consider the social, cultural, and ecological costs of life in cities and redevelopment, wondering if there could be a different, more ecologically balanced, livable, more community-based model for development. Could there be another story? What would be New York's story?

Social movements and creative activism are fundamentally about telling many different kinds of stories, engaging the polyglot nature of our society rather than submitting to the limitations of a single narrative. The practice and art of activism merges into a distinct mode of artistic activism, aimed at transforming urban spaces into living, breathing, mutable works of art. Some look to paintbrushes and graffiti. Others use their bodies or public spaces. Social sustainability takes place in countless forms. DIY culture—live music, spontaneous performance, art, graffiti—these gestures support an expanded image of what people can do in their environments. Through DIY culture, regular people find agency as active agents in history, experimenting with solutions to their own problems. A critique of capitalist accumulation, DIY points to an image of a city that values use over exchange (Duncombe, 1997; Foster, 2015).

This is a model born of a right to organize, share food, ride bikes, and plant gardens for a better city (Harvey, 2013). Cyclists view their efforts as part of larger thinking about ways cities can prosper, sustain themselves, and survive over the long term. Such thinking is a part of a growing movement of responsible development organized around a few distinct principles. These include supporting neighborhood identity and diversity; expanding neighborhood connectivity and public transportation; thoughtful use of resources; the interconnection of green spaces such as gardens, parks, and public spaces; support for social interaction; and participation between community and public and private sectors. Sustainable urbanism views neighborhoods as vital components of global cities, connecting global and local dynamics. Through participation in them, regular people support efforts grounded in dialogue and community engagement (Thorpe, 2014). All of this builds on a conversation that moves from the streets, through the Internet, to the halls of power, and back to the streets, where regular people paint a more livable, more colorful image of urban space.

CONCLUSION: GARDENS, BIKES, AND URBAN ECOLOGY

New York is a city connected between people and ideas, streets and green spaces, bike lanes and sidewalks, as well as those who yearn for public spaces where they can actually put their hands in the dirt—each of us sharing a delicate community ecology worth preserving and honoring. When we lose a green space, this balance is threatened. We lose our sense of community or self. The private invades the public. Everything is interconnected in this naked city. A close manifestation of this connection takes shape in reclaimed public spaces such as community gardens. For supporters, gardening is a form of resistance culture, as well as a model of social action connected to an expanding sustainable urban ecology (Eizenberg, 2013; McKay, 2011; Nettle, 2014). In many regions of the world, gardening and cycling are not just conscious decisions but a necessity, the only option to survive. The same can possibly be said in New York City, where gardens support a resilient urban landscape, including drainage and food security. They remind us that everything is connected in the city. But not enough people see that.

On Saturday, April 18, 2015, I left the house to make street memorials for pedestrians killed by automobiles and to highlight community gardens under threat in New York City. After spending the morning painting memorials, I dropped by a workshop on climate justice. "Everything is connected," declared a sign. And that's the point. We have to come to recognize the interdependence of humans with nature (Foster, 2000). All winter long, we pointed out that green housing is not built on green gardens and that community gardens help offer a solution to a city facing the threats of flooding, climate extremes, congestion, and rippling threats to sustainability. They should not be sacrificed for development. These spaces offer a wide number of benefits to our concrete jungle, including:

1. Providing food security, nutrients, and resources to underserved communities.
2. Reducing food and transportation costs.
3. Lessening the "heat island" effects in local areas.
4. Promoting civil engagement.
5. Reducing food waste via composting (Paisner, 2015).

They make cities better spaces in which to live.

In *The Dialectics of Nature*, Friedrich Engels referred to "the revenge of nature." If we cannot honor the interdependence of humans with the natural world, we invite this. Over time, movements the world over have come to understand that a collective struggle for an ecosocial transition involves moving away from human domination of nature, consumerism, and individualism toward an ecosocial sustainability (Foster, 2000, 2015). This begins with agency, as regular people connect their experiences and lives with larger stories and efforts toward change where people live. Here we understand that we cannot let what we cannot change prevent us from impacting what we can.

These stories and approaches point to forms of activism that impact everyday life. Through such low-threshold endeavors, everyone can take part in shaping their city as a livable work of art. All you have to do is get on your bike and ride, join your local community garden, or create your own solution. Here, social change moves through bodies of ideas, connecting people, transportation, green space, and an awareness of urban ecology fashioning one's own sustainable DIY spaces.

Chapter 3

From Gardens to Urban Libraries and a Struggle against the Negative

"We Won!" organizer L. A. Kauffman declared in a flyer produced by the Lower East Side Collective Public Space Group in spring 1999, after the extraordinary victory of the grassroots campaign to save New York's community gardens. Many of us got involved in that struggle because we recognized gardens as vital public spaces, open for everyone to learn and grow and build democracy together. Gardens, libraries, parks: these are all part of the commons of a healthy vibrant city. So, we organized, connected with broader movements supporting open green spaces, got arrested, used street theatrics, and helped push back the attack.

In the winter of 2014, Kauffman trumpeted another victory: "WE WON! New York Public Library Abandons Plan to Revamp 42nd Street Building," she posted on behalf of Library Lovers League, a group she formed the year prior with longtime activists including S. J. Avery, Zack Winestine, and a few supporters from the Lower East Side Collective Public Space working group, including this writer.

The Library Lovers League lit a fire under a lot of us, plugging in activists from the Illuminator Collective, the Puppets of Occupy Wall Street, Interference Archive, and the Billionaires, with the ongoing efforts of Citizens Defending Libraries, the Committee to Save the New York Public Library (NYPL), and other organizers already working on the issue. We came together to push back against the privatization steamroller, ready to blandify and homogenize the cultural landscape, erasing history, just as the old Lower East Side Collective Public Space working group had done fifteen years prior. At issue was a contest between use or exchange, memory or forgetting, remembering or reification. Sustainable cities are spaces where ideas flow from minds into cultural production, poems, and stories, some of which find themselves in the stacks of libraries where twelve-year-old kids explore, discovering new ideas, drafting their own chapters of the story of our city, light into darkness. Today, just as the eighth-century *Book of Kells* faced the desolation of marauding armies of Vikings before it found a home in the library at the Trinity College, Dublin, the books in the stacks of libraries around the country face a similar army of barbarian digitizers, privatizers, and developers hoping to displace them, to make way for condos and developer deals. Healthy cities need community gardens and spaces for piles of books and ideas. Considering the struggle to preserve such spaces, chapter 3 highlights conflicts between those who see urban space as a commodity and those who see it as a space for ideas and knowledge, bodies and expression, and use.

BOOK BLOC AND STRUGGLES AGAINST THE NEGATIVE

The struggle of books and gardens are all part of an elaborate dance, as supporters of open space analyze what is at stake in the struggle, historicize the roots of the conflict, envision a solution, and organize (Ollman, 2003, 69).

Figure 3.1.   The book bloc at the New York Public Library.

Source: Photo by Benjamin Shepard.

The effort to beat back NYPL's Central Library Plan is a testament to the efficacy of organizing.

A few days after the news broke that the NYPL was abandoning the Central Library Plan, I spoke with Kauffman, who helped break down the steps in the campaign. We talked about the ways this campaign connected with the struggle to save the community gardens. "To me, the library campaign was very much about the public sphere, about defending the commons and protecting public spaces," explains Kauffman.

"Then as now, is it a perfect victory? Of course not," acknowledges Kauffman, noting there are many unanswered questions about where the books will be housed at the 42nd Street Research Library and who will be held accountable. "But I'm in the camp that says it's important to claim and celebrate your victories. They are rare and precious. Then with the gardens, and now with the libraries, you say it proudly: Together, WE WON."

Kauffman continues, "The fight around the libraries was started and sustained by a dedicated group of scholars concerned about what would happen to the 42nd Street Research Library, one of the world's great public research institutions. But it was only won when it became more than that. The NYPL real estate plan would have damaged the library system in larger ways. We prevailed only when we were really able to make the issue not just about the fate of the research stacks but also about how the deal would take resources away from branch libraries and close the largest circulating branch in the US, the Mid-Manhattan Library."

Over time, the NYPL campaign evolved from an effort led by scholars to a broad-based coalition featuring many rank-and-file library users, defending the system as a public commons. A powerful combination of tactics—lawsuits, creative organizing, and coalition-building—propelled the victory. Kauffman describes the mechanics of the campaign:

> The lawsuits worked brilliantly at stalling the plan and buying more time to organize opposition. Over time, more and more cultural figures spoke against the plan, and not just about its effect on scholarship. You had, for instance, Junot Diaz decrying the effect on branch libraries and artist Molly Crabapple attesting to the importance of Mid-Manhattan in her education. A very crucial piece was pulling in some of the same forces who elected Mayor Bill de Blasio to ask him to block the plan—union leaders like George Gresham of 1199 and Hector Figueroa of SEIU 32BJ, and community groups like Make the Road NY and El Puente.

Breaking the story, *The New York Times* (2014) credits the turnaround with a change in administration, an honest assessment of the costs of the projects, and pressure from the public, including "critics dressed like books" who made "frequent appearances" at NYPL board meetings.

The night we received the news, a few organizers from the Library Lovers League, including Kauffman and Winestine, got together for a drink at Andrew Boyd's monthly Billionaires' salon to talk about the workings of the campaign. I first heard about it a year prior, plugging in fall of 2013 after one of our monthly salons turned into a planning session.

At the meeting, we agreed that the challenge facing the battle between the books and the billionaires needed to be dramatized. After a dozen years of Michael Bloomberg's billionaire rule, we were more than used to the logic of the billionaires and their ever-expanding proclivity to privatize the public sphere. Their zest to gut the public had become commonplace to the point of absurd. What we needed was a counterpoint to this logic, framing the argument from the point of view of the public, of the book users, the people who learn English in libraries, and the thirteen-year-old kid from Queens who finds salvation in a library. In other words, the books would need to speak back. We would have to make the clash between the books and billionaires a public spectacle for everyone to see.

Let's put together a book bloc, I suggested, describing a few of the book blocs in protests around the world. The idea clicked. We would stage a demonstration with displaced books converging, begging not to be moved. We'd set a date for the flash mob of books, planning working sessions at Interface Archive, organizing painting meetings for the next several weeks. We engaged our friends from the Puppets of Occupy Wall Street, as well as the Billionaires, who planned their own placards for the action.

The Billionaires, a theatrical group satirizing the role of money in politics, debated placard ideas and messaging, highlighting the class conflict at the center of the struggle. "Luxury Housing is a Right!" "Books: Can't Eat 'Em, Who Needs 'Em?" and "Private Libraries—Get Your Own." Somehow the book bloc resonated.

Before the action had even happened, I got a call from a friend, Gavin Grindon, putting together a show on book protest shields being held at the Victoria and Albert Museum in England asking for a copy of one of our book covers. We wrote a description for the book bloc we made for the December 16, 2013, rally to be displayed in the Disobedient Objects show:

"This is the 1962 cover of '*To Kill a Mockingbird.*' In the novel, Atticus, explains to his son after his friend passes, 'I wanted you to see what real courage is.'" His friend kept on, even when she knew her illness had become terminal. "Instead of getting the idea that courage is a man with a gun in his hand. It's when you know that you are licked before you begin but you begin anyway. And you see it through no matter what. You rarely win but sometimes you do." The struggle to save New York's libraries may be such a fight.

The issue seemed to strike a chord: save libraries, save our cultural history.

"Mon Dec 16, 2013 noon—Billionaires vs. Books on steps of NYPL! Be there! calling all billionaires!" declared Andrew Boyd's email to the Billionaires. "Books Not Billionaires Flash Mob to Save NYPL." It explained: "The New York Public Library is in peril. Plans are afoot to exile a large part of its legendary research holdings to storage in New Jersey. Why? So the nearby Mid-Manhattan Branch, one of the country's busiest libraries, can be sold to billionaire real-estate developers and replaced with a luxury tower. . . . Help stop this crazy 'renovation' by joining in a street theater flash mob on the steps of the 42nd Street Research Library."

Arriving at the steps of the NYPL on 42nd Street, a group of kids with book blocs were already contending with the Billionaires hurling their talking points and highlighting the class conflict at the center of this debate. "If people want books, they should just buy their own," noted one billionaire dressed as a yachtsman. "Or I'll tell you what—it's the holidays season, so I'll buy everyone here the book of their choice if they'll just stop all this fuss about preserving the library. How's that sound? You get a book, I get a luxury condo: it's a win/win."

Another billionaire spoke about the importance of real estate acquisition. "I think we can all agree that what the average New Yorker needs is another block of luxury condos that they can't afford to live in, not a library that serves everyone equally." Library acquisition would be particularly significant. "If we can get our hands on the libraries, just think of the possibilities for future acquisition. I've always loved the Statue of Liberty—why not put it up for sale to the highest bidder? America's huddled billionaires are yearning to breathe free! If I can afford it, I should be able to build myself a luxury penthouse in the crown . . . That's the American way, isn't it?"

Another billionaire expressed concern about creeping socialism. "Did you know that anyone who lives in New York can become a 'member' of the public library for FREE? This is an affront to anyone who supports uncontrolled capitalism."

"What are we teaching little Sally when we allow her to 'check out' a book for free? That knowledge is free and should be shared? Balderdash!"

Wearing my *To Kill a Mockingbird* book sign, I asked if I could go back into the library. Most of the books from the stacks had been moved out already, many to New Jersey.

The Billionaires ridiculed me. "Sending these books to New Jersey is a first step towards ending dependence on free book loans." He paused, adding: "Here, take a dollar."

"I don't want it. It's blood money," I replied, asking the reporters, "Why are real estate moguls calling the shots on real estate policy?"

The kids in the book blocs stood there in the cold for another hour, contending with the barrage of mock insults from the Billionaires, insisting they go to New Jersey. Most of the book bloc pleaded not to be sent to New Jersey. "Anywhere but New Jersey, anywhere," they said. "I'd rather die." By the end of the day, news about our action was tweeted around the world, with stories and videos sympathetically highlighting the plight of the displaced books in multiple news outlets.

By 2014, supporters were popping up in countless circles. *The Wall Street Journal* condemned the NYPL trustees for their lack of support for the organization they were charged to protect, and the Illuminator, a group which projects light images of protest messages in public spaces, shone images questioning the motives of the Central Library Plan. Every article on the project seemed to work against the NYPL's Orwellian argument that they were preserving the library by selling its largest branch. Like the Bush-era Clear Skies Act allowing for increased pollution, the Central Library Plan defied conventional wisdom or common sense. And the whole city seemed to know it. In the meantime, the sleeping giant of the campaign, moms with strollers and rank-and-file library users, got organized, meeting at rallies, speaking out, and sending some 6,000 letters to de Blasio. Each letter seemed to make the plan less and less tenable.

By May, the NYPL scratched plans for the Central Library Plan. This campaign was a testament that we can push back against big developers, even in New York City. Libraries and gardens, parks and streets—these are all our commons. They are places to build community, where ideas are preserved. They are also places for daydreaming, where a kid can go and find a book unavailable in her neighborhood and watch her mind explode with new ideas. Libraries do these wonders, helping us see cities as gardens.

INCREASE, REDUCE, WIN ONE, LOSE ONE IN MAY

Dialectical forces churn through history, our city, its story, and poetry. Increase, reduce. I am you and you are me—creating neighborhoods and their public spaces. As some survive, others are fenced off, bulldozed, and demolished. Abandoned buildings are squatted, occupied by the poor, ruins transformed into gardens, retaken by police and developers, sold off, and hopefully reclaimed. Gardens grow from wreckage heaps, opened up; bricks are cleaned up, taken away, and replaced with dirt. Kids play, until the owners come, retaking the land and setting up new fences, leaving us to bemoan our losses or ride through the streets, finding new spaces.

Throughout the spring of 2014, we'd fight for gardens and libraries—all extending our public commons. On one particularly heady day one of my favorite gardens, Children's Magical Garden (CMG) on Stanton Street in the

Lower East Side, watched half its lot fenced off—the same day we fought to reclaim an old space that was CHARAS, a squatted schoolhouse, long taken over by a developer. The very dream of retaking it brings everyone together. I loved CMG. My kids played there, digging in the dirt over long summer afternoons. Local community groups organized there. Occasionally, we heard rumors that the developer wanted the space back.

Yet the warnings this time felt real. "Cutting crew there now, developers putting up fence and destroying part of garden—please go there, document this, show up in numbers," read an email from my friend, gardener JK. Alarm bells sounded as they had when other community gardens faced the bulldozers.

Police surrounded the garden by the time I arrived. Standing there, I recalled roving garden parades, my kids cleaning up and planting inside. There was nothing like a Sunday afternoon in CMG. That morning, friends from the community arrived as bloggers and media descended on the garden. By lunchtime, new fences had gone up. It was retaken, divided. In this neoliberal city, no garden is completely safe. Gardens and community centers shuttered; the City restricts the public commons.

And we kept moving to rally for the return of old P.S. 64, formerly CHARAS/El Bohio Community & Cultural Center. We talked as we rode past Tompkins Square, to East 9th Street. The whole neighborhood had converged at the march. Fly showed me her new zine. We marched from CHARAS/El Bohio to Cooper Union, where they now charge tuition.

All week, we rode bikes through the streets looking for something of our city, for some lost heart, finding a pulse once more in the cobblestones, public plazas, music, and colliding stories, a dialectic of public and private forces shaping our city. Each walk to the gardens, bike ride over a bridge, rally for a community center, or dance ride through the streets—these small gestures shape an ever-expanding street ethnography of a secret New York. As Derek Sayer reminds us, each "meandering stroll through the highways and byways of the city that is necessarily directionless because it is driven by the hope of chancing upon the marvels hidden in the mundane. . . . This is an exploration that could begin anywhere and has no terminus" (2013, 5–6). It certainly does not here.

While I was on a trip to Prague later that June, we lost another garden in Brooklyn. The city is convulsing in front of our very eyes. Standing and looking at the fence outside CMG, I noticed a sign chalked there, stating, "Adam Purple Says Save the Garden!"

ADAM PURPLE AND THE GARDENS

The first time I met Adam Purple was on December 8, 2012, at the opening of the Museum of Reclaimed Urban Space, a museum located in the storefront of a squat, C Squat as it was known, on Avenue C in the Lower East Side.

Adam Purple gave a very funny rant about gardening and deep ecology with a Lenny Bruce twist. "Everybody shits," he says. "The question is where you shit." There is a law of return. Take food out of the ground and put it back. Purple told a story about how for years, once a week, he would take a bowel movement and bury it in his garden. "No one ever bothered me about that. They were following the squatters' bill of rights: LEAVE MY SHIT ALONE!" The room filled with laughter. It was not the only laugh elicited by a man who suggested we read books by looking at what is left out.

I never saw the Garden of Eden, his legendary community garden in the Lower East Side of Manhattan. But my neighbor Norman Green did. And he wrote about it in *New York Magazine* in 1979. We talked about the old article sitting out on a stoop in Brooklyn. I rode my bike up to Williamsburg to meet Mr. Purple, then residing in the Time's Up! space where I'd spent countless nights through the years, hanging out, organizing, planning, conspiring, and picking up supplies for our own garden down the street. But I never saw Purple, that was until we talked a few times at 99 East 6th Street, inside the bicycle co-op. There, Purple was rumored to have lived inside a closet behind the refrigerator. That afternoon, I walked in and there was the man often credited with starting the New York City community gardening movement, dressed in simply a pair of shorts, cleaning out a beer can for recycling, looking like an apparition. "Damned drunks," he mumbles to himself.

I introduce myself, asking if he has a minute to talk. He says he is busy. A minute later he pauses, asking me if I have ever taken my own bowel movement and buried it and watched bugs take it over.

"Sure, I have," I reply. I've been camping just like the next person.

"Good. It's the law of return," says Purple. "You take something from the land, you'd better put something back. It's a law that you dare not break. Any civilization which compulsively shits in its drinking water, will not survive!"

Marx pretty much said the same thing in *Capital*.

"Some people freak out when I ask them that," explains Purple.

"Why?"

"The City certainly freaked out when they heard that I buried one there once a week. I'm not stupid enough to ride my bike up to Central Park and back, three miles to get horse shit every day and not bury my own. I used saw dust. Dry shit does not smell. You never have to deal with it. You have no problems."

This was all part of the efforts to create the wondrous monument known as the Garden of Eden, a world-renowned garden and work of art that bordered Eldridge, Forsyth, Stanton, and Rivington Streets, until it was bulldozed on January 8, 1986.

"It's what was called eARThwork or land art. By definition, it's subversive because the rich cannot buy it and put it away in a museum. They don't like subversive art. It's also subversive because it goes in circles, which are anathema to the grid system." He looks around. "That's enough for today. I'll interview more if we can keep the interview to shit."

In between interviews, I read a few more articles detailing his efforts to create a livable space within the laboratory of the streets of New York City, eschewing electricity or paid work in favor of a life organized around recycling, reusing wastes, and creating compost.

"I'm teaching lessons about how to survive, an experiment on making earth," he tells Jesse McKinley (1998). "Of course you could do it outside the city, but the challenge is here." He pauses for a second, and then, as is his way, reconsiders. "It's the Athenian oath," he says. "The duty or responsibility of every citizen to leave the scene a little better than when they got there, to improve things" (McKinley, 1998).

Norman Green helps me compile a list of questions for Purple. Ask him what he means by "Your red shifts universe is on the psychic slips," suggests Norman.

"That's just a conflict with capitalism," says Adam the next week, with a shrug. He gives me a high five when I tell him I knew Green. Purple tells me about the ways gardens and libraries are really alike. They both open up ideas and secrets.

"Put down zentences.com," he adds, pointing me to a site full of number games and back histories of the Garden of Eden, as our talk meanders from radical ecology to literature, philosophy, and conspiracy theories. "Aldous Huxley used the phrase 'general enlightenment,'" explains Purple, referring to a sort of cultural soma. "Better than willful ignorance. Keep 'em ignorant. Keep 'em sick so they can be exploited." He points out texts for me to look up: "Go to the *Harper's Dictionary of Classical Literature and Antiquities* and look up under mysteries."

A subtext of the conversation is the modern world of technology in contrast with a premodern era. "There were orgies," he muses. "They were shut down. The Catholic Church did that in the age of darkness."

"Go to the New York Public Library, to the third floor, look in the little books for *Zentences*," he counsels. *Zentences* is, of course, Purple's book, which he self-published and stashed at the public library.

"Why Purple?" I ask.

"Purple is the name of a magic mushroom. It's the color of royalty," he answers, noting that he no longer wears purple, not since the city bulldozed his garden. But he's still enamored with the work of Empedocles, the pre-Socratic philosopher who wore purple and postulated that all life was made up of four elements—fire, water, air, earth—while love and strife account for their mutual attraction and separation from each other.

"There was a madam in Alexandria who wanted to give a story to the sex workers," he continues. "She gave them a trip to Eleusis in Greece. Each enjoyed a drink during the orgy. They walked by candlelight to Athens in a sacred celebration of life as we do not know it. Socrates got in trouble for making his own orgy with youth." Throughout our conversation, Purple hints at a kind of colonization, a system of reason encroaching into a more spontaneous, anarchistic cosmos. Only after Purple died and we heard about his history of sexual abuse of his children did I see there was more to what he was thinking and doing

I am not doubting the validity of accounts from his daughters or condoning Purple's reprehensible actions (see Anderson, 2015, 2016a, b). Still, through Purple's life we see an interplay between repression and expression, the kind of dynamic Nietzsche writes about in *The Birth of Tragedy*, with the logic of Apollo contending with the frenzy of Dionysus. In *Civilization and Its Discontents*, Freud suggests our world would fall apart if we let go of all inhibitions, allowing the id to run wild. In Purple's narrative one comes to see why. The conflict between the ego, superego, and id helps us form who we are. Superego helps remind us that there are others out there that we have to be concerned about; there is a social world and pain of others. Without much superego, his id ran wild. Purple apparently had little concern with this.

"Look up *LIFE with les(s) ego*," he urges. His point is that we, as humans, ask for too much; we hope to have more than we need. We "overshoot. The species overshoots, the environment we live in is caused to die off with our species. Look up homo colossus."

"Bill Clinton nearly destroyed Harlem," he continues, becoming more specific. "Why do you think I called it the Garden of Eden? These people can't stop with their machines." The garden was an antidote to this. Purple gave supporters poems if they contributed to the garden.

"Why do you ride your bike backward?" I ask.

"There's a reason for that," he notes. "If you ride with traffic you can get doored. You can get hit from behind. You gotta see what's coming."

"It's all gonna come to an end, this industrial world," he says, referring to a world with rising sea levels and too much development. In the dialectic of utopia versus dystopia, he cautions that the future may look more like the later. "The future may not be pleasant," he laments. "They say the universe is expanding. It's all coming to us. Death is not what is degrading. Life is."

"I have two or three libraries that are lost," he muses, linking a gentrification of space with the mind. "I have lots of libraries. I have had a virtual library but knowledge disappears just like gardens, don't have a credit card, that's a way to rob from people. The box puts you in prison. It's square. Yet, you'll find no straight lines in nature, none on the body. Lines are not straight. They are fractured," he suggests. "Consciousness means being aware of the environment. Frank Lloyd Wright said there is no pillar in the corner of a window. You are at liberty to look at one corner at a time. This is an idea that traveled around the world. You can look in more than one direction at a time. There is another system. There is meaning in these idioms."

In composting, reusing waste, and gardening, Purple offers an image of another kind of urban ecology.

"Get your shit together," he speaks, almost as in a soliloquy. "Ignorance of the law is no excuse. It's a parasitic species," he continues, referring to humans, who take without giving back to the land. "Our consciousness can expand. We can imagine something else," he suggests. "That's the only difference between you and I, consciousness."

"Go the library, see if it's there. *LIFE with les(s) ego*," he repeats. "You may have to move the book because the sea is rising, two miles of ice is melting. Gaia principle. The earth takes care of itself," he elaborates. "Living organisms have been here for a long time, adapting and evolving as a system always changing and impacting the chemistry, the conditions of living here. We have no one to blame but ourselves."

"What inspired you to create the Garden of Eden?" I ask.

"The first time I came to New York, I saw backyards full of junk, and little inspection. I was working on the backyard in Forsyth street." And he started gardening there in the mid-1970s. The site expanded and expanded, in concentric circles, moving out, eventually taking up some 15,000 square feet, composed of lilies and roses, raspberries and fruit trees. Publications including *National Geographic* as well as several foreign magazines ran stories about the garden. Some went as far as to compare it with the earth sculptures of artists such as Walter De Maria and Robert Smithson (McKinley, 1998).

"It was an absolutely astonishing creation," says Barbara Kirshenblatt-Gimblet. "Besides its natural beauty, the garden had an inherently political message. He made a garden out of a ruin . . . So symbolically it was an especially strong indictment of the failure of the city to do the same" (McKinley, 1998).

While residents and international journalists saw this as a work of art, the city viewed it as a vacant lot they had every right to build upon. "They got away with lies," notes Purple. "They held a hearing in August of 1985, a full evidentiary hearing." Nonetheless, "the garden started a revolution."

"Come back when you find the book," he tells me.

I never found the book.

That interview was the last time I saw Adam.

Over the next few months, I met more people who knew Purple. We even ran into Harvey Wang, the photographer who documented Purple's art for decades. Wang's wife Amy conducted an interview with Adam in 2006 for Storycorps at Grand Central Station (Purple, 2006).

"I looked out the back window of 184, they took down two buildings simultaneously that fronted on Eldridge Street, and so we had morning sunshine come into two vacant lots, which were brick rubble," he recalls, before he started the garden. "If you go to Rivington Street there's a large lot that it used to be a Synagogue, and the roof collapsed and if you look at that lot you'll see what kind of lot I started with. . . . So, when I looked out my window . . . before the buildings on Eldridge Street were taken down, I was watching mothers sitting in the back window of a tenement building look-ing at their children playing in the garbage . . . And I thought, wow, that's a hell of a way to raise children, with no place to put your feet on the dirt. So, over a period of the next five years I managed to get five lots converted from brick rubble into handmade night soil—into handmade topsoil made from horse manure from Central Park. Which I call Zentral Park, a slight change of spelling."

Purple describes the significance of the design. "Well, when you throw a rock in the water, circles go out. And the circle is historically a universal symbol, and you break the circle because you make like a labyrinth, you could walk in a spiral, you could walk out of the garden in a spiral and if you noticed from the pictures of it, the central yin yang was four pieces—that's a yin yang split into two. Two squared is four, that's an exponential function. The next circle was five sections, and the next one was six sections, seven, eight, nine, and so on. So, each time you laid another circle, the number of sections in the circle increased by one. So, that's an arithmetic progression: one, two, three, four, five, six, and so on." The yin and yang symbols at the center of the garden offer a sort of dialectical interplay between the rubble and green redevelopment of the city, also a way of considering Purple's life (Anderson, 2015).

"It was truly a community garden," he explains, "an open garden from beginning to end . . . you'd pick down into the brick rubble and, after all, bricks are made out of clay, and clay is one of the basic ingredients of soil. . . . So it was about 80 percent horse manure, and 20 percent brick rubble, and maybe five percent potash made from the wood that I burn from sorting out the brick rubble."

Purple stayed there, on the Lower East Side, even after the building owner left and the city kept trying to get him out. "I had started the garden in '75 and the landlord left in '76, I think, as I remember, but I had already started the garden and I wasn't going to abandon that because I could see other build-ings were going to come down, and so it was circular and it would expand and the circles would bump into buildings and knock the buildings down, metaphorically, which of course they did. I mean the buildings fell down, and of course the city saw what was happening and decided, well we gotta kill this for sure."

The lessons were many. "The most interesting thing, probably, was observ-ing earthworms at work. . . . They love shit and leaves and any kind of organic material that's rotting and turning back into soil and, after all, that's what topsoil is, it's decayed organic material. So, you learn to have a little respect for an earthworm . . . The soil in the garden was about four inches deep . . . [It] produce[ed] corn that was like five, six feet tall, and produced edible corn. . . . We had cucumbers and cherry tomatoes and asparagus and black raspberries on the wall on Eldridge Street, and 45 trees, including eight black walnut trees, half of which were fruiting. . . . But, it was an experiment in how to do it from scratch . . . That is, whatever you can use to make something else. And, it was very productive in terms of food."

Over time, the garden expanded to the size of thirteen greenhouses. "The idea for the greenhouses was that you could grow food year-round, you could live in the basement and use earth heat, and collect the water behind the building at 184 Forsyth Street. . . . Many buildings in New York, early in the development of New York had cisterns behind the building to collect the rainwater. Now it's all dumped into the ocean. Not that you'd want to drink rainwater, but rainwater is better than sewage water that's mixed in with the regular water that goes into the sewers. But, you can, it was a revolutionary outlook . . . and we don't allow you to grow food and make topsoil, either with your own shit or with horse shit from Central Park. That's a no-no, and they demonstrated quite well that that's a no-no."

Lots of people got involved with the garden. Yet not everyone felt welcome there. His family left. Purple famously turned people away who did not agree with him. An anarchist with control issues, his story had many contradictions.

In 1986, the city destroyed the garden. "The wall on the Eldridge Street frontage and on the south side of the garden took two days. . . . On January 8th of 1986 a large rubber tire highway construction vehicle with a scoop in the front ran over the garden for an hour and fifteen minutes. But they couldn't get in with that machine until they had destroyed the wall. . . . It took two days with a bulldozer to take the wall out, which had black raspberries growing on it. . . . On the map for the block I was in, all the area where the Garden of Eden existed it was labeled vacant. It was never officially recognized by the City as existing. They called it vacant. When in fact it was a work of art there. An earth work. And, incidentally, eARThworks and performance art are referred to as anti-establishment for the very simple reason, obviously, that the owning class cannot buy them and put them in a gallery somewhere and make them unavailable to the general public. There's a lot of artwork that's in private hands that the public never sees. So when you do something that is free, open, and costs nothing in terms of money, except human labor, you are a threat . . . And, obviously, I was aware of that. Well, the word revolution, if you put as I do in referring to rev les ego, I spell it r(apid) evolution: r(apid) evolution. What is revolution except rapid evolution? And, you don't have to have a revolution with guns. Only a gentle revolution will work . . . the Velvet

Revolution in Czechoslovakia, right? It was a good name for a revolution. That was a work of art that was also ecologically based, in terms of a human right to make earth and grow food. . . . We don't live in isolation from everyone else. . . . I take issue with the word gentrification, because gentry means landowners. And, I didn't own any land, I made land. But the gentrification process is a process of removing the poor. And you notice now that the poor are being removed from New York."

"It was the most majestic thing," says Lower East Side squatter Jerry "the Peddler" Wade, referring to the Garden of Eden. "It was a work of art. He'd get on a bike and ride up to Central Park [to collect horse manure] against traffic. In bright purple. He was spectacular. He inspired us."

Through Purple's endeavor, a neighborhood connected with a model of sustainable urbanism built around community gardens, libraries, and a public commons of ideas supporting an ever-expanding urban ecology. Purple was a dynamic thinker, even a revolutionary. His life was also a cautionary tale about abuses of power (Anderson, 2015). He was not an organizer. After the loss of the garden, other organizers, anarchists, grand-moms, and neighborhood members organized to preserve the gardens as part of an increasingly sustainable urban ecology.

Chapter 4

Community Gardens, Creative Community Organizing, and Environmental Activism

Community gardening is a way to fight the systemic injustice of poverty and other forms of structural oppression. Most gardens are in poor areas of the city, with much higher rates of asthma and lower rates of open space equity. Gardens offer a way for our community to heal itself and to recover a humanizing sense of itself in an otherwise very hard city.

—Friends of Brook Park gardener Ray Figueroa (Time's Up!, 2010)

In New York City, a huge amount of activism and creativity takes place within the community gardens (Carlsson, 2008; Eizenberg 2013; Nettle, 2014; Shepard, 2011; Wilson and Weinberg, 1999). To cultivate and protect these spaces, an environmental movement has found footing, engaging in a fundamental conflict between use and value of urban space. Gardeners support use, while developers exchange. The future of cities depends on sustainable use of this space. When cities support gardens, they acknowledge the need for an ecological balance in urban space and the world.

This chapter traces an informal history of the successful campaign to save urban gardens (mostly in the Lower East Side) of New York City after the loss of the Garden of Eden in 1986. Thousands of skirmishes, of green spaces created and destroyed from Little Italy to Queens, the Bronx to Coney Island, Bedford Stuyvesant to Harlem, are not covered in this history. Still, a story takes shape as a garden movement connects with community-supported agriculture, urban planning, and nutrition programs. Along the way, the movement expands into a process of community regeneration by planning, planting, weeding, and harvesting in spaces once filled with garbage and rubble. Through a close engagement between the physical environment and social world, gardeners open a space for difference, health, creativity, and organizing (Carlsson, 2008).

Located mostly in low-income neighborhoods, where asthma levels are high, housing is dense, and asphalt prevails, it is useful to consider the garden movement in relation to the politics of public space, uneven development, displacement, and neoliberalism (Carlsson, 2008; Schaper, 2007, Smith, 1996). Community gardeners have brought safety, food, beauty, fresh air, and a "sense of community" back to urban streets and people, for civic and social—rather than commercial—purposes; these public spaces face a myriad of threats from corporate globalizers and real estate interests. Much of the garden struggle is a fight to preserve public space for those at the margins to find solace in post-welfare neoliberal cities. Here in New York, groups such as Lower East Side Collective (LESC), More Gardens, Public Space Party, and Time's Up! have built a diverse coalition to defend community gardens. Their efforts represent a best practice in organizing toward sustainable urbanism.

URBAN SPACE, SUSTAINABILITY, AND SOCIAL JUSTICE

Over the years, community gardens have come to serve as a practical solution to the challenge of open-space inequity, including lack of access to play spaces in low-income communities. With minimal opportunities to experience the natural environment, neighborhood members created a network of community gardens out of the rubble of vacant lots, abandoned during New York's fiscal crisis of the 1970s (Lamborn and Weinburg, 1999). Providing much-needed green space, community gardens function as park and play spaces, supporting health, beauty, economic development, intergenerational exchange, and security (Raya and Rubin, 2006). Their status is always precarious (Kattalia, 2011). Many have come to see threats to gardens as a direct threat to spaces for healthy expression. After all, these are places where free thought and action thrives. Free play supports childhood creativity, problem-solving, executive function, resiliency, innovation, and space to exercise the body and mind (Shepard, 2011). Over and over this ludic activity is challenged by calls for more time dedicated to time (for standardized activities such as tests). The implications of this turn away from creative play include diminished innovation and increased obesity. Countless communities have no open spaces for play within walking distance (Raya and Rubin, 2006).

When the City of New York proposed eased protections on community gardens in 2010, community members spoke out: "Don't destroy our gardens. Don't destroy our communities. Gardens help us connect with both the earth and our communities, in ways which parking lots, coffee shops, and other urban spaces fail to," declared longtime Lower East Side activist Paul Bartlett. In making this point, Bartlett, a veteran of Lower East Side organizing, harkened back to a history of community gardening and activism dating back to the 1990s in New York City, when the mayor announced plans to sell off over 400 community gardens. In response, community members cried foul, using every tool at their disposal to launch a multipronged campaign to preserve the community gardens. Garden supporter Donna Schaper (2007) suggests growing gardens works in tandem with growing social change: "Gardening helps people with dynamite in their pants to change the world: it sustains us as we prod the world along" (xiv).

The campaign to support the gardens would take countless forms. Those involved engaged in a range of tactics to alter the distribution of power in an effort to save these green spaces. The battle for public space borrowed vitality from the struggle over old-growth forests on the West Coast with Earth First! "Many shuttled back and forth between the New York City community garden fight and old-growth forest blockades in remote Oregon," noted activist L. A. Kauffman (2004, 377). "The New York City community garden fight was one of the first times that Earth First!-style blockading techniques were used in an urban context. And they worked really well here, putting the gardens issue onto the agenda" (Kauffman, 377). Gradually, a local issue connected with a global movement to reclaim public space for the people (Shepard, 2011). One of those activists drawn into the garden struggle was Tim Doody. Having dropped out of college, he was concerned about what was going on in his community outside of Pittsburgh, Pennsylvania: "I started hearing people talking about the Allegheny National Forest, which is in Northwestern Pennsylvania, being clear-cut. The composition of the forest is being changed." The process threatened the biodiversity of the region, with an ever-expanding sprawl of corporate chains homogenizing the landscape, replacing mom-and-pop stores: "We just get Walmart, Barnes and Noble, Starbucks—the thing that makes the most money. And everything else has to go." Worried about what he was seeing, Doody started developing skills as an activist: "I went back and volunteered at Ruckus Camp [where activists are trained in direct action]. Rainforest Relief was there. 1999, I think. And some of the Ruckus climbers recommended this action. We were going to rappel down a banner and crash Giuliani's opening of City Hall Park. And I thought, I'll do it, let's go."

Once in town, Doody heard the community gardens were under threat, in the same ways as the old-growth forests he had seen outside Pittsburgh. Yet, activists were fighting back, and they were using many of the tools he had learned, including identification of an issue, research, mobilization, direct action, fundraising, legal and sustainability strategies, and play to make the campaign fun and creative.

"One of the most important steps toward defending your community garden is to have the support of your community, community gardens should be open to our communities!" (More Gardens! Coalition, 2002, 3). Garden groups gained the support of their communities through social organizing: holding pleasurable events such as parties, celebrations, and meetings, and making them convivial public spaces. At their essence, gardens are social spaces.

Writing this book grew out of reflections on growing up and coming to the city, where I fell in love with the green spaces of New York. My family had a farm in South Georgia for generations. My mom loved her gardens in Princeton and Atlanta. But I never saw these as contested spaces until I moved to New York, where they became a big part of my life. Here I saw public gardens facing a constant encroachment from the private. I first became involved with the gardens movement as a member of LESC. I was working in the South Bronx, where community members had looked to community gardening as a means for community revitalization in the years of Bronx burning in the 1970s. "Improve don't move" was the slogan. Creating gardens was a vital part of the process of rebuilding the community. The same process took place in the Lower East Side, where I lived. The organizing was very collegial. I recall running into members of LESC after an early meeting in the streets of the Lower East Side and getting a hug from one of the organizers I had just met. That was when I knew LESC was a kind space for friendships as well as organizing. Through it, LESC helped tap into the social capital of those in the Lower East Side: its people, their diverse experiences, and talents.

Throughout this period (from 1997 to 2000), activists developed strategies to preserve gardens as a dynamic component of public space and key community centers at a time when housing was being prioritized over environment and gardens. They connected housing and gardens, arguing for both as smart alternatives to previous models of urban renewal. LESC and the other garden defenders used a range of approaches, including street theatrics, media, legal strategies, and direct action in advancing solutions.

"At its best, direct action is where we advance the frontline of our movement work by visualizing the change we seek," notes Adrienne Maree Brown (2009) from the Ruckus Society. "Today, guerilla gardens are one example of a way to show that we know how to live more sustainably and we will push our leaders to catch up with us. It's about framing the issue in a way that inspires people to act, not just react . . . living a viable future and making it accessible to our communities."

From planting seeds in vacant lots to chaining themselves to green spaces about to be bulldozed, garden activists made masterful use of direct action to extend this environmental movement, refusing to disperse or sitting in, preventing their destruction, showing that gardeners were willing to use their bodies to defend green spaces (More Gardens, 2002).

L. A. Kauffman, of the LESC Public Space Group, describes the campaign and her work within the late 1990s. "I've been involved with a lot of organizing projects over the years, and there are very few where you can point to an absolutely concrete victory. I like looking back at the garden campaign as a way of considering how it is possible for us to win. That said, when you look at the last several decades of organizing, you see a pattern where we've learned how to win campaigns on a local level, but we've lost badly on the big issues around corporate control, the security state, foreign policy, and the state of our democracy. It's a paradox, and there's something both beautiful and bittersweet about carving out these local victories: We save 111 gardens while they steal an election in basically an undeclared coup. But there are parts of this story that I don't think have ever been told. As a campaign, it was a bit of a wild ride and an extraordinary one." Through Kauffman's narrative, we trace an often tense, conflicted history of the gardens movement in New York City.

"When I first got involved, LESC had only been around for a short time," said Kauffman, recalling the early days of this collective in 1997. "And some of us in the group were interested in working on issues of public space. Some folks from the Chico Mendez Mural Garden came to a LESC meeting to say their garden was threatened. The issue captured a number of our imaginations right away, as an issue about public space and real estate and privatization. A number of us decided to see what we could do. I had pretty much never grown anything. I was not a gardener." Kauffman would work to frame this as a public issue about cities and the privatization of space, not identity— gardeners versus non-gardeners. "Part of what was special was that LESC was looking for winnable local battles but bringing a broad perspective and analysis to them," explains Kauffman. "From the beginning, it was pretty clear that we couldn't save Chico Mendez Garden, that this first wave of gardens were likely to go down. The question was, how can we raise the friction around this whole issue so the larger garden-destroying agenda doesn't just move forward?"

To defend the gardens, supporters would draw a line. "They began with small steps, but it was clear early on that this was the beginning of a larger campaign by Giuliani," Kauffman continues. "Giuliani planned to sell off as much city land as possible, targeting the gardens first and foremost. All through that fall of 1997, the folks of Chico Mendez were trying to organize. And it was a challenging organizing environment. At that point there had been a lot of hangover from what had happened with the squats. There was a lot of paranoia and mistrust on the Lower East Side. And there was a way in which people were feeling very marginalized and hunkering down and turning inward."

The LESC Public Space Group pushed gardeners to open up their gardens, so they felt more public. "I can remember at Chico Mendez people would always be sitting hunkered in the middle of the garden, facing away from the street in a private circle, talking about what to do when the bulldozers came," she follows. "And we came in from LESC and said, 'If you want to fight this, you need to open the gates, welcome people to the garden, invite people in, put out a sign that says *Save the garden.* You've got to have a table outside that says, *Save the garden. Welcome, please come in.*' And you have to shift the framing. You had to shift away from the community garden issue being defined as just about the people who had plots in gardens and grew things there, broaden it into an issue about anyone who ever visited the gardens or benefited from them. On our leaflets, for instance, we used images of trees, not flowers or vegetables: Trees represented permanence and longevity. We worked to frame the issue so it wasn't just about who gardens, but who benefits from the gardens' existence."

Members of the LESC Public Space Group had countless influences, particularly queer activism, "what ACT UP had done," notes Kauffman. "David Crane had been in ACT UP. It wasn't the only group we looked to, but it had the best track record of concrete victories and that's what we were trying to get. Other influences included the Lesbian Avengers, Earth First!, and Queer Nation. We were looking to those early 1990s models, not 1968. Fierce, media savvy, not so concerned with its own purity that it wasn't going to make deals to win real victories."

The campaign was about clearly identifying winnable targets, which the group researched at length. "The deal that threatened Chico Mendez Garden—which was supposedly going to [replace] gardens [with] affordable housing—was being cosponsored by the New York City Partnership, which is New York City's Chamber of Commerce," Kauffman explains. "They immediately seemed like a soft target. They were not going to want a whole lot of bad publicity. Our first goal was to get them to pull out of garden-destroying deals. The assumption at that point when we were so small and marginal was that we were not going to be able to change Giuliani. Remember, this is 1997 in terms of levels of technology. I just started sending protest faxes to the Partnership. Back when ACT UP pioneered fax jams, you made a loop of paper that ran round and round in a fax machine so you could send the same page over and over. Well, it turned out you could make huge documents in Microsoft Word and fax them, so I made one that was something like a hundred pages of, 'Don't bulldoze the gardens. Don't bulldoze the gardens. Don't bulldoze the gardens,' with 'Pretty please' at the very end. And I would fax it straight from the computer. I just did that repeatedly. When I was bored, I would send out a few thousand faxes to the Partnership."

Outreach expanded the campaign. "Meanwhile, we were working to build community support," explains Kauffman. "We would go out to the subways in the morning, we would hand out flyers telling people about the crisis of

Figure 4.1. L. A. Kauffman, one of the masterminds of the garden campaign, in front of her "save the gardens" massive fax.

Source: L. A. Kauffman and the Fax Machine. Illustration by Caroline Shepard.

the gardens, with some numbers to call, and sign them up for a list we called the Email Army. And then we started asking people on the list to fax the Partnership, too. As more and more people did, that's when the Partnership got pissed off."

"So one night in August 1997, I was getting ready to go out to the opera when a pair of New York City detectives knocked on my door and ended up arresting me and leading me out of my building in handcuffs," recalls Kauffman, "charging me under a stalking law, for harassing the New York City Partnership."

As Jesse McKinley (1997) wrote in *The New York Times:*

In August, L. A. Kauffman, 33, a freelance journalist and part-time rabble-rouser, decided to tell the New York City Partnership what she thought about a plan to demolish a handful of community gardens in the East Village to make way for medium-income housing. Her sentiment was brief—merely "Leave our Gardens Alone"—so she thought she'd just fax it over.

And over. And over. And over. And over.

> During the next few weeks, Ms. Kauffman sent some 3,000 pages of faxes to the partnership, including a tome-like document, sent overnight by computer fax modem, that consisted of 499 pages of "Don't bulldoze the gardens!" in 14-point type, with the words "pretty please" on page 500.

The article highlighted the clash of ideas and thinking.

> Norman Siegel, executive director of the New York Civil Liberties Union, said the case would hinge on whether Ms. Kauffman had intended to enlighten or harass.
>
> "At some point, the communicative value of sending 2,000 faxes is slightly diminished," he said. "The first fax is clearly protected. The 2000th? I think that's probably the vanishing point."
>
> Ron Kuby, Ms. Kauffman's lawyer and a long-time civil rights attorney, disagreed.
>
> "It is an energetic flourishing of vox populi," Mr. Kuby said. "It should be encouraged."
>
> For those on the receiving end of the vox, however, the onslaught was bothersome. (McKinley, 1997)

Nonetheless, the article initiated a dialogue on the forces shaping the struggle. By "recogniz[ing]" their "causes," "situation[s]" are transformed, posits Paulo Freire (1970, 31, 32). Through the fax jam, Kauffman and others in LESC began such a process. "It was like a gift," confesses Kauffman. "Before that, we were just barely getting off the ground, we were like a mosquito in a tent—a small annoyance, nothing more. Once they arrested me, and we put it out on the email list and *The New York Times* covered it with a terrific little story, it became a full-blown controversy. Our email list must have tripled, and we suddenly had a lot more visibility and support. We knew the garden was going to get bulldozed. And enough gardens had been bulldozed in previous years in the winter, that we knew it would happen then, and probably in the middle of the night. And sure enough that's what happened."

The group could not stop the bulldozing, but they could "retaliate for the bulldozing," explains Kauffman. "That was when the first direct action happened. The garden movement was so small at that point that there were just three other people in addition to me who were willing to do something. We decided to chain ourselves across State Street, where the Partnership had their offices. It was me and Seth Tobocman and two other people. We bought a massive chain and chained ourselves across the street . . . On the day of the action it was such a surprise to the authorities that we ended up standing there for an eternity before emergency services arrived to cut the locks. And the action worked: After that, the Partnership pretty much backed out of sponsoring housing deals that destroyed gardens."

"So we did that Partnership action in early January," Kauffman continues. "We got a little media for it, but not much. It was the art of the possible for this small group. Twice, three times a week, we continued to go out leafleting, doing political education, building that email list. We were tiny. The bulldozing definitely radicalized and politicized people around the garden issue. Chico Mendez was a popular and well-used garden and it became a small *cause célèbre*.

"It was during the defense of Chico Mendez that Brad Will showed up in town from the West Coast, from Oregon where he had been doing forest defense encampments, bringing all these ideas about lockdowns, direct action, and blockades. It was when Chico Mendez was flattened that you started to see all of those ideas about garden defense come into the mix.

"So next the Giuliani Administration announced the March 1998 auction, which was the first time when a chunk of gardens was going on the auction block. There were just a few being sold, and only some were actually lively, vibrant, well-used gardens. We knew we didn't have the capacity to stop the sale, but you don't need much capacity to disrupt it. It was that Earth First! monkey wrenching idea, that even if you don't have much power, you can still cause friction and disrupt.

"So that first auction, Seth, Michael, and I decided to bid on properties, on the garden plots that were being sold. The atmosphere was very electric; we'd bid up the plots to something like a million bucks. When they came to get the cash deposit from me, I dug through my pockets and gave them 37 cents and a Metro Card. Needless to say, I got kicked out. The land was still sold, but it was something of a signal to them, that there was going to be resistance to what they were doing. Once those plots were sold, that was a new outrage we could organize around. We were no longer saying the city is *planning* to bulldoze gardens, we could say the city has bulldozed these and sold off these. They were doing it at a slow trickle, but we knew the plan was to sell off more.

"For the next land auction, in summer 1998, there were quite a few gardens on the docket as well as the CHARAS Community Center. We were working closely with CHARAS and we had also built a strong alliance with the city's affordable housing groups. We had a press conference with the Metropolitan Council on Housing, supported by all the leading tenant and affordable housing groups, expressing support for preserving all the community gardens and saying that gardens aren't getting in the way of affordable housing, Giuliani is.

"During this time, we would also go to the GreenThumb Grow Together and to the Community Garden Coalition gatherings. We developed really positive relationships there."

Throughout the campaign, members of the LESC Public Space group did outreach, lots of it, citywide. Kauffman elaborates: "We created something called the Bulldozer Hotline for people to call if their garden was being destroyed—Francoise Cachelin, who was an insomniac, took the phone calls—and we made fridge magnets with the number that we sent to every community garden in the city.

"We were constantly doing public education, old-style education on the issue. My favorite poster was the 'Which Kind of Worm Would You Prefer in Your Neighborhood,' which showed a real estate developer and a common earthworm. It was a takeoff on ACT UP's infamous 'Know Your Scumbags' poster."

In July 1998, LESC heard the city had plans to sell off a number of lots where gardens grew, as well as a community center in the Lower East Side, CHARAS/El Bohio. So, they came up with a rather creative response. On July 20, 1998, twelve activists entered a public auction with envelopes full of crickets to disrupt the proceedings (Shepard, 2011). Kauffman describes the scene: "We needed to come up with something new, we couldn't just bid on properties again, and we wanted to do something that would be splashy and disruptive. There were these legendary tales of tenant activists back in the day releasing rats in rent-control-board meetings. We wanted to come up with something that would be disruptive but mirthful, something no one could claim was actually dangerous or threatening. I don't remember how we came upon the idea of releasing crickets, but the more we thought about it, the more perfect it seemed. In our press release, we called it 'nature's revenge against greed' and called ourselves Jiminy Cricket, after Pinocchio's conscience: We were the conscience of the city. It was pre-9/11, and the level of security at police headquarters, where the auction was going to take place, was obviously much lower than it is today. David Crane and I had made envelopes with mesh air holes and we went down and tried going through the metal detectors. It worked great: their exoskeletons didn't show up on the X-ray machine. But when we were riding back on the subway, David suddenly gave me this look, and it turned out the crickets had escaped and were crawling up his arm! I got this enormous shipment of crickets—10,000 in my apartment. I acted like it wasn't unusual—I had a pet turtle, it could have been food for her—but wow did they smell bad. We stuck the boxes in the air shaft overnight and unfortunately once the crickets got comfortable, they all started chirping loudly—my neighbors later complained about it. The day of the auction—July 20, 1998—we transferred them all into the little envelopes and we all went down dressed in business attire."

With thrift store suits, none of these Lower East Side squatters looked like developers, said Tim Becker, one of the participants, recalling Seth Tobocman's suit trying to go inside. "It was obviously a borrowed suit because the pants legs were at least 40 percent too short. And he had stolen the tie. It was some polyester number that he had gotten from somebody and it looked really bad. And I said to myself, the police are going to watch the [closed circuit] TV in the back and they are going to know that something is going on. This guy is not a developer. It doesn't say money to me. If you call this guy money, it doesn't work" (Shepard, 2011).

"It was a hot July day, and there was a long security line," continues Kauffman. "And those poor crickets got too hot inside their envelopes, which makes them sleepy. So the auction finally begins and someone, maybe it was the head of Citywide Administrative Services, gets up and makes a big stern announcement that anyone who is making a false bid will be arrested. And we are giggling to ourselves because we know we're not going to use the same playbook. There's tension in the air, they're expecting something, they don't know what. We had a cue for when we were going to start releasing the crickets, and somebody totally flubbed it, so we're suddenly all scrambling to release our crickets and they're all totally overheated. They didn't jump out. But it didn't matter that the reality was different than the perception. The release of the 10,000 crickets *did* disrupt the auction—for hours. But it wasn't like they were hopping all over the place. Even so, as we predicted, it was really comical."

Several people were arrested, but only two were people who had actually released the crickets—Jason Grote and Tim Becker. The others were usual suspects that the police swept up just assuming they were involved. Jason and Tim reported the police laughing when they were going through the system. The news stories were great: "Police Headquarters was jumping yesterday after activists unleashed a fields worth of crickets after a land auction." That was the *Daily News* in an article titled "Activists Bugged by City Land Auction" (Cauvin, 1998). This was *The New York Times*: "Cricket invaders turn auction into madness."

The LESC storyline found its way into the press reports and the future of the campaign. "The goals of the action were to get publicity and to help build the movement, both of which it did," Kauffman followed. "But we were also hoping we would make Giuliani mad enough that he would show his hand. We knew the policy intention was to destroy the gardens *en masse*, but so far it had just been dribs and drabs. The next auction was a long time away. It wasn't till almost a year later, May 1999."

Over the next year, the organizers challenged New York mayor Rudy Giuliani's rotten apple narrative that the city was in decay and either one supported his plans or supported decay. With the gardens, activists shifted the discourse. "Many community gardens had started out as land squats that could be tarred by squatting, the gardeners could be portrayed as marginal characters," noted Kauffman. "That was what Giuliani meant when he famously said 'the era of communism is over' about the community gardens. We were countering that message with flowers and crickets, disruption and mirth. We were putting together something really different. Eventually Charas was sold, but LESC got their hands on one of the bidding forms and found out who had bought the property. The following day CHARAS supporters put up signs asking: 'Who sold CHARAS?' The newspapers were sympathetic to the case, supporting the neighborhood argument that gardens support rather than hinder the neighborhood. Nevertheless, despite the protests, the city announced plans to sell off another hundred gardens the following spring. After the announcement, plans were underway to delay and disrupt the scheduled auction of 119 garden sites."

"At some point in this, More Gardens! got going," explained Kauffman, describing the group started by Michael Shenker and Harry Bubbins to defend the gardens. "The LESC Public Space Group never put our name on things. More Gardens! did, which is why their role is featured in the histories and ours really isn't. More Gardens! came along saying the 'save the gardens' message was too negative. They wanted something more positive and ambitious. They were a more countercultural, prefigurative group of folks, who were passionate about saving the gardens and were living out a life of principle and seeing gardens as a model of a human society they wanted to create. They were younger. We were more punk and coming out of the queer punk direct action tradition; they were more hippies, coming out of an environmentalist and deep ecology background. The issue was much bigger than it had been at the start by the time they came along, and they made it even more so. And it ended up being a terrific collaboration. I don't remember the date when the properties for the auction were being announced. It was clear we had pissed off Giuliani. So he put a whole bunch of gardens—111 or 112—on the auction block. There are provisions for how far in advance city real estate sales have to be announced, which was a fairly long lead time.

"It gave us all a wonderful organizing opportunity. More Gardens! organized a terrific little sit in at City Hall, which was the first time you had large numbers of people, maybe 30, ready to go to jail. That was February 1999. That was when things really began building. One of the things that made the campaign really work was it was colored by the flashy direct actions that we did but was deeply rooted in old fashioned organizing."

LESC printed Spanish and English outreach packets for each neighborhood impacted. "The level of engagement was definitely growing. City Council members were getting called, the Coalition was increasingly active. When we started having rallies to save the gardens in the spring, the turnout was not only larger than it had been in the past, but also a lot more representative of the city—not just white radicals from the East Village." Throughout the campaign, Kauffman took note of the diverse experiences of the activists, many with long histories of engagement, as Young Lords and Black Panthers, who'd organized survival services decades prior, got involved. "You had all of these strains coming together over one seemingly local, seemingly limited, seemingly special-interest campaign," she recalled. "So by the time of the final weeks before the auction, all of these pieces have been put into place, all of these folks are in motion. Reclaim the Streets did a garden party in the street about a month before and that really inspired that group of folks. Under the rules of the city, they had to have a pre-auction seminar, where they explained what the rules of the auction were. That's when we had our 'earth-shaking protest,' a pretty classic street sit-in. More Gardens! had shown that there was a core of white middle-class folks who were willing to take arrests. So we thought there would be a lot of folks who would do it, and it was indeed a big action, over a hundred people."

Several members of the Lower East Side Collective, including this writer, joined in. "It got good press," elaborated Kauffman. "And then a few days later Matt Power did his brilliant tree climb in City Hall Park, saying he would not come down until he spoke with the mayor or the auction was canceled. That got huge publicity. Brad Will and another activist and I locked our ankles together in the office of the agency that runs the auction. It all worked together to create a sense of rising crisis around the auction, exactly what we wanted. There was a strong sense that the movement was on a roll, with new actions every day. All of them bold, showing this movement was pretty fearless. And we were openly vowing to disrupt the next auction. Part of the beauty of the cricket action was we wanted the Giuliani Administration to think we were crazy motherfuckers who would do just about anything. At the earth-shaking protest, we handed out a leaflet that we wanted to make sure the police saw. It was a list of auction disruption techniques. We came up with a list of ways that people could disrupt the auction that might get them kicked out but couldn't be stopped, because they have to let the public into a public auction. Come in with lots of metal, to slow down the security line, stand where you are not supposed to, wear disruptive costumes, that kind of thing. But the big one was a call for a puke-in: If the auction makes you sick, eat a big lunch and take some ipecac syrup right before going in. We wanted them to know that if they thought the July auction with the crickets was a mess, this was going to be a madhouse. It was going to be a huge embarrassment. And sure enough: at the very, very last minute, they cut a deal and canceled the auction. All the gardens [on the auction block] were saved and never again did they put a huge block of gardens up for auction. Gardens were bulldozed after that, and there will be new threats. But it was a beautiful victory."

The campaign that spring of 1999 set a tone, pointing out to the city that if they go after any set of gardens, people are going to fight back, doing the research to point out that there are other lots available. "It was a remarkable turnaround from gardens being a pretty marginal issue, associated with squatters, to being this truly diverse uprising against privatization," Kauffman elaborates. "These real estate fights in New York mean something in themselves but also as symbols and models for the rest of the country. That was May 1999, it wasn't long before people started talking about Seattle and people started mobilizing. It was a moment when that combination of street theater and spectacle and broad radical analysis of economic relations were coming together."

ESPERANZA GARDEN OF HOPE

Throughout the campaign to save the gardens, activists used every tool they could to create new situations, new ways of considering urban spaces. Interventions included demonstrations, sit-ins, and bulldozer hotlines, as well as land trusts to purchase the land. One of the gardens not saved in May 1999 was Esperanza Community Garden, on East Seventh Street, which was destroyed in February 2000 after a long defense. More Gardens!, LESC, and Time's Up! organized a twenty-four-hour-a-day vigil to defend the space.

"I started calling the Attorney General's office," explains garden supporter Susan Howard, direct action and legal strategies working in tandem, activists holding the space and lawyers agitating. "I had Foster Mayer from the Puerto Rican Legal Defense Fund, who had been on the CHARAS lawsuit." It was the same case argument as had been used with CHARAS. This was public space: "We sent in evidence, maps, etc. They said they did not know. Yet, it was very compelling." The plan was to get a temporary restraining order (TRO) on bulldozing gardens until legal arguments were resolved. In the meantime, the city started moving in on Esperanza, where supporters were holding a twenty-four-hour vigil and bulldozer alert. Throughout the campaign, direct action combined with a joyous theatrical model of organizing, which compelled many to participate. This social action lulled and disarmed audiences with stories that seduced rather than hammered, shifting the terms of the debate.

The week after Howard's contact with the attorney general's office, I received a message from the phone tree for the garden noting that "no parking" signs were being put up all over East Seventh Street. "That means something in this long struggle," notes Howard, a veteran of the Lower East Side squatting and gardening scene. "We assumed they were going for Esperanza. We started begging the cops not to participate, to back off. There is going to be a TRO from the Attorney General's office."

I had put my name on the phone tree as one of the "arrestables," to block bulldozers from destroying Esperanza. Tomorrow would be the day, the messages confirmed. El Jardin de la Esperanza (Garden of Hope) had grown from the rubble of a neighborhood reeling from the 1970s fiscal crisis. Alicia Torres turned a vacant lot on East Seventh Street between Avenues B and C into a garden where two generations of her extended family had celebrated birthdays, weddings, holidays, hot-dog roasts, and the change of seasons. It was a safe place for children to get off the streets of a Lower East Side once overrun with drug dealers. Now that the land was cleaned up, the Giuliani administration wanted to make a buck with it, selling it to developer Donald Capoccia, who had donated some $50,000 to the mayor's campaigns.

Some 100 people were at the garden when I arrived at 6 am, 150 by 8 am. A police car blocked traffic at the corner of Avenue C. Tim Doody had already made his way over to the garden, where he met those from LESC, More Gardens! the anarchists from the neighborhood, and this writer; the police surrounded the space. "The first street blockade I've ever been to was the More Gardens! blockade that we did together," recalls Doody. "All through that process, there was such a whimsical amazing element that combined the residents of the long-time Puerto Rican homestead, who were caretakers of the Esperanza Community Garden." Punk youth and grandmothers, it seemed the whole neighborhood got involved: "People gravitated around the huge Coqui." In Puerto Rican legend, this tiny frog was fabled to "let out a shrill cry rumored to scare the invaders away," notes Doody:

Here was this huge giant tree frog of Puerto Rican lore that activists had erected to vanquish larger foes, looming, as activists prepared to lock down, keeping vigil. It added an element of play and spirituality into the struggle, a galvanizing point, and garnering tons of media. Organizers put together picnics and parties and all-night vigils. The art of the campaign helped draw supporters and media. The research supported the claim that the garden should be preserved. Direct action helped draw media attention to the issue and legal action helped fortify the short and long-term gains. The Coqui watched from above. "Can you help me distract the driver so I can get under the bulldozer," Brad chimed in as Tim and I talked with Doody and company inside the garden holding the blockade. Howard leaped in a cab to go to the New York Attorney General's office, where she informed them:

"There is a firestorm in the Lower East Side," recalls Howard. "They are going to bulldoze Esperanza Community Garden." The receptionist was unable to help. Just then, the elevator opened and out came the lead attorney, Chris Amato. Howard tells him. He said "follow me and tells some of the other lawyers what was going on." The Attorney General's corporate counsel called the city and said: "We hear you are going to bulldoze a community garden in the Lower East Side. Hold off until we hear from a judge." A representative from the city retorted: "We're going to go ahead unless we are delivered a stop work order." By this time, the Attorney General's office was totally committed: "They went out to find a judge to put on a TRO."

While the attorney general's office was out trying to find a judge, those inside the community garden on East Seventh dug in. Activists locked themselves down in any way they could. It was the day after Valentine's Day, February 15, 2000. Garden defenders had been there all night. "It was like a painting," recalled Tim Doody. "Everybody was in the garden playing drums, getting into their lockdown positions and singing and chanting. And you just saw these hundreds of cops and like snipers on the rooftops." Those inside the garden felt they were building the world they wanted within the garden blockade. The police said we were trespassing. No injunction could go into effect until 2 pm that afternoon at the earliest—but if activists could stall the police and bulldozers all morning, there was a chance the garden could be saved. Some activists locked themselves to the surrounding fence with bicycle locks around their necks; others locked down to "sleeping dragons," pipes connected to concrete blocks buried deep in the ground. Another group locked themselves to a forty-five-foot-high steel tripod in the shape of a sunflower. And, of course, five activists locked themselves inside the Coqui, hoping to save Esperanza.

Police swarmed the front of the garden, while a bulldozer loomed in the distance. "Protect and serve the garden, protest and serve the people," we chant. The police moved in, tearing down the fence in front of the garden, sawing off an activist who'd chained herself to it. Then, one by one, the police arrested twenty-five activists who had locked themselves down to the garden or formed human chains with each other. In all, thirty-one people were arrested, many for the first time.

It took the bulldozers fifteen minutes to demolish the twenty-two-year-old garden. Those arrested were put through the system, many of us spending some thirty hours in jail, mostly in the holding cells in the basement of the Manhattan jail. In jail, we heard that Attorney General Spitzer had successfully procured a temporary restraining order on development of all Green-Thumb gardens.

The night in jail was long and ugly, but I was glad to be inside with Brad Will, Jerry "the Peddler" Wade, Aresh, Michael Shenker, and Tim Doody, instead of on the streets where the destruction of the garden was taking place. I thought of my friends putting their bodies on the line, saying they would do anything necessary to save this small community space, and the Coqui. Never have I felt more joy and connection with New Yorkers from all walks of life than standing in a blizzard, smiling by a bonfire during the winter encampment, sharing stories at Esperanza. The community built fighting for the garden was something that was going to last.

Attorney General Eliot Spitzer later remarked that the mayor had "subverted the legal process" by going ahead to bulldoze the garden just as the case was being heard in court. The City's actions and the community response eventually translated into a deal with the city to save many gardens for well into the next decade. "Despite this ruling, the City continued seeking to destroy gardens, and in some cases, was successful," notes Howard.

GARDENS AND THE POLITICS OF PUBLIC SPACE

In 2001, activists with More Gardens! spent the summer collecting signa-tures to sponsor a ballot referendum to make the gardens permanent. "The whole argument was to create a public campaign to have people support the gardens," explains Susan Howard, who took part in the signature collection process. Throughout the campaign, the activists brought a jigger of play. One petition driver even dressed as a rose bush, dancing at our tabling events.

By September 17, 2002, a deal between the attorney general's office and the new mayor secured the gardens in New York City: "The Stipulation of Agreement and Order was signed between the State of New York Attorney General Spitzer and the City of New York," says Howard. "The agreement covered only 546 gardens, with 100 of the gardens actually small open spaces supported by GreenThumb," a program of the New York Parks Department initiated during the fiscal crisis in the 1970s to provide support for over 500 community gardens. Over the next eight years, the city would become more and more expensive, many forced out as property values increased, placing more pressure on gardens as spaces for development.

With the 2002 garden agreement set to expire in September 2010, the NYC Parks Department published a draft of a new set of rules for the gardens, with few of the protections outlined in 2002. I had been going to New York City Community Garden Coalition meetings. A draft of the new rules was leaked to *The New York Times*. A subsequent article outlined many of these concerns (Moynihan, 2010a). Susan Howard gave me a call after the new garden rules were published in the *City Record*. Fearing the limitations of the rules, we called upon friends from More Gardens!, LESC, and Time's Up! to attend a meeting at ABC No Rio, a social center that was founded in 1980. In mid-July, the group held a meeting to talk about strategies. Throughout the discussion, activists outlined a common goal: make the gardens permanent. The meeting turned into a focus group on the benefits of gardens, including reduction in asthma and absorption of carbon and increases in social cohesion and property value with a converse reduction in crime.

"The community gardens are up for review again and we need to come up with some strategies to save them," wrote Bill from Time's Up! in an email blast after the meeting. Much of the struggle would take place through a battle over the story of the new rules. The working group from the meeting drafted a position statement in support of the gardens: "Green Means Gardens: Preserve,

Preserve, Preserve" read the first lines of the Time's Up! Statement on New Garden Rules. Time's Up! urged the city to make a final commitment to a green city by making all the gardens permanent once and for all. To support this goal, the group came up with a plan for three actions: a bike ride to the mayor's house calling for him to make the gardens permanent, a trip to City Hall for harvest day with crops from community gardens, and a tree climb in City Hall park. We planned the actions, coordinating with the press as we went. The day of the Paul Revere Bike Ride to Save New York's Community Gardens, the press was already writing about the event (Weichselbaum, 2010). The rationale for the Paul Revere theme of the ride was simple. When Paul Revere rang his bell to warn that the British were coming during the American Revolution, all he had was his voice and his bell to sound the alarm: "The British are coming!" In the case of the July 29, 2010, Paul Revere bike ride, the group was aided by modern media—the Internet, email, text messages, and newspaper reports—to sound the alarm about the City's move to eliminate protective status and endanger hundreds of community gardens. "The developers are coming," cyclists screamed riding through the city, followed by police, who had been calling and pestering me about the route for the ride all day long. Cyclists rode "horse-cycles"—bicycles with cardboard horse heads attached to the front—to several Lower East Side gardens, before heading up to Mayor Bloomberg's house to contend with a phalanx of police. Arriving at Bloomberg's townhouse on East 79th Street, a wall of the top brass of the police in white shirts walked toward the group of riders. It felt like a scene from the movie *Gunfight at the O.K. Corral*. Rather than wait or be told to stop what we we're doing, we rode past them. Walking straight up to the mayor's door, a group of us delivered the flowers and a sign asking the mayor and the city to please live up to his call to make this a green city.

"Mayor Bloomberg, please make the community gardens permanent for our children's children." Media were there to photograph and tape the discussion, and the story of activists pleading with the city to save the gardens went around the world. The following Monday, word of the group's work had found its way back into *The New York Times* (Moynihan, 2010b).

At 10 am on August 2, 2010, Jessica Sunflower, a garden supporter, climbed a tree in City Hall Park to call for the city to preserve the community gardens. Sunflower was surrounded by garden supporters from Time's Up! with vegetables from the community gardens as well as signs declaring: "Support the Gardens" and "Make the Gardens Permanent." Sunflower's gesture of direct action to affirm the need for community gardens harked back to decades of nonviolent civil disobedience, from Gandhi's Salt Satyagraha to the Civil Rights-era sit-ins and ACT UP's "zaps." The action garnered media attention city wide. After some twenty-six hours in jail, Sunflower shared a statement about her twenty-six-hour ordeal in custody and why she climbed the tree: "Heartening was being handed the *NY Times* editorial against the new rules when I walked out of the courthouse. *The Times* editorial from August 3, 2010, literally echoed the argument of activists, calling for the gardens to be protected, not transferred for development. The city was starting to lose control of the story."

"I am very proud to take part in making our collective voice heard," said Sunflower. The New York Garden Coalition held a press conference two days later, further condemning the new rules. It was clear that the city had lost the battle of the story. One by one, city politicians published comments critiquing the new rules while calling for protections for the gardens. The attorney general's chief of staff even helped Susan Howard and I meet with his legal staff, where we implored them to push the city to strengthen the rules. By early September the city published substantially improved rules for the gardens. In a later meeting, the attorney general's office would concede that the city was angry that they had had to make so many changes. They made just as many as were necessary to avoid litigation. "You got a lot," we were told. "Go to court if they go after any of these gardens." And that is exactly what activists would do when the next city administration went after the gardens.

CONCLUSION

The organizing used to build a coalition to defend the community gardens represents a best practice in the study of community organization. Here, a practical claim combined with a willingness to mobilize and use direct action and multiple media forms—including street theater, social media, and play—to support the campaign. Built through direct action and sweat equity, community gardens are places for neighborhood members to meet, share, and plant the seeds of community. These are spaces for people to be introduced, be creative, discuss issues of mutual interest, prioritize use over exchange, bridge a gap between work and play, and fashion a distinct model of sustainable urbanism.

POSTSCRIPT ON ADAM PURPLE

In September 2015, Bill Time's Up posted a message titled "Remembering Adam Purple." He wrote: "Yesterday, September 14, 2015, we lost one of New York's most well-known and colorful environmentalists. Adam Purple died of a heart attack while riding his bicycle over the Williamsburg Bridge . . . His commitment to a sustainable lifestyle was unrelenting and all-encompassing."

A MEMORIAL FOR AN ICON

The memorial for Adam Purple was held in La Plaza Cultural Community Garden in the Lower East Side of Manhattan. Adam Purple, born David Wilkie in 1930 in Missouri, was a white-bearded and purple-clad fixture of the Lower East Side and, later, Williamsburg, Brooklyn. His Garden of Eden was "eARThWORK," which he began creating in 1975 in a vacant, garbage-filled lot between Forsyth and Eldridge Streets. It was destroyed in 1986.

I had heard that Purple was gone as I rode to a meeting of Public Space Party, a direct action group that uses street performance to highlight issues of sustainable urbanism, cycling, and public space. It was like seeing a ghost to run into him at Time's Up!

"I remember seeing him when I was a kid in Central Park," recalled Catherine at the meeting. "I was like nine and there he was in his purple tie-died outfit, picking up horse manure. He was like a hundred then and that was 1979. And then I saw him at Time's Up! years later." Everyone had stories about Adam Purple and the community garden that he created.

Today, stories about sustainable urbanism are everywhere. This is the idea that cities can be mutable works of art, as the Garden of Eden demonstrated. They can be places to slow down and just live. Today, as another mayor, Bill De Blasio, plans to bulldoze community gardens to make way for housing few can afford, the story of the Garden of Eden is worth recalling. This garden artwork brought community resilience and care, green space and ideas. It was a place for water to seep back into the earth, opening a model of cross-class contact, recycling, and green community development.

As Sarah Ferguson (1999) writes, "By the early 1990s, some 850 gardens had been established—more than 60 of them on the Lower East Side. Yet these plots were becoming increasingly threatened . . . Inspired by the destruction of Adam Purple's world-renowned Garden of Eden . . . Felicia Young began hosting pageants to dramatize the plight of the area's green spaces. Every spring, throngs of glitter-and-gauze wrapped dancers, giant puppets, and mud-caked performers wind their way through the neighborhood's eclectic spaces, re-enacting the gardeners struggle to keep their land."

Today, that dance still continues; so does the struggle for the gardens. The Garden of Eden reminds us that cities are more than spaces for accumulation and overdevelopment. They can be places to conserve, reuse, and renew.

John Penley notes: "One of the things I remember about Adam Purple is that he was recycling things in large quantities before most people had even thought about doing it or even called it recycling. He was a true pioneer in this respect. I remember that after he was evicted from his Forsyth Street. . . . I went and was amazed at all the different things he had in the building and it was separated into different rooms . . . It was pretty amazing and things were orderly and separated but there was a massive amount of stuff he had collected over the years . . . His garden was like no garden I have ever seen before and he used organic garden techniques before any of us had even heard the phrase 'organic gardening' used."

"People thought he was crazy," says Harvey Wang, who photographed Purple. "But Adam was speaking the truth when the truth couldn't be heard."

Ray Figueroa of the New York City Garden Coalition welcomed everyone and set the stage. "How many of you are feeling good in this garden?" he asked, referring to the garden where the memorial was taking place, La Plaza Cultural, at the southwest corner of East Ninth Street and Avenue C. Everyone raised their hands. "As you enjoy it, remember, this happened because visionary lovers of the earth were out organizing, getting arrested. We need to not forget this history. We need to stay vigilant in the face of those who say affordable housing is at odds with community gardens. Today, we need more sustainable models of development. If it means anything to you, you have to come out. This is a romance."

George Bliss groaned thinking about the false debate between housing and gardens. "I am horrified to hear that the same ploy is being used today." When the garden was finally destroyed, Bliss saw Purple standing looking at the last tree. He summarized the lesson of Purple's life: "We have to create what is right, not react to it. But create it, connecting with everything . . . Bringing it here was a gift. So I decided to paint footprints to remind the world about the garden," George confessed. "Following the loss of the Garden of Eden, Bliss painted purple footprints that lead to the former location of the garden."

Wendy Brawer of Green Map System notes: "So sad to see this. Adam's purple footprints drew us to the neighborhood in 1986, and he taught deep ecology at the very first Green Map event in 1992. Special thanks to Time's Up! for housing him, and helping us all stay in contact with this learned activist."

Howard Branstein, who runs the 6th Street Community Center, and was active in land trusts on the Lower East Side in the 1970s, says that Purple insisted, "I'm not going to deal with the city. They stole the land from the Indians in the first place." Those listening at La Plaza broke out in applause. Howard pointed out that Purple was not always practical. When he stayed in his building after the owner left, he was unable to organize the remaining tenants, many of whom were vegetarians. Many around him left or were turned away for ideological reasons.

"They would not shit in the garden," Purple told him.

"Well that's not helpful," noted Howard. Still, "he was a messiah and inspiration for the garden movement. In 1986, when beauty died, a stronger garden movement was born. When El Jardin's fate was put up for a vote, the whole community board supported it, as a consequence of the loss of the Garden of Eden."

"Reclaiming urban land, that was Adam's idea," explained Bill Weinberg, a radical historian and editor of *Avant Gardening*, who got to know Purple in 1985. He described the destruction of the garden as a "political hit." The city went after this garden. "There were vacant lots [owned by the city] everywhere. It was chosen for political reasons. Finally, they came in the dead of winter and took the garden. It was a political crime. They tried to do the same thing with La Plaza and the community fought back. We need to keep organic culture here in the Lower East Side."

Father Frank Morales says, "Adam was the most thorough revolutionary that I know. He was all of it, one-part Karl, another Groucho Marx. I'm still in denial that he's gone. I keep thinking he'll be coming back on the third day."

"He was an urban survivalist," notes Chris Flash, editor of the *Shadow*, a Lower East Side radical newspaper. Flash was frustrated that Purple did not organize more to save his home, but that was for the Michael Shenkers of the garden movement, who helped outline a model for organizing to save the gardens, connecting direct action and legal advocacy. Countless lawyers who followed this model were there to support these efforts.

Alan Moore recalled those days in the Garden of Eden, where he listened to a man speaking quietly among the trees. Moore didn't expect to address the assembly, although he'd lived in Purple's squat when he first came to the city. He slept in a back room, just off the garden, and was scared at night someone might come in the building, which was largely abandoned. Purple told him not to worry as long as he could hear the crickets. When they stopped chirping, then someone might be coming.

In the days and months after his funeral, stories about Adam continued, offering more and more messy details, as the interplay of repression and expression in his life story expanded. Over time, the narrative would become more and more complicated in the yin and yang of the garden and Purple's life, with darkness sometimes overtaking light.

Toward the end of December, *The Villager* newspaper ran an article, naming one of Purple's stepdaughters as a source, and a second in which all four daughters use their full names and confirm one another's account of what their father did to them. In it, the paper aired the claims of the daughters that Purple was a sexual abuser (Anderson, 2015, 2016a, b).

No one is only one thing, chimed a few observers on Facebook.

"I suppose he made some difference, but I had a bad reaction to him," recalls Bill Koehnlein, who was banned from Purple's Garden of Eden, and from entering the premises on Forsyth Street, after a disagreement, "especially the way he treated two or three of my friends, plus I couldn't abide by the fawning people did over him—and the way he relished it and lapped it up. A cult is a cult, no matter if it's Donald Trump, Bob Avakian, or Adam Purple."

"Not very surprised!" noted Alan W. Moore. "As an artist, he was a classic 'monstre sacré' . . . An extreme personality who, finally, created an incredible work of art."

After the publication, Purple's daughter Jenean, who went on record in the article, wrote thanking the author for considering Purple's work in the totality of his life, suggesting the world, "Consider my father as a whole person, not a monster or hero, just a man who lived life according to his values. Yes, he hurt some people along the way, but don't we all?" (Anderson, 2015). Well, some more than others.

"*The Villager* was not wrong to bring it to light," Bill Weinberg told *The Villager*. "If the daughters chose to go public, their wishes should be respected. Let this be an inoculation against 'heroes.' Every human being has the capacity for evil. Maybe it even says something about Hegel's paradoxical unity of opposites that the same man who created something so beautiful on Eldridge St. apparently had such a dark side" (Anderson, 2016b). The light and dark, yin and yang symbol at the center of garden, the discontent certainly changes our understanding of the artist who created the Garden of Eden. Such opposing forces change ideas and cities. They inspired Freud's narratives of psychoanalysis, linked with the Frankfurt School's conversations about Marxism (Marcuse, 1955). Eros and Thanatos are part of urban spaces, their impulses interwoven into efforts to move forward through time and space. The story of the garden is a cautionary tale not to follow blindly. Flux is constant; we have to move. Adam Purple's last efforts on the planet took place as he rode his bike home over the Williamsburg Bridge bike path. The following chapter considers a few of the struggles to navigate this urban terrain, between cars, bodies, and ideas about cities.

Chapter 5

Dialectical Times: On the Movement for Nonpolluting Transportation and Sustainable Urbanism in New York City

"Today urbanism's main problem is ensuring the smooth circulation of a rapidly increasing quantity of motor vehicles," Guy Debord quipped (Merrifield, 2002a, 94). Both Debord and his mentor Henri Lefebvre worried that the modern metropolis of drab order was gradually suffocating the life-affirming creativity of the city (95). Like the Dadaists and Surrealists before them, Lefebvre, Debord, and the Situationists recognized the potential for a new kind of city, defending the urban mix and rejecting the rationalized urban sphere, in favor of "daring, imagination and play in social life and urban culture," notes geographer Andy Merrified (96).

Today, advocates of sustainable urbanism consider nonpolluting transportation a vital component of their efforts to mold a livable city. Countless groups in New York City follow up where the Situationists and the Dutch Provo left off, supporting efforts to rid urban space of the undue influence of automobiles and their harmful effects on people and the environment (Shepard and Smithsimon, 2011). The stories cyclists in the city involve intersecting narratives of a culture clash between those who see urban space as a space for the free flow of polluting automobiles and those who see it as a place for nonpolluting transportation, bicycles, community gardens, and people-based uses. In short, it involves a dialectical interplay between Robert Moses' suburban vision and Jane Jacobs' vision of eyes on the street in urban space. This is a story about cities as do-it-yourself (DIY) spaces, urban life as mutable, influenced by multiple social actors, moving from pedestrian uses toward automotive transport, back to a space linked by rail and cycling (Duncombe, 1997). Such advocacy is part of a distinct pro-urban politics, fashioned around its own "right to the city" (Furness, 2010; Harvey, 2013; Horton, 2006).

CYCLING, SOCIAL MOVEMENTS, AND PUBLIC SPACE

"Before cars came along, the streets were often a common, a place of popular sociability, a play space for kids," notes David Harvey (2013, 74) in his work *Rebel Cities*. Harvey (2013, 74) makes his point with a caveat. "Streets that get clogged with traffic make that particular public space unusable. . . . This kind of a street is not a common" (74). Sadly, this is too often the case in today's cities, as the commons are rendered unusable, filled with cars and shopping carts, privatizing space. This need not be the case. In response to expanding systems of privatization and automobility, a generation of cyclists have looked to streets for alternate expressions as well as instrumental uses. Seeing the streets as places for friends and strangers to meet, play, talk, ride, and create a social world within our commons, cycling advocates suggest there is more to urban living than going to and from work (Shepard and Smithsimon, 2011).

The stories here serve as a case study in environmental justice and DIY urbanism; each engaged in a clash of visions of urban space, bikes versus cars, Jacobs versus Moses, open versus closed space, growth versus degrowth, neoliberal versus sustainable urbanism. Offering a lens into the ways cities are organized, the push for street justice builds on an expanding debate about neoliberal urbanism, with local actors lamenting the negative dynamics associated with globalization seen in cities, including inequality, pollution, and dependence on fossil fuels, while looking for alternatives (Harvey, 2013; Sites, 2002; Vitale, 2008).

Aiming at reversing some of these dynamics, including fast cars and unsafe streets, community organizers have taken to charting an alternative path built around environmental justice (Shepard, 2014; Vitale, 2008). Here, degrowth is framed as a community-building model seen in contrast with a model of capitalism that Max Weber (2002, 121) saw as an all-consuming machine, pulling most everyone or thing into its trajectory. This seemingly carcinogenic model of capital expansion is posed in contrast to progressive solutions associated with emerging social movements aimed at fostering sustainable models of urbanism, built through community development, infrastructure for nonpolluting transportation, public space, as well as efforts to foster resilient urban spaces.

To support these endeavors, organizers engage in a range of efforts, including social action, forensics, direct action, and data analysis, assessing crash data from when cars collide with cyclists and pedestrians. Such community practice extends into core areas, including dialogue and deliberation to examine options for meeting the challenges, remediation to fix what is wrong, prevention and development to stave off problems while creating alternatives, and social action to fashion direct action-based solutions (Shepard, Totten,

Homans, 2012). This is a model of community building born of imagination and conversation, assessing what is wrong and what might be done to right it. "Dialogue cannot exist," posits Paulo Freire (1970, 76–77), "in the absence of a profound love for the world. . . . The naming of the world, which is an act of creation and re-creation, is not possible if it is not infused with love." Social action grows through such conversations.

NONPOLLUTING TRANSPORTATION

Through these efforts, organizers have engaged in a project of experimenting with what sorts of sustainable urbanism really work. A prime example of such efforts involves nonpolluting transportation. Since 1999 I have been a volunteer with groups involved in this movement, including Time's Up!, Right of Way, the Occupy Sustainability Committee, and Public Space Party. These efforts support a distinct lineage of cycling activism extending from the Women's Movement to European Socialism, the Dutch Provo to Reclaim the Streets, and the Occupy movements organizing for a "right to the city" (Furness, 2010; Harvey, 2013; Horton, 2006). Henri Lefebvre (1996, p. 158) saw such efforts as a "demand . . . [for] a transformed and renewed access to urban life." This is a spatial demand, says critical geographer David Harvey (2013). Countless movements have translated their goals in terms of equitable access to public space (Shepard, 2014).

CYCLING FOR A RIGHT OF WAY—ACTION
AND RESEARCH

Much of this story began with the groups Time's Up! and the Occupy Wall Street (OWS) Sustainability Committee. These groups used cargo bikes to transport food waste and compost from the occupation downtown to community gardens throughout NYC. Cyclists brought bike generators to power the occupation in the park. A year later, this experience proved invaluable to post-Sandy organizing efforts. Cyclists organized relief rides with cargo bikes bringing supplies and sharing food under the slogan "Mutual aid, not charity." Cyclists moved thousands of pounds of food from Brooklyn to Queens, pointing to the possibilities of biking as a vital resource for post-disaster cities (Shepard, 2013).

Over the next year, cyclists testified at the City Council about the importance of cycling for disaster relief, but issues of safety continued to get in the way. So, we looked to another social movement, the Dutch "Stop de Kindermoord" (Stop the Child Murder) movement, for insight. Pedestrians and cyclists are killed every thirty-six hours in NYC; 265 lives were lost to traffic violence in 2014, more than in comparable locales such as Amsterdam, where only six cyclists are killed a year, on average (Orange, 2013). In Amsterdam, the city puts the onus on drivers to support safe streets for everyone. Cities such as Malmö and Berlin, where only fifteen cyclists were killed on the road in 2012, follow this trend; others, such as Delhi and London, which suffered 78 and 118 cyclist deaths in 2012, respectively, suffer higher losses (NHS, 2014; Orange, 2013). Few seem to compare with the New York experience.

While cycling in Holland has become increasingly safer, cycling in New York still involves navigating contested terrain. Just to ride to work or to the park, cyclists take part in an intersecting narrative of twisting, congested corridors of blocked passages, plotting Jane Jacobs' (1961/1992) image of small-scale streets, in contrast with Robert Moses' image of cities as spaces for smooth movement of automobiles (Harvey, 2013). Since the 1970s, many New York streets have come to look like highways, while the Dutch have reduced traffic deaths by creating a network of streets designed to be safe and convenient for pedestrians and cyclists alike. "The superiority of the Dutch approach" is "dramatic," says Ben Fried (2013). "In 1975, the traffic death rate in the Netherlands was 20 percent higher than in America, but by 2008 it was 60 percent lower. About 22,000 fewer people would die on U.S. streets each year if the nation had achieved safety outcomes comparable to the Dutch" (Fried, 2013).

For years now, New Yorkers have been fighting for safer streets. In 1987, the city of New York attempted to ban cycling in midtown Manhattan, inspiring a wave of activism often referred to as "The Bicycle Uprising." Charles Komanoff (2012) saw that the 1987 midtown bike ban was "motivated by scapegoating of bicycle riders (bicycle messengers) for endangering pedestrians." He and other bicycle activists turned that logic on its head by researching and publicizing the fact that motor vehicles were striking and killing two orders of magnitude (100) times as many pedestrians as were cyclists. But the alleged slaughter of pedestrians by "kamikaze bike messengers" led City Hall to attempt to suppress cycling, which set off a chain of events that ended up galvanizing bike activism in New York. Activists first ferreted out the statistics of "Who's Really Getting Hurt" and published the findings (Komanoff, 2012, 9). In addition, waves of cyclists defied the ban through a series of group rides, demonstrating the power and possibility of group rides to transform streets from car-dominated spaces into alternative sites for nonpolluting transportation. Thanks to waves of direct action, data analysis, dissemination, and research, the bike ban would not last for long.

The livable streets group Right of Way was formed in 1996 to help ensure the right of way for pedestrians. "Frustrated by officials' chronic refusal to acknowledge the dangerous and debilitating environment for walking and cycling in New York city streets," cycling activists, such as Charles Komanoff (1999, 54), "understood that the few initiatives underway to improve human powered travel were being overwhelmed by the relentless growth in motor traffic." The group's mission:

> The fundamental human right to move about in public space without being intimidated, injured, or worse is the "right of way." On the streets of New York City, drivers routinely violate this basic right of others. Right of Way uses direct action to highlight this issue and rectify it. Our mission is to assert the public right of way and turn the streets into vibrant public space for all. (Komanoff, 1999, 54)

Charles Komanoff (2012) recalls those days when he first started collecting and analyzing data on traffic fatalities. The August 19, 1991, crash, in which a car rushing through traffic to keep up with a motorcade for a religious leader ran a red light, careened onto the sidewalk, and killed seven-year-old Gavin Cato, the son of two Guyanese immigrants, ignited three days of upheaval known as the Crown Heights Riots of August 1991. It also compelled the group to act; Right of Way started making street memorials, spray-painting them on the streets where people had been killed by cars all over New York. The group put individual names and causes of these crashes on street memorials. That would lead to the group's identification with the victims and their families.

The group knew too many people dying in the streets of New York, yet the city was not forthcoming with accident data (Komanoff, 1999). They wanted to understand what was happening with New York traffic fatalities. "After our first half-a-dozen stenciling forays, we 'graduated' to wanting to stencil in a more focused way," notes Komanoff. The group tracked "people killed in the Brooklyn City Council district represented by the anti-bike, pro-driver head of the City Council Transportation Committee." They filed a Freedom of Information Act request for data on crash fatalities from 1994 to 1997 in New York. Initially ignored, the help of a local congressman moved the request forward. Komanoff felt sheer excitement when he got the boxes of files from the city. "Once the boxes arrived, we saw we were sitting on top of a gold mine of data." Komanoff and company put together a database with 947 cases and accident reports and 60 categories, detailing who was getting killed, where, how, and by whom—"an amazing cross section killed," notes Komanoff. "There was an almost dialectic relationship between the data we were analyzing and the direct action." People of all walks of life in New York were impacted. The result of the research was the Right of Way book *Killed by Automobile*: *Death in the Streets in New York City 1994–1997*, by Komanoff and Right of Way (1999). Data and direct action overlapped and supported the group's efforts, combining street art, legal analysis, testimonials, and emotional pleas from those impacted by traffic violence.

The group experienced a renewed engagement in the fall of 2013, lasting into spring 2015, as members of Time's Up!, the Cargo Bike Collective, Transportation Alternatives, Public Space Party, Make Brooklyn Safer, and others, including this writer, collaborated, adding a new pulse to a burgeoning street justice movement. Together, we pushed cycling activism from direct action into research, City Council hearings, and back into the streets, from stenciling to testifying to bike riding with banners while painting badly needed bike lanes in the streets. The aim was to create a safer city for all New Yorkers. We testified about the need for the city to investigate car collisions with cyclists and pedestrians and continued to paint memorials for cyclists and pedestrians killed by cars, reminding the world of their lives and the reality that the New York Police Department (NYPD) did little to investigate the causes of their deaths. We organized Critical Mass rides celebrating nonpolluting transportation and pushed cars out of bike lanes (Shepard and Smithsimon, 2011).

The group's energy was renewed with the installation of a guerilla bike lane on Sixth Avenue from 42nd Street to Central Park as a "gift to the city." The reason was simple. On Thursday morning, August 22, 2013, cab driver Mohammed Himon drove onto the sidewalk on this stretch of Sixth Avenue where he said he intentionally stepped on the gas because he had gone blind with rage during an altercation with a cyclist. On the sidewalk, Himon ran over pedestrian Sian Green, severing her leg.

"While accelerating into a cyclist and onto a sidewalk is unacceptable and we hope Himon is charged with serious crimes, sometimes basic infrastructure can calm traffic and save lives," said organizer Keegan Stephan (2013–2015).

"In this case, a continuation of the Sixth Avenue Bike Lane from 42nd Street to Central Park could have created the space and distinction needed to prevent Himon's atrocious actions. If someone had done this sooner, Sian Green might not have lost her leg. We celebrate the amazing work the DOT has done over the last seven years to make our streets more safe and livable, but the work is never done. That is why we gave this bike lane as a gift to the city."

With each action, Right of Way supported an expanded movement in sustainable urbanism, born of a right to organize, ride bikes, plant gardens, connect neighborhoods, and fashion a better city (Harvey, 2013; Thorpe, 2014). For cycling advocates, it was all part of a dialogue.

On September 30, 2013, Keegan Stephan and other cycling advocates testified at the City Council Oversight Hearing on the NYPD Collision Investigation Reforms, chaired by James Vacca of the City Council Transportation

Committee. Vacca opened the hearings with a vengeance, noting that everywhere he goes, people come up to him to complain about cars. "It's not the Daytona 500 out here. They have no regard for anyone, pedestrians, cyclists, or other cars," asserted Vacca, in comments at the hearing (Shepard, 2013–2015).

"Negligent drivers are getting off the hook, while the NYPD continues to only investigate crashes involving fatalities, not injuries. This is a low standard. Crashes involving cars deserve expeditious investigation of critical injuries." "Reckless endangerment is a misdemeanor which needs to be enforced," added Peter Vallone Jr., chair of the Council's Public Safety Committee, noting New Yorkers are more likely to die than see the NYPD follow the laws on the books (Shepard, 2013–2015). "Failure to exercise due caution is also a criminal charge."

Keegan Stephen (2013–2015), of Right of Way, followed, testifying:

In just over six months, 63 people—more people than in this room—have been killed by automobiles while walking or biking in NYC.

In two-thirds of these deaths due to automobiles, the NYPD declared "No Criminality Suspected" within hours of the crash, before the Crash Investigation Squad (CIS) reports could be thoroughly completed.

In six of these, the pedestrian was killed on the sidewalk.

In nine of these, the pedestrian was killed in the crosswalk and the driver was admittedly turning, clearly failing to yield right of way, and still no charges.

This clear disconnect between the strong circumstantial evidence of driver culpability and the premature exoneration of the drivers by the NYPD, make the other 26 cases in which the NYPD declared No Criminality Suspected, themselves suspect. This calls for an expedited, reliable disclosure of crash investigation material to the public.

To deter traffic violence for the safety of all, the NYPD

1. Must do a better job of investigating deadly hit-and-runs.
2. Must not declare the absence or presence of criminality at the scene of a crash, or allow anonymous leaks to the press.
3. Must charge for crimes in a much higher percentage of crashes than they are.
4. Must be required to release their reports to the public.

ACTION

A few weeks after the hearing, on October 13, 2013, the group led a group bike ride to dramatize the human costs of the problem, riding out to eight locations in Manhattan, Staten Island, and Queens where children under eight years of age were killed by an automobile. Over the day, we rode more than fifty miles, through four boroughs, to stencil eight sites where the children

Figure 5.1. Allison street graffiti.

Source: Photo by Benjamin Shepard.

were killed by automobiles that year. In five of these cases, the NYPD filed no charges.

One of the most intense moments of the ride took place in Queens, where we made a memorial for Allison Liao, age three, who was killed walking with the light in the crosswalk at the corner of Main Street and Cherry Avenue and the police declared "No Criminality Suspected." On arriving we saw a memorial already in place for Allison. I kept on imagining the child's last glimpse up at a car, riding straight at her, and her grandmother's reaction as she was crushed.

A CALL FOR PREVENTION

A few weeks later, members of the group would testify when the City Council Transportation Committee was debating Int. No. 535, a local law designed to reduce the speed limits in residential areas in NYC.

My friend Wendy E. Brawer, another Right of Way supporter, offered written testimony. "It's been proven that 97 percent of people on the street can survive a 20 MPH crash," stated Brawer. "Only 80 percent can survive a 30 miles per hour crash" compared with the "30 percent who can survive a 40 MPH crash" (Shepard, 2013–2015).

I thought this would be just another hearing. But when I saw that the first group to testify was the family of Sammy Eckstein, the boy recently killed by a car in Park Slope, I knew this was not going to be the usual hearing, as the movement for safer streets took a new urgency and emotional resonance.

"On October 8th at 5:11 pm, my 12-year-old son, Sammy Cohen Eckstein, was struck by a van just across the street from our home," related his mother, Amy Cohen, a social worker, during the hearing. "He died a few hours later. As best we understand it, he crossed into the intersection from Prospect Park with the light to get a soccer ball. While he had the light when he entered the intersection, it quickly changed and he slipped and was hit by a van approaching the intersection at full speed" (Shepard, 2013–2015).

The tone of the hearing was radically altered with the words of the slain boy's grieving mother, father, and sister. Each lamented his passing just days before his bar mitzvah, calling for the City Council to do something to prevent future deaths by lowering driving speeds on residential streets. Most everyone in their Brooklyn neighborhood of Park Slope mourned for the boy. His parents brought that grief to the City Council.

"Around the world, it's been proven that lower speed limits save lives," noted Transportation Alternatives executive director Paul Steely White during the hearing. In September of 2013, London joined Paris and Tokyo in lowering the speed limit to twenty miles per hour (MPH). "New York City would greatly enhance the safety of all its residents, motorists and pedestrians alike, by adopting a similar measure," White said. "A one-mile-per-hour reduction in average speed on pedestrian-dense urban streets with low average speeds will lead to a 6 percent decrease in traffic crashes. And New York is home to the most dense urban streets in the country," White concluded (Shepard, 2013–2015).

I was the last person called to speak. With little need to review the statistics everyone had already cited, I spoke as a father, driver, cyclist, and pedestrian. "I have seven and ten-year-old daughters who ride and play along the same Prospect Park where Sammy died. I don't want any of these kids to be the next casualties. This legislation will prevent future incidents. Motorcycles and cars would race up my street like it was a speedway, only to careen to a stop at the red light. Recently I moved to the Gowanus, where we have been designated a safe zone. And the policy works. When I drive and my mind is on other things, the 20 miles per hour signs remind me to slow down. The policy should be expanded citywide" (Shepard, 2013–2015).

Vacca concluded by stating he was going to move the bill.

SOCIAL ACTION

The dance of the dialectic between data and direct action would continue all fall. Shortly after the hearings, members of Right of Way demonstrated how easy it could be for New York to change the speed limit in the city. On a freezing Saturday night, November 23, 2013, the group installed "20 Mile Per Hour" signs along Prospect Park West, where Sammy was killed by a car driving much faster. The group viewed their gesture as a second "gift to the city." The 20 MPH speed limit signs on Prospect Park West—where the Park Slope Civic Council's application for a Slow Zone was rejected by city officials the previous year—were a simple response to a crazy situation.

"This is not enough," said Keegan Stephan (2013–2015). "We need complete street redesigns, speed and red light cameras, and vigilant law enforcement to eliminate traffic deaths. But even signs alone can save lives."

"The city could lower the speed limit on most of New York City's streets tomorrow," noted Stephan (2013–2015). "This would inevitably slow down traffic, allowing the NYPD to focus on people who continue to speed and engage in other life-threatening criminal driving, such as failure to yield."

"While these signs are not permanent," said Stephan (2013–2015), "we have put them up to show the city just how easy it is." A subtext of the action was a call for the city to slow down, to degrow, so this could be a livable city.

The group would spend the fall putting the signs up in neighborhoods across Brooklyn and elsewhere in the city. The argument had been "It's expensive to put these signs up, it's going to take a lot of work and take a lot of approval, but the cyclists were here to say, 10 cyclists can put these signs up in an afternoon and we know that this saves lives. That was the point" (Shepard, 2013–2015).

Throughout the winter and spring of 2014, activists in the traffic justice movement pushed as the city seemed to be responding. The year 2014 would bring a new mayor committed to a Swedish "Vision Zero" approach to reducing traffic fatalities. New York could be a pedestrian-friendly city, argued members of the group. We walk to the subway, ride bikes to work, and play in our neighborhoods. But with the suburbanization of New York, more and more cars have pushed into these streets, damaging neighborhoods, the environment, and people (Hammett and Hammett, 2007). At a Candlelight Vigil for Pedestrian Safety held in Queens, Amy Cohen argued we need a paradigm shift in our streets (Shepard, 2013–2015). Everyone seemed to agree. But would the city change?

In order to change the speed limit in New York City, we would need permission from the state government in Albany. So activists pushed, organizing a gathering to demand home rule for speed limits. Some 100 people carried "20 is Plenty" signs in support of bills in the NY State Assembly and the NY

State Senate pushing for "Home Rule"—allowing the city to lower the speed limit to 20 MPH. The argument was simple. Lower speeds save lives. When drivers aren't speeding, they have more time to brake when something unexpected happens. Lower speeds mean that even when a driver or pedestrian makes a mistake, there is time to avoid a crash and, if there is not enough time, the penalty is in most cases not death. Cycling activists citywide converged at Grand Army Plaza to make a plea for our own model of sustainable urbanism in global Brooklyn.

"This is a crucial step in Mayor de Blasio's push toward Vision Zero," said Keegan Stephan (2013–2015).

By the fall of 2014, the fight had heated up, with a mix of politics and urgency. The rules of the road were changing. The city could finally celebrate a breakthrough with the passage of legislation in Albany reducing the speed limit in NYC to 25 MPH. This change "could prevent 6,500 injuries to pedestrians and bicyclists in the next year," noted Transportation Alternatives (2014). Further, the city passed the Right of Way Law, making it a crime to hit a pedestrian or cyclist with the right of way (City Council, 2014). Cyclists' advocates would summarize the breakthrough as the result of a combination of street-based direct action and research in support of their case, media work, as well as legislative advocacy, including testimonials from family members who lost their children to traffic fatalities. "Forensic data analysis and direct action gets the goods," said Charlie Komanoff.

A RIDE OUT TO QUEENS

Riding with Right of Way, I've heard countless stories of preventable deaths on the streets of NYC. Yet, few of the deaths strike quite the same chord as the story of Allison Liao. The young child was walking with the right of way as she held the hand of her grandmother when she was killed by a car that swerved into the lane on Flushing's Main Street, running her over. We painted a memorial for her on my first ride with the group. Years later, her story still resonates. In January 2015, a few of us attended a Department of Motor Vehicles hearing for the driver, Ahmad Abu-Zayedeha, who killed Allison. On a snowy morning, Charlie and I took the 7:41 am train out to Queens for the hearing. We arrived an hour before the hearing began, meeting Liao's parents and other street justice activists supporting each other while trying to change the system that allows these deaths to continue.

Waiting for the hearing, a few of us talked about what had happened that day in October 2013. The driver, Ahmad Abu-Zayedeha, took a left turn into traffic and ran into Liao. At the time, the driver was charged with failure to yield, which was a violation. The charges were later dismissed in a minute-long hearing. The driver said he thought she broke away from her grandmother, without watching the video evidence showing she was holding her hand. As result of this case, the city passed intro 19–190, Local Law 29, also known as the Right of Way Law, making it a crime for a car to cause injury to someone with the right of way (City Council, 2014). That law went into effect in August 2014. Yet, it had only been enforced eight times as of the hearing that day in January. It is one thing to have a law; it is another to change hearts and minds. That's part of the dilemma. People have to look out for each other. The city has to enforce it.

"The whole system needs to be redone," argues Dave "Paco" Abraham, another supporter. Few of the transportation advocates are pushing for more punishments, but rather "to see some accountability," notes Charles Komanoff (Shepard, 2013–2015). Allison's parents spoke to a group of reporters before the hearing:

> We hope the outcome of this is to suspend his license. For him, it's an inconvenience. But that's all. Our life is shattered. We hope this can shed light on this problem. Allie's gone. His behavior took her. It was preventable. He drank before he left. He's a reckless driver. He put his needs ahead of ours. We're going to ask to have his license taken away. This isn't something we're going to get over. (Shepard, 2013–2015)

Liao's grandmother testified at the hearing: "There was time for me to walk. I looked from left to right. And I started walking. My heart beats. There was no traffic and the car hit us from behind. My family is suffering" (Shepard, 2013–2015). By the end of the month, the DMV revoked the license of the driver (Aaron, 2015). In this small way, the traffic justice movement helped the city feel more livable and accountable. But there is much more to do to achieve the paradigm shift needed in the streets.

CONCLUSION

Urbanists Jane Jacobs (1961/1992), Henri Lefebvre (1996), and David Harvey (2013) have long argued that cities can and must be understood as constellations of living, pulsing, active neighborhoods, rather than merely spaces that accommodate the smooth, efficient movement of automobiles. Neighborhoods depend upon safe streets, allowing kids and adults alike to stroll, to stand at a crosswalk, or to walk to a garden without fear of being hit by a speeding automobile. There has to be more to urban space than means of necessity, they argued, echoing Herbert Marcuse (1955). Sustainable urbanism posits urban spaces can be livable, self-correcting entities, organized by regular people favoring people-based, not car- or building-based, uses.

Through such actions users foster a model of urbanism aimed at making cities livable over the long term. Here, regular people aid cities through spatial efforts emphasizing connection between neighborhoods, government, and education, fostering public awareness, cooperation, and partnership with multiple stakeholders. In this, cities are viewed as hubs of interconnected neighborhoods, with accessibility by foot, bicycle, or public transportation (Thorpe, 2014).

In the same way Mothers Against Drunk Driving helped redefine the issue of alcohol consumption and driving, the traffic justice movement has helped us reimagine what the streets can and should look like.

Yet, the problem of traffic fatalities has only increased, with spikes in deaths among cyclists, up to 28 in 2019, at the hands of drivers not paying attention, or failing to yield the right of way, among 218 total traffic fatalities, including 121 pedestrian deaths (Fitzsimmons, 2020). In comparison, London suffered seventy-three pedestrian and six cyclist fatalities, while Oslo, Norway, had no cyclist or pedestrian fatalities and only one traffic fatality (Ralson, 2020; Schreiber, 2020). More and more people are recognizing cycling is an ideal alternative to driving or crowded public transportation.

Throughout this chapter, we traced a story of people forming a community and a constituency which identified a neighborhood problem—traffic violence—and turned it into the issue of street justice. They organized around the issue. In doing so, they influenced perceptions and policy. Direct action and data analysis functioned in a synchronistic manner, moving the issue forward toward a solution of safer streets and infrastructure for cyclists, pedestrians, and other commuters. After all, streets are for sharing. These are our most vital public spaces. They need to be safe for everyone to walk, ride, breathe, play, and build community. The majority of the people in the world today live in cities. Through sustainable urbanism, cities can become spaces in which we all can participate, move with the right of way, and thrive.

A subtext of these actions is that everyone needs a safe way to move from home out to the world and back. Bikes help us navigate this ecology. In the winter of 2015, Austin Horse, a veteran of the sustainable movement in New York, delivered seven bikes to Syrian refugees in Jordan, helping them move and navigate from their camps to the world around them and back. Bikes are solutions. But more than that, everyone needs a home.

Chapter 6

Gardens Are Homes, Gardens Rising

When Lower East Side squatter Jerry "the Peddler" Wade walked me through the squats and community gardens of New York, he explained: "Gardens and housing—we need them both. Gardens are our commons." The point, of course, speaks to the biggest schism in the garden movement today. Whenever the city mentions they want to bulldoze the gardens, they claim they are doing so to make way for affordable housing. They did it with the Garden of Eden and Esperanza, and they do it with gardens today. Most suggest healthy cities need both. Today, gardens are thriving, while the city refuses to offer a comprehensive list of empty housing units in New York City. Still, from Smiling Hogshead Ranch to La Plaza Cultural, regular people are transforming the public spaces of New York while challenging the notion that cities must pit housing against gardens. Could the one step up, two steps back dance between housing and gardens be the point that everyone needs a home? Healthy cities need green space and housing. Gardens help sustain neighborhoods, offering food security, preventing floods, supporting resiliency, creating oxygen, and growing community. Gardeners, squatters, and public space advocates have long collaborated. This chapter considers a few reasons why community gardens are an essential ingredient of sustainable urbanism; after all, gardens are homes.

The false divide between housing and gardens dates back to the 1980s and the struggle over the Garden of Eden. It stretched through the Koch, Giuliani, and Bloomberg administrations, finding new fury during the de Blasio administration when the city Department of Housing Preservation & Development (HPD) announced plans to develop seventeen active community gardens citywide to make way for, surprise, "affordable housing." In response, Public Space Party created a banner declaring "Gardens are Homes!" and carried it to garden events around the city.

After one of these events, a few of us found ourselves talking about this strange state of affairs. "Developer giveaway," "corporate welfare," "scam"—these are just some of the terms people bandy about when you hear the tired argument that the city has to deprive the community of beloved open green space to make way for housing community members quite often cannot afford. People want real affordable housing and green space, not developer giveaways. Merging the two forces creates homes.

Tired of the endless debate, a few of us thought it might be a good idea to offer HPD a proposal in the winter of 2015: Save the seventeen gardens on the HPD list or turn their office into a garden. For many, the HPD space is vacant of new ideas or ways to support New York neighborhoods in dire need of real affordable housing and green infrastructure. HPD likes to suggest gardens are vacant lots best used for housing. Garden advocates see otherwise. With a small gesture, Public Space Party hoped to help everyone rethink the situation.

Thursday, February 19, 2015, was the deadline for development proposals on sites owned by the New York City office of HPD that included community gardens. So a few of us, most notably Public Space Party activist Michael "Ziggy" Mintz, drew up a proposal for HPD: swap your office for community gardens or take the seventeen gardens off your #HPDLIST. We even filled out a proposal on the HPD application to develop the lots:

FORM A: Completeness Checklist

REAL AFFORDABLE HOUSING
  Proposal FORM B: Neighborhood Preferences Narrative

1. REAL AFFORDABLE HOUSING
2. AND COMMUNITY GARDENS

Given the extraordinary social rate of return for community gardens HPD itself should be turned into a community garden. Community leaders and garden activists know that these gardens are not getting in the way of affordable housing. Quite the contrary, gardens are homes to the birds, butterflies and dreams for a better city that brightens our lives. Gardens support community capacity building, reduce asthma, increase fitness, support social equity, help cool the planet, curb global greenhouse gases, reduce storm water overflow, increase biodiversity, provide fresh produce in "food deserts," etc. The benefits are endless. And none of these issues preclude supporting affordable housing. There are vacant lots owned by HPD throughout the city that can become sites for affordable housing.

Most garden activists know that supporting rent control is the best way to support affordable housing. More developer giveaways will not support long-term affordable housing, and in this case, the short-term trade off will lead to rent increases and displacement all too soon. There are hundreds of vacant city-owned sites NOT included in HPD's list, so there's no reason for the inclusion of these community gardens. We desire gardens AND affordable housing and they are not mutually exclusive. Moreover, the affordable housing programs where all of the sites are located have income thresholds much higher than what most people can afford. Most local people could enjoy the health-imparting social enrichment of a community garden instead of an apartment they can't afford. New York rejects this tale of two cities—pitting housing vs open space needs. We need both. We need more open spaces and gardens, especially in low-income communities. It's up to you HPD, support the gardens and take the 17 thriving gardens—including Tranquility Farm, Harlem Grown, Electric Ladybug Garden, Imani Community Garden, Harlem Valley Garden, EL Garden Bushwick, and many more—off your RFP list or turn your space into a garden. It's up to you.

This was our letter to HPD.

On Thursday, February19, 2015, we brought our proposal, dirt, chairs, plants, and other garden props to set up a "displaced garden" in front of the HPD office at 100 Gold Street, where we'd erect the HPD Garden. There, in the cold, we conspired, pulled together garden materials, and created our mock community garden on Gold Street. A few of us walked inside to bring a copy of our proposal to Ms. Arielle Goldberg of HPD. After going through security, we waited and waited and waited for someone from HPD to finally come down and talk to us. At first, HPD would not accept our proposal without an envelope, so we ran out in the cold to get one.

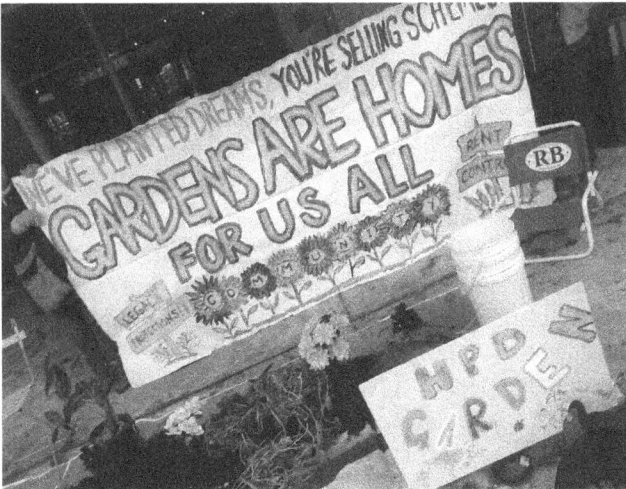

Figure 6.1. Scene of the HPD Garden outside their office.

Source: Photo by Benjamin Shepard.

Public Space Party mastermind Ziggy explained: "In the end, I gave our proposal *in hand* to Ms. Goldberg. I even had to sign an official document stating HPD received our proposal. Unbelievable!" No one was sure what HPD would do with our proposal. We hoped they would take the seventeen gardens off the HPD list. As follow up, the group signed petitions calling for Mayor de Blasio to take the gardens off the HPD list, organizing a bike ride to all the endangered gardens in Brooklyn, and working with garden and housing advocates to make the point that New York should not have to choose between community gardens and affordable housing.

Throughout the day, several activists, including squatter and artist Seth Tobocman, dropped by as we set up our garden in front of HPD. Squatters have long understood that gardens are homes, defying norms of accumulation, favoring community use.

They certainly are for those who create them. I learned this after visiting a new garden in Queens the summer before the seventeen gardens were put on the HPD list in fall 2014. I'd been traveling all summer long, hiking the Camino de Santiago with the family. My first few nights back in town, I rode my bike out to see my friends at various locations over town, such as the 169 Bar, Coney Island, ACT UP, and Queens. On my way, I dropped by the Mayday Convergence space for a prop-making session for the Bike Bloc, a working group preparing for the Climate March on September 21, 2014. Later, I rode from the Mayday Space in Bushwick to Queens, where my friend Gil Lopez showed me a vacant plot of land owned by the Metropolitan Transit Authority where he and a few of his friends had started an urban farm called Smiling Hogshead Ranch three years prior. He'd lived there, sleeping there for weeks. Lopez (2014) told the story of starting the garden. "In the late winter of 2011, a dozen gardeners convened on a trash strewn parcel of land in an industrially zoned area of Long Island City. Then and there, we quietly decided to transform the place into an urban garden," he explained. Over the next three years, Lopez and company did just that, planning, planting, organizing, and creating an open space. For Lopez, this work is about "restoring the commons, connecting people with soil and creating the world that we choose to live in." Over the winter, the gardeners registered the site as a nonprofit organization, putting the pieces together to "enter into our Garden License Agreement with the property owner."

While touring the space, Gil talked about the garden as a place for cycle repair and organizing, demonstrating the possibility of a sustainable urbanism, built out of a distinct DIY ethos.

The next week the makeshift garden was making its official opening, with the support of the city. On Saturday, September 6, 2014, Gil welcomed everyone for the ribbon-cutting ceremony. "Thank you all for coming out to celebrate with us here at Smiling Hogshead Ranch." Lopez (2014) told the story of the garden. "What started, for me at least, as an urge to get back into the soil after a growing season lost. Then discovering that the quickest way to garden in NYC just may be to start a new garden from scratch. I was brand new to the city, I barely knew the landscape and had only met a handful of like-minded people. After conveying my need to start a garden before putting my name on a waiting list for a community plot, Stephanos Koullias roped me into a group of really great Western Queens folks that wanted to get stuff done. If these founders didn't do this, then who among us would have? I hope you are all saying to yourself, ME. I could do this. I would do this. . . . It doesn't have to be starting a garden, but I encourage all of you to think about where your passions lie and spark your imagination, ignite your issue, fuel your fire with knowledge. Do it individually or find a like-minded group. But do it! . . . Doing something like 'guerrilla gardening' is a form of direct action known as Alternative Cooperation. Generally, this is where an end goal is envisioned (usually not one that would normally be allowed to happen by law or by rule) and you go ahead and create that reality without permission because you know it is worth it. So, while we have permission now to actually BE here, we still have our eyes firmly set on goals in the distance. So the direct action continues."

The garden began with a simple act. "It was early March, 2011," explained Lopez. "I met most of the folks Stephanos had gathered right over there (motioning) by where row 14 is now. We talked about the results of the soil test, we talked about the legality of it and how we would share the cost and work. We agreed to move forward, the following weekends we cleaned the trash, cleared the brush, worked the soil, removed stones and more rubbish. Spring turned to Summer and we continued to weed and water. That first Autumn we had a nice Fall harvest. At that time Occupy Wall Street was setting hearts and minds aflame across the country and was not lost on us. We decided to give it a go again the following year, with even more passion and urgency. Then, in the heat of the 2012 Summer, I got a call from the MTA's Real Estate Division. Who, what, when, where and why, it was a litany of questions. I thought the fun was over. Early on, we had decided not to ask the property owner if we could remove the trash and plant a garden. But I calmly explained, in my most professional voice, that 'whoever owns the land, we knew they wouldn't have let us move forward with this project. And we knew that we weren't going to hurt anything anymore than we were going to help. We waited for the chance to ask for forgiveness.' The voice on the other end began to yield. It is true, we would never have let a group do this in the past, he said. But we are decommissioning the remaining line on that property soon and we don't have any plans for the parcel. Some of us have heard about this urban agriculture but that's not our business at the MTA. We were actually kind of pleased to see this happening already. They wanted to let us continue to do the work we were doing but we had to sign a contract. Later that day, sitting in my inbox, was a hastily cobbled together Garden License Agreement. It was so messy, written to me, Gil Lopez, as the licensee. With language I could barely get through, I believe it is called legalese. The founders mulled it over and decided we would stall for a bit. But we no longer had to be so hush-hush, the property owner knows now, nothing left to hide. So we announced workdays on Facebook and Meetup groups like Crop Mob NYC. As new faces came and worked with us interest grew, teachers wanting to bring their school groups, non-profit organizations asking to team up and do green jobs. We regrouped and decided that it would be best if we figure out how to make this real. We had reached out to 596 Acres early on and now. Paula Segal really helped us revise and interpret the Agreement. It was revised and we came up with a game plan to make it happen. We needed to incorporate and we finally found a 501c3 fiscal sponsor to accept the money from our benefactor. We finally got our stuff together and incorporated as a non-profit. We negotiated the Agreement and on August 1, 2014, we received a countersigned contract from the MTA. All that paperwork was a distraction for some, an annoyance to most. We rationalized the learning curve involved with all this legal legwork because New York City has too many vacant lots for there to be wait lists for community garden plots. If this is what has to be done then so be it, we stepped up to the plate. What we are all here today taking part of is a truly urban farm. The Ranch is different from a community garden, with a different ebb and flow. Yet it weaves together so many aspects of the city, from the nearby Long Island Expressway, Newtown Creek, the soon to be completed Skillman Ave. bike lane, the Sunnyside Rail yard across the street, warehouses, manufacturing, materials processing and handling facilities. . . . But this area is bristling with vital activity, we want to add to and enhance our neighborhood. I have a vision of Smiling Hogshead Ranch as a collective of collectives, running a farm, offering some bike workshops and basic services, reclaiming organic by-products from nearby kitchens to build and clean the soil . . . how about a community tool lending library. We also dream of taking over that rail spur once it is deactivated and transforming it into a green industrial park."

Lopez envisions this urban space as a place for bioremediation, cleaning, and healing: "To reimagine our 'waste' streams and see them as they really are, resources that we are wasting. Imagine the storm water coming off the elevated portion of the LIE a couple blocks away being diverted from the sewers, where they just combine with real sewage to create our urban phenomenon known as Combined Sewage Overflow into the Newtown Creek. Instead, we could have that water go through a series of natural filtration processes, known as a water purification chain. Starting with a settling tank to separate out solids, then, living filters that grow algae, followed by planted areas where microbes in the plants' rootzone continue cleaning the water, eventually that water can support fish. It would be the first source of freshwater to the Newtown Creek in decades. What I have just described is one means of bioremediating polluted water. It is not a new idea and it is not a radical idea, it's just a little out of the ordinary. Well we want this bright green future! But we want it now, in the present. There is no time or reason to wait. We are already informally bioremediating the soil with the mycelium of mushrooms back there underneath the railroad tracks . . . In the urban ecology of our city's green infrastructure landscape, the Ranch is developing air, water, and soil remediation techniques while building cultural meaning and social capital by reskilling a segment of the citizenry. . . . Our moment has come and our time is now. As individual citizens, we must take personal interest in our surroundings and neighborhood conditions. But the state must also let us take active interest in our communities conditions. 596 Acres is providing a lot of information for people and offering transparency tools for better governance. Hogshead is just one manifestation of what can happen when passionate people work together toward something bigger than themselves. We have just begun. The hardest part of making this dream come together is sustained imagination of what can be and cultivation of THAT world in which we want to live. Our story is one case amongst many that are demonstrating a positive shift in the undercurrent of our society. But it is up to all of us, not only the renegades or the squatters, but we were the ones who made this happen, through the calculated use of rule breaking, good old fashioned hard work, some charm, and lots of enthusiasm. We have transformed this forgotten corner of the city into something worth celebrating. . . . So here we are, cutting this ribbon in ceremonial."

Talking with Gil afterward, I told him that I loved his point that the space was not trash; it was full of trash. "We have to rethink our relationship to trash," he explained. This thinking is what the story of all the gardens is about. Today, more and more of us are starting to see gardens as more than vacant lots. The process of reclaiming this space, the narratives included here, traces a few pieces of this story.

SANDY AND GARDENS RISING

While Lopez and company were busy cleaning out the lot that would become the Smiling Hogshead Ranch, organizers in the Lower East Side with Time's Up! and C Squat on Avenue C were busy creating a museum dedicated to this process. The museum would be dubbed Museum of Reclaimed Urban Space (MoRUS). It would be organized as a practice as well as a place to learn about the history of the gardens and the squats of the Lower East Side. Just a few days before the museum's opening, the waters of Superstorm Sandy flooded the space. In the weeks to come, squatters and gardeners shared food, cooking it out on the street, offering it to neighborhood members as they cleaned up from the wreckage, charged cell phones with an energy bike connected to a marine battery, and demonstrated the possibilities of community-based support.

Bill Weinberg, a MoRUS tour guide and the author of *Tompkins Square Park: A Legacy of Rebellion*, and I talked about the ways the gardens have changed the city.

"Did you just see the piece in *The Villager* about the gardens?" he asks. "Gardens now seen as key part of future storm defense plan," said the November 5, 2015, article by Ferguson (2015) in *The Villager*. The governor's Office of Storm Recovery gave a $2 million grant. The folks at La Plaza Cultural Community Garden are actually trying to create a model, trying to restore the natural hydrology systems in this hyperdeveloped cityscape. And they actually created this "French drain" to catch runoff.

In this way, the gardens support neighborhood resiliency. "They are creating bioswales," notes Weinberg. He read from the article by Ferguson (2015), noting these bioswales "utilize plants and stones to divert water and allow it to be absorbed more slowly into the ground." That's what they were doing all summer in La Plaza. They were developing a French drain and a bioswale and "Hugel beds of organic matter that absorb water." Through such innovation, we come to see gardens as the future of cities coping with flooding. They make cities livable. To do so, designers are looking at the city's past. "Actually starting to restore our natural hydrological systems here in the big developed cityscape," explains Weinberg. "This to me, this is what the future should look like, not Uber and Airbnb and cell phones and Citibike and Facebook. I say we need an induced implosion of the entire world industrial apparatus if there is going to be any kind of sustainable future on this planet." Weinberg is quick to note he learned this term from Hans Joachim Schellnhuber. "And the gardens are starting to do it—creating the sustainable alternative to the industrial apparatus. I find the fact that they just got this big grant to be a big step in the right direction and very inspiring. Mind you, in the grand scheme of things, it's but one very small counter-friction against the machine, which is working overtime to destroy the planet day in *and* day out. But you know what are you going to do? I'll take what I can get."

The Gardens Rising Storm Recovery Grant was announced at La Plaza Cultural on Ninth Street and Avenue C in Manhattan. The New York City Community Garden Coalition (NYCCGC) explains: "Gardens Rising—will combine community-based participation with engineering expertise, to develop a green infrastructure study and Master Plan to increase the permeability and storm water capture within forty-seven neighborhood/community gardens located in Lower Manhattan. This is a two-phase project, the first phase is to develop a Master Plan to combine the best of gardener expertise, landscape design, engineering, and creative thinking with cost effectiveness and sustainable practices. The project team will examine the feasibility, costs, benefits and impacts of proposed storm water capture locations and methods to increase permeability and green space in the neighborhood gardens to better absorb storm water and runoff. The study area is roughly bounded by 14th Street on the north, the East River on the east, Delancey Street on the south, and the Bowery/Fourth Avenue on the west, and is home to forty-seven (47) gardens measuring approximately seven (7) acres. The majority of the gardens reside within an area that was severely flooded during Superstorm Sandy and many were impacted directly by the storm. When completed the Plan will identify projects that will implement green infrastructure and storm-water capture systems to better outfit these gardens and neighborhoods. . . . This is a huge step forward for our community gardens, which are finally being recognized as a vital environmental asset. It puts community gardens at the center of the greening movement in New York City. We intend to parlay this grant into other funding to build other sustainable systems throughout the five boroughs . . . Gardens Rising should be interwoven with permaculture, solar energy, rat abatement policies, composting practices, citizen science, and other ideas and practices that will evolve with this process" (2015).

LA PLAZA CULTURAL AND CLASS STRUGGLE

A great deal of this innovation expands from the creative work of the community gardeners and squatters and one specific garden that pulled them together. "This corner of Ninth and C is the location for several community gardens, including La Plaza Cultural," says squatter and gardener Jerry "the Peddler" Wade as we walk through the neighborhood.

"La Plaza itself was one of the first projects of the CHARAS group of activists, who occupied the corner lot in the late 1970s," notes Alan Moore, a squatter who lives in Barcelona. "While their center on the same street, called El Bohio, was evicted, the garden of La Plaza remains."

"The Purple Parade put up teepees in the squat," says Wade, recalling the struggle to save the garden. "They were feeding people here. There were three weeping willows. This was a people's space." Wade and company heard about construction workers coming to 327 Eighth Street, across from the garden. "We egged them with two dozen eggs we'd dumpstered," confesses Wade with a sparkle in his eye, noting the eggs were pretty smelly. "The cops also got egged." Jerry smiled, explaining that the gardens were spaces people saw as part of their neighborhood homes, part of the solutions to the problems they faced in their lives. "We built a soup kitchen in La Plaza with the Rainbow Family feeding people rice and beans."

The defense of La Plaza grew directly out of the lessons of the loss of the Garden of Eden. At Adam Purple's funeral, several observers noted that if people had not organized after the Garden of Eden disappeared, we wouldn't have these gardens now. The death of the Garden of Eden seemed to be a catalyst to support the other gardens.

"It certainly mobilized a lot of people, including myself," says Weinberg. "My first interaction with community gardens at all was in support of Adam. That was the first struggle to save a community garden that I was involved in . . . the Garden of Eden back in 1985." Today, Weinberg sees this loss as one of the most powerful experiences he ever had with the gardens.

"The day they destroyed it, there wasn't any confrontation," recalls Weinberg. "They sort of came in in the wee hours in the dead of winter in a sneaky way. That's what they tried to do in the Esperanza Garden in 2000, but people headed them off . . . There was actually somebody sleeping in the tree house the night the bulldozer showed up. There was a confrontation, but the garden was destroyed." They lost the battle there but seemed to win the larger war over the gardens, at least in the Lower East Side.

"And then the whole struggle over La Plaza, which was actually being squatted for a while," notes Weinberg. This was a home. "There was actually an encampment in La Plaza for around three years when the garden was in open *resistance,* after the city had given approval for the housing project to be built there. There was a sort of hippie encampment. The Rainbow People— they came in and established an encampment from around 1988 to 1990, that same period, the class war period. And they established a soup kitchen. Hundreds of homeless people were lining up to get free food. They built a teepee in La Plaza and they started calling it People's Park East, in reference to People's Park in Berkeley California."

The city just watched. "The city had a lot on its plate," explains Weinberg. "Basically, at that time, the city was getting out of control. The city had their hands full with Tompkins Square Park in that same period, which gave a little breathing room for La Plaza Cultural. Ultimately, we won. Ironically, what saved La Plaza was one of the many scandals of the Reagan Administration which are little remembered today, which was the scandal at the Department of Housing and Urban Development, the department of the federal government that funds housing projects in the cities. It came to light that there were bureaucrats who were on the take, who were getting kickbacks from the developers. It was less about real estate exactly than it was about federal money. These were all so-called 'poverty pimp' organizations, as we anarchists in the neighborhood derided them, who were building low-income projects for the poor. This is what they did with Adam's garden. You couldn't get away back in the late 1970s through the class war period with destroying a garden to make market-rate or luxury housing. Later, that became possible. And they did it—for instance at Esperanza. But back in that period it wasn't possible, for two reasons. First, the Lower East Side was still considered a 'bad neighborhood' and the rich didn't want to come here yet. And second, there was enough working-class power in the neighborhood—a political machine linked to the left wing of the Democratic Party—that you couldn't get away with it. So they used this divide-and-conquer ploy. They needed to break up the community gardening movement because they saw there was all this land that had fallen out of bureaucratic control and they wanted to move ahead with their plan to 'redevelop' the neighborhood. They would say, 'We don't need this land to build a luxury project. We need it to build low-income housing.' And this was a means of dividing the gardeners against the housing advocates. And a lot of them were the same people. A lot of the housing advocates were gardeners. But this was a means of driving a wedge between the two groups. And in the case of Adam Purple's garden, it worked. The community really was divided. With La Plaza Cultural, there was more unity around the garden . . . partially because Adam Purple's Garden of Eden really was kind of a one-man show. He really was this kind of loner and can-tankerous old curmudgeon, whereas La Plaza Cultural is more authentically a community garden."

Through the losses, gardeners and squatters, such as Michael Shenker, started developing strategies to defend the gardens, built around direct action, legal support, arts, and fundraising for each garden. "Ultimately we bought time," explains Weinberg. "And they tried the same ploy at La Plaza as at Garden of Eden—'OK, we need this land for low-income housing.' But it came to light that the project which was slated for that site was one of those that was tainted by the scandal. And the project was abandoned. At that point, the city said, 'OK, we give in. You can have your garden.' And they brought it into the GreenThumb Program. That's how it worked. The encampments and resistance bought time, and that was critical."

Reflecting on the organizing used to save the Lower East Side community gardens, Weinberg confessed: "I'm proud of the neighborhood. Certainly, La Plaza Cultural. Adam Purple's Garden of Eden was destroyed. The Esperanza Garden later would also be destroyed. Some other gardens would be. But La Plaza Cultural survived, despite the fact that it's really big and takes up a lot of real estate. It survived. We saved that garden. And now these incredible visionary things are happening there like bioswales and Hugel beds. I'm pretty damn proud of that. I didn't have anything to do with it, except that I was there, and I witnessed it and I wrote about it and I cheered it on. I'm proud of the fact that the neighborhood got organized and saved that garden. And that they are doing a lot of visionary things there."

Doing so, these gardens are pointing to what cities need to be doing all around the world, honoring green space, bioremediation, bridging the divide between the city and the town. Small changes add up to bigger changes. This makes change seem possible. This is a bottom-up sort of a movement. Through his work with MoRUS, Weinberg has wanted to acknowledge the radical history of the neighborhood. "There are still struggles going on to save the community gardens."

The seventeen gardens placed on the HPD list for development in 2014 mark a continuation of this struggle. For Weinberg, the Lower East Side class struggle period may be over. But the struggle for the gardens continues. The dialectics of gardens fostering community development, which improves neighborhoods, green space, increases gentrification, pushing up rents, which displace bodies, leading to further speculation, continues ad infinitum. The story of gardens lost and found reverberates throughout the city, where gardens rise, draw enough support to survive, or face the same fate as the Garden of Eden.

Aziz Dehkan (2015), of the NYCCGC, posted a notice about the gardens and the HPD list on the last day of the year in 2015, regarding the plan to destroy nine community gardens. "These community gardens were a direct result of sweat equity that neighbors used to improve their neighborhoods," wrote Dehkan. "And it seems undeniably wrong to destroy the very asset that makes neighborhoods livable and a place where developers subsequently seek to build. We ask once again that Mayor de Blasio give all community members a place at the table to make NYC livable . . . HPD has an abundance of potential sites on which it can develop affordable housing. Less than 10 percent of HPD's vacant lots contain flourishing community gardens. Given these numbers it is clear that destroying community gardens forever is not only wrong, it is patently unnecessary."

From Smiling Hogshead Ranch to Gardens Rising, community gardens and neighborhoods ebb and flow in constant motion. Dehkan (2015) writes: "Community Gardens have for decades been an integral part of the fabric of New York City. These gardens are living symbols of unity built by neighbors who joined together to turn abandoned, trash-strewn lots into vibrant community oases. Community Gardens in the City represent a truly holistic, resilient, cost-effective neighborhood-based source of sustainable food production, increasing people's access to locally grown fresh produce, while negating effects of climate change by reducing carbon emissions. Open, vacant lots should be prioritized as buildable over those with active uses such as community gardens. The Mayor should pursue policies to create community gardens while at the same time creating affordable housing units in New York City for our children and future generations." After all, gardens are homes, but they are not easy to maintain in this neoliberal city.

Chapter 7

Primitive Accumulation and a Movement for a Home in a Neoliberal City

On June 11, 2015, I joined a group of housing advocates and some squatters outside the offices of the governor of New York. Rent control laws were up for renewal and many feared they would lose their homes. They were there to block the entrances and disrupt business as usual. "It's the only way policy-makers listen to disenfranchised people," said one of the eventual arrestees.

"I came to New York in 1976 as an art student," explained Seth Tobocman, one of the organizers. "Now I am a teacher. There was affordable housing then. It was possible to start a life here. But every year the rents have gone up, making it near impossible for artists to get a start here. We need to stop vacancy decontrol. We need a rent rollback and home rule for New York housing issues." Building on decades of squatting, he expressed a degree of optimism about such organizing. "We got our initiation in a very conservative period. We can do more than we imagine."

"We are tired of being displaced, extorted, harassed, and ignored. We will continue to bring our grievances to the doorsteps of the powers that be until we are heard," said Sara Quinter, another New York resident taking part in the demonstration.

"There is a housing crisis in New York," notes Jessica Rechtschaffer. "Politicians in New York are whitewashing the entire issue. The rent regulations are up for renewal and they are there doing last minute horse trading. Yet people's lives are at stake. We need to keep rent control and HDFC. If that went away none of us would be able to stay in our buildings. We need affordable rents for regular people, not billionaires," Rechtschaffer explained as she prepped for the action.

"I'm here because I'm a fourth generation New Yorker and I'm watching the city that made me being stripped away," noted Quinter. "In a word, it's greed," she concluded.

By 9 am, the group blocked the entrances to the governor's office at Third Avenue and 41st Street, many holding pots and pans and others with signs.
"Once I pay my rent, all my money's spent," chanted activists.
"Fight fight fight, housing is a right!"
"Governor Cuomo, you can't hide, we know you're on the landlords' side."
Passersby cheered as the chants escalated. The police warned activists blocking the doors. Gradually, they started arresting each activist sitting there.

"People are losing their homes," Tobocman repeated over and over as he was being arrested. Regular people can barely afford to live here. Vacancy Decontrol has eliminated 300,000 rent-regulated apartments, the majority of which housed low-income people and people of color. Affordable units are few.

Perhaps the greatest chasm in the city involves the influx of bodies and the scarcity of housing people can afford. No struggle better embodies the contradictions of the neoliberal city than this. There seem to be condos everywhere, yet few can afford them. Rent costs are going through the roof, yet building after building holds vacant units. The human struggle for a home must contend with the age-old phenomena of primitive accumulation, today seen in rising rents and foreclosures, wherein people are displaced from their homes and communities. The housing crunch feels like a manufactured mess of the neoliberal city, maximizing profit by the inch instead of making room for everyone. Use duels with exchange value throughout the recent history of housing in New York, which includes the neoliberal reshaping of cities from "urban renewal" through disinvestment in the 1970s, deindustrialization, white flight, the hollowing out of cities, and the "write down" of land values (Fitch, 1993; Fraser, 2012; Smith, 1996).

Still, how is this dialectical activism shaped by capital? Squats and gardens are made from abandoned buildings, with rubble cleaned out and made into livable neighborhood spaces because of disinvestment and neighborhood decline. The Eros and creativity of the human spirit bridges DIY politics and sweat equity to remake the city. Social capital, bodies gathered, creates innovative responses as people demonstrate a capacity to survive and thrive. The activity is partly "produced" by reshaping through capital, as activists create gardens and squats, which draw still more social capital, which they later have to defend from the inflows of capital drawn to these revitalized neighborhoods. During the last two decades, gentrification has become the order of the day. Primitive accumulation finds new intensity with global capital flows, displacing bodies and undermining rent controls (Sites, 2002; Smith, 1996). But what actions are needed to shape responses, to balance forces? Here, a dance of the dialectic involves a tango between countervailing forces, as social and financial capital are left to contend with conflicts between people and profits, those on the margins making things, providing services for those working in banks, pricing them out of neighborhoods, each a part of this ever-flowing totality.

This is a story repeated again and again. "Money itself . . . intervenes in this process as itself as a highly energetic solvent," explains Marx in *Grundrisse* (1973, 507), "and to that extent assists in the creation of *plucked*, objectless, *free workers;* but certainly not by creating the objective conditions of their existence; rather by helping to speed up their separation from them—their propertylessness." Displaced from land and the capacity to earn a living, these "free workers" are pushed into the "labor market . . . dependent on the sale of its labor capacity or on begging, vagabondage, and robbery as its only source of income," only to find themselves "driven off the road by gallows, stocks and whippings" (507). These conditions are produced and reproduced, a part of the "exchange market . . . separated from their direct connection with the mouths of the retainers and transformed from use values into exchange values, and thus fell into the domain and under the supremacy of money wealth" (507). It did not start with capital so much as with primitive accumulation, with capital as a relationship that permeates all, displacing bodies, forcing us into a subordinated relationship to capital, pulling people apart, as journeyman are driven out of their shops, and landowners displace workers. To make sense of these dynamics, Marx considers preconditions and result in history, investigating motion, capturing movement from the present to the past into the future, to get a handle on modes of production. Studying the issue of homelessness, we see a history of workers released from land, thrown out of their homes, and turned into vagabonds when landlords wanted to grow a money crop. These were itinerate laborers desperate for new work, their homelessness a cause and condition of capitalism (Ollman, 2016). Capital has changed social relations before but social relations can transform capital anew. Over and over squatters have reversed this trend, taken control of their lives, means of production, and the fruits of their labor. Use value puts restraints on capital, while exchange value seeks to commodify everything from public spaces to homes.

The clash takes place every day. It is the story of New York and cites everywhere. Faced with this struggle for a place to call home, regular people have taken the solution into their own hands, squatting in vacant buildings, creating social capital, whether the city wants them to or not. This chapter considers the struggle for a home in New York. It begins with the story of the squatter movement, active in rebuilding the neighborhoods after Superstorm Sandy. The story of squatters and post-storm activism points to models of mutual aid combined with efforts to secure both housing and a sustainable future of cites. It highlights a few activist approaches to respond to the crisis of housing, highlighting the uses of DIY organizing and squatting as approaches to fashion a sustainable image.

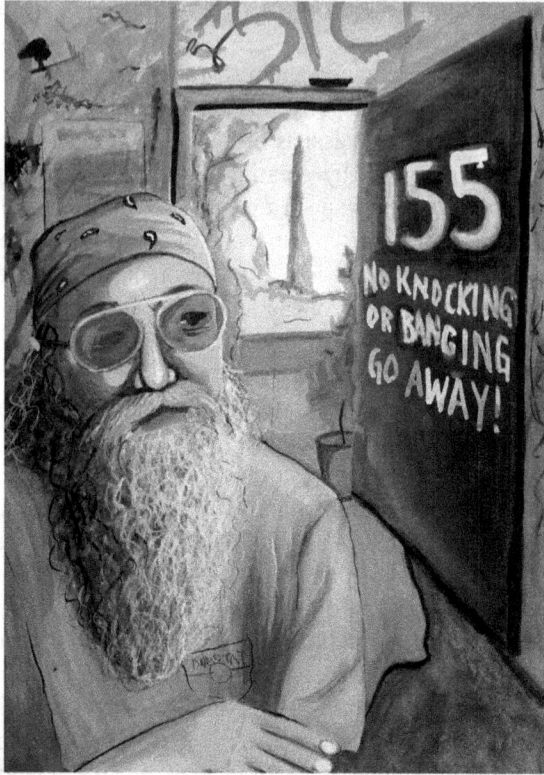

Figure 7.1.   Jerry "The Peddler" Wade outside of C Squat.

Source: Illustration by Caroline Shepard.

A DIY CITY

"You have to imagine the history. It was empty down here," says Jerry "The Peddler" Wade, looking around Avenue C and 9th Street. The squatters helped build this neighborhood. "It is the right of the tax payer, food, housing, healthcare, and clothing." Strolling through the streets of the Lower East Side, Wade traces an alternate history of New York, built of the sweat equity of regular New Yorkers. "This was a swamp. This was a landfill," he explains, pointing to the river where there were once dry docks. "There was a neighborhood down here. The first flag was Jolly Rogers."

This was very much a DIY movement. "Starting with the assumption that the world is fucked up and realizing that this could be done," explains Fly, an artist and squatter who has lived here since 1988. So she and company explored what could be done for their neighborhood. "Punk was an instigator in that, growing up and forming your own opinions. I could see that I had a responsibility. It's not just that you are on your own. But it's the realization that I have to do something." And so she did, joining the squatting movement at the peak of the class struggle period, building things and repairing her eventual home at 209 East 7th Street. She had long been an art punk, learning a DIY ethos from her dad, who rationed during the war, never wanting to waste anything. Through her dad, she learned to repair and create. "I inherited his power tools. DIY making stuff—that was in me. DIY—that is the essence of this apartment. I chiseled that window from a brick wall, looking six floors down. My sweat and blood is literally in this building," she says. Both she and her friend and neighbor Michael Shenker had terrible accidents in the building, suffering, creating, fashioning a neighborhood and a home along the way.

With roots in movements extending back to Dada and Emma Goldman's anarchism, DIY culture has become an increasingly important tool for anti-authoritarian organizers, finding its way into countless social and cultural movements (Duncombe, 1997). It's as old as the human impulse for liberation, and now it's one of the most recognizable and effective ways for urban activists to mount resistance by creating counterculture.

"The DIY movement is about using anything you can get your hands on to shape your own cultural identity, your own version of whatever you think is missing in mainstream culture," writes Amy Spencer (2005). The "enduring appeal of this movement is that anyone can be an artist or a creator. The point is to get involved." Through DIY culture, activists, punks, poets, organizers, junkies, and community gardeners have built their own buildings, groups, structures, and forums, using counterpower to fashion spaces and counter institutions of their own design. Doing so, they prefigure a new world of their own creation within the shell of the old. That was certainly the case with the Lower East Side squatters.

RUMBLINGS FROM TOMPKINS SQUARE PARK

In the 1980s, much of the movement for a home in New York made its way through Tompkins Square Park, a 10.5-acre public park on 10th Street in Alphabet City, where radicals have long debated, organized, pontificated, planned, squatted, and even rioted over a right to a place to sleep and call home. From 1874 until the summer of 1988, riots and unrest have been frequent here.

New York historian and writer Bill Weinberg recalls a moment in 1980: "It was the big turnaround year in my life. It was the year that I graduated from high school. It was the year that President Jimmy Carter, in response to the Soviet invasion of Afghanistan and the Iran hostage crisis, brought back draft registration. I was in the first crop of 18-year-olds that had to register for the draft, post-Vietnam. That was something that I was not very happy about. That prompted my first experience with political activism *per se*. I got involved with an anti-draft group my senior year in high school. That was the turning point. That summer I went cross-country for the first time. I found myself at the Survival Gathering, in South Dakota, hosted by the American Indian Movement. That got me further along in my trajectory.

"I started hanging out in the neighborhood [Lower East Side] in about that same period, coming in to go to punk rock shows and whatnot in my senior year in high school and hanging out in the neighborhood more and more, and later getting interested in the struggle around Tompkins Square Park and writing about it as a journalist. I was doing a weekly column for *Downtown*, which was a sort of poor man's *Village Voice* which was around for a while back in the 1980s."

There, Weinberg stumbled into a distinct lineage of activism: "I first gravitated into the orbit of the latter-day Yippies over at #9 Bleecker Street. I guess through them I became aware of the squatters. Through the anti-draft effort I became aware of the Yippies and through the Yippies I became aware of the squatters and through the squatters I became aware of the whole Tompkins Square scene, even though I wasn't living here yet.

"I was at the 1988 Tompkins Square riot, but I was living in Brooklyn at the time. I was covering it, and I was writing about it and had lots of friends who were squatters. We all knew there was going to be a riot that night. I bicycled in from Brooklyn to see the riot."

The buildup for the riot was gradual. "First of all, there was a generally apocalyptic atmosphere, with crack and AIDS and all that that was going on back in the 1980s," explains Weinberg. "Alphabet City was very, very rough at that time. There was landlord abandonment, and people lining up to get their heroin in empty buildings. It was being sold openly in the street, shooting galleries and so on.

"And then the homeless took over the park and started an encampment in 1988. And there was all this contestation and a growing sense of tension. We knew that the shit was going to hit the fan. I was living in Park Slope at the time. I just remember biking in that evening, and thinking. 'OK, I guess there is going to be a riot tonight. I'll be there to witness it.' I didn't throw any bricks or anything. I was skirting around the outskirts on my bicycle, trying not to get hurt."

Then, as now, in New York, the homeless seemed to be everywhere and the city seemed incapable of solutions. "The homeless in the park weren't saying, 'Oh yeah, we want to live in the park for the rest of our lives.' That wasn't the point," says Weinberg. "The point was, 'We don't have anywhere else to go. We consider the HRA [Human Resources Administration] shelters to be more dangerous than the park,' especially at that time. Shelters were really, really crowded, with lots of violence and antibiotic-resistant tuberculosis. The slogan at the time was the 'shelters are death camps.' Hopefully they are not as bad today as they were then. The attitude was, 'We don't have anywhere else to go, the park is less dangerous than the shelters. And we're here to speak truth to power. We're here as a public protest demanding that the city actually do something to address the homelessness crisis, to provide people with actual dignified homes.' Nobody was saying camping out in the parks was a solution. It was a means of *demanding* a solution."

Jerry "The Peddler" Wade helped organize the squatting movement. "The first community gardens and a dog run were here. There was also a tent city in Tompkins Square Park in 1975," he recalls. "When I got here, people lived here. In June 1988, the city wrote in white paint that the park closes at midnight. We called for a demonstration on July 30th. I debated Robert Downey Jr. that night and got paid. I came down at 11:30. I had $200.00. I got a case of beer and then another, giving it to my friends. Cops followed me, with my beer in my hand. Everyone had moved to the lawn. I set the beer down by the Gaia Tree, turned around at the cops and screamed, 'Pigs out of the park' spraying four cops with a shaken-up beer. Four people were arrested that night. I got out 24 hours later. I called for another demonstration, brought police whistles and noise makers for chaos." That night police panicked and beat people, with over a hundred going to the hospital, explains Wade. "Activists didn't get beaten, it was the people who got beaten."

THE TOMPKINS SQUARE PARK RIOTS, AUGUST 6, 1988

"The word was going around that the cops would enforce the curfew that night," notes Bill Weinberg. "I bicycled in from Park Slope where I was living at the time. It was really hot, sweat coming off me in sheets as I biked across the Brooklyn Bridge in the late afternoon. Everyone in the park seemed to assume the shit was going to hit the fan. I got a plate of pierogies at the Kiev. While I was eating, Allen Ginsberg walked in with this fresh-faced young farm kid that looked like he just got off the bus from Kansas and was obviously completely in awe of him. They happened to sit at the table next to me. From their conversation, it was clear they were going over to the park to check out the action after dinner, as I was.

"Back in the park, tension was building steadily from sunset, with anarchists beating on drums and rallying their troops, the cops occupying Avenue A and rallying theirs. You could feel that something was going to explode. I got a sense that at 1 AM the cops would move into the park to evict and that would be the spark. Just before 1, the anarchists marched out onto Avenue A to confront the cops . . . I don't have a clear recollection if bottles were thrown or nightsticks were swung first. But all of a sudden the tension broke. And the explosion arrived. The crowd burst outward in every direction as the police attacked. Bottles were flying and the businesses along Avenue A were shuttered. I retreated to Second Avenue, swept along with a wave that surged west up 7th Street. I walked up a block and the clock in the bank at St. Mark's and Second Avenue said exactly 1 AM. I could hear police sirens converging on the park from all directions. There were refugees streaming up St. Mark's toward me. I walked up 9th Street for better access. It was relatively quiet. But I got no further than First Avenue when I saw a police van with several cops on foot, their nightsticks in the air, chasing a young wiry Black guy, dressed only in cut-off shorts, who was tearing up the middle of the avenue for all he was worth. The van overtook him and swerved south *against the traffic*, cutting him off. The cops were on top of him in seconds, flailing him savagely with their nightsticks, not stopping even after he had fallen to the ground. He curled up in a ball to ward off the blows, but I could tell he was getting totally fucked up. I felt ashamed and helpless for just observing. But there was no one there to back me up or even to witness. I retreated to Second Avenue, trying another street again for approach. That's how it went with me for hours. I confess I didn't make it back to Avenue A again. But I caught glimpses of the battle raging as I approached again from the side streets, then retreated, generally swept along with westbound waves driven towards me by police charges. At one point on 6th Street, there was a helicopter overhead, its blades turning the street into a whirlwind of dust. At around 4 AM, I bicycled home. The battles were still raging. I got home just before dawn, dazed, exhausted, and grateful to be in one piece. The next day I went out and bought all the papers. There were horrible, horrible photos of what I had witnessed the previous night. One account mentioned that among the arrested was a young houseguest of Allen Ginsberg from Kansas."

WALKING TOUR OF THE REPUBLIC OF 9TH STREET AND THE BEGINNINGS OF THE SQUATTING MOVEMENT

The riots of 1988 were flashpoints in a civil war with thousands of skirmishes. One of the drivers of this movement is Jerry "The Peddler," a larger-than-life character in the neighborhood. He traced his history squatting in our conversations. I first met him in 2000 when we were arrested and put through the system together defending Esperanza Garden. A decade and a half later, Jerry and I met at his home at the corner of Avenue C and 9th Street for a tour of the neighborhood. He recalled garden legends Chino and Liz Christie, who started a garden at 9th and C, in the heart of the Squatter Community. "It all started here," he recalled, standing at 643 9th Street.

What brought you to New York, I asked him. "I was really a child of the 1960s." Born in 1940, Wade left Texas, wanting to get away from what he saw as the three Rs—"right wing, religious, red necks"—and joined the Army, seeing the Prague Spring firsthand. They wanted him to go to Vietnam. "I knew it was us against them. I was in the front and thought what the fuck am I doing. If I get out of here, there will be no more of this for me." For much of Jerry's life, his organizing has been about creating solutions. "That's what we do. It's always solutions. You need a home. Take one. There were hundreds of buildings, thousands of apartments." It made no sense to him. He started organizing meetings.

Jerry walks me through his East Village world. Pointing at 544 13th Street and Avenue B, he noted, "Beatniks were here. Ed Sanders, author of *Tales of Beatnik Glory*, he lived at 377 East 10th Street. Tuli Kupferberg, of The Fugs, was here. They published *Fuck You* magazine here. These guys were hippies, not revolutionary hippies, but cultural hippies, Up Against the Wall Motherfucker. They were class based." Jerry is a countercultural activist. "The world is against us," he explains. "It's hippies and bums and beatniks against the world."

As we walk, Jerry describes the history of public housing in New York and the neighborhood. A great deal of the housing from 14th Street to the Williamsburg Bridge was built in the 1940s and 1950s. No new public housing was built in the 1980s. In the 1990s, a little bit more was built, Housing Works, Avenue D and 9th. "Casa Victoria was built on 8th Street not on La Plaza. They got their senior housing. And we got our garden. We saved it because of the soup kitchen. We just did." He suggests this was just a very 1960s solution: "Back in the 1960s, the adage was everything for everybody. Housing and food for the poor."

Story after story, he takes me, building by building. 327 8th Street was built after Rock against Reagan in 1984, he tells me. "They came to find me. They asked me, how do we squat? Do you have a door, I asked. We grabbed a sledgehammer. We had two lookouts. And we opened another squat here."

"319 8th was the home of Michael Shenker, one of the original squats. Willie went to get a piss bucket and poured it on the cops. 327 sent their water to 319 with a garden hose and a PVC pipe."

There were countless battles, with commons ebbing and flowing. A low point was when the city took the bandshell from Tompkins Square Park. "This was a central meeting space. When they took it the movement lost momentum." Without public space, movements have a hard time sustaining themselves. It is a lesson repeated again and again.

Wade first became a squatter in 1984 in the East Village of New York City, sharing food, weed, beer, and organizing around the simple idea that everyone deserves a home. Home rather than shelter, he says. Disability is inhumane. In February 1984, he became a squatter after he was evicted from his home the month prior. "I became a squatter walking up from C Squat. Squatting puts the tools in people's hands. Everybody knows gentrification. Squatting is the answer to it."

Many of the most iconic squatters joined the movement in 1984. "I've never considered myself an organizer," confessed Michael Shenker, in an interview before his death. "Sometimes it's necessary to organize people to maximize the impact potential. Through squatting was where I learned how to do that and that it became an absolute necessity for people to organize in order to defend their homes." Shenker joined the squatting movement after moving around the neighborhood for years. "Before then, I came to the Lower East Side in 1971,'72. Back then, apartments were cheap, relatively affordable. You could get an apartment for $100.00. They hadn't burned the neighborhood yet."

And then things changed in the neighborhood. As a way to explain these changes, Jerry unpacked a theory, called spatial deconcentration, often referred to by anarchists in the neighborhood, to describe the movement to push the poor out of the city. "After the 1960s, they put together a commission. The Black population had been concentrated in the inner city. There was white flight. And the city was pushing out people of color. The city was closing hospitals, libraries, buildings are burning in the streets. The city is allowing a whole generation to die in the gutter."

By the mid-1970s, New York was broke. So, the city scripted a model of "planned shrinkage" to rid its streets of undesirables. "Our urban system is based on the theory of taking the peasant and turning him into an industrial worker," New York Housing Commissioner Roger Starr, one of the plan's architects, argued at the peak of the fiscal crisis of the 1970s. "Now there are no industrial jobs" (Fitch, 1993, viii). The first signs of the crisis could be seen in the public spaces of New York, vacant lots everywhere, empty buildings, and so on. The squatting movement grew out of this, transforming vacant lots into gardens, vacant buildings into homes, with the city sponsoring homesteading programs.

"The new wave of the squatting movement was just getting started then," notes Michael Shenker. Before that some people had made some moves with their buildings in the late 1970s.

In 1984, Jerry and a few others took over much of the corner of Avenue B and 13th Street, squatting buildings at #533, 35, 27, 39 E, and 44 across the street, dubbed "Sucker's Hole." The group took over these buildings, renovating each. They would stay in the buildings for the better part of a

decade until the city started the evictions. On July 4, 1995, the city brought
in a tank. "I was drinking beer all day in Dos Blocos," a squat with a garden
on East 9th Street, says Jerry. This was a community space. "By the time the
beer was gone," Jerry went to Sucker's Hole and dropped a banner that said,
"'Home Sweet Home.' We said we had taken it back. I took a corner room.
The headlines with helicopter in the background declared 'SIEGE.' 'Squatters
Seize City Tenement,' was the story in the *Daily News*. July 5, 1995. We had
it that night. I looked down the street. People are dropping bricks. I throw a
brick from six stories up. I was up in the Tombs (New York Central Booking)
with charges of reckless endangerment, felony riot, and attempted murder.
I did less than 36 hours in the house. Usually it's 36 hours or so. I said let's go
with the Legal Aid Lawyer. He comes up to me, says, 'My name is Angel and
I'm gonna get you out.' We were close to choosing a jury when the DA says,
I will give you time served. I jumped on it. Class B Burglary that another
court threw out was my only charge. Always go with the Legal Aid Lawyer.
Always make the court date. If you miss the date, return on your own. You
don't want them to come get you."

The clash continued for years. In my 2005 interview with Michael Shenker, he reflected on the difficulties of the squatter movement. "Our struggles
in the buildings sometimes came down to physical confrontations, beatings;
cops got beat; it wasn't something to rejoice about," he said. "The result of a
failed action had a direct impact, which was that people were in the streets.
Sometimes they go to jail and they get out, all their belongings have been
taken out of their home." Paradoxically, Shenker smiled and acknowledged
they "had a blast."

By 2002, a new administration was in power in New York. The Bloomberg
administration established the groundwork for a settlement with the squatters.
"No one was aware we were tired of fighting," confesses Wade. "We made a
secret deal. Both mayors took credit for the deal in 2002."

Michael Shenker notes, "Three of them [the squats started in the 1970s]
are part of the current Urban Housing Assistance Board (UHAB) deal. As of
today, it's 11 buildings," says Shenker. "The apex is right now because we
are codifying the entire process, which means we are going to be signing
some contracts with the city and the state government. And these contracts
summarize the struggle because they are going to be binding for 32 years or
whatever. And so we'll see what's in writing, you know."

Through all this work, the activists took control of the outcome of their
labor. "They did actually do it," explains Weinberg. "When the movement
was at its peak there were something like 25 squatter buildings. Eleven survived. Today they're homesteads. Probably the decision to negotiate the fate
of those 11 buildings which hadn't been evicted was seen as a compromise
by both sides. The city administration under Giuliani had this real hardline

intransigent position, 'These people are squatters. They took over these buildings illegally. They're anarchists. They don't have any right to be there. I'm
not going to legitimize them by negotiating with them.' And the squatters
took the same attitude. 'Yeah, damn right! We're squatters. We're anarchists.
We don't recognize private property. We don't recognize the city's authority.
We're not going to legitimize *them* by negotiating with *them*.' But ultimately
both sides decided to negotiate. The city realized that the squatters were no
longer a threat to the gentrification. By that time, the gentrification had happened. It's an already-established fact on the ground. And the city realized
that buying them off and bringing them into the system might be a way of
domesticating them and keeping them quiet. And the squatters realized that if
they didn't negotiate they were going to be evicted. They were going to lose
their homes and everything they had fought for ten years. So until this time
in the distant future when we overthrow capitalism, there isn't any such thing
as purity in this world. The squatters made a decision. They aren't as opposi-
tional as they used to be. And technically they aren't 'squatters' anymore. But
nonetheless, they kept their homes. They kept their fucking homes, and that's
a victory. And for a period of nearly 20 years, from when the first squats were
established in the early '80s to when the deal was finalized in 2002 or 3, when
we had Bloomberg in, there's a space of 20 years when they were occupying
space outside the law. That means something."

A DIY spirit propels the stories of Fly, Bill Weinberg, Michael Shenker,
and the other squatters discussed here, including Jerry "The Peddler" Wade.
"It was everybody that was the movement. It was a vanguard movement.

"There was leadership in everyone, not one vanguard. Everybody was doing
their own thing and created a movement," explains Wade. "I was no good with
speeches. But give me a mob and a bullhorn. I'll lead you to hell." There
was leadership in a leaderless movement. Finishing the tour after walking for
some two hours, Wade looked around East 9th Street, where our squatting
tour began. "We've come full circle. This is where we started, Dos Blocos and
the beginning of the squatting movement and its end on its eviction in 1999."

MORUS OPENING

The end of Jerry's tour was the beginning at Museum of Reclaimed Urban
Space, located in the basement of the C Squat. Walking through New York,
we traverse the footsteps and stories of friends and comrades. Sometimes
these narratives take me through special places—across community gardens
and squats, over bridges, between buildings—through the imagination of
the city. Some involve bike rides, protests, and tours of secret places. Each
action inspires a new conversation, overreactions, and counterreactions. On

December 8, 2012, we continued the conversation at the opening party of the Museum of Reclaimed Urban Space.

"Much of the activist perspective on this history is being whitewashed away," says Bill DiPaola, echoing Sarah Schulman's point from the *Gentrification of the Mind* that positive social changes are not given because politicians are nice; they happen because people have fought for them using direct action. AIDS drugs were not released because the US government became nice. AIDS activists forced them to do the right thing. Gardens of the Lower East Side were not preserved because the city likes them. They survive because people fought for them. Founded by Laurie Mittleman and Bill DiPaola, the genesis for MoRUS is conversations like this, many of which took place during one of the Time's Up! community garden tours. Knowing this history, Laurie and Bill helped open the museum to highlight the neighborhood's real activist history. This alternate history is the subject of the Museum of Reclaimed Urban Space. The museum highlights the local histories of the Lower East Side, looking at the ways regular people impact our city, its history, and public spaces. The museum would shed light on activist culture, efforts to save gardens, support for nonpolluting transportation, and squats and activist-organized bike rides making the streets safer years before the city created bike lanes.

Downstairs in the basement of the museum, Bill would place signs from Zuccotti Park, pictures of squats, and a cardboard bulldozer we used to theatrically bulldoze the building which was constructed on the site of the Esperanza community garden. MoRUS would be a space where regular people could commemorate *our* creation of a more sustainable city.

Shortly before its proposed opening, MoRUS was flooded out by Hurricane Sandy. I walked down into the basement of the museum the day after it was flooded and found that old bulldozer soaked. But we were very lucky—immediately after it was flooded, people from the community came to help support the space, while also offering free meals to those in the neighborhood from food procured from dumpster dives. Time's Up! set up energy bikes and charged people's phones. The direct action of the day was care and connection.

In the days before Sandy, we talked about how to support each other, of being there for each other if things became dark. I found myself in Melody Lanes in Sunset Park Brooklyn the afternoon of the storm. Dark clouds were brewing. As the kids enjoyed the bowling, I walked to the adjacent bar to catch some of the Jets game. Serving drinks to the clientele stood a short bartender with long white lamb chop sideburns and a beard. Ordering drinks, it felt like Isaac Asimov was pouring; life and fiction blurring in an afternoon Ray Bradbury would love. It was Monday night; the wind howled outside as we all played Bertell Ollman's old class struggle board game. Friends messaged on Facebook, "I just saw a light flicker. I'm brewing some coffee now. I can stand a lot, but not without coffee." The storm was supposed to hit from 8 to 10 pm. By this time my wife Caroline is putting up tape on the windows. Throughout the night, messages flood in from throughout the city. A Chelsea gallery is underwater, millions in art lost. Water has breached the West Side Highway. Trees are down throughout Brooklyn. Oil and sewage from the Gowanus Canal has flowed up Second, First, and Sackett, stirring our neighborhood's polluted foundations. It now becomes easy to remember that Newtown Creek is the site of the largest oil spill in U.S. history and that the Gowanus is a superfund site. We can smell it. Avenues throughout the Lower East Side, Brooklyn, and Staten Island are flooded with water.

The city is devastated. This is the second hurricane in New York within a year, in addition to a tornado. Walking through it all, I imagine this is the *new climate chaos*. After the storm, Time's Up! move their energy bikes out from the now-flooded Museum of Reclaimed Urban Space. They set up the bikes that had been in Zuccotti Park during the peak of the Occupy Movement to power the encampment. Now they help people who've lost the ability to recharge cell phones. Riders peddle to generate energy used to charge phones. Smiling, crowds stand there helping out, happy to be active and helpful. Others are glad just to charge their phones.

Bill DiPaola is there. We go to the flooded basement. MoRUS's offices are destroyed along with the cardboard bulldozer. "Maybe we should save this one as a model," Bill notes. "Try to keep it steady," George notes as I jump on the energy bike. Sixty watts will recharge a phone, 120 watts can power a laptop. If you ride too fast or too slow, you blow a fuse. A Japanese film crew films us peddling. I tell them it feels good to burn calories, build community, and help people stay connected with their families. The museum is also a public commons, where people share ideas and innovations, conversations and solutions. Throughout the week, the group cooked free food for everyone. Jerry "The Peddler" arrives now, setting up a table with more food.

"This is just what we do," he explains.

MoRUS is also a place for conversations, organizing, and mutual aid. It's a place where people share ideas. In the days after the storm, more and more of us make plans for survival relief efforts modeled around the Common Ground Collective. This would be the genesis of Occupy Sandy. Others would plan for a parade. And others would offer free food and supplies to their neighborhood. MoRUS would become a hub, as would other squats such as ABC No Rio on Rivington Street. At ABC, a group of punks are barbecuing; a "free food" sign hangs on the social center. E-bikes are pumping. The free food distribution by the punks of ABC and the energy of the bikes are all parts of a DIY sustainable urbanism. "Once again, it was hippies and punks and beatniks and bums to the rescue," notes Jerry "The Peddler," standing outside, offering free food to the community.

Later that December, the museum finally opens. Seth Tobocman was beginning his "War in the Neighborhood" talk, about the squatter movement, as I arrived. I remember first seeing him with this book at Charas back in 1999 before we were kicked out of that space. We always knew we had a better chance of winning if some of the squatters showed up for the fight. Accompanied by stark images from his graffiti-inspired murals and live music, Seth narrates:

> A space opens up with care, seizing control of the gardens, housing, and those things which control our lives.
>
> Every lunatic a philosopher, everyone for president, a democracy of cement, stolen scaffolding, flying bodies in the night. . . . and these are the best moments of our lives.
>
> The moment passes. . . . We tore the walls down, now we're putting them back up.
>
> Is it any surprise we have become the mirror image of our oppressor?
>
> . . . Aren't we the descendants of slaves, of fugitives, have any of us known freedom?
>
> . . . What would any of us know of democracy?
>
> If any of us can look at a vacant lot and see an image of a garden, then why can't we think of a better way of treating each other.
>
> You don't have to fuck each other over to survive.

The internal relations between people and the squats they live in are anything but simple.

I was supposed to read shortly after he finished. But hearing Seth, I knew I would need to keep my talk swift, tight, and engaging. His talk and many others were very, very powerful. I tell the story of the crickets, narrated in chapters 3 and 4.

While MCing, Fly follows Seth's talk, noting, "I wanted to mention something Seth said. This is a living museum. It puts activism into practice. This is a very, very proactive organization, proactive not an institution. We have to celebrate. But we also have to keep on fighting for these buildings, gardens, and spaces we've created and saved. We have to continue the struggle."

"Squatterlyness is next to Godliness," says Father Frank Morales in his talk. "Because land is life, the struggle for a home through squatting is synonymous with the struggle for life itself, like a bird in her nest and a fox in his hole, we're gonna get home somehow." Situating his story, he listed name after name of friends in the squatting movement. "Back in the mid-1980s Cathy, Robin, and English Steve . . . hundreds more made a decision to struggle for a home, to struggle against the bone chilling freeze of empty, windy, and rain soaked, often time roofless rat-filled derelict houses without juice, without permission and made something out of nothing. Made a decision to fight the power, the corrupt normal, to defend each other and throw down and have a good time, outside the bounds of bourgeoisie time and space where freedom subverts and joy thrives. And lo and behold, we are still here!

"Today the good people of MoRUS . . . are all here to inaugurate a new and beautiful space to recollect that history, the LES squat history and all the diverse radical history associated with the scene here, which is a continuation of the radical history of this neighborhood, the Lower East Side, Loisaida, the place I am proud to call my home from the days when I was a kid living on 12th and D in the Jabob Riis projects. Recollecting that history so that enquiring minds a century from now like the Odyssey will have an accurate and colorful rendering of our battle for a space to come home to, or even have one like . . . the hundreds who said 'fuck the shelters' and who squatted the park, creating a miracle crazy symmetry of Woodstock and Hooverville, if only for a brief moment. Nausea and the Radicts blasting 'squat or rot' from the bandshell . . . a call for class suicide amidst an open call of insurrection for all . . . What an adventure: Sipping tea at 545 13th street with Ginsberg who loved the squats, chess with Yuri on his roof, Drooker beating the drum, Kirk blowing his horn, John the Commie blowing his, Seth's virtual tank bowling over the keystone cops who I'd seen so many years earlier running up Avenue B with a thousand bottles flying in the summer of 88, just like Jerry's flyer predicted, cops sprinting, just ahead of punks and Puerto Ricans, Blacks and squatters, homeless and poets, later squatter women and men unwitting models for fashion and *Rent*, the play, and *Stomp*, our metal jams. I remember workdays on 8th Street, when the whole block was abuzz in the heat of summer sweat communal barn-raising, Dwight and Red, Rosemarie and Willy, veteran of Stonewall, piss buckets on the landlords heads, six buildings on the block then, they said it couldn't be done, they said no trespassing, they said get away, we said no way, cause we knew that the land was ours, like Woody said when he and Leadbelly lived on 10th Street and the casitas were everywhere, and the gardens grew, and the fences came down, and Taito y Esperanza fought back, and 319 fought back, and 5th Street fought back, on the rooftop clenched fist dark shadow in the sky stood Brad Will RIP forever luchando, forever dreaming. . . . And we remember today our friends and comrades who have passed onto that great squat in the sky here with us: El Maestro Mike Shenker, whose squatter opera you should hear, and our beautiful African brother Ruta . . . Bimbo and El Coco que habla whose poetry reverberates through outer space still, all who live in these bricks, who walk these streets still. Yes, some kind of history . . . but mostly, the feeling of weightless soul in flight in airy vacant spaces, dirty gritty saintly bandits free, skating on a canvas all our own, renovating our spirit, an almost inexpressible real living post-capitalism in the now!

"And we're still making history! That's right! Cause we gotta keep actualizing the human right to a home through squatting some more. All the vacant houses sitting a few blocks down from those displaced by Sandy, all those vacant houses sitting around town are waiting for homeless families to move in . . . sitting there waiting . . . waiting for what: to have their locks cracked, to be occupied, that's right! Occupied: We took that word literally decades ago! So now the 21st century squatters must be born, and like weeds spread unstoppable all over the country, in those dozens of shrinking cites where mass abandonment is threatened by mass demolition, a race against the machines, monkey wrench the bull dozers, let's keep on squatting, public housing for the people, the land is life and squatting is the life force, fun with no compromise, no turning back. So put a new wing on this museum, we are about to fill it anew! We have no choice but to dream the impossible and make it real!

"So let's be thankful for making this happen, for telling all of our story, a beautiful story, a heroic story I think, the squatterliness next to godliness story . . . and good luck to the MoRUS. Let's all do what we can to support it and keep our history alive, and keep on making it!" Finishing his talk, Father Frank invites everyone to sing about an earlier moment: "In 1649 at St. George's Hill."

The stories of sprouts of anti-capitalism in our capitalist moment pour forth for hours and hours. My favorite was by Fly, a member of the World War III collective started by Seth and Peter. They were sort of "direct action artists," explains Fly. "Being part of that collective is how I got my start in drawing commix in the early '90s. I was very intrigued by using art as a form of activism—a tool to tell the people's version of the news and to promote social justice of the news and promote social justice locally and globally. World War 3 artists took part in many demonstrations creating beautiful banners and props and often getting arrested for not backing down. I liked the idea of protest being creative and theatrical and not just reactionary and aggro." At MoRUS, Fly narrated from her Unreal Estate show, a slideshow of images, drawings, and comics tracing her years as a squatter, recalling houses that disappeared and that were burned down and a June 1993 riot at Cooper Union when Father Frank was denied a chance to speak, so squatters fought for the mic, stood up for themselves, and struggled for the Glass House.

"Glass House was a big abandoned glass factory on the corner of Avenue D and East 10th Street squatted in the early 1990s," explained Fly. "By 1993, there were a lot of people living there but the city was trying to give the building to a nonprofit group that we suspected of being corrupt. So that spring and summer was dedicated to fighting for Glass House. Finally, it came down to the last Community Board 3 meeting of the summer on the solstice, June 21. We had an eviction watch meeting at Glass House the night before. Everyone agreed that if the board tried to end the public speaking segment before we had our say, we would have to use any means necessary to shut the meeting down. A bunch of us stayed up all night painting banners to unroll when the shit hit the fan. It was really hot and tense but everyone was ready to work together, feeling optimistic, like a big dysfunctional family finally uniting, ready to defend Glass House. The next day me and Arrow headed to the meeting together, sharing a forty on the way. Not talking much, just anticipating the mayhem. The meeting was in the auditorium at the Cooper Union, a very enclosed space with way more than usual police at the entrance and inside. Later it would be suggested that the Eviction Watch Meeting had been infiltrated and that one member of our dysfunctional family was in fact an informer. But for now everyone was just nervous but ready and confident that we had each other's backs. When we walked in, the public speaking portion of the meeting was already in full swing. JT at the mic talking about Glass House while the squatters in the audience applauded and cheered. We took seats near the back close to the exits, a deliberate strategy as the police can converge quickly on a consolidated group. Frank Morales was next in line to speak and everyone was excited but as he stepped up the chairman of the board, Louis Solar, grabbed the mic, announcing that public speaking was now over. Then there was one of those sudden eternal moments of silence and incomprehension. Time Stands Still. That's when Arrow jumped up and stomped to the front of the auditorium, right up to the chairman. It happened really fast. Like we were all suspended or dead while Arrow was the only one left in real life. He was yellin: 'No, no we're not done. We haven't even STARTED!' Then he just plucked the mic out of the chairman's hand and started delivering a speech; 'NOW is the time to ACT and we will NOT BE SILENCED!' Then suddenly all hell broke loose. The lights went out, the emergency lights came on, banners were unrolled, tables and chairs were overturned. Someone dropped a stink bomb and someone else hit the fire alarm. Everyone was yelling and screaming. Trying to get out or trying to get closer in. The police started closing in from all sides with their clubs swinging. Arrow with fist in the air, arm and arm with Sleepy Sean. I saw Arrow go down under a pile of cops, like a cartoon. They just all kept jumping on top of each other until it was a big pile o' pigs. The auditorium was very enclosed and in the middle of the fray I started getting that claustrophobic panic. Things were happening really fast. The chairman of the board was yelling for the cops to arrest people and the cops were following his orders. He even told them to arrest Margarita Lopez, a member of the board, because she was telling the cops not to beat people up. But soon all the cops were jumping in on the action. Then we were all in the middle of the fight with fists flying.

A big seething mass of people crushed together. Lots of punching, screaming, and squirming as we slowly got shoved up the stairs and out the glass door. We all went flying sporadically onto the concrete where more cops proceeded to jump on people and toss them over barricades. I went sprawling onto the sidewalk, gouging my knees and elbows but we were all up and running in a second to avoid getting night stuck. Brian Trash yelled 'Fuck the Police' and a bunch of cops went after him. He made it halfway up 7th street before they wrestled him to the ground. It was three white shirts and they pounded him for a minute then threw him into the paddy wagon, later charging him with inciting a riot. They were dragging a lot of people into the paddy wagons. Arrow was still inside, and I wanted to wait for them to bring him out but the cops had started jumping and arresting any stragglers so we all had to make a run for it. A pack of a couple dozen punks running up St. Marks Place pulling garbage cans and any other available junk out into the road and dumping them to block police vehicles from chasing us. Screaming and howling and throwing garbage at the advancing gang in blue all the way east to Tompkins Square Park. More police cars were quickly arriving at the entrances to the park along Avenue A. They were to corner us. Running beside me was Piper and he kept yelling 'I'm a pacifist. I'm a pacifist.' It was time to scatter, make it thru the park and regroup at La Plaza. I managed to duck and dodge my way through the main entrance at St. Marks and Avenue A and ran east through the park towards 7th Street. Once in the park the cops weren't chasing us anymore. They were blocking the entrances on Avenue A, but they weren't into the park and I couldn't spot any of them on Avenue B. I tried to walk calmly and blend in with the normal people who had not just come from a riot. By the time I got to La Plaza there was already a congregation of Riot Escapees, catching their breath and pumping themselves up with the typical post-riot regalia. 'Dude! Did you did you see me unarrest myself? . . . Can you believe we pulled that—Fuck Yeah Duuuude!' Everyone was feeling safe again as we all caught our breath. The stories started getting more elaborate as everyone figured out how much exaggeration they could get away with. Some people went to get forties and that was when Chaos drove up in his van and yelled to everyone that 'Glass House is being evicted RIGHT NOW!' Which turned out to be another massive exaggeration.

"A week later the Community Board convened another meeting to replace the Riot Meeting. This time they did not even let us in the door. We all camped out on the sidewalk wearing signs saying 'Future Homeless.' A lot more happened after that," Fly concluded, recalling high-octane moments of building homes, laughing at cops, eluding social controls, and telling stories. "After a riot you have to hang out and tell stories about how you hit a cop over and over again." Looking around I saw my friend Jess, who has had her share of Critical Mass run-ins with the NYPD, smiling in recognition. The slideshow combined comics, images of comrades such as Brad Will, and graffiti that first drew me to the East Village when I was a twelve-year-old kid digging through piles of records and zines at Metamorphosis records on Greenville Avenue in Dallas.

A theme of Fly's talk involves recollections of the life and philosophy of squatter icon and her neighbor Michael Shenker, who always supported her efforts. I had known Michael through the Esperanza Campaign and the Anti-War Movement. "One of my favorite people ever," she confessed. "He was a master electrician and hooked up most of the squats directly to the street manholes to pirate juice from Con Ed. I want to mention here that when we did get our legal hookup we were able to negotiate with Con Ed to repay them for the electricity we had pirated. But in the meantime, we had a very contentious relationship with Con Ed. I think this was after we had had to evict a violent resident and he had then started calling all city agencies as we were getting visits two or nine times a week from the fire department, HPD, and had to disconnect for a while (street lamp—turn off 6 AM—turn on 6 PM). Then we finally reconnect to the manhole." Fly and Shenker took turns, parking a car on the manhole, so they could access it at night, with Fly on lookout and Shenker in the hole. Some days, Con Ed would leave notes for Shenker. "One morning the power suddenly went off and I looked out my front window and there was Con Ed pulling out our wires. I went to get Michael but he was already on the fire escape."

Fly sees the whole effort of saving the building as a vast DIY cultural project. "I loved the idea of working on my own space with a collective and having control over every aspect of my own space and design," she explained. "I also loved the idea of community and working together to make a better world—I was a bit idealistic in my youth but I think that it has served me well." Fly and her fellow squatters referred to their efforts as "sweat equity." Through it, they actually enjoyed the outcome of their efforts, without their labor translating into someone else's surplus value.

"We did a lot of art. And visual artists were particularly effective," explains Michael Shenker. "We did a particular amount of propaganda, which was influential for people. It created sympathy. It opened up people's minds. So visual arts were particularly effective, concerts sometimes being done."

Done with her apartment, putting down floors, decorating, and so on, Fly looked around and saw that there was not much natural light. She wanted a window. But knew it was not OK to just cut a hole in the wall of her apartment. She'd need approval. So Fly called her neighbor Michael Shenker. The two talked about the pros and cons of the effort, before Michael finally conceded that she had a choice, "Do you want to be safe and live in the dark or take a chance and live in the light?" She made a window. For Fly, this is what Shenker did for the whole neighborhood: he helped everyone take a chance and live in the light.

"We had a blast the whole time," confesses Shenker a few years before his death in 2010. "It was like fun. Yeah, it was a pain, but the other side of that was great joy and pleasure. Incredible culture too, smoking parties and stuff like that." He lived in his own apartment, a part of a community that had actually built their own world. "What did you need? You needed a place to live," explains Shenker. "You needed a place to hang out. You needed a place to touch nature. We won pretty much all of those. We won buildings; we won gardens to a large degree; and we won ABC No Rio. And we pretty much used the same sets of tactics in all three of those struggles."

I loved knowing Shenker, laughing with him as he made fun of me for voting for Democrats as we sat up all night talking after our arrests at Esperanza Garden. "Well, you're in the Tombs now, buddy," he laughed. We all laughed, Brad, Jerry, Michael, Tim Doody, and I.

"What happened in the 1980s in New York was like Shay's Rebellion, the Whisky Rebellion," concludes Jerry "The Peddler."

"History never ends," Weinberg continues. "So obviously it's ongoing. But the period of real confrontational struggle—what I call the 'class war period,' which was at its climax between August 1988 when the Tompkins Square riot happened and Memorial Day 1991, the final riot followed by the park being ordered closed—that's history. Then after that, there was the whole struggle to save the community gardens." Many of these stories are documented in memorabilia of the squatters, gardeners, and cyclists in the Museum of Reclaimed Urban Space. "There are these criticisms of the museum as commodifying this struggle, I acknowledge," notes Weinberg. "But it's not like anybody is getting rich off of this commodification. And again . . . there isn't any purity. We live under capitalism. And the other side of this is that few people would be remembering this history as it goes further down the Orwellian memory hole each year. The museum—along with the squatters themselves, sitting around telling war stories, and people who are doing academic research—is one of the ways that that historical memory is being preserved."

The struggle for a home in a sustainable city would expand into countless directions over the following years. Between the squats and the gardens, activists helped organize and create social capital, green their neighborhoods, rebuild the housing, and watch financial capital displace bodies from the very neighborhoods they helped revitalize. Direct action helped save these spaces again and again, as conflict transformed social relations. In the following decades, the clash would take on multiple dynamics with activists wondering what was the best way to make an impact. Sometimes these debates took places in meeting spaces or corridors of power. In others, they were staged and performed among bodies in public space, calling for sustainable, people-based uses and expressions in this global city.

Chapter 8

Contested Urban Space, Union Square, and Dispatches on Voluntary and Involuntary Arrests in New York City

"Arrest him," the white-shirt policeman tells another officer, pointing at my friend Chuck, who was serving as a legal observer at a Reclaim the Streets action in New York's financial district in June 1999. Several notable activists from the previous chapters, including Arrow Chrome and Brad Will, are along. "I am a legal observer. I choose not to be arrested," Chuck replies. "Put my name on the ticket," orders the policeman in a white shirt, looking at the long-haired, aging New Jersey public school teacher with a big tie and legal observer cap. Laughing, Chuck is handcuffed and ends up spending the night in jail with friends from his affinity group Reclaim the Streets. While the experience was generally a positive one, it certainly was not the plan for the action. In a clash between the subject and object, the subject sometimes has little interest in the object locking him or her up and being sent to jail. Often, the object has other plans in this ongoing dialectic. There are times when arrest is not part of the show, as the exchange between Chuck and the white-shirt officer indicates. But sometimes arrest *is* part of the show, seen as a means to forward a campaign, garnering media coverage, shifting discourse, and drawing new participants.

Similar clashes take place every day in New York's public spaces, from Tompkins Square Park to Zuccotti Park to Union Square, just off 14th Street. "The Pavilion is our country's temple to free speech and free assembly. All the heroes of the working class have gathered here and spoken here, from under the arches of that very building. Turning the Pavilion into yet another pricey restaurant is a crime against history," says Bill Talen, also known as Reverend Billy. Throughout the park, privatizers and supporters of a public commons debate competing storylines, with capitalists promoting freedom of ideas, of resources, and the rights to compete for things out of most people's grasp, while proponents of public commons see the city as a place to imagine, grow, connect, find solace, and support democracy. In few places in New York, does this tale of two cities find expression like Union Square (Ollman, 2003).

This tension has long informed the story of Union Square. After 9/11, regular people created a public space peace vigil, until the mayor had it taken down, advising everyone, "Take a day off . . . go shopping" (Zukin, 2004, 1). A public commons of ideas is always at odds with those who see cities as optimal spaces for profit maximization (Merrifield, 2002a, b; Ollman, 2003). Our commons is a public trust; from community gardens to streets to parks, from the skies to the water, this is our space (Linebaugh, 2014). This is our world. The idea of the commons dates back to the Magna Carta. It is part of what John Winthrop talked about when he considered the U.S. experiment in democracy as a city on a hill. This is an idealized green space, open for all to speak and congregate. What it is not is a privatized shopping mall with its ticky-tackies and restrictions on speech; this is open space, accessible to all—for art, public assembly, creativity, and democratic engagement. Public space is a fundamental right. Our democracy, our city depends upon it.

An intersection of ideas and bodies, it is also a site for class conflict. Contending with the space between what is and what could be, what should and what could be done, Marx saw cities as spaces where internal relations between social forces lingered, his subject was change and interaction among competing forces (Ollman, 2003, 1–3). This contested space is an incubator for ideas, stories, direct action, and democracy itself. "The law that protects us there, the First Amendment, won't save you from being frisked, harassed, or even arrested," explain public space crusaders D. Savitri and Bill Talen (2011, 136). "The only real authority in public space is public action. Bodies in space, talking and listening: the freedom starts there." This chapter considers a few of the competing narratives of this public space and the conflicting social relations propelling them.

VOLUNTARY AND INVOLUNTARY

"I didn't expose myself—I exposed everybody else," says performance artist Holly Van Voast. She'd successfully litigated against the New York Police Department (NYPD) for arresting her for walking around public spaces of New York topless (Calder, 2013). On one occasion, she was busted for strolling in front of Hooter's topless, wearing a mustache and a Marilyn Monroe wig during the twentieth anniversary of the New York Court of Appeals decision, which found women have the same right to stroll topless in public space in New York as men do. "After experiencing a number of busts, we are pleased to announce that Holly Van Voast has received compensation," notes her lawyer. "The policy of the NYPD has been changed as result of Van

Voast's experiences, and now the NYPD has been properly instructed as to the proper handling of bare breasts" (Calder, 2013, 7).

Arrest can be a highly dramatic means of confrontation, communicating moral courage, as well as contributing to high-octane conflicts. Such performative gestures have a long and important history. Days before the final show of the Living Theater in the Lower East Side of Manhattan, I chatted with Judith Malina about theater and direct action. During its peak years, it was located off Union Square. "We are all a part of the Living Theater," she explained. "It is everywhere. Every policeman, actor, student, activist, anarchist, every school teacher, and homeless person, we are all part of it."

"But what about with an arrest? What happens if the police disrupt the show, halting the performance?" I ask.

"You announce now the police are arresting me," she follows, explaining that the police have to be seen as part of the show. There is no separation between life and performance. Malina would know. Her performances often left her in jail.

I first started attending shows there when my friend Monica Hunken was performing there. The first show I saw there was *Maudie and Jane*, starring Monica and Judith. I was taken by Malina's tenderness and openness performing with Hunken. When Hunken was arrested on the sidewalk in the winter of 2012 while dressed as a clown during one of the Occupy performances in front of a bank, she kept on clowning and felt free even with the police handcuffing her. She kept on skipping, staying ever in character.

The line between art and life is never simple or smooth. The city is a living theater—a space where tragedy overlaps with play, dreams, hopes, revolutionary theater, arrest, children growing up, community gardens, elders returning to the earth, struggles over public space, and hopes for something better.

When I first started going to ACT UP meetings in the 1990s, I heard the expression "demo diva." It was a campy way of describing a distinct sensibility queer activists often bring to activism, performance, and street protest, tracing a line from the cabaret and the picket line and the sex club to the art gallery, and back. Arrests were always part of the show. "We knew from the anti-war and civil rights movements that demonstrations that include peaceful civil disobedience actions that involve risking arrest receive far more media attention than simple street marches or political rallies," notes one of the group's founders Eric Sawyer (2002, 89–90). "Television producers seem to think that pictures of police arresting demonstrators make interesting television news. Thus, ACT UP tried always to include some action in our demonstrations that would get us arrested." For ACT UP, risking arrest was always part of the performance. It was a gesture linked to resistance to oppressive mechanisms of everyday living, and it used the city as a work of art.

Figure 8.1.   Monica Hunken arrested at the height of Occupy. She stayed in character throughout the ordeal.

Source: Illustration by Caroline Shepard.

For members of ACT UP, civil disobedience was a form a theater, as well as a means of resistance to oppressive social mores. "They started telling us about hell, and I was so busy jerking off all the time and stealing from the donation plate, that I knew that was not the place for me," recalls longtime member Andrew Vélez (2004) in an interview with the ACT UP Oral History Project, describing his childhood. "So I headed right for the theater, and that's where I found my first tribe," confesses Vélez. "I auditioned for something and got into some off-Broadway play, when I was in my teens."

ACT UP members laid their bodies down and on the line at Wall Street, at the offices of the CDC, in the Halls of St. Patrick's Cathedral, and anywhere else where they could focus the nation's attention to the silences, which allowed the AIDS epidemic to rage unabated. Here, activism blurred with performance art, the use of bodies, and the sense of urgency leaving the door open to a richer, more embodied, queerer, more delicious, daring, and defiant form of high-octane radical street performance.

"Who do you have to fuck in this town to get arrested?" groused David Feinberg (1994, 47) during an office takeover at the Food and Drug Administration when it seemed no one could get arrested, bringing a life-affirming gallows humor to the better to laugh than to cry spectacle of AIDS activism. Members of the group brought their activism and defiant form of radical street performance into streets, offices, bathrooms, jails, opera houses, sex clubs, and even the theater.

Visual AIDS artist Hunter Reynolds was an early member of ACT UP and a founder of Art Positive, an affinity group to fight homophobia and censorship in the arts. Dragged through the streets, and bound like he was being arrested, his performances linked AIDS activism, queer political performance, and direct action.

Arrested at St. Patrick's Cathedral in ACT UP's famous Stop the Church action, he explains: "I was not able to be in the die in so the police arrested me on the street . . . I told them I want to die," he continues, directing the police about where he wanted to lay down for his arrest. In the months after that iconic action, several of Hunter's friends got sick. For those engaged in queer political performance, the line between the club and the street, the stage and the jail cell, and the backroom and the bedroom connects their lives, linking spaces for performance, activism, arrest, social change, and even life and death. And arrest was most certainly part of the show.

REVEREND BILLY AND CRITICAL MASS

If there is one activist whose performances have invited a strong reaction in New York, it is Bill Talen, performing as Reverend Billy, a self-described "aging Elvis impersonator" with an anti-consumer message. When I first met Talen in the late 1990s in New York, he was performing in Times Square. We would engage in invisible theater performances about sweatshops in the lines at the Disney Store or Starbucks. A group of us organized a performance with Talen, inviting arrest at the Disney Store in November 1999. "It is my civil right not to live in a shopping mall," I declared while being hauled off by police for sitting down to block the line to the cash register at the Disney Store. The sit-in at the Disney Store invited a police response. Over the years, this has been the case with Reverend Billy shows, especially with gestures of free speech increasingly viewed with suspicion rather than as constitutionally protected activity.

Take the monthly Critical Mass Rides that meet at Union Square Park on the last Friday of every month. For years, the ride went on without incident in New York, until 2004, when the Republican National Convention led to the mass arrest of bicyclists. In the following years, the city continued to arrest those taking part in the rides. Meeting in a public park for a bike ride, this peaceable assembly seemed to be a simple First Amendment protected activity. In the summer of 2007, just before July 4, Independence Day, Bill Talen arrived to support Critical Mass in Union Square, a public park where Paul Robeson used to sing, Emma Goldman spoke, and the Living Theater performed *The Brig*. Hundreds of police were also there. So, Talen started reciting the lines of the First Amendment of the U.S. Constitution. Over and over again Talen and his partner Savitri Durkee recited the words: "Congress shall make no law with respect to the right of the people to peaceably assemble." They were screaming at the line of police, who eventually moved in and arrested Talen. Recalling the scene years later, he describes how the "45 magic words" of the First Amendment started to pour out of his mouth: "I started to shout it. Feeling so much anger at the new rules in New York." Talen saw attorney Norm Siegel standing watching the scene and knew he had a solid witness. "Being there with Robeson, Emma Goldman, writhing up so full of anger, we started to have an audience. We didn't go to get arrested. It was an authentic performance. It was the emotion." In the weeks to come, the story about getting arrested for reciting the Constitution spread around the world. Talen and company successfully fought back, suing the city for damages, while making a point about infringements upon public expression in the public commons (Savitri and Talen, 2011).

Over the years, we would continue to fight against the privatization and hyper control of the public commons of Union Square. So would a generation of activists, as movements ebbed from a peace and justice movement converging there after 9/11 through the Black Lives Matter movement and a campaign to fight the privatization of the space itself. The contest only intensified with the battle of Critical Mass at Union Square.

Barbara Ross explains, "The NYPD has arrested me twice and confiscated my bicycle three times for the so-called-crime of bicycling without a permit." The use of public hysteria to justify preemptive arrest and the control of mobilization structures witnessed during convergence actions, including the New York RNC, was only increasing. A total of 1,800 people were arrested at the 2004 RNC, more than Chicago 1968 and every other convention in U.S. history. A total of 264 cyclists were arrested while taking part in Critical Mass on August 28, 2004. I will never forget seeing the undercover police with the smell of whiskey on their breath swinging batons at the crowd of cyclists trying to get inside St. Marks Church In-the-Bowery. Few of my friends or I would make it through that week without finding ourselves in jail.

Over the next year, the NYPD's Raymond Kelly and Paul Browne would continue to justify the crackdown with highly inflammatory rhetoric, linking cycling with anarchism. Kelly argued that the Critical Mass ride was "hijacked by groups of cyclists intent on disruption" in an op-ed article published by the *Daily News* on October 28, 2004, and later in the *New York Post* on July 21, 2006. Years afterward, depositions from a lawsuit would prove that Raymond Kelly's allegations against Critical Mass bicycle riders were made without credible evidence, based on information from unknown sources and used to rationalize the NYPD's multimillion-dollar campaign to follow, ticket, and intimidate Critical Mass bicycle riders every month.

"The last Friday of every month, the NYPD turns Union Square Park into a prison yard," says Madeline Nelson, a bike supporter, before the May 2005 Critical Mass ride.

"Why are you doing this?" the Reverend Billy asks a policeman as he prepares to arrest a group of bikers before the March 2005 Critical Mass. "Well," the officer confesses, "everything changed after 9/11."

As the years passed, Reverend Billy and the Church of Stop Shopping focused on environmental concerns. In the fall of 2013, he performed an "extinction sermon" in the lobby of a Chase Bank on 56th Street and Sixth Avenue in Manhattan, with others playing the role of "Golden Toads" rendered extinct by the policies of the bank. Singing and dancing, the toads passed out information sheets about the impact of Chase investments on the environment. The group exited to the subway, where Talen and Nehemiah Luckett, the music director of the Stop Shopping Choir, were arrested and later charged with "riot in the second degree, menacing in the third degree, unlawful assembly, and two counts of disorderly conduct." New York's district attorney would request one year in prison for "this criminal stunt." As the Friends of the Church of Stop Shopping recount, in their petition to keep Talen out of jail: "Wylie Stecklow, defending the two activists, insisted that the '15 minutes of performance art about the earth's crisis' was well within 'expressive political activity' protected by the First Amendment of the US Constitution. The lawyers went back and forth: 'Art!' 'Crime!' 'Art!' 'Crime!' 'Art!'" (2014). In court on December 9, 2013, "Nehemiah and myself stood with our lawyers today and our jaws dropped," recalls Talen. "The bizarre District Attorney dropped our suggested sentence from a year in jail for 'Riot' 'Menace' and other crimes . . . to nothing at all for Nehemiah and an afternoon of community service for me." The arrests had not been planned, but they exposed a system of injustice.

Eleven years after the crackdown on Critical Mass, Mellow Yellow and a group of cyclists met at Union Square for the monthly Critical Mass bike ride. Mellow Yellow was riding a sound bike with amplified sound. Peddling around Union Square at nightfall, the police walk up to Mellow Yellow, asking for his identification.

"Why are you here?" asks Mellow Yellow. "You're here to tell me to turn down the radio? What about cars that are killing people?"

"Look I don't care about the cars killing people," the policeman explains.

"You don't care about cars killing people?" wonders Mellow Yellow, his voice escalating. The police's priorities became clear as Mellow Yellow's simple performance continued—they moved in to handcuff him, pushing him to the ground, where a group of police piled on, and sent him to jail, where he would stay for the next twenty-four hours.

The spectacle of a leaderless Critical Mass opened a whole new way of thinking for Mellow Yellow. "I was raised Catholic. My teacher punched me in grade school and then she sided with my bully. I told him his riddle was wrong. She sided with him. If the teacher was wrong, authority was wrong. If they say Freddie [Gray] killed himself, then they are wrong. Critical Mass was a space to connect with people. I loved meeting people there, talking with people . . . even in New York in our darkest days, to meet and connect with people. The other thing that appealed to me was the critical collective consciousness, informal networks as opposed to an organization."

"My first Critical Mass ride I was behind Chris Long," notes Mellow Yellow, reflecting on his years of riding in New York. Chris Long was a New York cyclist who was arrested during the July 25, 2008, Critical Mass bike ride as he rode through Times Square. The police charged Long with attempted assault and held him for twenty-six hours in jail. Only after leaving jail, did Long find out a video of the ride that showed Long being violently knocked off his bike by a rookie policeman. A tourist filmed the incident and passed the video onto Time's Up! The group, in turn, distributed it to the world, eventually leading to the policeman's dismissal from his position and a significant settlement for Long.

"I was playing the game. I asked the white shirts what we could do," says Mellow Yellow, talking about the police presence at Critical Mass. "They said ride in the bike lane. Take away the joy of the experience." These police seemed ready to disrupt this field of bountiful activists. "The night of the Chris Long incident, seeing that had a huge impact. We all reconvened; the three groups met downtown. It became my practice. It was the place I met for all of my rides: the Beach Ride, Moonlight Ride, Critical Mass."

"I was outspoken. I asked, 'Why are you doing this?'" The police came to know Mellow Yellow, not finding his irreverence to their liking, threatening him when he came to hearings or spoke up for bike safety.

"We're not afraid, you're just getting paid. Cars vs bikes. NYC streets are owned by pedestrians," riffs Mellow Yellow. He saw group bike rides as a clash of ideas and social forces, between what he saw as free people versus those enslaved to the system. "NYC Critical Mass, a pleasure community, a free ride on a human-powered machine. The contrast is with the police and their message that everyone has to disperse. The people vs sound cannon, cars vs bikes, free-moving machines. A car is a giant box that is violent."

Critical Mass is where Joe met many of his New York friends. "It's an embattled space. We want freedom of assembly. That's my mandate." This is an image of the world we hope to live in. "We have to dismantle the police state first," concludes Mellow Yellow. "New York is so saturated. Yet, there are so many possibilities."

He sees the reaction to Critical Mass at Union Square as a form of panic. "I was commuting from Brooklyn. I rode with Transportation Alternatives and Time's Up! I saw the police panicking. I was inspired by Billy's defense after he was arrested for reciting the First Amendment at the Critical Mass. I was basically doing Critical Mass testing the ground, talking with the white shirts, pointing out that the whole thing was essentially a question of free speech."

"My first ticket was during a Thursday ride through Times Square." Vlad was filming for Global Revolution. "I said to Vlad I am not a leader but you can follow me. I turned. I was given a ticket. I lost my trust in the cops. I saw the incompetence."

"This is their training exercise," he explains, reflecting on events, such as 143-plus arrests the night before our conversation after the Freddie Gray rally at Union Square on April 29, 2015, as activists stepped out of the park into the street. By that point in the spring of 2015, activists with the burgeoning Black Lives Matter movement had been marching for days, blocking bridges, staging die-ins at train stations, and marching against traffic with their hands in the air, declaring, "Hands Up! Don't Shoot!" and "Black Lives Matter," in rallies that often started in Union Square. Some days, activists step off the curb without a hitch. On others, they barely have the opportunity to move. Yet, they were still drawn to Union Square.

UNION SQUARE AS OUR COMMONS

In June 2008, Reverend Billy and supporters dropped a banner from the historic Pavilion of Union Square Park, declaring, "Union Square Not for Sale." With bullhorn in hand, Billy delivers a sermon entitled "A Shout from the Pavilion":

> What is our commons?
> What do I own with you and you with me?
> And what is our place—if not this place—The place with one name
> That names us all . . .
> It is our Pavilion, our reviewing stand,
> On the north end of Union Square in New York City. It is that place
> in the passing of American time

And we are the workers parading by it. We see Paul Robeson singing on it
And Dorothy Day praying on it
And Emma Goldman shouting above a sea of fedoras . . .
What is our commons?
What do we all own at once?
Can we actually send this Pavilion back . . .
The decades of tens of thousands chanting and marching?
We accepted the gift of this place that they risked their lives to create
We use its freedom every day.
The Pavilion is designed by the First Amendment.
Its wide-open rotunda, its colonnades and symmetry—
It is a body of a building made for wailing, beseeching, demanding . . .
We cannot sell this place and let all those heroes die standing up
In a tastefully-framed photograph on a restaurant wall.
What is our commons?
What do we possess together?
We hear our name in a shout from another century
A hundred thousand workers in a fervent unison in Union Square
Our name rising from the reviewing stand called the Pavilion
We hear it and take a breath to shout it forward into time
To keep the gift going.

The streets and corners, alleys and parks, apartments and buildings of New York remain in constant flux. Go away for a week and return to find your favorite watering hole closed, signs for a building permit in front of a familiar street corner, or a fence with a "Keep Out" sign on a once-inviting public park. In summer 2008, Reverend Billy and company started holding "education and agitation" events at Union Square, by the construction site of the Pavilion. This group of activists (including this writer), dubbed Save Union Square (SUS), vowed to stop the conversion of the historic Pavilion at the north end of Union Square into a private, upscale restaurant. Over the previous year, the plans to privatize this landmark historic park moved through a review and approval process that seemed rigged from the outset. In response, community groups issued a lawsuit that stymied the process. The group saw the plans as part of a larger pattern of development by the Bloomberg administration, of turning public resources over to private hands with little to no regard for the rights of the public to utilize public space, and no respect for history.

"The New York City Parks Department under Mayor Bloomberg has a repeated pattern of making drastic changes to our popular city parks," with little to no concern about community sentiment, says New York activist and blogger Cathryn Swan.

When Judge Jane Solomon, a New York State Supreme Court Judge, heard the number of procedural oversights, she put an indefinite stay on the development. No one knew how long the temporary restraining order (TRO) would last. Still, concerned New Yorkers wasted little time to rally public opinion about the project during the stay on construction.

Save Union Square supporters organized weekly events to raise awareness about the park, to draw people to their cause. Wednesday at 5 pm, they met in the park, assembled with images of Union Square's past—Sacco and Vanzetti, Emma Goldman, and Paul Robeson—to speak out, build community, and recite the First Amendment. Looking at the Pavilion, Billy seemed to see Paul Robeson singing, Dorothy Day praying, his heroes everywhere.

"For over a century, Union Square has provided an important forum for public gatherings and protest. Its design, with a mix of green and wide open space, and its central location have made it a key gathering point," notes Jessica Rechtschaffer, a member of the Radical Homosexual Agenda, lamenting the fence now surrounding the space. "During the Giuliani and Bloomberg regimes, public space has repeatedly been given to private interests. At the same time, public protest has been suppressed." Union Square has always been a space to witness change and interaction among competing forces. Emma Goldman preached for abortion rights there, in 1916. The eight-hour workday was won there. And, in 1997, the park achieved landmark status. "Union Square Park has been designated a national historic landmark," a plaque in the square reads. "The site possesses national significance in commemorating the United States of America. Here workers exercised their rights to free speech and assembly and on September 5, 1882, observed the first Labor Day."

"The only people who will bring back the commons are the people who insist on democracy," pleads Bill Talen. "Reclaiming our commons may sound to you like the most sensible thing to do—but the stakes are very high. The police and the courts often side with the privatizers." Without public space for people to bump into each other, talk, assemble, or lament, democracy dwindles. The struggle over the space extends far and wide, a democratic right to the city in stark contrast with a view of public space as a source for accumulation and growth.

In December 1999, over 1,000 homeless activists converged there to fight Rudy Giuliani's homeless policies, which involved mass arresting of the poor. In January 2000, I spent the night in the north end of the square with City Council members as well as Sylvia Rivera. The Giuliani administration was planning to arrest anyone sleeping or even laying their head in a public space. While Rivera was famous for decades of queer activism, she told me she considered sleeping in the street that night to protest cutbacks on homeless services as one of the most important things she had ever done. "We're not free till everyone is free," Rivera maintained. "Part of our mission statement is to be out there for all oppressed people." Many saw the policy as a thinly veiled threat to freedom of assembly. The plan eventually fell apart.

With community centers shuttered, activists contended that there were too few places to gather in New York. For example, when the anti-war group United for Peace and Justice wanted to organize a rally in Central Park in 2004, the city favored protecting the grass and rejected the proposed rally ending in Central Park. Without accessible public space, opportunities for free public assembly are vastly curtailed.

On August 11, 2005, Rosie Mendez, the city councilwoman for the district, wrote the following note to Parks Commissioner Adrian Benepe: "A commercial venture within the pavilion would take away over 2,000 sq. ft. of scarce space needed by the public and the community would be deprived of the long-awaited opportunity to reinstate multipurpose public uses of the pavilion rather than commercial ones," noted Mendez. "There is great concern regarding the potential restriction of free assembly and free speech, should a restaurant be located on the park's border facing the north Plaza. It is very likely that the concessionaires would be unwilling to close-down business in the event of a protest or large gathering outside of their establishment. Police are likely to be called upon to keep crowds away. As a consequence, the rights of the concessionaire, using public space for private gain, would be protected over the rights of the public."

Much of this view changed when an anonymous donor offered seven million to renovate the space, with a small caveat about a restaurant.

Few heard about the plan. Even the New York State Assembly was precluded from deliberations on the transformation of the space. The community around Union Square has the lowest concentration of public parks and play areas and the highest concentration of restaurants in the city. "If you are going to use parkland for a non-park purpose, you have to get state alienation approval," explains Geoffrey Croft, the president of NYC Park Advocates and the Union Square Community Coalition, referring to the concept of alienation, an eighteenth-century common law doctrine. "The city tries to get away with as much as possible without it. It's a tactic and that happened in this case . . . The real problem here is that the city does not protect its parkland. That's the job of elected officials. In this case, there is a great deal of public support," he concludes.

On June 5, 2008, SUS held a rally outside a meeting of the Union Square Business Improvement District held near the square. Several actors reenacted historic moments in the park. I played George Washington, who brought his exhausted Continental Army to converge on the spot in 1783 when the British finally left the island. "Beat back the BiD!" we chant. "Beat Back the BiD! Parks for the Public!"

When Rosie heard about the rally, she made a brief appearance. In between jeers and boos, Mendez tried to explain why she shifted her position.

"How about no restaurant," one activist screamed.

"We're fighting for freedom, not French fries!" the crowd began to scream.

Mendez made the case that all renovations, including one million procured from her predecessor on the council, Margarita Lopez, would be lost without the restaurant plan.

Two weeks later, on June 19, we all stood on the City Hall steps passing out flyers, doing outreach at the annual LGBT Pride event at City Hall. The doors of City Hall were open for what looked like a cocktail party. We asked everyone entering City Hall to request that Rosie help in saving Union Square from being turned into a restaurant. Some didn't know much about the issue. Others gave snide comments. One man who had had a few cocktails asked that we not stand on the City Hall steps. Another man said, "Well, if you want Rosie, there she is." Mendez was just walking through the City Hall security. With my two daughters, one on my back the other in tow, I walked up to Mendez, thanked her for coming to our June 5 event and explained we do not need another restaurant, we need an open and accessible Union Square. I handed Mendez our flyer (with the story of the anonymous bidder and the words "extortion!" "corruption!"). "Please help us save Union Square," I ask. "Please Rosie, we need open space, not another restaurant. It's not too late." As Rosie walked away, she gave another uncomfortable look. Fifty or sixty people were now watching.

The goal was to challenge the steamroller of big real estate paving over our history. Throughout the mid-1990s, the Disney Company tried to create an amusement park on a Civil War battlefield in Virginia. They lost that battle but won when they lobbied for the City of New York to clean up Times Square's red-light district in exchange for their business there. Blandified urban space seemed to be expanding in concentric circles from 42nd Street, with corporate profits posited against the city's urban color, its intersections of high and low, the boogie-woogie of New York's public spaces losing out to the bland. New Yorkers live, eat, and play in public space, members of the group would contend. They need this mix of bodies and ideas.

Over the next five years, SUS challenged the Parks Department and Union Square Partnership plans to install a restaurant in the historic Pavilion. Sometimes the struggle took place in court, with preliminary injunctions preventing the operation of a restaurant or the installation of fixtures for a restaurant. Lawyers argued that without state legislative approval, the restaurant would be an unlawful alienation of parkland. The city moved to dismiss the case, claiming it was both unripe and nonmeritorious.

In September 2008, a business improvement group held a private party at Union Square. SUS organized a counter rally, bringing noisemakers and smashing pots and pans outside the fenced off event. I started throwing paper airplanes made from our flyer over the fence into their event. Enjoying the

Figure 8.2.   The author being arrested for throwing a paper airplane over a fence at Union Square. "Public space for the people . . ."

Source: Illustration by Caroline Shepard.

revelry, feeling a sense of freedom, I let my guard down, lapsing from my usual practice of eyeing police, as I usually do at demonstrations when I do not want to get arrested.

"I'm sorry, Ben," Tim Doody said as the police approached from behind, pulled my arms behind my back, putting cuffs on, and arresting me for throwing paper airplanes at Union Square. The performance ended with arrest. The police had taken their part in show, demonstrating the restrictions on access to public space for debate or dialogue. To an extent, this was the point—the performance was about the privatization of public space, after all. Before that night, I thought getting arrested by plainclothes police for putting up stickers during the Republican National Convention was the most ridiculous arrest I had ever experienced. But getting busted for throwing paper airplanes with Billy, who was arrested as well, topped that. Sitting in the police van I thought of Arlo Guthrie, who sang about going to jail for littering in "Alice's Restaurant." A few years later when the Occupy Movement started, a friend was arrested for "furtive eye movement" while looking at a police officer. Another Occupier was arrested for chalking on the sidewalk. In New York, absurd arrest became the norm.

OCCUPY

One of the most remarkable aspects of Occupy Wall Street (OWS) was its capacity to ground a movement in a literal struggle for the public commons. The vitality of OWS took expression in the movement's public presence—this contested terrain, subject to competing claims. In New York, the very gesture of reclaiming public space takes shape through an interplay between those seeking to privatize and maximize profit and those claiming it as a space favoring convivial social relations and democracy. Within its efforts to occupy public space, the movement found a space in the social imagination and a position in the public discourse that fall and spring from September 2011 to 2012. Doing so, OWS opened a conversation about inequality and democratic living.

For many involved in the movement, Zuccotti Park was our agora. "The Agora (Greek: Ἀγορά, Agorá) was a central spot in ancient Greek city-states," notes OWS activist Morgan Jenness. "The literal meaning of the word is 'gathering place' or 'assembly.'" The agora was the center of athletic, artistic, spiritual, and political life in the city, notes Jenness. "Many suffer from 'agoraphobia,'" says Jenness, defining the term as "the fear of participating as a full citizen in the commons (or agora) as well as fear of what may evolve from the discourse that happens there from those who wish to suppress it."

The NYPD made every effort to shut down this movement, just as they did with Critical Mass. But activists pushed back. Cyclists litigated. And, the city was found to be guilty of violating cyclists' basic rights. In fall 2010, the city agreed to pay cyclists attacked on Critical Mass Rides $965,000.00. Yet, instead of apologizing, the city set its target on cyclists, and later OWS protesters taking another stab at reclaiming public space. "We won the bike lanes, but lost free speech," Mellow Yellow contends, reflecting on his years of struggle against the police to make sure the ride happened. Some years he was arrested, others he eluded their social controls. Every year these rides become a site of contestation, a clash between free bodies and police hell-bent on control. Today, they are larger than ever.

"Bike power has come a long way," Mellow Yellow reflects. "We're past Critical Mass with bikes. But we need a free speech critical mass. You need people power. I wanna ride, be contrarian, and reject authority. Still the bikes on the street, the practice of a critical mass is sharing space, same as a body of people." Speaking about the Black Lives Matter movement, which organizes bike rides across the city, he argues, "We found a core issue—police protests, challenging an issue, of brutality and abuse—dating back to the Mayflower and slavery." When the NYPD gets donations from banks such as Chase for their support in suppressing Occupy, one has to wonder who are they protecting and serving.

The police have been arresting public space advocates for ages. Cyclists were arrested during the Occupy eviction night in November 2011 trying to remove the Time's Up! energy bikes from the space before the police confiscated them. The following January 2012, Keegan and another Occupy activist were arrested for sitting on a park bench in Zuccotti Park, a park zoned for 24/7 access. And on the six-month anniversary of the movement, March 17, 2012, police arrested members of the group as they congregated in Zuccotti Park, a privately owned public space zoned for twenty-four-hour access. The same day as the rest of the city celebrated St. Patrick's Day, hundreds were handcuffed and arrested. A woman having a seizure was arrested. These involuntary arrests tore at the fabric of this movement. Still, the show and the satire went on. When members of Time's Up! lampooned the police, mock arresting cyclists for filming them as they ate donuts in front of the 7th precinct, they were promptly arrested and charged with reckless endangerment. Barbara Ross and Keegan litigated and won a $22,000 settlement (Sledge, 2014).

Throughout the ups and downs of the movement, observers suggested that activists involved in Occupy endured a persistent pattern of arrest. In November 2012, the Organization for Security and Cooperation in Europe (OSCE) issued a report finding that U.S. authorities' responses to the OWS movement involved excessive police force, unjustified mass arrests, disproportionately large numbers of police, and violation of the rights of journalists.

"The OSCE report confirms recent findings by U.S. groups of violations of protest rights, and demonstrates the urgent need to reform the way some cities, including New York, regulate and police protests," says Professor Sarah Knuckey of New York University School of Law, who co-led an investigation into the treatment of OWS.

"There is no part of the world where suppression of protest is not a problem, and the U.S. is no exception," says Maina Kiai, the UN Special Rapporteur on the rights to freedom of peaceful assembly and association. "Fighting for a meaningful right of free assembly is vital because there can be no democracy without this right," concludes Kiai.

March 21, 2012

11:52—Midnight, Union Square

Audio from Global Revolution livestream, nearing midnight, after the "Million Hoodies" demo at Union Square, for Trayvon Martin:

> The park closes at 12 O' Clock. You have to leave the park. The NLG reporting over 500 or more cops surrounding the park. There will be massive arrests. There is a massive police force. You have to exit the park at midnight. Whose

Park? Our park? It's important to note that every effort to quell the movement has failed. And now it's the American Spring. In eight minutes there will be a mass arrest. I've never seen this many cops. This is similar to the raid . . . This is the absolute meeting place for the park. Five, four three two one. [people roar] A anti capitalista. [claps] Crushing people's rights or courtesy professionalism, respect. We have a right to peaceable assembly, freedom of assembly. You guys don't hurt us. We're not criminals. We're citizens of the United States. Get up, get down, there is a revolution in this town. [crowd] More high ranking officers than I've seen since the raid. The locals say this is open 24 hours a day. People are always here drinking, smoking. The NYPD can evict people from the park, but they cannot stop this movement. People are coming from around the country. This is bottom up. Take off that riot gear, we don't see no riot here. People were playing chess in the park last night, but their game was interrupted by a check mate by the police. Every time they try to sabotage us, they just make us stronger. [chants] One we are the people, two we are united, three, this occupation is not leaving. Where is my freedom?

CONCLUSIONS

Social movements are fundamentally about public space. From Zuccotti Park to People's Park to Union Square, movements find inspiration in a place to meet, organize, share stories, break isolation, dance, plan, build mutual aid, and create a bit of care and civil society in an otherwise tough and alienating world. As the stories about protests over critical masses and aesthetic choices, evictions, and involuntary arrests attest, the ongoing clash between subject and object takes a dynamic shape in public space, as the individual encounters the other. "When we consider and reflect upon Nature at large or our own intellectual activity at first," Frederick Engels (1877) suggests, "we see the picture of an endless entanglement of relations and reactions, permutations and combinations, in which nothing remains what, where, and as it was, but everything moves, changes and comes into being as it passes away." At issue within these ever-evolving social relations is a question about what kind of a city this will become. "We see therefore at first the picture as a whole with its individual parts still more or less kept in the background," Engels continues. "We observe the movements, transitions, connections, rather than things that move, combine, and are connected."

Throughout this chapter, we've explored a tale of two cities taking place in public spaces of New York City. Debates between those seeking to maximize profit by the inch and those seeing public spaces as commons extend from Tompkins Square Park to the community gardens, from Union Square to Zuccotti Park. They take place everywhere regular people are arrested for getting in the way of an ever-blandifying better business climate. Still, activists push back, spurring waves of environmental resistance and human rights movements, agitating and winning significant settlements for arrests, including for impersonating police officers. After years and years of claims and counterclaims, lawsuits and protests, a seasonal restaurant finally opened in the Pavilion in Union Square Park, connected to a vibrant park for kids, but not without significant concessions, prohibiting it from extending into the square. Its presence did not seem to hinder the budding Black Lives Matter movement, with unpermitted parades and die-ins erupting from the space, summer after summer. Through the mere act of resistance, regular people help animate the space as this tale of two cities takes on an urgent expression. The dance between open and closed space, expression and repression, churns forward.

In 1649, the Diggers, a group of landless commoners, claimed St. George's Hill, outside of London, as their own. "The symbolism of taking back as common land what had been enclosed (i.e., privatized) overshadowed the negligible material value of planting corn in barren soil," notes Steve Duncombe (2002, 10). "But what these outcasts of Cromwell's New Model Army did hold dear was the community created in their act of resistance; it was a scale model of the universal brotherhood they demanded in the future." Similar struggles are currently found in spaces such as bike lanes, community gardens, public piers, and even parks where convivial social relations take shape. Such spaces are increasingly contested. So are ideas about who should stand where and why.

Chapter 9

From Emma Goldman to Riot Grrrl, Sex Work, Autonomy, and the Transformation of Streets: Reproductive Autonomy, Public Space, and Social Movements

In the first chapter of her autobiography, *Living My Life*, Emma Goldman (1931) recalls hearing the news that the Haymarket Martyrs had been executed: "The terrible thing everyone feared, yet hoped would not happen, actually occurred. Extra editions of the Rochester papers carried the news: the Chicago anarchists had been hanged!" Despairing, Goldman went to bed. She woke the next day, as if "from a long illness, but free from the numbness and the depression of those harrowing weeks of waiting, ending with the final shock." Her world had changed, and so had she. The losses offered something

Figure 9.1.   Emma Goldman portrait.

Source: Illustration by Caroline Shepard.

of a break and an opening. "I had a distinct sensation that something new and wonderful had been born in my soul. A great ideal, a burning faith, a determination to dedicate myself to the memory of my martyred comrades, to make their cause my own, to make known to the world their beautiful lives and heroic deaths" (Goldman, 1931).

Goldman saw the plight of the Haymarket Martyrs as her plight and cause, viewing other exploited workers and freedom fighters in the same way. Outsiders were marginalized and excluded, over and over, often by the state itself, so Goldman pushed back, framing her engagement in terms of anarchism. In the subsequent years, she connected workers' rights with the struggles for autonomy of bodies from the state, noting that sweatshop workers received $6 per week, an average wage of $280 per year. Under such conditions, why would anyone be surprised that people turned to other means to make a living, including sex work, wondered Goldman (who briefly worked the trade) (1969, 179). For Goldman, such labor was best viewed as "the direct result, in many cases, of insufficient compensation of honest labor" (180). It is among the few ways out of a second-class life as a sweatshop worker, a mistress, or a servant. When she suggested that there was no difference between marriage and prostitution, the U.S. government deported her to Russia. Soon enough, she began writing similarly scathing indictments of the revolution. The Soviets deported her. In subsequent years, her writing and activism explored the links between sex and labor history, anarchism and movements for the liberation of sexuality, connecting the women's movement, sex work, and an anti-prohibitive ethos later to be described as queer theory (see chapter 11). For Goldman, sex work was contested labor. So she and future generations of sexual civil liberties activists connected it with battles for public space, struggles against capitalism, and global justice activism, opening up a space for engagement between social theory and queer activist social knowledge. Countless others built on Goldman's readings of the meanings of sex work. A few of these perspectives and debates are considered here.

This chapter explores debates over anarchism, sex work as precarious, contested labor, and ways of responding to questions about this form of work. Here a dialectic of sex takes countless forms. "Everything is and is not, for everything is fluid, is constantly changing, constantly coming into being and passing away," notes Friedrich Engels (1877). Movements ebb and workers are stepped on, killed, and made martyrs, out of which new movements arise. In Emma Goldman's (1931) life, movement closings offered openings.

From anarchism to the women's movement, this process has only continued. "It is everywhere. The division of yin and yang pervades all of culture, history, economics, nature itself; modern Western versions of sex discrimination are only the most recent layer," argues Shulamith Firestone (1970, 1).

"There is a whole sexual substratum of the historic dialectic that Engels only dimly perceives" (6).

"I'm just tired of sex workers being, pretty obviously, people we're generally more willing to be ok with being abused, used, or murdered," notes Ashe Maree, a sex worker, in a tweet on February 25, 2015. The abuses women endure are considerable. Misogyny is everywhere. Some condemn the practice of sex work; others the people. Over and over, competing narratives shape understandings of sex work; some view it as autonomous work while others see it as exploited labor, a way to use or be used, among those with or without choice, active agents or victims.

People judge, condemn, abhor, valorize, and even idealize the practice from any number of points of view. After all, the way one sees the world is quite often determined by social standpoint (Harstock, 1998). Marx argued that in capitalism, there are two basic viewpoints from which to consider reality: for those who own and those who don't—determining how one sees the world. Such standpoints expose points of view. Dominant groups have little to no interest in knowing or understanding the subjectivities of others around them. Subordinate groups, on the other hand, must have double vision, so they can see both their own realities and those of the dominant group. Race, gender, and class inform what and how we see. The women's movement has often divided loyalties between class and identity-based alliances, with each offering their own distinct vantage points. And sometimes they conflict, with economically privileged women condemning sex work and sex workers themselves instead of seeing them as sisters (Hollibaugh, 2000). Standpoint theory helps us to see two things: the importance of location and of consciousness.

Marx studied vantage points, highlighting the importance of the place where we are at as a form of abstraction. He used it to pay attention to materials we are trying to understand. In his study of economy, he kept changing the vantage point, even in one sentence, as he looked at interconnections from vantage points in space and time, past and present, and ways of seeing. He studied history back and forward, from the present to the past, looking at today to wonder about what happened in the past to explain how it functions in this way, looking at modes of production, from the preconditions of capitalism—feudalism—into the past. Capitalism and its interrelations go back hundreds of years, he argued, pointing to both class history and history of class, aiming to reveal as he "labor[ed] the law of motion in a modern Capitalist society" (Marx, 1846; Ollman, 2016).

In terms of prostitution, Marx suggested we all compromise ourselves in the face of capital. "*Money* is the pimp between need and object, between life and man's means of life," he argues in the *Economic and Philosophical Manuscripts* of 1844. "It is the *universal whore*, the universal pimp of men and peoples." From such abstractions, our understandings grow. "We have to grasp the essential connection between private property, avarice and the separation of labor, capital and landed property; between exchange and competition, value and the devaluation man, monopoly and competition, etc.; the connection between this whole estrangement and the money system," writes Bertell Ollman (1976, 63). Capitalists take work, make surplus values from the labor of others, and create profit. Capitalism has spread with commodification of the world. The mode of production in capitalism infects others and us (Ollman, 2016). Such vantage points inform conversations about sex work (Hollibaugh, 2000; Mattilda, 2004).

Some see sex workers as unfree, their labor creating surplus value for others (especially when kids are involved). Others see them as entrepreneurs enjoying the fruits of their own efforts on their own terms, using the free time off work to create counter-narratives of living on their own terms (Hollibaugh, 2000; Mattilda, 2004). These multiple standpoints propel today's sex wars and their ever-shifting terrain. Yet, the voices of those from the front lines tend to remain largely absent from the debate (Showden and Majic, 2014). The Emma Goldmans, who'd engaged in the practice before writing about it, remain few and far between. "Nothing about us, without us," declares the sex worker blog *Bound, Not Gagged*. Yet over and over again, the police and moralists set the terms of debate, instead of the workers involved in the practice (Chateavert, 2014).

Raids and arrests have long been part of the conversation. Over the last few years, they have moved from the streets to the Internet, where advertisements on Craigslist and Backpages have been shuttered. And then came the raid of Rentboy.com in the summer of 2015, when the debate took an intense turn. My family and I had been traveling through Spain and Portugal, where sex work and drugs had been decriminalized. Consequently, demand plummeted as the state moved from policing to framing these issues in terms of public health and labor safety. The United States is far from this position. Prohibition rarely stifles demand. The experience of Prohibition reminds us of this.

Checking in on Facebook, I saw word about a crackdown in New York City. With offices near Manhattan's Union Square, Rentboy.com, a nearly two-decade-old website for male escorts, was raided on August 25, 2015, by Homeland Security agents in concert with NYPD. The acting U.S. attorney for the Eastern District of New York, Kelly T. Currie, was prosecuting seven individuals for felonies in a high-profile case that quickly drew criticism around the country, including from *The New York Times* editorial board. A call for the decriminalization of sex work was made by Amnesty International, Human Rights Watch (HRW), the American Civil Liberties Union (ACLU), the World Health Organization (WHO), the UN Special Rapporteur on the Right to Health, the UN Development Program, UN Women, and UNAIDS, among others.

The raids ignited a vast conversation. "Rentboy.com was closed because the government thinks I need to be saved," said David (2015), venting. "Few people have ever assumed that my choice to engage in sex work was anything other than a choice—that is, until the US government rounded up the staff at Rentboy.com, claiming that they were an 'internet brothel' exploiting poor, stupid sex workers like me. Rentboy was hardly 'prostituting' me: not only did they offer community and peer-to-peer support to sex workers, but they offered us practical assistance through workshops on, for example, how to secure healthcare and how to file taxes." Rather, "as a grown man, capable of making thoughtful decisions about my own life, I should not be placed at risk of jail for choosing to be an escort. Nor should the men and women at Rentboy.com now risk jail and penalty because they sought to support me and my work."

As my friend John Welsh explains: "There are so many different kinds of sex work. Some of it is coerced or forced and some is not. When people claim that every sex worker is exploited or victimized, they patronize and disempower people. People have the right to use their bodies as they want—whether others think that use is a form of self-abuse or not. Sex work needs to be outside of the context of law enforcement. Law enforcement should focus on people who force others to do anything against their will."

On September 3, 2015, I attended a rally decrying the arrests at Rentboy. com, outside the U.S. Eastern District Courthouse in downtown Brooklyn. There, New York LGBT activists, civil rights organizations, the HookUp Collaborative, and other supporters denounced the arrests of Rentboy.com staff, demanding that the U.S. attorney stop the prosecution of Rentboy.com, drop all charges after the raid by Homeland Security and NYPD, and decriminalize sex work. Most everyone there condemned the raid and what looked like selective prosecution of sex workers. Why was the government wasting time and money to persecute escorts? The harassment seemed to endanger the workers and their clients, rather than protect them. Others just felt like it was another punishment of poverty, targeting the poor and people of color for still more incarceration.

Arriving at the rally, Bill Dobbs, one of the veterans of SexPanic!, a late-1990s New York City sexual civil liberties group, was on hand, giving interviews (Shepard, 2009). A panic over sex and bodies seems to bubble up to the surface every few years, with debates about sexual civil liberties clashing against a wall and dictating how much difference of expression our democracy can tolerate.

At the rally, I greeted my friend Jim Fouratt, who has been part of these battles for a long time.

"You have the best sign," he said, pointing to my hand-painted placard. We chatted about why he was here. "I carried the Gay Liberation Front banner because controlling one's own body was/is a core value in GLF, the first multi-issue post-Stonewall progressive political organization. Controlling one's body is not just a sex work issue. What consenting adults do with their own body is their own business Not the state, not the city, not Homeland Security, not the local officials, not the police, unless someone is harmed. . . . Employees in this raid should be let free unless they are charged with a serious crime and or aiding and abetting the owner and his business partners in laundering money and/or evading taxes. There are important questions to discuss: Is prostitution estimable? Does the high cost of living make sex work more viable a survival job for young people, artists, or students who are poor?"

My friend Randolfe Wicker, a veteran activist who joined the Mattachine Society in 1958, was on hand carrying a sign of his friend, trans icon Marsha P. Johnson. "We should not have minor arrests for pot or sex work," he tells me. "They are never wiped clean of your record. You get arrested and you cop a plea. And you don't get bail. But the case follows you for a lifetime. I know a man arrested for hustling, copped a plea and the arrest popped up on a background check when he was applying for a job 18 years later. You plead guilty to get out. But you are getting marked. No student loans. Does anyone know why they did this raid?" he asks. "To me it's the biggest waste of taxpayer resources I have ever seen. They are cleaning up the town. Now it's too clean."

"Sex worker rights are human rights," chant those in the picket line.

"I hustled on Hollywood Boulevard in 1959," confesses Wicker. "I wanted to hang out in the coffee shops with the Beats. I learned more that summer than I ever learned at University of Texas. They put you through hell if you are caught. I wanted to get a job after that. Inspector Seymour Pine, who lead the raid at Stonewall, said sex workers and queers are easy targets."

Jack Waters, of Petit Versailles Community Garden, was marching with his partner Peter. "I'm here to support human rights and to oppose the criminal targeting of sexual minorities," says Jack, explaining why he had come.

"Sex worker rights are human rights," says one sign.

"You cannot spell homeland without 'ho,'" reads another, adding satirical splendor.

"Sex expression is free speech!"

"Keep your laws off my body," we chant, an anarcho-libertarian sensibility pulsing through the crowd.

"Look out kids, here come the whores," chimes in Bizzy Barefoot, a radical faery in New York. "This is a subject that is close to my heart and on all sorts of levels, many listed on this sign," notes Barefoot.

Finishing the rally, Andy Humm and Bill Dobbs pull everyone in for a circle.

"It's great to be with Randy Wicker, who built a community of sexual minorities," notes Dobbs, pointing out there are countless arrests each year for this. It is all part of an ongoing war on sex. There are arrests of cruisers in Prospect Park where there is no money involved. The buck stops with the mayor, who seems to be emulating draconian Rudy Giuliani in his aggressive policing of public space, with threats to close pedestrian plazas on 42nd Street because of topless women, shut health clinics, and crack down on homelessness.

Randy Wicker is standing giving another interview. "It's just universal discrimination," he explains, referring to the raid. "Discrimination against trans people, who cannot find other work. You run away from home and come to New York and find there are 12 beds for runaway LGBT youth," who become homeless. Wicker recalls his rebel friends Sylvia Rivera and Marsha P. Johnson, who coped with these struggles for years. "No jobs, no bed, literally forced into the streets. Then you do a background check years later and the arrest is still there. In today's digital world it lasts forever."

More and more people are speaking out about the need to stop the arrests, to decriminalize this work.

"I've never seen so many men come out to show their rage about the treatment of sex workers," says Dede, who is wearing a Margo St. James "outlaw poverty, not prostitution" T-shirt.

After the rally, I talk with ACT UP member Michael Tikili about the raid and the interconnections between sex work and AIDS activism. "It's a conversation that is long overdue," he says. He suggests AIDS activists have to look at the attack from a broad intersectional, human rights perspective. "This is a matter of urgency," he continues, "people finding a way to survive." After the raid, people lose a way to make a living. The process only became more complicated after Congress passed and the president signed the Stop Enabling Sex Traffickers Act and Allow States and Victims to Fight Online Sex Trafficking Act, otherwise known as the FOSTA-SESTA package, on April 11, 2018, cracking down on online platforms.

"Now they have to look for new platforms. Now you can barely survive. You have to fight so hard to get it," says Tikili. He has long worked to make such connections. "I've strived to bring movements together. We need to do a better job of coming together. People are too insular. We've been good at Occupy, with ACT UP. I'd like to see more synergy between Black Lives Matter, with movements for healthcare, environment, post-Katrina activism . . . The next fight for HIV is decriminalizing drug use. Criminalization puts us all at risk," Tikili continues. "We cannot stop the AIDS crisis if we continue to see sex work criminalized." Wars on drugs and sex work leave people incarcerated, exposing them to HIV and other related diseases. Decriminalizing sex work and ending the wars on drugs are essential steps forward.

Advocates suggest sex work be seen from a materialist perspective as a form of labor—that the practice is both an act of free will and very difficult work, not as an activity to criminalize. Many reject representations of sex work in terms of trafficking, favoring a view of sex workers as active agents. Still, the practice is worth considering in terms of vantage point, carefully distinguishing between someone moving to San Francisco after college making some extra money and the kid in India forced into the business as a child. There is exploitation of sex workers, as with all workers, but many reject "the totality of that framework. This contest is necessary given the near stranglehold that the trafficking and victimization framework have on public policy making," note Showden and Majic (2014, p. xv) in their work *Negotiating Sex Work*. Far too many policy designs have "favored efforts to 'rescue' women," they note. "This is most apparent in the United States, which is leading global efforts against human trafficking" (xviii). These efforts have resulted in an array of unintended consequences, including a "global gag" rule accompanying federal money for international anti-trafficking work that impedes HIV/AIDS prevention work by requiring those funded by the Global AIDS Act to explicitly condemn sex work and trafficking, thereby limiting the range of service providers and interventions (xix).

In her essay "The War on Sex Workers," Melissa Gira Grant (2013) recalls a trip by Gloria Steinem to a red-light district in India in which she condemned "sexual health services and peer education programs in brothels, programs that have been recognized by the U.S. Agency for International Development as best-practices HIV/AIDS interventions. Steinem described the women leading those health and education programs as "traffickers" and those who support them as 'the trafficking lobby.'" Sadly, Grant contends, "in the name of 'protecting' women, or even ensuring their 'rights,' feminists are eager to take away their jobs and health care."

Subverting the victim and whore debate, Showden and Majic call for "a new model of knowledge production" (xxiv), favoring the voices of sex workers themselves as active agents challenging social mores, prudery, and hypocrisy, changing cities, supporting broad-based social movements, and helping redefine norms of public and private space. "Nothing about us, without us" (243).

A generation of sex worker advocates, labor organizers, and sexual civil liberty activists, such as Call Off Your Tired Old Ethics (COYOTE) and the Exotic Dancers' Alliance, have forced changes in laws and organizational arrangements for sex workers (224). Some formed unions arguing for labor rights; others called for cultural changes and rights-based supports for sex workers. "Our Convention is Different, we want everyone to COME," says a poster by Margo St. James at the COYOTE "Hooker's Convention" of 1974 (Chateavert, 2014, 78). Activists and sex workers themselves have long changed laws and social mores.

Melinda Chateavert (2014) contends that sex workers have been at the forefront of social justice movements for the past fifty years, building a movement that challenged ways of thinking about sex, work, labor, freedom, autonomy, urban space, women's movements, queer theory, anarchism, fashion, and sexual self-determination. From Emma Goldman to Margo St. James, and from Carole Lee to Riot Grrrl and Slutwalk, this movement has linked conversations about sex work with broad-based, universalizing discourses favoring worker and human rights while challenging capitalism, sex phobia, and sexual violence. Emma Goldman (1969) suggested that most everyone has sold themselves in one form or another, especially married women. Countless sex workers have echoed this sentiment, pushing social movements from feminism to gay liberation and HIV/AIDS to engage questions about sex work. Their entreaties have not always been welcomed. For example, in the years after Sylvia Rivera's calls for solidarity among sexual outsiders, queers, gender non-conformists, and sex workers in the early 1970s, the Gay Liberation movement came to favor a politics of sameness and marriage, supporting whorephobia in the guise of respectability that "stigmatized those who trade sex for money or support" (Chateavert, 2014, 10). This is "a type of sex panic that reflects deep seated belief that identity politics and civil rights requires weeding out members for gender nonconformity, sexual deviancy, and drug dependency. The LGBT movement should include sex workers because many sex worker activists are queer and some queer activists support themselves through sex work" (10). Generations of sex workers have impacted this movement, helping to create spaces where they found respect and dignity. "They want safe spaces that respect all sex workers, no matter where or how they work, or their class, race, gender, or sexuality," notes Chateavert (2014, 19).

In the decade after Stonewall, COYOTE simultaneously fought unjust laws, built social service programs, and arranged assistance by and for those in need. The group helped change social mores and pushed the feminist movement to see that sex as pleasure was a rightful aim. To do so, notions of sex and social justice had to overlap. Without pleasure there is no justice and vice versa, said Carter Heywood (1989). Others resisted the charge, as sex wars raged. Still sex work advocates expanded their pro-pleasure coalition, rejecting paternalistic calls to rescue or save those involved, supporting notions of women's sexual freedom in the broadest terms. "It encouraged women to be angry about whore stigma and slut shaming for pursuing sexual pleasure or trading sex for money," notes Chateavert (2014, 49). Margo St. James told *Rolling Stone* magazine in 1974: "As a woman/whore, I feel equality will never be reached until women's sexuality ceases to be the source of our shame—until the men are forced to stop their pussy patrols" (49). Unfortunately, those patrols did not stop. The movement challenged a criminal justice system that penalized women, rather than the men committing far more insidious crimes from Wall Street to K Street, with far more significant social and economic consequences. The impacts of the sex worker movement were far-reaching, with some eleven countries legalizing prostitution. It created a movement based on human rights and cultural politics, which would sustain itself for decades to come. By the 1990s, a new cohort of activists would reengage Goldman's (1969) call for solidarity among social outsiders, anarchists and sex workers, and queers and kinksters. "The people perverted, will never be converted!" they chanted when the mayor pushed for a new anti-sex zoning law to push public sexual culture, sex, and sex workers from New York's streets. "Giuliani scared of sex, whose he gonna censor next!!!!" sexual civil liberties activists, including this writer, screamed, linking sex activism with struggles for social justice and free expression. While the forces of censorship formed strange bedfellows with developers and feminists, the prohibitionist rhetoric would not last, as the naked city found its swagger again.

New York's latest mayor, Bill de Blasio, has supported efforts to decriminalize prostitution, reducing penalties and referring sex workers to social services rather than jails. After all, "putting the blame on 'sluts' and 'whores' excuses the criminal justice system" while "allowing police to ignore violence" against sex workers, women, Black men, and other outsiders (Chateavert, 2014, 158). For decades, women have pushed against this, simultaneously supporting cultural efforts, DIY movements, punk shows in support of women's self-defense, and discursive efforts to transform the way the world looks at sex. "I'm a slut and I vote. So does everyone I sleep with," declared a poster by Incite on International Women's Day 2012. Chants of "Politicians out of my poontang" and "Keep your government off my pussy" could be heard outside the Democratic National Convention in 2012 (184–5). Activists with the Riot Grrrl movement made T-shirts and underwear declaring "Girls Kick Ass" and "Girls Rule." Through flyers and zines, punk shows, memorials for sex workers, postapocalyptic self-help sing-alongs, and trainings, the movement created a space that rejected both slut shaming and violence against women. "Girls constitute a revolutionary soul force that can and will change the world for real," exclaims the Riot Grrrl Manifesto (200).

Increasingly, the movement has expanded beyond discussion of decriminalization and prostitution-related laws into broader conversations about the prison industrial complex and multi-issue organizing. "In this millennium, activists in the sex workers' movement are involved in many issues: harm reduction, the defense of public sex venues, the prison industrial complex, police violence, immigration, homelessness, welfare 'reform,' the war on drugs, labor organizing, feminist porn, HIV/AIDS criminalization, hate crimes against gays and transgender people, and anarchist and 'lavender left politics,'" argues Chateavert. "Their work consistently crosses over the not-so-neat, identity-based categorizations that once dominated Cold War civil rights struggles" (206). Sex workers understand that crackdowns on street people, on outsiders, overlap with a neoliberal effort to colonize and blandify public space by pushing them to the margins, sanitizing our streets of the pulse, which makes them real and vital.

Today the war on sex workers is a war on human rights. The crusaders of the right, of the Comstock-like anti-sex forces, are always ready to push in this moral tug of war. "In Louisiana some women arrested for prostitution have been charged under a 200-year-old statute prohibiting 'crimes against nature,'" notes Melissa Grant (2013). "Those charged—disproportionately black women and transgender women—end up on the state sex-offender registry." Sex worker rights are human rights. Increasingly, this frame has become a central discourse of sex work organizing. From Emma Goldman to Slutwalk, sex workers and their supporters remind the world that sex overlaps with social justice in mutually reinforcing ways. Still, sexual outsiders, people with HIV, homeless queers, and sex workers are all criminalized. What happens in prisons matters, notes Judith Malina (1984). For the world to survive, we need other ways of looking at punishment, healing, and the very nature of reality. Vantage point helps remind us to think about who is speaking, who is silent, on what terms, in what conditions. "Nothing about us, without us." If we listen, we can hear bigger stories out there that connect us all.

Chapter 10

Between ADHD and the Desert of the Real: Confessions of a Teenage Ritalin Junkie

"Welcome to the desert of the real," Morpheus greets Keanu Reeves, playing Neo in the 1999 movie *The Matrix*, waking him from a computer-generated virtual reality. In the previous scene, Morpheus has offered Reeves a choice: take a red pill and live a synthetic hyperreality, akin to soma, a mind-numbing sedative in the novel *Brave New World*, or take the blue pill and live in the real world. Neo takes the blue pill, navigating a war-torn, yet often spectacular landscape, sometimes wondering if he should have taken the other pill. It's a question many are forced to face—a contrast between notions of the real, that is, the world, and simulated synthetic spaces, the matrix of pills and pharmacology products altering moods and consciousness. Scene after scene traces philosophers' questions about the nature of the material world— Marxism, Buddhism, feminism, gender studies, and postmodernism. One question hangs over the entire story: what is real (Irwin, 2002)?

Both the line from *The Matrix* and the title of Slavoj Žižek's (2002) book *Welcome to the Desert of the Real* borrow from Jean Baudrillard's (1981/1994) *Simulacra and Simulation*. "It is the real, and not the map," writes Baudrillard, "whose vestiges persist here and there in the deserts that are no longer those of the Empire, but ours. The desert of the real itself." For Žižek, the film traces a "passion for the real," often sublimated within a postmodern "simulacra" of television news, medications, and horror movies that all served to leave the system intact, precluding conversations about alternatives beyond capitalism. It's a point he's made over and over, echoing it at Zuccotti Park during the peak of the Occupy movement. We can imagine colonizing new planets, but we have difficulty imagining postcapitalist realities. Instead, we go back to the matrix. This is not a new observation. Much of the United States is plastic, posits Umberto Eco in *Travels in Hyperreality*. "The ideology of this America wants to establish reassurance through imitation. But profit defeats ideology, because the consumers want to be thrilled not only by the guarantee of the Good but also by the shudder of the Bad," Eco concludes (1976/1886, 57).

The exchange between Neo and Morpheus highlights contrasts of modern living: reality versus fantasy, disorder versus the normal, hyper versus well behaved, safe versus dangerous, high versus low, medicated versus sober, healthy versus sick, numb versus feeling. In *Letters to a Young Poet*, Rainer Maria Rilke (1934) suggests there are lessons to gain from sadness and depression, if only we look at them and embrace them, let them make their way through us, much like the opposing forces in the dialectic, moving between positive and negative, through nightmares and dream journals, making their way toward some sort of insight or recognition of interconnection between sane and insane selves (DuBrul, 2013).

We all face such questions. Do we endure the real and the pain? Do we take the red pill or the blue pill? When my best friend's dad put a gun to his head and pulled the trigger, he had taken medications when depression grasped him. And he never really came back. Not the same; he was someplace else. Was it the pain or the feelings from the desert of the real, which preceded that moment?

A couple of years ago, I ran into a friend from childhood whom I took MDMA and synthetic variations with for years in the 1980s. "Are you on anything?" she asked as we sat chatting. In Los Angeles everyone is on something, she confessed. Sometimes these chemicals augment experiences. Synthetic realities peaking on MDMA, with Depeche Mode blasting as we drove around town in high school, helped pump me up through highs I had only now just started to return from. Beyond too much beer, coffee, orange juice, and statins, I was not on anything that exciting, I explained. The realities of years of experiments with LSD, mushrooms, MDMA, AIDS activism, harm reduction, and syringe exchange all informed both a weariness and a great respect for these chemicals and the desert of the real, where we really feel, even if they are sometimes more than we can bear. We all take medications to reduce pain when we go to the dentist's office. But when do these medications dim the lights or separate us from what is beautiful about feeling?

Today, questions about which pills we take are everywhere, as parents drug their kids to perform in school, my clients eat hormones or antiretrovirals, and friends take various antidepressants. Morpheus' question informs both who we are and the very nature of reality. At least it has for me.

If there is one enduring memory from my childhood, it is a small porcelain bowl containing three little white pills. The pills were as ubiquitous as morning orange juice and cereal.

"Ben, don't forget your Ritalin," my mother would remind me as I rushed to meet my carpool. "Don't forget your Ritalin."

On any given day, millions of children and adolescents in the United States are given a psychostimulant of one form or another. The theory is that these drugs help young people handle their emotions, feelings, and reactions. This situation is like no other in the world. More American children and adolescents receive diagnoses of attention-deficit disorder (ADD) than in any other country, and these diagnoses are often followed by prescriptions for medications such as Ritalin. The United States and Canada together account for some 95 percent of the global market for Ritalin for the treatment of ADD. The number of kids prescribed these medications has only accelerated in recent years.

Ritalin first came on the market in 1955. Some seventy years later, millions of prescriptions have been written for it to treat ADD, or "hyperactivity," as the condition was generously described back in my day. Of these, millions of prescriptions have been for children who have little choice but to take these medications, regardless of how doped up the drugs make them feel. There was no Morpheus out there offering options. Ritalin (methylphenidate) has the same effect on the brain and behavior as other forms of amphetamine and may cause side effects including irritability, psychosis, hallucinations, mania, and aggression. I used to hear a chorus line of voices babbling in my head for hours and hours. Other users of the drug find themselves feeling worn down, even lethargic or depressed. In addition, Ritalin may promote suicidal thoughts and can lead to addiction; some research suggests a link to cancer. Thus, it is not surprising that Ritalin may actually cause the same problems it is purportedly intended to address: poor attention, impulsivity, and even increased hyperactivity. Most disturbing, the drug has been linked to changes in brain functioning that remain long after the therapeutic effects have dissipated.

I was diagnosed with dyslexia as a "hyperactive" child in the spring of 1976. I squirmed, bounced out of my seat, and had a difficult time with my schoolwork. I spent the next three years—second through fourth grade—in schools for children with learning and speech disabilities, sharing classrooms with kids with hearing aids, and other tools. Medications were a core part of my treatment.

I was prescribed Ritalin and Dexedrine to help me settle down and get to work (toward getting into a competitive prep school, college, job, and producing kids who could do the same, ad infinitum). Even at that age, the social push to succeed and compete was vexing. School is, after all, a socialization process, churning ever forward. Ritalin and Dexedrine function quite nicely within this milieu. By fifth grade, in 1980, I was mainstreamed. My medication dosages increased, and so did the side effects. My doctors prescribed Ritalin and Dexedrine, both "uppers," in an effort to help me calm down. In practice, they made me crazy. I'd stay up all night once or twice a week. Voices echoed through my head like bells chiming in a cathedral.

I could hear multiple voices and conversations chattering away in my head. Some days there were so many voices inside that I could not hear or respond to questions from the external world. It was hard to say which was more real or important.

Even now, almost four decades later, I still vividly remember the intensity of those overlapping monotone voices. The chats were so busy inside my head that even talking with other school kids, something that had never been a problem before, became difficult. Oddly, this never merited a peep of concern from any of the cavalcade of doctors, psychiatrists, family therapists, and social workers I met during those years. It was all supposed to be very common. "The voices are getting worse," I explained to the doctor who prescribed the pills. He was not all that interested in listening.

The synergistic doctor and patient partnership—in which patients and doctors consult with each other—was not really in place in 1980, prior to the era of AIDS activism. Even now, I doubt this democratic process applies to ten-year-old children and their doctors. The pills just kept coming, and I continued to feel sped up and muddled down at the same time.

In 1982, when I was in seventh grade, the film *Quadrophenia*, based on the album by The Who, was showing at a local repertory theater. It told the story of a British youth pulled in so many different directions that he felt not just schizophrenic—with a personality split in two—but also quadraphenic. Jimmy, the protagonist, was a Mod, a member of a British youth subculture known for fighting with a rival youth group known as the Rockers and terrorizing everyone else during British sea weekends on Brighton Beach in the early 1960s. Mods wore zoot suits; Rockers wore leather. I immediately gravitated toward the Mods. Jimmy and the other stylish Mods ate handfuls of pills—reds, French Blues, all mostly amphetamines—and zipped around town on their scooters in between street scuffles and chance encounters. For all I know, they were eating Dexedrine itself. It was the first time I had ever seen an image of the pills, which had become such a fixture of my life, featured in popular culture. Yet instead of fulfilling the tedious aim of socialization, these pills fueled the high-octane fun, fights, highs, lows, sex, fashion, and riots between the Mods and the Rockers. Like everything else, the pills were a commodity. They functioned like currency. When Jimmy had pills, he also had girls and friends. Maybe it could work the same for me. By eighth grade, in 1983, I took the lesson of the Mods to heart, imitating their fashion and their enthusiastic use of stimulants. I had access to any junkie's dream— an endless supply of prescribed speed, with a doctor happy to provide bottle after bottle. Instead of following prescribed dosages, I began to use the pills as speed and basically stopped sleeping for the next four years. If I was running late completing a school paper, I would pop a couple more pills and stay up all night and into the next day without a blink.

Once I began using the pills as speed, the strange isolated internal feeling faded. I started giving them to girls, and my problems with social issues receded. If pills were a currency, eighth-grade biology lab was a currency exchange. Everyone had access to their parents' medicine chests. On some days we'd try Valium and Ritalin; on others it would be Xanax. I could eat Xanax like popcorn and it didn't do a thing. Yet it wasn't bad with a nice Chablis on the rocks over *Masterpiece Theater* with Mom.

I stopped taking the pills out of pure boredom when I entered college in the fall of 1988. By then, it was some ten years since I first started. Certainly no one had put a gun to my head to force me to take the meds. Most days, I was up until the middle of the night; then I took a few more pills to wake up, and a couple more throughout the day to restimulate myself. I was never quite sharp. Actual class time was pretty fuzzy. Whether this was from the lack of sleep or from any of the pills, inhalants, joints, or other compulsions, such as high school football, I do not know. But within a couple of years with regular sleep, my interest in and ability to actually take in class materials increased.

When I got out of school, I found a job working with people with HIV and AIDS in the early 1990s, before effective treatments. Many told me about their battles with doctors over medications, wondering which pills were right for them, if any. Which pills could they reject? Many were informed they had to take AZT, despite the side effects that many doctors ignored complaints over.

"At one point everyone wanted me to take AZT," Marija Mrdjenovic recalled in her oral history. "Well, I had had a very dear friend, who had AIDS, and had died after he'd been given 1,200 milligrams of AZT. A complete overdose. At that time, as is now the case, the drug companies tend to go to the high end when they're testing their drugs. There have been so many people who have died of drug overdoses in clinical trials. You apply that to women and not only are they lower in body weight, they have a whole different immune system. You're giving them something that is even more than an overdose, it's an over-overdose. One doctor wanted me to take these huge amounts of AZT and I refused. He said, 'Well, if you don't take AZT I'm going to stop seeing you as your doctor.' There was that attitude of, 'I know what's best for you.' I was convinced that AZT was not the answer. They wanted me to take like 600 to 800 milligrams and nowadays the optimum dosage is something like 300 to 600. They're still trying to push it up so they can sell more of the drugs, but literally, 300 was enough to give me arthritic symptoms and enough to bring my white cell count down" (quoted in Shepard, 1997).

"I took AZT for about three days once and then I threw the bottle out my kitchen window," said Nancy Lemoins. "That was like when it cost so much money. It just made me throw up constantly. I was much healthier. I had about

700 T-cells so it didn't even seem imminent. At that meeting last night all the women had taken it for like a week and then they quit" (Shepard, 1997). I felt a strange kindred spirit with these AIDS activists forced to make their own choices about their health, willing to reject the red pill and the blue, finding their own path, even if it meant death. Maria died shortly after our interview.

LOOKING BACK

I'm glad I stopped taking the pills. Other people I know from those days are still on some form of pharmacological treatment for dyslexia, but now the medication is combined with antidepressants. In this respect, Ritalin is like a drug manufacturer's dream. Find a caring and concerned mother like mine, have a doctor tell her there's an answer to her child's problems, and the kid starts a medication, which may be the beginning of a lifetime of pharmacological solutions to life's difficulties. These pills become part of the body chemistry.

As a proponent of harm reduction, I am opposed to the harms associated with drug use, not drug use (of either over- or under-the-counter medications) per se. What is difficult to swallow is the idea of trading good parenting and creativity for Ritalin. There are other schools of thought that call for stimulating and supporting the interests and imagination of children, rather than controlling their behavior. The United States is the only country in the Western world that routinely treats normal childhood high energy with medication. In the years since I last took Ritalin, the number of prescriptions for the drug has increased exponentially. While I was diagnosed with dyslexia, the "hyperactivity" I experienced is now referred to as a distinct disorder: attention-deficit hyperactivity disorder (ADHD). According to the National Institute of Mental Health, ADHD is the most frequently diagnosed childhood disorder, affecting 3 to 5 percent of all grade school-age children. Other sources suggest the number is closer to 10 percent. And in some regions of the country, fully 50 percent of children are diagnosed with the condition. However, the question that's rarely asked is, why is it that so many young people cannot adjust to what is considered normative behavior, and normative behavior according to whom? Few are talking about the legalized amphetamines children are prescribed every day. While the War on Drugs continues to enjoy generous support from Congress, the *Journal of the American Medical Association* has documented an inordinate increase in the number of two- to four-year-olds taking Ritalin and other mood-altering drugs. It is not a stretch of imagination to understand that legal mood-altering medications often lead to misuse, dependency, and overdose. I could not have been the only kid out there sharing the pills with buddies. Although Ritalin is packaged with a warning against use by children younger than age six, doctors across the country continue to prescribe it—and one rarely sees the vice squad invading their offices.

BACKLASH

I'm certainly not the first writer to suggest that the governmental, corporate, and medical support for the overprescription of mood-altering medications resembles the official attitude toward soma, the drug that controlled people's thoughts in Aldous Huxley's *Brave New World*. "Why don't you take soma when you have these dreadful ideas of yours? You'd forget all about them. And instead of feeling miserable, you'd be jolly. So jolly," one character advises another in the novel. But highs and lows are part of life. Red pills sometimes mix quite nicely with blue pills. But eventually, reality is odd enough, offering innumerable moments of the sublime, often hidden between the secrets in the seaweed, treasures on the garbage. If we miss them, we miss the moments of poetry. Yet too much reality can be too much, as Neo experiences in the Matrix. The dance is anything but simple. Still, the current impulse to medicate away the high energy of youth with Ritalin, the pain of grief with Prozac, and everything in between limits these possibilities. Instead of addressing these issues, kids are being given prescriptions for more medications to keep the complaints down. Whether or not we're dealing with a new breed of youth, there has to be another way of working with those the school system designates as "problem" children besides feeding them drugs.

In a recent review of Stephen Rose's *The 21st-Century Brain*, Jacob Stevens (2005) offers a materialist framework for the use of Ritalin: "The drug does make the majority of children calmer in class, but without addressing the causes of disruptive behavior. The trend, as Rose argues, is towards the privatization and chemical suppression of a range of societal issues: 'trying to adjust the mind rather than adjust society.'"

Within such a context, it is difficult not to oppose the frenzy-like social experiment understood as the Ritalin fix—and its sedation of a generation (Stevens, 2005). Moving to New York years later, I started to see the decision about which pill to take as part of a larger conversation about where we find ourselves in this world, and how we see reality. How do we navigate the desert of the real? Do we medicate? The crack users at our syringe exchange hung out on the couches upstairs, while the heroine users stayed downstairs in our drop-in center. Each had their own rituals and cultural ties connected to their use. Like the Mods and Rockers, movements and subcultures shared their pills, approaches to pleasure, aesthetics, and organization. Each informed a disposition. Some people took none. Others took both blue and red pills. Out for drinks after an ACT UP meeting, a friend talked about anarchist organizing amid a conversation about harm reduction, heroine, and speed. I had never even heard of anarchist organizing. It seemed like an oxymoron. I was intrigued. The anarchists seemed to understand that the plastic pills did not really help things all that much. They were not sustainable. Take them if they are fun, as the Mods did. Reject them if they hurt or control. The pollutants in the mental and physical environment had their costs. The merging was the interesting part, as dialectical activism offered spaces for new connections between the AIDS activism credited with getting "pills into bodies" worldwide and the anarchism seen as energizing global justice movements. Running through the streets or digging gardens, the anarchists opened new stories and connections between feelings I had had all my life about the dangers of prohibition and repression. More than anything, anarchism opened a conversation about the links between multiple movements, building and growing from each other. The following chapter considers a few of these overlapping movements of ideas and bodies through time.

Chapter 11

Bridging the Divide between Queer Theory and Anarchism

The other night, I took a stroll into St. Mark's Bookshop in the East Village of New York City.[1] First, I perused the queer studies section. Unlike a decade ago, there were very few new titles, with the exception of works on gay marriage and fitting into the system. Next, I walked over to the section on anarchism and it seemed to have quadrupled since my last visit to the store. While the dearth of books on queer theory compared to works on anarchism could be explained away with any number of excuses about academic press distribution, it seemed to reflect a growing concern about the relevance of queer theory to movements for social change (Kirsch, 2000). While anarchism has increasingly supported and informed social movements (Graeber, 2004a, b), queer theory has suffered from a seeming inability to speak beyond the confines of the academy or itself (Hall, 2003; Mattilda, 2004; McLemee, 2009). There was, after all, a time when queer activism and theory informed each other and the movements they supported (Crimp, 2002; Warner, 1993, 1999). Yet, just as anarchism has become further rooted in global movements, queer theory has come to feel distant from the politics that once fueled it. Some have come to argue that queer theory needs to reinfuse itself with authentic social struggles (Kirsch, 2000; McLemee, 2009). This chapter proposes queer theory embrace its philosophical interconnections with anti-authoritarian organizing. It explores the historic links and conflicts between anarchism and queer politics, considering the divide between queer theory and anarchist activism, as well as their interconnections via distinct case examples of anti-authoritarian organizing involving rejection of social controls, vice squads, and criminalization of protest and dissent. Queer and anarchist politics overlap in any number of ways. This interconnection between movement narratives fuels movements for change, adding a chapter in a history of dialectical activism. Here, questions about Eros and connection dating back to Freud and

Emma Goldman intermingle with anarchist and even Marxist questions about both freedom from want and personal autonomy (Ollman, 2016).

Throughout the last decade I have participated in the cross-pollinization between queer and AIDS activism and anarchist-inspired global justice movements in New York, with all its fits and starts and its occasional successes. Throughout the reflections and interviews, this chapter strives to highlight the ways such activists contribute to a multi-issue, multigender, anarchist queer organizing ethos that Emma Goldman helped articulate as she romped around the city a century ago.

QUEER AND ANARCHIST POLITICS

Queers and anarchists have long shared a similar disposition toward sexual politics. Sharing a kindred spirit with the early Victorian sex radicals in the United Kingdom (Sears, 1977), anarchists were particularly influenced by the campaigns to end the British Contagious Diseases Act of 1864. Faced with a law that authorized police to "investigate and inspect," quarantine, and criminalize suspected prostitutes, activists embraced an anti-statist approach (O'Kelly, 1993a, b). Influential anarchist queer writer Daniel Guerin (1970, 13) suggests that at its core anarchism is a "visceral revolt" against such models of state control (also see Berry, 2004). In the years to follow, homosexual desire and sexual freedom became primary topics for anarchists, who developed common cause with sexual outsiders (Kissack, 2008).

Conversely, early gay liberationists organized in a fashion that echoed anarchist sentiments toward freedom of the mind, body, and spirit. Yet, this could only take place when the Gay Liberation Front (GLF) rejected a Mattachine politics of respectability in favor of an anarchist impulse toward radical egalitarianism (McLemee, 2009). The anarchist queer chant "2-4-6-8, Smash the Church, Smash the State!" was a constant at early gay liberation rallies and actions (Teal, 1971, 1995). A report on GLF's thirtieth anniversary was titled "Anarchy Inc" after the nickname one of the members for the group (Blotcher, 1999).

Author J. P. Harpignies (2009), who lived in New York at the time of the Stonewall riots, recalls this feeling in the streets of June 1969. Harpignies was organizing with a group at New York University (NYU) called transcendental students (TS). Self-described anarchists, the group transformed an old restaurant, Harouts on Waverly Place, into a community space. Not that long into TS's managing of the Harout's space, members of GLF dropped by after a run-in with the police. There, "what seemed like a few hundred of NYC's wildest drag queens and militant gay activists at the height of their early excitement about their emergence as a potent social force, poured in and began to dance wildly and to party ferociously," recalls Harpignies. "Their energy and their variety of appearance and dress and plumage was truly extraordinary." Harpignies stared "mouth-agape. . . . It seemed like a typhoon that was so powerful the idea of trying to rein it in never even came up. I've never seen that wild a scene again in my life." Few in TS had witnessed such an ethos of sexual freedom and anti-authoritarian politics. "We had never seen people as totally rebellious and seemingly fearless as these folks, so we felt a sort of awe and respect for them."

In years to come, Gay Liberation would expand into a global movement (Teal, 1971, 1995). Its aim was not just liberation for queers but liberation of sexuality for everyone (Altman, 1972). The movement borrowed from a range of influences, including anarchism, to help articulate the meanings of its aspirations. "Thanks to Emma Goldman for the title," Gayle Rubin (1975) wrote in her essay "The Traffic in Women," acknowledging the influence of anarchism on her thinking. With this essay, Rubin incorporated anarchism into sexual politics and an interplay between Marxism and psychoanalysis in a way that anticipated and influenced queer theory.

None of this is to suggest the interconnections between anarchist thinking and queer activism have been smooth. Liberal-minded gays actually departed from GLF to form their own group, the Gay Activist Alliance (GAA), shortly after GLF was formed (Teal, 1971, 1995). In the years to come, the split between assimilationist-minded gays and queers who hoped to link gay liberation with broad-based movements for social and sexual freedom would only grow (Crimp, 2002; Sedgwick, 1990). Liberals and radicals battled each other throughout the ACT UP years, echoing the previous generation's conflicts (Crimp, 2002; Shepard, 2009). Assimilationist-minded gays would disavow their movement's linkages with broad-based social movements for social and sexual freedom, instead favoring the rights of gays to just fit in, shop, marry, and join the army (Goldstein, 2002; Warner, 1999). Queer activists challenged this line of thinking, railing against the cultural erasure of assimilation (Brown, 2007; Mattilda, 2004). People are different is the first axiom of Eve Sedgwick's (1990) queer theory. Yet, this thinking had become increasingly isolated; its influence felt separated from political debate.

BETWEEN THEORY AND PRAXIS

Certainly intellectuals and academics helped infuse a critical theory into the work of ACT UP and SexPanic! and vice versa (Crimp, 2002; Halperin, 1995; Hall, 2003). Yet the field and the activism supporting it seemed to hit a creative brick wall when facing the politics of neoliberalism, urban space, and quality-of-life politics in the late 1990s (Crimp, 2002; Duggan, 2004).

And some suggested that the field retreated when it was unable to influence such developments (Shepard, 2009). It is easier, after all, to theorize about a problem than to solve it (Kirsch, 2000). Others argued that much of queer theoretical writing had disengaged from activism and had become obtuse and accessible only to academics (McLemee, 2009; Rogue and Shannon, 2008).

A few examples help illustrate the point. "So many people are so constipated," says Jay Blotcher, a longtime observer of the queer scene in New York. "They think that they have a handle on sex but they are lobbing grenades from the ivory tower." Thus the embodied aspects of queer world making are obscured. "They apply a lot of polysyllabic words to the experience. And that's a distancing factor."

"Let me give you a salient moment where academia fell short of the reality of it," Blotcher continues. In the early 2000s, NYU sponsored a symposium titled "Queer Nation, What Happened?" It included not just academics but also activist Alan Klein, one of the founders of Queer Nation. "Alan got to speak first. Alan is as far from an academic as you can get. But he knows his stuff," notes Blotcher. "Alan said Queer Nation began because ACT UP was becoming crowded with agendas. Therefore, the occasional queer issues that found their way into ACT UP . . . were looked upon with much more selectivity," Blotcher elaborates. "Alan got together with his lover, Karl Soehnlein, [and some others], and said 'let's create another group that can address this.'" Klein related this story and passed the mic. "Well, it is as if he hadn't talked," recalls Blotcher with disappointment. "The following speaker ruminated, 'the reason Queer Nation began was because of the Zeitgeist, the dialectic this,' blah, blah. . . . And Alan looked like he'd been slapped across his face," Blotcher remembers. "Sometimes reality is less glamorous than you want it. Queer Nation sprung from queer pragmatism. The rest came from that." The academics ignored Klein's direct experience with the group. "It reinvigorated my distrust and sometimes disgust with intellect, academia specifically, when it comes to on the ground, in the trenches activism," Blotcher concludes.

The details of this story are less important than the sentiment. The story Blotcher relates is anything but uncommon. In recent years, any number of observers have had similar experiences (see, e.g., Mattilda, 2004; McLemee, 2009; Nyong'o, 2008). Part of the problem is that much of academia seeks to distance itself from the politics or culture of anti-authoritarian activism, which has so profoundly influenced queer organizing and vice versa (Brown, 2007; Graeber, 2004a, b; Nyong'o, 2008; Ritchie, 2008). While queer theory has relegated activism to its periphery, anarchism has increasingly linked its critique within activist practices. "It is primarily concerned with forms of practice," writes David Graeber (2004b). Yet, if the examples above suggest anything, it is that in many circles queer theory has come to ignore the practices Graeber describes. While there are any number of queer activists involved in direct action and anarchist(ic) movements, many theorists seem to have walked away from the practices, writings, or questions involved with the activism, which once fueled queer theory.

There are any number of ways to interpret this. Yet, one could argue that queer theory faces a divide between theory and practice, resulting in a diminished praxis. The term "praxis" is generally used to describe a "kind of self creating action," writes Martin Jay (1973, 4). "One of the earmarks of praxis as opposed to mere action was its being informed by theoretical considerations" (Jay, 1973: 4). Social change activism is thought to involve "the unifying of theory and praxis" (4).

ANARCHIST QUEER

Jamie Heckert (2006) writes: "Were queer theory to draw upon the rich heritage of anarchism and acknowledge the anarchistic elements of its own heritage," it just might find its way out of this impasse (14). "What might 'street' queer theory look like?" Rogue and Shannon (2008) wonder. It might reflect some of the queer and anarchist organizing practices taking place in squats, gardens, small towns, and social movements across the globe. While queer theory and anarchism are often viewed as mutually exclusive terms, they need not be. They share a great deal of common ground, built of an active crossover between anarchist and queer issues and actions. The following highlights a few overlapping themes.

Rejection of the paternalistic state—Queers and anarchists alike view the state with a basic skepticism. When the state proclaims civil liberties must be sacrificed in order to protect citizens from social outsiders, both camps share a similar critical disposition. Both favor self-organization in the pursuit of alternative spaces for social connection (Graeber, 2004a, b; Warner, 1999). Within their support of DIY approaches to community building, use over exchange, and pleasure over procreation, they both share a similar critical view of capitalism (Brown, 2007; Duggan, 2004; Mattilda, 2004). This is not to suggest such a disposition is monolithic; it is not. There are LGBT and even queer activists as well as anarchists who preclude an anticapitalism from their analysis (Goldstein, 2002; Guerin, 1970). Yet for the most part, both camps share an emphasis on the use of space for alternate means to accumulation; they approach building space with an emphasis on pleasure and direct democracy rather than profit making (Amster et al., 2009; Brown, 2007; Holtzman et al., 2004).

Both anarchism and queer theory borrow from a range of influences to support *a politics of freedom*. Here, freedom supports collective self-determination, mutual aid, a rejection of patriarchy, and space to make choices about one's life (Brown, 2007; Goldman, 1969; Highleyman, 1988, 1995; O'Kelly, 1993a). "Both projects argue for a need to move beyond hierarchical and naturalized arrangements of socially constructed identities," note Rogue and Shannon (2008). This is a politics organized around the realization of respect for people's needs. Rather than individualism, it is about the seeking of freedom via a wide range of expressions. While much of life under capitalism involves disciplining of the body, this politics puts a premium on explosive experiences, dynamism, and experimentation. Herbert Marcuse described such a politics in terms of "polymorphous perverse" sexuality, which extended from bodily experiences into an abundant approach toward social change. The Red Butterfly Collective, a splinter group from GLF, is a good example. "Human liberation," it argued, "in all its forms, including Gay Liberation, requires effective self-determination, i.e. democracy, in all spheres of social life affecting the lives of people as a whole." The collective's motto lifted directly from Marcuse: "Today the fight for life, the fight for Eros is the political fight" (quoted in Escoffier, n.d.).

Anarchism and queer politics support *a critique of the normative* assumptions about the world (Goldman, 1923, 2001; Kissack, 2008; Warner, 1993). Both emphasize practices rather than fixed social or cultural identities (Amster et al., 2009; Hall, 2003; Sedgwick, 1990). Both support free will and choice, favoring the consent of those involved, and not the approval of government or religious institutions (Highleyman, 1988, 1995). This sentiment echoes Emma Goldman's (1919/1969) argument that matrimony was another form of wage slavery and exploitation. Rather than marriage, anarchist queers support alternative social groupings, sexual self-determination, and safer promiscuity (Brown, 2007; Highleyman, 1988, 1995; Mattilda, 2004; Ritchie, 2008).

Concurrently, anarchism and queer politics share a mutual *respect for pleasure* (Ritchie, 2008). Mikhail Bakunin lay the groundwork for an anarchist rejection of fruitless forms of social and sexual prohibition, later taken up by anarchists such as *Joy of Sex* author Alexander Comfort. "Liberty alone can bring moral improvement," writes Daniel Guerin, paraphrasing Bakunin's work (1970, 32). "Far from checking the spread of immorality, repression has always extended and deepened it," Guerin (1970, 32) elaborates. Contemporary queer theory echoes the anti-authoritarian rejection of social and sexual prohibitions Guerin describes. "There is an ethical urgency about queer theory that is directed at the damage that sexual prohibitions and discriminations do to people," Eve Sedgwick explains (cited in Smith, 1998, B9).

As opposed to sexual shame, both fields argue that fantastic possibilities take shape when people share social eros. Such eros can be thought of a social connection and attraction among minds, spirits, and bodies of people (Escoffier, n.d.). Not necessarily sex, social eros speaks to the possibilities that take shape among people free to build alternate social relations around care, adventure, pleasure, and responsibility for each other and the communities in which they thrive. "Anarchism stands for a social order based on the free groupings of individuals for the purpose of producing real social wealth," argues Emma Goldman (1969, 62), "an order that will guarantee to every human being free access to the earth and full enjoyment of the necessities of life, according to individual desires."

In order to achieve the levels of "full enjoyment" Goldman refers to, anarchist queers have fashioned a politics based on autonomy from state social controls, as well as coercive social mores. The implications of such thinking are many. "To be autonomous is not to be alone or to act in any way one chooses—a law unto oneself—but to act with regards for others, to feel responsibility for others," write the anonymous authors (Katherine Ainger, Graeme Chesters, Tony Credland, Andrew Credland, John Jordan, Andrew Stern, Jennifer Whitney) of *Notes from Nowhere* (2003). "This is the crux of autonomy, an ethic of responsibility and reciprocity that comes through recognition that others both desire and are capable of autonomy too" (ibid., 110). People are different; they have different needs and desires as Bakunin argues (quoted in Anarcho, 2001). What one person finds repulsive, others find delicious, tantalizing, and risky.

"Sooner or later, happily or unhappily, almost everyone fails to control his or her sex life," writes Michael Warner (1999, 1). Yet, it is typically those on the margins—the sex workers, sexually generous queers, and women who have had children out of wedlock—who must contend with the ramifications and condemnations. "Shouldn't it be possible to allow everyone sexual autonomy, in a way consistent with everyone's sexual autonomy?" Warner muses (1). One would hope. Yet, as Kissack (2008) and Sears (1977) point out, queer anarchists have long struggled for sexual self-determination, often out of necessity. Sexual autonomy, after all, requires more than rejecting social restrictions, controls, or unjust laws, Warner notes. "It requires access to pleasures and possibilities, since people commonly do not know their desires until they find them" (1999, 7).

The result of such explorations is an abundant approach to sexual self-determination and community building, in which sexual self-determination is a very part of movement organizing. "Women should be building our movement the way we make love—gradually with sustained involvement, limitless endurance—and, of course, multiple orgasms," anarchist feminist Jo Freeman put it in 1972. More than physical experience, Freeman refers to an ethos of desire, expression, and the possibility that people can do things on their own terms. Such a politics connects notions of pleasure and direct democracy, experienced in multiple forms.

The theatrics of the Stonewall-era queer performance group the Cockettes embodies such an ethos. "From the very beginning everything was fun, nice way to be together, be ourselves and do our bit for sexual freakdom," Scrumbly, one of the Cockettes, reflected. "Anarchy ideally is a wonderful system. If it feels good, go along with the game" (Tent, 2004, 18). "It was total sexual anarchy," John Waters recalls (Gamson, 2005, 55). Rejecting pre-Stonewall repression, the Cockettes tilted the scales toward creativity. In doing so, the Cockettes offered a theater of transgression, their shows performances in sexual liberation, via a topsy-turvy carnival-like interplay as audience and performers shared a space for social connection, pleasure, and democratic exchange. Theirs was an embodiment of a liberation-era ethos of communal living, mutual care, disdain for capitalism, and respect for pleasure (Gamson, 2005; Tent, 2004). More than sexuality, the Cockettes reveled in a distinct and absurd politics of play.

Crafted and created by such activists, play offers solutions to myriad challenges. It connects activism with camp, irony, humor, and a respect for pleasure and group solidarity. This approach perfunctorily rejects a macho brand of activist heroics (Crimp, 2002). Play is not a rejection of activism but rather a unique amplification of it. Linked with aesthetic and organizing projects, play becomes an arena in which to explore alternate social and cultural possibilities (Shepard, 2009).

While queers have long recognized pleasure as a resource, they share this disposition with anarchists (Brown, 2007; Ritchie, 2008). *Fifth Estate*, an anti-authoritarian magazine, recently ran a special issue dedicated to play. "Party like its 1929," says the lead editorial. "To discuss the radical persistence of pleasure might seem rather decadent," the editors note. But, "we want to remind our readers and ourselves that one facet that has always distinguished anarchists and anarchy from other flavors of resistance and visions of society is our insistence of the revolutionary nature of joy" (3).

Over the years, queer anarchists have built on this ethos to support *a culture of resistance*. While anarchists refer to the DIY spaces they create as forms of dual power, in which autonomous publics coexist within the structures of state power (Graeber, 2004a, b), queers have come to recognize these public commons as counter-publics (Mattilda, 2004; Warner, 1999). Such networks are buttressed within an emphasis on mutual aid and families of choice, which support close ties between the collective and the individual (Brown, 2007). Whether supporting a public sexual culture, a street party, a zine, or other forms of direct action, these symbols of freedom contribute to cultures of resistance (Ritchie, 2008).

Much of this cultural project takes shape via a DIY approach, which emphasizes various forms of creative direct action (Duncombe, 1997; Highleyman, 1988, 1995; Holtzman et al., 2004). The efficacy of such practices involves the space for people to find agency, engage, and speak out (Goldman, 1923, 2001). Such approaches involve not only challenging unjust laws but also organizing alternative solutions. A few examples help demonstrate the point. The final section of this chapter highlights campaigns in which queer and anarchist activists shared common cause while building on an anti-authoritarian organizing agenda organized around rejection of social controls, vice squads, and criminalization of protest and dissent.

CASE 1—SEXUAL SELF-DETERMINATION REPRODUCTIVE AUTONOMY: FROM EMMA GOLDMAN TO THE CHURCH LADIES FOR CHOICE

On May 31, 2009, Dr. George Tiller, a U.S. doctor who provided reproductive health services, including abortions, at a clinic in Wichita, Kansas, the home of Operation Rescue, was shot by an opponent of the procedure (Hegeman, 2009). After he heard of the incident, New York anarchist James Nova (2009) responded:

> Also tragic is that only when someone gets killed does anti-abortion terrorism get any press. when they burn clinics or smash windows, spit on, punch, and tackle defenders, employees, and patients it warrants no coverage. I've had hunting knives pulled on me, been tripped, shoved and witnessed others being assaulted many times over the years. these psychos have the total support of nearly every local police department across the country. I have seen cops kneel and pray with the attackers. but they aren't classified as terrorists because they are CHRISTIAN!

The first case study considers the efforts of queer and anarchist activists to defend such clinics and reproductive autonomy thought necessary for freedom and sustainability in a rapidly populating world. The coalition has deep roots. Emma Goldman (1916), after all, was arrested for speaking about abortion in violation of the Comstock Law in New York.

Over the years, queers and anarchists would continue to battle the prohibitive politics of Comstock's ilk. Between Goldman's arrest in 1916 and Operation Rescue's Summer of Mercy protests in 1991, when the group sent thousands of activists to block access to abortion clinics, debate over the practice has continued (Hegeman, 2009). "When I was at Berkeley, my political involvement was basically with women's reproductive rights," explained queer activist Brian Griffin, who went on to join ACT UP. "To me homophobia and misogyny are the same thing. It's all about hating the female and boys acting like girls."

A central tactic of abortion opponents is to organize a vigil at an abortion clinic. The Students for Life of America (SFLA) (2007) lists steps to organizing a clinic vigil: (1) "Choose a Clinic," (2) "Announce the vigil," (3) "Know the laws," (4) "Gather materials for your vigil . . . with pictures of both living and aborted babies," and (5) "Be a witness for life at the clinic" (SFLA, 2007). What SFLA does not mention is the efforts of abortion opponents to harass or intimidate clinic clients, often screaming, "You're murdering your baby" (Bader, 2005). In response, queers organized clinic defense, setting up a clash of ideologies, with the police serving as intermediaries. But as James Nova points out, they make their position clear. I have been threatened with arrest for stepping even close to the street at clinic defense.

Over the last few years, I have attended clinic defense at the Ambulatory Center in South Brooklyn. In November 2007, I went with the Church Ladies for Choice, an ACT UP spinoff group, members of the Radical Homosexual Agenda, the New York Metro Alliance of Anarchists, and the Brooklyn Pro-Choice Network. The Rude Mechanical Orchestra performed that overcast Saturday morning. The Church Ladies and company stood on one side of a barricade at the entrance to the clinic. On the other side, a group of pro-life activists held rosaries and a replica of a dead, bloody fetus; they offered diapers to those willing to be turned away. The Church Ladies juxtapose that energy with a display of silly humor, undermining the atmosphere through irreverent songs. Most of their songs are culture jams of classic melodies rewritten as pro-choice anthems. One crowd pleaser is "Christian-fascio-Nazi-nutso-psycho-right-wing-buuull-shit," written to the tune of Mary Poppins' "Super-cali-fragilistic-expialidocious" (Church Ladies, 2005).

"My church lady name is Harmonie Moore," explains Brian Griffin in an interview in 2006. "Back in the early days of ACT UP, a chant was invented, 'how many more have to die?' And after chanting it repeatedly, hours on end, at demonstrations, it became 'Harmonie Moore have to die?' And people used to say, 'Who is this poor woman Harmonie Moore and why does she have to die?'" So, as the Church Ladies were coming together, Griffin adopted the chant as his own moniker and became Harmonie Moore. Each of the Church Ladies shows highlight the implicit links between women's health, reproductive autonomy, choice, and HIV prevention. Yet, they do it with a politics that links the lessons of queer activism and feminism translated through jokes and songs.

The Church Ladies are part of a long lineage of DIY queer perfor-mance groups, dating back to the Sisters of Perpetual Indulgence and even the Cockettes. "I was always fascinated with the Cockettes," says Griffin. "I think the Church Ladies go over much better in New York than say the Sisters of Perpetual Indulgence. . . . I think we fit well here in New York. . . . We're far more given toward irony."

"When I moved to New York one of the things in terms of get-ting involved with this city, I noticed everywhere I was going there were these boys with 'Silence = Death' and ACT UP T-shirts," Grif-fin explains. "I thought I should go to a meeting because these are the people that are looking where I'm looking and I'll probably make friends there," Griffin continued. Most of Griffin's friends volunteered with New York's Gay Men's Health Crisis, a highly formalized orga-nization. "And that's not me," Griffin says. ACT UP's culture of play was far more appealing. "So combined with the fact that I was seeing all these attractive men that I wanted to meet, I started going to ACT UP meetings." Once there, he was absorbed into the activist culture, espe-cially after he met future coconspirator and reproductive rights activist Elizabeth Meixell. "When Elizabeth came up to me to say she wanted to have the Church Ladies for Choice, I swear it was like a lightbulb," Griffin recalled. "I know exactly what I want to do with this. I know it's the next step through the Cockettes, through the Sisters of Perpetual Indulgence."

So, Griffin and Meixell founded the Church Ladies with a group of activists from Women's Health Action Mobilization (WHAM) and ACT UP. The first demonstration was at an event WHAM had planned out-side of St. Patrick's Cathedral. Karen Finley showed up as the Mother of God. "And there were four of us," Griffin explained. "I had a red dress and a sign. We had this moving picket and we would laugh and giggle with Elizabeth feeding us chants."

Someone walked up to Griffin and asked, "'Aren't you making fun of religion?' I said, 'Well, yes.' She had no comment. 'Yea, what's the problem?'" While only a few of the Church Ladies are anarchists, the group cohered within an anti-authoritarian stance. "When in doubt, make fun of the Religious Right" became their creed. Much of the potency of the Church Lady repertoire involves its camp embrace of bad taste, the subversive possibilities of humor and play. Another popular song at clinic defense is "Chop It Off," an homage to Lorena Bobbitt, a U.S. housewife who castrated her abusive husband. The song takes on the misogyny of a culture of rape, using humor to delight in the lessons of a woman who fought back. Staring straight at the "antis" during clinic defense, the Church Ladies sing to the tune of "Jingle Bells":

> Listen up you boys
> We don't want to confuse
> There's something that you have
> That you don't want to lose. . .
> So you should *always* ask!
> And be polite, you see,
> Or clap won't be the only thing that hurts you when you pee!!
> Oh!
> *Chorus*
> Chop it off! Chop it off! Use a kitchen knife
> Teach him he can't rape you just because you are his wife
> OW!!! . . .
> If he tries to rape you . . . well, he has to sleep sometime!
> (Church Ladies, 2005)

Harmonie Moore's favorite moments as a Church Lady are when he's actually able to make the antis laugh. Here, humor takes on any number of meanings. After all, those who laugh tend to participate in a shared meaning. Such humor undermines ideas, morals, and authority (Woodside, 2001). It helps regular people break through feelings of inhibition to act and play, liberating us from the confines of rationality and reason (Holt, 2008). And it gives us a means to engage. At least, it feels like this when the Church Ladies perform.

Throughout the years, different Church Ladies have moved through the group; yet, the group has maintained an abiding faith in sexual self-determination, the importance of humor and culture as tools of resistance, and a belief in the freedom to speak out. Over time, even the struggle for public assembly would become embattled.

CASE 2—PUBLIC ASSEMBLY

Throughout the 1990s, many traditional meeting spaces for queers came under attack. In recent years, this process has only become increasingly pronounced. Driving the frenzy was a conservative urban regime that successfully justified its power grab as a morality campaign. Queer meeting places for social and sexual congress were shut down (Crimp,

2002). In response, queers would work with anarchists to defend, create, and preserve such spaces. Some were sex clubs, squats, cruising areas, and community gardens; others took shape as forms of public assembly, including street demonstrations, parties, and Critical Mass bike rides.

One of the groups to queer the right to public assembly is New York's Radical Homosexual Agenda (RHA), an affiliate of the New York Metro Alliance of Anarchists. From 2007 to 2009, the RHA (2008) used direct action to champion notions of liberty. To do so, the group announced a 2007 Parade Without a Permit after the city council speaker, lesbian Christine Quinn, cut a deal with the police department to curtail freedom of assembly for groups of twenty or more. "Just as the police have the power to grant permits, they also have the power to deny them," the RHA would note (RHA, 2008). "Why do the police decide who can assemble and who cannot?" Over the next two years, the group held parades, zapped politicians, disrupted city council hearings, and participated in unpermitted drag marches as well as many other forms of direct action.

For the fortieth anniversary of Stonewall, the RHA organized another Parade Without a Permit. "Join us in the streets as we assert our freedom to assemble and celebrate our liberation," the call for the parade declared, highlighting the point that Gay Liberation began when queers fought back against abuses by the NYPD and inspired a riot (Teal, 1971, 1995). "Today, the infamous NYPD vice squad which raided the Stonewall bar in 1969 is still out in force entrapping and arresting queers." It noted, "Though [Mayor] Bloomberg and Quinn have worked hard to ensure that the NYPD repress the freedoms of straight and queer New Yorkers, our lives and our rage won't fit in their heavily policed parade routes," echoing the anarchist motto "Our Dreams Won't Fit In Your Ballot Boxes!"

On June 19, 2009, the night of the action, I walk around Washington Square Park passing out flyers, announcing our parade, stopping to chat. "You know the deal," I say when I stumble into a group of friends from Queer Fist and Reclaim the Streets. "You guys are coming, right?" "Of course," they assure me. Carrying a sign declaring, "The Stonewall Veterans Never asked for a Permit," we walk around Washington Square toward the exit. I was thinking we would take the streets once we got to Seventh Avenue, but when I look behind I see my group of friends has cheerfully succeeded in taking it as we walked out of the park. "Liberation, not assimilation, fuck that assimilation!!!" the group chants. The campy declaration, "We're here! We're queer! We're fabulous! Don't fuck with us!" follows. This spirit resonates throughout the night air. "We will not be quiet! Stonewall was a riot!" we scream as we approach the Stonewall Inn. The rally moves down Christopher Street, where a nightly street party takes place off the piers most every night. Many join the parade. "One onlooker stepped to the front of the banner and unleashed his inner baton twirler as the RHA drum core pounded out a rhythm and led us in the chant, 'This street is for faggots. F-A-G-G-O-T-S!'" (WeWANTYou, 2009). Members of the NYPD trail behind most of the night. Fortunately, no arrests accompanied this celebration of a culture of resistance. The RHA were not the only group fighting the police in New York in 2009. The final case study highlights efforts to push back the new vice squad.

CASE 3—FIGHTING THE VICE SQUAD

"When the handcuffs clicked on my wrists on October 10, 2008, an energy was released within me that connected me directly to the spirit of the Stonewall rebellion in late June of 1969," recalls Robert Pinter, a victim of a false prostitution arrest. In the weeks and months afterward, members of ACT UP, the RHA, and the Queer Justice League joined in coalition to fight the ongoing ravages of the New York Vice Squad. Still, the arrests continued. Throughout 2008, the NYPD Vice Squad entrapped at least thirty men for prostitution after exiting Manhattan adult video stores with undercover officers who initially approached them for consensual sex. The city uses these false arrests as the main evidence in pursuing nuisance abatement suits against the stores to close them down. The arrests are part of a nearly two-decade-long quality-of-life campaign sanitizing signs of public sexual culture from the city streets (Crimp, 2002; Shepard, 2009). In response, Robert Pinter founded the Campaign to Stop the False Arrests in December 2008. The group held rallies from February through June 2009. Its work drew the notice of local and national media, highlighting a crackdown on cruisers, visible signs of public sexual culture, and the overpolicing of public space (Humm, 2009; Osborne, 2009).

Andrew Vélez, a longtime member of ACT UP, helped organize a few of the rallies around the false arrests. "One thing one has to give up with such activism is a sense of good taste," notes Vélez, describing an ethos that runs through queer activism. Of course, this requires letting go of shame, learning to speak up, and coping with embarrassment. Yet, he suggests, it is worth it. As an example, Vélez describes a brainstorming session during the meetings over the false arrests. "It's both scary and fun planning these things. You never know when you would come up with something," ruminates Vélez. "Like just recently . . . I was at a meeting and they were talking about an upcoming rally and whether they should get a permit for a rally in Sheridan Square"—before answering himself with a "No," one should not get a permit, just as RHA did not in their Parades Without a Permit, which he attended. The action in question was scheduled in three weeks. "And I'm like, 'What are you waiting for? Too much time. . . . You know what? Valentine's is coming up. I think we need to give the mayor a Valentine. We should go to his house on 79th Street.'"

The following week, a relatively modest number of people, including myself, attend the rally in the freezing cold. "But it happened to be a day in which the media was hungry for something," Vélez continues. There were as many journalists as activists. "We got huge coverage and a meeting the following week with Christ Quinn and the mayor's office. It was mostly damage control." While the NYPD had been harassing queers for cruising and cracking down on visible signs of public sexual culture for years, suddenly they were apologizing. "We embarrassed the mayor who wants to be god and be reelected," Vélez explains. "The sign I made said, 'DUMP the MAYOR.' So, it's his nightmare coming to life. That's not stuff he wants to hear, even from crazies. That's why that meeting came about. And [NY Police Commissioner] Kelly has backed off." The charges were dropped against Pinter.

The actions gained vitality as the Coalition to Fight the False Arrests expanded to include a number of groups, including Sex Workers Outreach Project—NYC (SWOP-NYC) and Sex Workers Action New York (SWANK). Here, the actions built on historic theoretically informed critiques used to build solidarity among sexual outsiders. The work of SWANK within this coalition continues a long tradition of anarchist queer sexual civil liberties activism (Kissack, 2008; Sears, 1977). Here, current activists build on Emma Goldman's (1969) anarchist theory of prostitution and sexual freedom, which frames sex work in terms of workers and autonomy, as well as sexual civil liberties. Such activism links campaigns against the vice squad within a framework for challenging unequal and repressive relations between the sexes, races, and classes, as well as rejecting oppressive social norms. Finally, it builds on an anarchist queer tradition of rejecting "all forms of exploitation" (O'Kelly, 1993b).

CONCLUSION

This chapter has explored the interplay of ideas and approaches to theoretically informed direct action. In the first case example, the Church Ladies highlighted the interaction between a culture of resistance, creative direct action, and the insurrectionary possibilities of humor in a campaign for reproductive autonomy and environmental sustainability; the second, RHA's Parades Without a Permit, highlighted the link between queer traditions of defiant and playful street performance and efforts to elude social controls; and the third explored the politics of rejecting prohibitive politics in favor of engagement with new forms of sexual self-democracy. What these small examples suggest is that queer activism and anarchism are mutually reinforcing, with issues and ideas overlapping and interconnecting. Queers benefit from the anarchist connection with global movements; conversely, anarchism gains strength by borrowing from queer approaches to direct action, community organization, rejection of patriarchy, and the pragmatic organizing strategies Jay Blotcher, Brian Griffin, and Andrew Vélez describe. The discipline of queer activism, buttressed with research, flexibility, and pragmatism helps support movement action in any number of ways. While not all anarchists agree with such approaches, anarchism and queer organizing often meet on the ground within a flexible approach to actually creating and sustaining alternate public commons. Both share a propensity toward taking power via direct action. This approach injects a vitality into multiple movements. Yet, for queer theory to value these ideas and practices, it could benefit by stepping off the sidewalk and back into the streets. The challenge for queer and anarchist politics is to mutually support an ongoing commitment to a rejection of authoritarian and or prohibitive politics in favor of the political possibilities of pleasure ebbing through multiple movements for social change.

NOTE

1. Established in 1977, St. Marks Bookshop closed on February 28, 2016, unable to pay rising rent.

Chapter 12

Harm Reduction as Pleasure Activism

In 2004, organizer Adrienne Maree Brown (2004, 20) described the links between pleasure and harm reduction. "Some people think I've spent the last several years of my life working with raising awareness about HIV/AIDS, destigmatizing drug use, and ending overdose, but really it's about breaking down barriers to pleasure. So I'm a pleasure activist." Certainly, Brown is not alone in this sentiment. "I don't think we do acknowledge the pleasure though," explains Allan Clear, "not as much as we should" (Shepard, 2009). The following takes up where Brown and Clear leave off, considering the anarchism of harm reduction and the pleasure of sexual civil liberties activism and their crosscurrents. Both anarchism and queer activism have long challenged anti-pleasure ideology (Kissack, 2008). Through decades of social struggle, the two overlapping movements have come to share an embrace of the insurrectionary possibilities of pleasure, a rejection of social controls and formal hierarchies in favor of mutual aid networks and DIY community building, the use of direct action, and a culture of resistance (Shepard, 2010). Pleasure activism manifests itself in any number of these crosscurrents. It involves core questions. How do we contain or reduce the harms of modern living? How can people be encouraged to love instead of kill each other? In a world with far too much violence and repression, the release valve opened by pleasure offers an important step toward regeneration as opposed to destruction, Eros instead of Thanatos (Marcuse, 1955). This chapter highlights age-old clashes between forces of expression and repression, order and chaos, the autonomy of bodies in space and those aimed at curtailing them. The result is a dialogue between ways of imagining public space, prevention, and reproductive autonomy, connecting approaches to desire with models of health and regeneration.

The relationship between harm reduction and pleasure is anything but simple. "Take yir best orgasm, multiply it by twenty and you're still fucking miles off the pace," writes Irvine Welsh (1993, 1996, 11) in his novel *Trainspotting*, musing on his romance with heroin. "The passion for destruction is a creative passion, too!" Bakunin (1842, 2002, 57) famously argued. Thus, the paradox of pleasure is often pain, as the characters in Welsh's novel soon find out. Still, this right to pleasure finds its roots in any number of movements for sexual freedom, as well as the intersections between drug use and anarchist and queer movements (Shepard, 2009). Often obscured, the need for pleasure fuels the imperative to reduce harm. What inspired the movement's formation but a struggle over expression and desire. Drug use is often about numbing pain, yet it is also fundamentally about pleasure seeking and sensuality (Kennedy et al., 2010). Finding the pleasure in harm reduction is akin to queering the anarchist at its foundation.

Harm reduction has long been recognized as an anarchist direct action movement (Crimethinc, 2017). And there are good reasons for this. In the same way Gandhi challenged social mores to make salt, even when the practice was outlawed in colonial India, harm reduction activists have challenged penal codes to create syringe exchange programs in the spirit of direct action (Springer, 1991). Such gestures of freedom are a fundamental part of anarchist practice.

"You may already be an anarchist," Crimethinc suggests:

> Whenever you act without waiting for instructions or official permission, you are an anarchist. Any time you bypass a ridiculous regulation when no one's looking, you are an anarchist. If you don't trust the government, the school system, Hollywood, or the management to know better than you when it comes to things that affect your life, that's anarchism, too. And you are especially an anarchist when you come with your own ideas and solutions. (Crimethinc, 2017)

Part of this impulse involves breaking down socially imposed barriers to pleasure. Such thinking helped queers invent safer sex when the AIDS epidemic began (Crimp, 2002). Direct action was also the inspiration for the proliferation of harm reduction programs around the world; here, sexual risk reduction and drug use practices shared common cause (Springer, 1991). "I have often pointed out, the importance of considering the essential role played by pleasure in drug use—even in the most chaotic use—and its life-endorsing 'usefulness,'" explains Walter Cavalieri (2010), director of the Canadian Harm Reduction Network, "as well as the need to draw on the parallels between the gay liberation and the drug users' rights movements."

At their core, harm reduction and anarchist queer movements embrace pleasure, autonomy, and self-determination. In doing so, they challenge core elements of a social structure bent on social controls. Anti-pleasure ideology, after all, has deep roots. From the Temperance Movement to Prohibition, over and over, authorities have sought to curb expression of pleasure or consumption of intoxicants. Yet, few movements have built on the lessons of the failure of Prohibition. The following pages consider some of the history of anti-pleasure ideology as well as forms of pleasure activism that have challenged this thinking. Case examples from drug users, HIV prevention, and social organizing are explored. Through them, I consider core questions: How can we create an agenda to support both the affirmation of pleasure and the rejection of prohibitive politics? What would such an agenda look like? What are obstacles and best practices? How can harm reduction take up the issue of pleasure, linking understandings of multiple forms of pleasure with a progressive agenda aimed at rejecting prohibitions that support war and violence, rather than affect and care, and pleasure and abundance?

ANTI-PLEASURE IDEOLOGY

The history of struggles over pleasure involves an ongoing dialectic between expression and repression. While the Dionysus cults embraced intoxicants, drink, wine, and collective expression of ecstasy, the Romans recognized that these pursuits represented a fundamental challenge to power relations. The authorities sought to crush the cults (Ehrenreich, 2007). Yet those who embraced pleasure continued to find their way into trouble. Adam ate the apple and anti-pleasure religious doctrine took hold, which we are still grappling with today.

Deep within his dissent to the *Lawrence v. Texas* Supreme Court ruling repealing U.S. sodomy laws, Justice Antonin Scalia offered a telling clue about the continuing phobia conservatives experience concerning the practices in pleasure. "If sodomy laws are unconstitutional," Scalia wrote, then so are "laws against bigamy, same sex marriage, adult incest, prostitution, masturbation, adultery, fornication, bestiality, and obscenity." Few assumed that any laws against masturbation were still on the books anyway (Hertzberg, 2003). Well, not technically. But for those with a keen eye on hierarchies of transgression, the seemingly trivial topic takes on inordinate meaning. To make sense of Scalia's dissent, it is useful to look back to thirteenth-century Christian theology, specifically St. Thomas Aquinas' categorization of "luxuria," signifying crimes against nature, in which masturbation signaled the beginning of a slippery slope leading to sodomy, adultery, and bestiality. For Aquinas and the rest of the "every sperm is sacred" crowd, masturbation is a sort of gateway pleasure, like marijuana is to heroin. It is not very dangerous in and of itself. Yet, left to the active imagination, it is capable of opening doors to a vast arena of possibilities (Laqueur, 2003, 142–3). Hence, Scalia's reference to the subject in a Supreme Court decision about sodomy. While one would assume Aquinas' *Summa Theologica* is not applicable to American law, given the quaint notions of the separation of church and state, its cultural influence cannot be underemphasized. However deeply flawed they remain, teachings on crimes against nature have established the basis for laws that continue to criminalize countless sexual practices, including homosexuality. Concurrently, they propel abstinence-only sex education, which fails to acknowledge either evidence-based practice or the complexity of sexual expression.

The roots of anti-pleasure ideology stretch far and wide. From Aquinas to Calvin, Cotton Mather to Comstock, a puritanical streak permeates U.S. politics. When Republican senate candidate Christine O'Donnell recently spoke out against masturbation, she was participating in a storied tradition. The Puritans famously condemned those who deviated from their religious doctrine and emphasis on work rather than play, torturing religious nonconformists. Yet, there were those who fought back (Beckman, 2014; Russell, 2010).

The founders had many reservations about the threat of the widespread expression of sexual desire and drunkenness seen in the colonies. Thomas Jefferson famously warned those in the new nation not to visit Europe, where one "is led by the strongest of all human passions into a spirit of female intrigue . . . for whores . . . and in both cases learns to consider fidelity to the marriage bed as an ungentlemanly practice, and inconsistent with happiness" (Russell, 2010). When the founder of U.S. psychiatry, Benjamin Rush, was not busy experimenting with torture devices designed to treat mental illness, he railed against bodily pleasure as "a disease of the body and the mind" (Russell, 2010).

Over the years, this prohibitive logic has only gained steam. The nineteenth-century Temperance Movement sought moral reform and the prohibition of the consumption of alcohol (Gusfield, 1986). The Eighteenth Amendment of the U.S. Constitution was ratified in January 1919. The era set in motion a cavalcade of unintended consequences as markets for alcohol consumption moved from legally regulated commerce into the province of an unregulated black market, which involved sublegal approaches catering to market demand. Violence and crime followed. What did not occur, however, was the reduction of the consumption of alcohol. And, by 1933, the Eighteenth Amendment was repealed. Throughout the period, a queer public commons took shape in places such as San Francisco, where Prohibition was not enforced (Shepard, 2009).

Over the next three decades, the welfare state expanded simultaneously with social movements involving labor, civil rights, women, and people on welfare. By the mid-1960s, these movements started to encounter a backlash over the expanded welfare rolls. With his unsuccessful presidential campaign of 1964, Goldwater introduced crime as a panic issue. While it failed in 1964, crime succeeded as an election issue in 1968, and Nixon was elected with the help of his "Southern Strategy," which racialized crime, welfare, and poverty. Policy emphasis shifted to crime control, rather than welfare provision or prevention. Nixon's election marked a striking policy shift, with a new emphasis on a prohibitive approach to crime under a new "War on Drugs." Rather than provide services to alleviate poverty, the new emphasis was on criminalizing it. The Rockefeller Drug laws of the early 1970s are a prime example.

Faced with increased attacks on social movements under the new administration, a number of groups sought to fight back. The Black Panthers organized a food program to support their community in Oakland. The Young Lords, a Bronx-based direct action group of the same vein, organized a number of forward-thinking, audacious acts of direct action aimed at cultivating a more responsive system of public health for social outsiders. In 1970, the group took over Lincoln Hospital. The group's list of demands included calls for Spanish-language translation for services, acupuncture to aid detox services, and a consumer bill of rights. Most would later become common practices and policy (Shepard, 2009, 2011).

One of the early members of the Young Lords was Sylvia "Ray" Rivera, a leader in the transgender movement. Rivera was also a veteran of Gay Activist Alliance and the Street Trans Action Revolutionaries (STAR). Much of the gay liberation impulse shared common cause with the anarchism of the era (Kissack, 2008; Shepard, 2010). Pleasure activist Charles Shively (1974, 2001) described "indiscriminate promiscuity as an act of revolution." Through this organizing, gay liberationists challenged the social system, rather than embrace marriage, militarism, and law and order social policies. Instead, the movement fought homophobia, sex phobia, and anti-pleasure ideology. It borrowed from Wilhelm Reich's (1980) argument that anti-sex politics support the docile bodies linked to fascism as well as anti-sex ideology; such thinking only fuels abstinence-oriented policies, sexualized and racial fear, prohibitive politics, and disconnection from the body.

Throughout the early years of the AIDS epidemic, activists grappled with core questions about the appropriate approach to HIV prevention. While some suggested HIV prevention should include a Temperance-era abstinence approach, which called for strict prohibitions of sexual contact (Gusfield, 1986), others called for a more humanistic, sex-positive approach. Dr. Joseph Sonnabend, Richard Berkowitz, and Michael Callen worked on an HIV prevention pamphlet in New York in the early 1980s. They recognized that if one asks gay men, much less anyone else, to give up sex, the result is usually anger. All or nothing propositions result in variations between hysteria, repression, and inevitable lapses. For many, a world without sex is not worth living in. Prohibition is often more dangerous than acknowledgment, careful expression, and prevention. In response, the three recognized that latex was the life-saving compromise needed. From here, Berkowitz and Callen built on the lessons of gay liberation to draft "How to Have Sex in an Epidemic." The result was a revolution allowing for personal and political protection and cover for both sex and the liberation movement, which dismantled the shackles around it (Berkowitz, 2003). The lessons of the tract became core principles of HIV prevention activism during the next two decades. "Our promiscuity taught us many things, not only about the pleasures of sex, but about the great multiplicity of those pleasures," noted pleasure activist and ACT UP veteran Douglas Crimp (2002, 64), reflecting on the invention of safer sex. "It is that psychic preparation, that experimentation, that conscious work on our own sexualities that has allowed many of us to change our sexual behaviors . . . it is our promiscuity that will save us."

Yet, over the years, the use-a-condom-every-time code started to wane. In a 2007 podcast, Donald Grove, a veteran of ACT UP's syringe exchange committee, reflected on this moment and its lessons for the harm reduction movement:

The mere fact that society disapproves of something does not mean it isn't going to happen. For me harm reduction is about working with drug users where they're at. Which means recognizing that lots of them are very interested in stopping, but until you can provide them with the kind [of help or alternative] they need they aren't going to stop, or can't stop. Therefore, you need to address the fact that drug use is an ordinary part of their daily lives. And not only that, but I think where it becomes really particular and really special is it's an ordinary part of their daily lives. It is highly stigmatized, something they have to do in secret, something they have to do with a lot of other dangers and harms piled on top of it by the legal system and that this is going to impact everything else about their lives which isn't stigmatized. We as a culture approach the impact that the drug use, we take the impact that those things have on the rest of their life and say, "Well that wouldn't be happening if you weren't using drugs." What I keep coming back to is, but they are using drugs. When I was still in my early thirties, thirteen years ago, I realized that we have a lot, including in the gay community, a big dialogue around how you ought to be doing things rather than how you are doing things. And what happened to me in the back room of the Wonder Bar, after a decade of impeccably safe sex, I was sucking off a guy in the back room and he came in my mouth. And I swallowed it, and it was as though I had been struck like a gong. And I vibrated for days after that, because I realized how much I had missed for so long. . . . And I realized that this was something I did not want to stop. And you know it was a struggle. I talked to some of my harm reductionist friends about it. I learned to put it, everyone wants to talk to me about what I ought to be doing, and no one talks to me about what I am doing. And I see that as the essence of the harm reduction approach when interacting with drug users who for instance need sterile syringes. So that's the essence of harm reduction for me, is to say, accept people, or work with people based on what they are doing rather than what you believe they ought to be doing.

Through Grove's narrative one can see the lessons of Crimps's (2002) thinking intersecting with a burgeoning harm reduction movement pioneered through syringe programs, such as ACT UP's illegal exchange in New York (see Springer, 1991).

Throughout the period, activists came to build a movement around the recognition that abstinence is unsafe and repression unhealthy. As queer theorist Eve Sedgwick explained, "There is an ethical urgency about queer theory that is directed at the damage that sexual prohibitions and discriminations do to people" (quoted in Smith, 1998). Building on these practical understandings, the U.S. harm reduction movement organized to support the needs of drug users in the United States. A group of activists moved to change the way cities around the United States cope with policies such as syringe exchange. Like a condom, harm reductionists recognized syringe exchange as lifesaving intervention (Springer, 1991). The Harm Reduction Coalition defines the practice as a set of interventions that seek to "reduce the negative consequences of drug use, incorporating a spectrum of strategies from safer use, to managed use, to abstinence."

One of the primary activists involved with the early syringe exchange programs in New York was Greg Bordowitz (2002), who worked with ACT UP's syringe exchange committee. Bordowitz reveled in ACT UP's ethos of pleasure.

Looking back on it now, it was a place you could have romance. Well, everybody was in love with everybody. There was this intense sense of comradeship and closeness. We were all brought together and felt close because of the meaningfulness of the work, and the fact that people were dying, and people in the group were getting sick. It created this feeling, a heightened intensity. Emotions were very powerful within the group. . . . And also, that fuels Eros. That fueled attraction that—people clung to each other, not necessarily in a desperate way, but people found comfort in each other.

For members of ACT UP, pleasure was a resource (Shepard, 2009).

Yet, over the years, syringe exchange programs would increasingly become entwined with departments of health, funding, and the pitfalls of the nonprofit industrial complex. Today, much of harm reduction is about evidence, science, linear thinking, service provision, struggles with funding, and collaboration. But where did the pleasure go? The plenary of the 9th Social Research Conference on HIV, Hepatitis C and Related Diseases, Australia, 2006, was titled *StigmaPleasurePractice*. Here, participants asked: Why is it difficult to consider pleasure in drug policy and practice? What are the consequences for practice? How might a greater focus on the pleasures of drugs invigorate harm reduction (Holt and Treloar, 2008)?

To start the process, it is useful to reconsider the ways direct action practices inform anarchism and sexual civil liberties activism and, by extension, harm reduction (Shepard, 2010). "I joined Sex Panic! because there's no group making the same connections between the renewed sexual repression of the past several decades," explained Chris Farrell in 1998. Here, we question the logic of punishment. "The failure of the left to identify pleasure as a political principle worth fighting for does a lot to explain the moribund state of progressive politics." Here, Farrell calls for the activists to "return sexual pleasure to the progressive agenda. . . . Until the left learns the function of the orgasm, our fight against repression is doomed" (Shepard, 2009).

From sex worker organizing to parties celebrating public sexual culture, examples of such practices are many. Groups such as AIDS Prevention Action League and Jacks of Color have helped support a broader push for safer promiscuity with large-scale parties, which support pleasure. The late sexual civil liberties activist Eric Rofes rejected paternalism while writing that gay men are far more comfortable and capable of embracing complicated choices. Through events such as the Artgasm Big Bang Party (2007), pleasure activists have supported both harm reduction and public sexual culture: "We are a group of radical queers who are creating a space that is sex-positive, gender-inclusive, anti-capitalist, affordable, size-positive and feminist where we can fuck, make art, engage in kink, dance and play." To do so, this sex party depends on "a radical definition of consent." Here, consent is recognized as "the presence of 'yes' and not just the absence of 'no,' with the understanding that everyone can change their mind, stop, or back up at any time. Consent must be established each and every time sexual activity happens." Through such endeavors, pleasure activists have taught us that without justice there can be no pleasure and vice versa.

Throughout the movement, leaders such as Housing Works cofounder Keith Cylar helped keep the expression of pleasure as an integral component of harm reduction. Squatter Louis Jones started Stand Up Harlem within the same spirit of anarchism. "That to me felt so incredible. You talk about emotions. I just felt such pleasure. Everyone thinks about pleasure in terms of decadence, but there was more to it than that. I was moved. . . . It brought fulfillment. I felt animated. We were living together, sleeping together, and working for change." Yet, more to it, "Using was dying with dignity—with dignity because it was my choice. No one was making it for me. I took a stand for those I knew who chose drugs when they were facing death."

At CitiWide Harm Reduction, where I worked for four years, we grappled with pleasure as part of a tragicomic continuum of human experience. When a member died, we said goodbye in a circle. Here, grief was transformed into a space for care, song, drumming, and happiness. And members knew they had faced the negative, moved through it, and come out the other side. The tenacity of those in the circle made the scene one of the most pulsing spaces I have seen. In their daily transforming of the negative into a new way of living, those in the program achieved a kind of magical power (Shepard, 2009). In this way, harm reduction is understood as a place where members build healing communities, spaces for care, and solidarity. Through such connections, they challenge the insurmountable and they share lives and authentic experience together outside of the prohibitive logic of criminal justice and coercion.

Building on these lessons, one can come to see components of an agenda for pleasure, care, and just human relations. In *Three Essays on Sexuality*, Freud rejected Puritan mores by suggesting that everyone has some form of perversion in them (Tatchell, 1989). There is no shame in it. This is part of being human. Yet, shame exists and causes harm. To do away with shame and the repression it fuels, pleasure activists pushed to transform the social order (Reich, 1980; Tatchell, 1989). They recognized that we sustain ourselves through acknowledgment of human need rather than endless conflict. Here, we make friends with the other. Rather than us and them, suit versus slut, a philosophy of harm reduction and internal relations reminds us of the interconnections between us; it teaches us that we are all connected (Ollman, 1976). These relationships matter. To be effective at these ends, the process must include a respect for self-determination, choice, and pleasure. If we do not acknowledge the importance of pleasure, we risk mirroring the prohibitive politics we reject (Holt and Treloar, 2008). After all, what we are protecting is a right to social imagination that rejects paternalism while opening spaces for alternative social relations and ways of embracing experience outside the realm of capitalism and rational experience. The failure of the political left to articulate a pro-pleasure argument is nothing short of a failure of the political imagination. It leaves a huge void to be occupied by moralists. Many of us know, there is another route to pleasure and freedom, beyond a clash of civilizations.

Chapter 13

Urban Spaces as Living Theater: Toward a Public Space Party for Play, Poetry, and Naked Bike Rides (New York City, 2010–2015)

Art and activism overlap in countless ways, connecting lines between life and the game of modern living intersecting throughout the history of social movements. This chapter builds on the interchange between expression and repression seen in the previous chapters highlighting tensions between play and work, wherein, urban space is opened up for multiple uses, conflicts, and possibilities. Along the way, humans clash and connect with objects and others, working, playing, and laboring on the verge of agency or becoming machines. "Capital absorbs labor into itself—'as though its body were by love possessed,'" writes Marx in *Grundrisse* (1973, 704). But how do we find our way out? Where do regular people find a space for agency? How do we contend with the encroaching of the private into the public? What can public spaces offer us? What do they tell us about our lives or metropolitan areas? Are they spaces for poetry and performance, or condominiums and reification, for animation or repression? Where do these clashes lead us? And what does the answer suggest about what cities can be? The following considers a few of these questions.

"When I walk down the stairs into the Living Theater I feel like I'm walking through into another world," I said to Judith Malina the Friday before the final performances at the Living Theater's run on Clinton Street in February 2013. "There is no other world, just this world," Malina replied, insisting that there could be no separation between art and life. We are all part of it—all contributing to the beautiful anarchist revolution she has imagined and supported since the late 1940s.[1] Malina's life project has found expression in the street actions, stories, performances, poems, and ways we all reimagine urban public spaces, the way we use these spaces and spend time there. Spaces need

art; they need poems. To feel alive, cities need this. The mission of the Living
Theater has long been:

> To call into question
> who we are to each other in the social environment of the theater,
> to undo the knots that lead to misery,
> to spread ourselves
> across the public's table like platters at a banquet,
> to set ourselves in motion like a vortex that pulls the spectator into action,
> to fire the body's secret engines,
> to pass through the prism
> and come out a rainbow,
> to insist that what happens in the jails matters,
> to cry "Not in my name!"
> at the hour of execution,
> to move from the theater to the street and from the street to the theater.
> This is what The Living Theater does today. It is what it has always done.
> Living Theater (ND)

This chapter considers street clashes between liberation and social control,
revelry and labor. Case narratives from recent social movements in New York
City review naked bike rides, poetry events in community gardens, and bike
liberation events as examples of play-based movement that works toward
transforming urban spaces into a living theater. Exploring the workings of
play in public space, it traces lines between "different ways of knowing,"
opening "space between analysis and action" to consider official and subjective forms of knowledge (Conquergood, 2002, 145). The first part of the
chapter explores philosophical reflections on work and play, followed by an
ethnographic retelling of different radical street performances from New York
City between 2010 and 2015.

THE MEANING OF PLAY

While Marxism offers a telling assessment of the mechanics of labor, it has
also concerned itself with work's other, namely play or leisure. From this vantage point, play has been granted an idealistic, almost liberating dimension,
beyond the rules and regulations of everyday life. Herbert Marcuse focuses
more on the philosophy of play than his Marxist contemporaries. He suggests
that play is a dimension of freedom, a "self-distraction, relaxing oneself, forgetting oneself and recuperating oneself" (Marcuse, 1973, 15). For Marcuse,
play is a dimension of freedom; it serves as a critique, because of its position
outside the conventions of the everyday.

For the purposes of this chapter, play can be thought of as a spirit, which encompasses theatrical presentation as improvisation, motion, and an ethos of action, eruption, and liberty (Schechner, 2002, 79). But it is also paradoxical, sometimes pushing forward, sometimes backward between liberating and repressive purposes, sometimes highly organized, sometimes open for improvisation. In its less formal incarnations, it can involve hula hooping by the pool or poetry readings in the park. From time to time, it departs from the mundane, expanding into a status quo-threatening endeavor—offering the possibility for emancipation from alienating reified social relations. In this way it is seen as a threat. The Western fear of people gathering together dates back to the conflicts between the orgiastic Dionysian cults and the more orderly Apollonian ways of looking at the world (Maffesoli, 1996). People are only free when they play, posits Georg Lukacs, citing Schiller's famous lines on aesthetic education in *History and Class Consciousness* (Lukacs, 168, 138).

Borja-Villel, Valazquez, and Bringas suggest, "The work time/leisure time binomial . . . is fundamental to the life of the Western subject." The clash between "bourgeois and revolutionary ideals, between the social classes linked to the accumulation of capital and the possibility of social change and the new forms of coexistence and sociability" (9) involves not only conflicts between freedom and social control but "between 'self' and 'other'" (9). Many of these conflicts take place in the city. Here, play is often synonymous with the use of public space for alternate means to capital accumulation. People gather, plan, occupy, and find each other. "The city has become the space conductive to the playful event, a place for desire, open to the possibility of Rimbaud's injunction to 'changer la vie'" (10–11).

In the United States too, the specter of fun involves tensions about play and public space involving questions of otherness and democracy. "How has such a tumultuous public, historically riven by deep social differences (class division, racial prejudice, partisan politics, culture wars) ever gathered in peaceable activity?" ponders John Beckman (2014, xiii). "The answer is by having fun—often outrageous, life-threatening fun." Activists have long understood this, looking to transform public spaces into spaces for play and other liberating activities. Art and activism overlap in countless ways throughout the history of social movements, often merging in a carnivalesque playground. Here, social reality is imagined as a game, in which social actors play in irreverent, often humorous ways, adding a sense of festivity and release, freedom and surprise. "By its repudiation of the possibility of suffering," Sigmund Freud suggests, humor "takes its place in the great series of methods devised by the mind of man for evading the compulsion to suffer" (quoted in Morreall, 1987, 113). Connected with social movements, subversive humor and pleasure disrupt monotony, liberate, and disarm systems of power (Critchley, 2002; Holt

2008; Morreall, 2012; Sanders, 1996). Through humor and play, social actors challenge the rules of the game of modern living, highlighting alternate ways of imagining social reality.

While the concepts of humor, play, and fun differ and should not be used interchangeably, they overlap in instructive ways. The opposite possible effect of humor and play is deflection, denial, and violence (Sanders, 1996; Schechner, 2002). "Understanding humor as play helps counter the traditional objections to it and reveals some of its benefits, including those it shares with philosophy itself," notes John Morreall (1987, 168). "Sudden glory" is the disposition that takes place when we react to pain or sadness with a surprised laugh. Such disruptions are similar with play and humor (Sanders, 1996). In *Passions of the Soul*, Descartes suggests laughter overlaps between some six emotive states including sadness, wonder, joy, love, hatred, and desire. More often than not, laughter can be seen as a form of ridicule. Sometimes, the point is to make fun of opponents, to take away their legitimacy. Such forms of guerilla theater have come to be described as "radical ridicule" (Bogad, 2005). "We have hatred for this evil, we have joy in seeing it in him who is deserving of it; and when that comes upon us unexpectedly, the surprise of wonder is the cause of our bursting into laughter," notes Morreall, suggesting such humor can be understood in terms of theories of superiority, relief, incongruity, play, and comedy (Morreall, 1987, 168). A pressure valve is released when we laugh and play, in distinct and overlapping feelings.

Exploring the workings of play in public space, this chapter deploys an auto-ethnographic narrative, making use of the researcher's feelings, thoughts, and reflections as subjects of consideration in and of themselves, as well as in combination with other data. It connects multiple layers of analysis, linking play and performance, the cultural with the personal, moving backward and forward between observation of individual and larger social forces (Conquergood, 2002; Trahar, 2009).

I first started thinking about play in social movements when the city in which I live, New York, officially sought to cut down on such practices through a new mayor's temperance-like quality of life campaign in the mid-1990s. From performance art to street activism, creative outlets for play seemed to define the contours of public space and private life in cities from San Francisco to New York (Bogad, 2005, Ornstein, 1998). It seemed to be everywhere throughout the city. Community organizing here took countless ludic dimensions. Over and over, it helped open spaces for civic purposes and political mobilization, allowing people to meet and occupy public space in meaningful ways. Play has long been a resource for social movements, extending from Dada to Surrealism, Situationism to ACT UP and Occupy and Black Lives Matter (Shepard, 2009, 2011); it adds a life and joyousness to the process of social change. Without a little play, the possibilities for social change are often limited, opportunities for transformation and release diminished (Duncombe, 2007).

URBAN POLITICAL PROTEST, PLAY, AND PERFORMANCE

Much of the contemporary ludic spirit of social movement practices dates back to Dada and the Yippies, who used pranks as a means to intrigue and seduce, to lull and invite people into the process of social change, bringing humor into the discourse of progressive politics (Duncombe, 2007). While there are certainly urban activists who do not consider creative protest to be useful,[2] play has long been used by social movements to increase their visibility and broaden their audience. To take but one example, social movement scholar Doug McAdam (1996) suggests that Martin Luther King and his fellow members of the Southern Christian Leadership Conference had a knack for "strategic dramaturgy" (McAdam, 1996, 338–56, 339–40). They understood that street activism had to be framed as a performance, capable of speaking to a number of potential publics.

There are countless often contradictory motivations behind political performance, including (a) expressing dissent, (b) self-definition, (c) showing movement strength, (d) recruiting new members, and (e) convening and opening space for expression (Bogad, 2005). What they have in common is that they open up alternative ways of experiencing, forming, engaging, staging, and sustaining community. They challenge social hierarchies while demarcating parameters between inside and outside, spectator or performer. Political performances create a sense of gravity, which connects those involved. Here, activists step out of their roles to remind us of the staged quality of our experiences and performances, nudging spectators into a more critical disposition toward the framed nature of our reality (Bogad, 2005).

In 1990s and early 2000s New York, much play-based political protest was taken up through decentralized practices such as Critical Mass, unpermitted, political protest bike rides aimed at reclaiming public space around the world. It has since inspired other forms of political protest, such as the New York City World Naked Bike Ride, which combines political protest, street theater, a party on wheels, public nudity, and clothing-optional recreation.

NAKED BIKE RIDES AND OCCUPY GEZI

According to its organizers, the New York City World Naked Bike Ride celebrates "a future free of indecent exposure to the toxic world of auto and oil

Figure 13.1.   Naked rider biking down Broadway, June 2013.

Source: Photo by Benjamin Shepard.

dependence." "Ride as 'bare as you dare,' keeping mindful of your own comfort level and local laws. Celebrate the beautiful diversity of our bodies," they
declare. Through individual participation, riders take part in a debate about
urban space between those who, much like twentieth-century urban planner
Robert Moses, see cities as spaces for the smooth circulation of automobiles
and those who, like Jane Jacobs, suggest that cities can be places where we
talk with people, becoming "the eyes upon the street" (Jacobs, 1992).

Mellow Yellow is the first person I know who talked about organizing a
naked ride, back in 2010. Just new to town, he thought that such an event
could bring people into a broader conversation about the ways cities work.
Aware of the 2004 attacks on Critical Mass,[3] he still wanted to put together a
powerful mass of bodies in the streets. Everywhere he went, he would chalk
up the message, painting it on his body or streets. Some were more receptive
than others. Sometimes people were offended. Mostly they were intrigued
with his enthusiasm. "I'll see you at the world naked bike ride," he would
remind everybody.

"More ass, less gas," we chant during the first ride. More than a celebration of nudity, our slogan connects people's bodies with a larger story about
sustainability. We zoom up to the UN and down to Washington Square Park.

"Empire State of Mind" blares out of the sound bike as we make our way
down Broadway, all of us singing, "In New York . . . New York, New York."
We were all leaders, pulsing through space in a semi-clothed critical mass of

bodies. This wasn't just any protest; it was an invitation to be part of a plea-sure community. "More nude, less rude," those riding begin to scream. No one is sure who starts the chant. But it seems to harken to an anti-Puritanical ethos in movements for sexual freedom dating back a century (Shepard).

"If you're doing it, we can too," notes one observer, disrobing. The ritual space between music and dancing bodies opens up New York to a different set of colors and experiences. Participants create a moving amoeba, a carnival-like liminal space between order and openness, in which people are more comfortable with each other than the closed, clothed every day. The event makes the point that the body can be a vehicle for free speech, thus demon-strating the centrality of bodies in performance (Schechner, 2002).

Mellow Yellow sees the individuals taking part as supporters of a radi-cal alternative, a "free ride on a human-powered machine, free-moving machine," he notes. "That was a choice I made when I was 16 in San Jose, California. Get away from cars," he explains. "I say it as a global warning. You guys are destroying the future. Bikes are a solution." It is a message that is only expanding.

Each ride is different, though. In 2013, the 3rd annual New York City WNBR overlaps with various campaigns around public space, including Occupy Gezi, a movement protesting the transformation of Istanbul's Taksim Square from a public space into a shopping space. The plan for the Square feels very familiar to New Yorkers. When Mayor Rudy Giuliani planned a "quality of life" crusade to clean up and sanitize Times Square and New York, many of us recognized this policy as a code for class cleansing, used to justify pushing the poor from public view, criminalizing homelessness and poverty, while vilifying social and sexual outsiders, and turning the commons into a shopping space. "The conflict over public space is always about control versus freedom, segregation versus diversity. What's at stake is more than a square," writes Michael Kimmelman in *The New York Times*. "It's the soul of the nation" (Kimmelman, 2013).

In June 2013, a pushback seemed to be taking shape in the rapid ascent of the Occupy Gezi movement and solidarity actions around the world. Finish-ing a skirmish, a group of Turkish activists open bottles of beer and raise a mock toast to their prime minister. "Cheers, Tayyip!" they declare, mocking a proposed law prohibiting the consumption of alcohol in public spaces. In the United States, activists with the Occupy movement joined the street actions for Occupy Gezi in Zuccotti Park. Several carry signs declaring "From Zuc-cotti to Gezi, you are not alone. We are with you. Don't give up Istanbul." A young woman stands up starting a mic check. "We need our public spaces," she declares, calling for both the mall proposed for Taksim Square and the crackdown on activists to stop. "We demand that the park remain a park. The attempts to demolish the cultural center must stop. Those who support violent suppression should be removed from their posts. Use of tear gas should be prohibited around the country."

"Around the globe," a man screams.

"Around the globe," we follow.

"Detained protesters should be released. The restrictions on the right to protest, to meet in public spaces should end. We should honor the right of people to the streets."

Occupy activists post a statement:

> We are artists, students, intellectuals and citizens of New York City. Together with supporters of Occupy Wall Street, we are here in Zuccotti Park to show solidarity with our friends and brothers and sisters who are occupying Gezi Parki in Istanbul. This is a peaceful event. Our goal is to attract public attention to the protests in Istanbul Gezi Parki and the consequent police brutality of the Erdogan/AKP government! Since Monday, May 27th, citizens of Istanbul from all backgrounds have been staging a peaceful resistance in Gezi Park, the city's largest public park, protecting it and its trees from a large gentrification project to transform a public park into a shopping center. The demolition of the park should be understood as another incident of the government's ongoing appropriation and privatization of public resources. Since the peaceful occupation started three days ago, the Turkish police have repeatedly intervened, with each intervention more violent than the last. . . . Today, hundreds of thousands of people in Istanbul are resisting the AKP government's neoliberal policies and the brutal attacks on the protestors continue. #occupyGeziNYC

Activists around the world support them.

Finishing the rally, I jump on my bike to meet Mellow Yellow and several other activists for the Hot Pants Ride we were organizing for later that afternoon. "In solidarity with World Naked Bike Ride (WNBR), wear your hottest, fiercest hot pants on this clothing optional extravaganza through the streets of New York," we urge, our pleas for freedom in public space overlapping. Our message:

> Climate change is real and it ain't getting any cooler out here. Get comfortable in our future climate and show some skin. We love short shorts! Mask up, pants down! As comfortable as you please. Reclaim your body! Reclaim your streets! Reclaim your planet! Ride your bike! The Hot Pants Ride is a safer space for all bodies to ride free of harassment or pollutants in the physical or mental environment. To participate each rider is asked to respect that the liberation of bodies requires freedom, autonomy, and justice for all. This begins with joy and commitment to self-determination. And of course bikes!!! What: An afternoon of fun, free community, and direct action, including a clothing-optional bike ride. We celebrate our bodies, celebrate cycling in NYC! (WNBR, 2010–2014)

That Saturday, June 8, 2013, everyone gathers at Grand Ferry Park on the Brooklyn Waterfront, riders from across the city planning to join us. Biking up Broadway, I was going to call Keegan about the sound bike when he screams hello from the fish truck he was riding. We make plans, talking at lights. The ride and its politics of self-determination are never simple, making sure it is fun and celebratory without being creepy or male-dominated. Mellow Yellow and I arrive at Grand Ferry Park at 5 pm, well before the ride is to begin. After a full write-up in the *Daily News* the day earlier, the park is teeming with people and police. Unlike the previous year, when the ride had gone under the radar, this year it is fully in the consciousness of the city, and by extension the police who promised to escort (control) us. There, we remind photographers to ask for permission before taking shots. Still they hoard in—attracted and revolted at our celebration of bodies in space. But still we organize, hold our consent teach-in, paint slogans on bodies, and hit the road, careening up and down the Williamsburg Bridge with hundreds of fellow semi-clad cyclists, through traffic, past the police, making our way. People dance in between lights. The music and the chants hit a crescendo riding down Broadway with more and more naked cyclists. Downtown we zoom past Zuccotti Park, where we had not planned to ride, but the amoeba of the ride pulls us, the leader the body of the movement of bikes guiding us.

"Dig your body, ride your bike," we scream.

"Whose streets, our streets!"

The scooter cops soon join, instructing Keegan to turn off the sound bike, telling us not to ride outside the bike lanes they are blocking. The unpermitted ride is breaking apart, with the police scolding us at every turn. It is like a fun house or one of those 1970s television shows, *The Banana Splits*, with the police villains chasing the short-shorts wearing riders in a theater of the absurd.

"We gotta get back to Brooklyn where things make sense," shouts one rider.

Eventually, the cyclists move east through the West Village. We lose the scooters, reconnecting with other riders by text, and ride back, deep into the night, listening to hip-hop and dancing, as we finish the best WNBR we had had in years. Steven Menendez posts on Facebook: "This was one of the most FUN and Liberating days of my life! Feeling blessed!"

Through Naked Bike Rides, rallies, and solidarity actions, ride participants and Occupy Gezi activists come together as bodies in space, sharing their lives, dreams, heartbreaks, and ambitions. With each gathering we hope to see and be part of something larger than ourselves. As Michael Kimmelman puts it in *The New York Times*:

> So public space, even a modest and chaotic swath of it like Taksim, again reveals itself as fundamentally more powerful than social media, which produce

virtual communities. Revolutions happen in the flesh. In Taksim, strangers have discovered one another, their common concerns and collective voice. The power of bodies coming together, at least for the moment, has produced a democratic moment, and given the leadership a dangerous political crisis. (Kimmelman, 2013)

Today, more than ever we need our public spaces, where we can imagine a different, more authentic form of democratic living. Here the dialectic of work and play reveals itself as a question about what is important about modern living, as people wonder if modern living offers something larger or more abundant than just going to work.

PUBLIC SPACE PARTY FOR POETRY AND PRANKS

In his 1960 preface to *Reason and Revolution: Hegel and the Rise of Social Theory*, originally published in 1941, Herbert Marcuse concludes: "Poetry is thus the power 'de nier les choses' (*to deny the things*)—the power which Hegel claims, paradoxically, for all authentic thought" (Marcuse, 1941/1960, x–xi). "Dialectic and poetic language meet, rather, on common ground," Marcuse elaborates. "The common element is the search for an 'authentic language'—the language of negation as the Great Refusal to accept the rules of a game in which the dice are loaded" (67).

Over the last few years my cycling friends and I have held several poetry jams in the streets of New York under the aegis of Public Space Party (PSP), both a practice and a group dedicated to supporting democracy, fun, joy, justice, and full participation in a vibrant public commons.

We came up with the idea for the first ride in the spring of 2013, while working in the community garden we were starting with Time's Up!, an anarchist-inspired environmental group based in the Lower East Side of Manhattan. Biking through NYC, stopping to read poems and create spontaneous interaction, JC, the ride organizer, described the event as a "living interactive experiment of word, sound, and movement." Motion grows, swirling, mixing, moving, and evolving through a dialectic and interconnections between bodies and social relations. In this whirlpool of ideas, different conditions are expanding, ever-altered by this interaction. These connections may not be immediate, but they are part of capitalism's essence, ever-moving, interacting, and undergoing change over time (Ollman, 1976). Poetry would help us come to grips with this motion.

"So happy to hear that one of Nuyorican Poets founding padres, Jesus-Papoleto Melendez will be joining us Sunday," declares JC before the 2013 ride. "Prepare for something special." The event would start at 3 pm at the

Washington Square Arch on April 27, 2013. I start the day cycling to the garden everyone was creating. The space is alive. We greet volunteers and turn wood boxes into composting crates. Only weeks before, it had been a vacant lot. After a little love from the community and a few volunteer days, it has become a garden, albeit a temporary one. Leaving, I ride over the Williamsburg Bridge to Manhattan to join the poetry jam. Riding through the Lower East Side, I see JC and Brennan with the sound bike in tow. We meet everyone else at Washington Square Park.

"We sound our barbaric yawp and burst forth in kinetic inspiration," pronounces JC. Standing under the arch, he welcomes everyone, reminding us of Marcel Duchamp's 1917 performative declaration of a "free and independent Republic of Washington Square" from this very spot. Artists and poets climbed on the top of the arch, had tea, and established an occupation of poets and artists. Some of the rest of us follow, there were poets and bikes everywhere. The multitextured action combines stories and memories, words and movements like a Deleuzian plateau.[4]

I read *Howl* as we leave the park, screaming out stanza after stanza, riding, taking breaks for a stanza at each stoplight, a clusterfuck of cars, bikes, and bodies in the streets. The words make their way through the air, floating, finding a space, bouncing among the cars, bikes, pedestrians, horns, hordes, and hustle and bustle of the city. It all felt right, as the jazz of the city felt like a crescendo.

"We are not on drugs, we are the drugs," JC screams, riding us down Seventh Avenue. While meandering through the Greenwich Village streets, we pay homage to Edna St. Vincent Millay at her former home on the corner of Bedford Street and Commerce Street.

Judy Ross reads E. E. Cummings. I read Rumi. Brennan plays an audio recording of St. Vincent Millay reading, her voice reverberating from the sound bike. And Jesus-Papoleto Melendez declares: "I will jump out of the window if that's what it takes to please you sexually," pausing, "only if you live in the basement." He then reads from Pedro Pietri's poem "Telephone Booth 905 1/2." Feeling the words vibrate through me, I think about the poetry of the garden we are creating, the stories already growing from there, of the work of making a family and a garden grow, as well as the poems and bike rides that occupy my Sunday afternoons. Riding home, water from the fire hydrant pours on the flowers in the garden, helping them grow, helping us all, the city seeming to be coming alive.

Over the years, we have more and more poetry rides, often taking place in spaces under threat, such as community gardens in vacant lots throughout the city. With each one, poetry makes its way through the streets, into the nooks and crannies of the sidewalk, where the earth wakes and the wild weeds make their way back between the cracks into our presence. We carry banners, recall gardeners, and continue our procession through the years, through the trees in our concrete jungle, letting the poetry mingle, between texts, green spaces, and memories. With more and more people joining the readings, the poetry fuels countless interactions between parts of the body of the city (Ollman, 2003, 17). Sometimes we march, sometimes we ride. Through the poems, the city comes together as a story of our own invention. As Jane Jacobs (1992, 238) reminds us, "Cities have the capability of providing something for everybody only because, and only when, they are created by everybody." Reading these poems, it is hard not to imagine the city as a living theater, to feel it; it feeds us, pulsing with ideas and hopes, ambition and heartbreak, cars and conflicts.

BIKES, CARS, AND EXPERIMENTS WITH PLAY
IN BIKE LANES

The streets are constantly changing and evolving along with our approaches to navigating them. As much as anything, play opens up in between spaces, where tensions between disorder and order, public and private, and connection and social movements help us reimagine public space. The dialectic of cars versus bikes initiates a conversation about the very nature of cities. A little humor helps us imagine new ways of seeing the space between the streets and sidewalk.

In October 2012, for example, a group of cyclists dressed like explorers, discoverers, sleuths, pirates, and bloodhounds meets at the Manhattan side of the Williamsburg Bridge to explore what to do when the bike lane off the bridge ends in the Lower East Side. An activist friend, Monica, is dressed up as Jacques-Yves Cousteau, while I dressed up as Sherlock Holmes. Leaving the bridge, we survey the territory, looking for an easy way across the zooming cars along Delancey Street, locating a bike lane on Clinton Street, riding about fifteen feet before encountering a parked car. Our bikes crash into the car. The driver is not amused to see a bunch of explorers pull out magnifying glasses in order to analyze what exactly is obstructing our designated lane.

"What are you doing? Don't touch my car!" the driver screams.

"What is this and what is it doing parked in a bike lane?" I ask.

"It does not look like a bike," notes Monica. A few of us inspect the car, crawling under it, before careening away, feeling a sense of pleasure at simply facing a driver in the solidarity of a group of friends and fellow riders. Huizinga suggests that a tension and release is part of the embodied experience of play (Huizinga, 1950). It certainly feels that way as we navigate between construction, cars, and people in the lanes. "The ideal public space for play promotes innovation, experimentation, the transformation of categories, and the renegotiation of boundaries," notes Kenneth Tucker (Tucker, 2012, 83). While bike lanes may not be ideal places for play, they are public spaces. Through ludic adventures, this group of cyclists temporarily transform these contested spaces into places of health, hope, and possibility for a sustainable city where we daydream and imagine something else (Huizinga; Morreall). Sadly, temporary autonomous zones rarely last. The regular returns to the fore and the city feels more and more like a shopping mall.

On the morning of November 2, 2015, this group of cycling advocates from Public Space Party take part in another ride, explicitly setting out to address the issue of cars illegally parked in bike lanes. The city of New York had recently celebrated the installation of more than 1,000 miles of bike lanes, but they were often impeded by motor vehicles, all too often police vehicles, flouting the law.

The cyclists meet in Fort Greene Park, where we talk about the greatest hindrance to safe cycling in New York City and what is needed to be done about it. While the city has laid out a Vision Zero safety program aimed at reducing traffic fatalities to zero, lack of enforcement of traffic violations in bike lanes impedes these steps forward, creating unsafe riding conditions. The cyclists head out to the busy corner of Hoyt Street and Schermerhorn Street in Boerum Hill, where multiple police vehicles are double-parked in bike lanes across the street.

Carrying air horns and wearing colorful clothes, cyclists crash into the cars parked in the bike lanes, holding out signs declaring, "Warning: Cop in Bike Lane!" and calling 311, and reporting bike lanes illegally blocked by NYPD vehicles, including outside of NYPD precincts.

The Rules of the City of New York, RCNY § 4–08 (e)(9) plainly state, "It is against the law to park, stand or stop within or otherwise obstruct bike lanes." Nonetheless, police vehicles are parked in bike lanes—from Schermerhorn Street, to Jay Street, to Coney Island, to Sixth Avenue—all over the city. On Schermerhorn Street, the police go as far as painting their own parking spots over the bike lane.

Throughout the action, PSP draws attention to this illegal and dangerous practice by the NYPD, and to how it relates to the greater culture of lawlessness in the city's police department. Six police cars parked in a bike lane are given a PSP "Bike Lane Parking Ticket," reminding them of NYC traffic rules.

At the corner of Hoyt Street and Schermerhorn Street in Boerum Hill police officers acknowledge they are in violation of the law. Asked why they were not informing other motorists double-parked there not to park in the bike lanes, they explain that it is a lot of work to do so. They promise to do more in the future, however. Other police are less interested in taking part in a conversation and walk off.

"Impunity is a key ingredient in the police violence and malfeasance being outed now in social media," notes PSP activist Owen Crowley on November 15.

This is a practice that I witness almost daily. Police cars running red lights without cause, personal cars parked illegally and encroaching into the street in front of police stations, police cars parked or standing in bike lanes. This creates hazards for pedestrians, cyclists, and civilian drivers. On top of that, it is an exercise that reinforces a culture in which police are above the law.

The police occupy a unique place in this space, as both referees enforcing the rules and as inverters breaking their own rules, ignoring the rules and enforcing the rules as they see fit. Getting police cars out of bike lanes is an essential first step in Vision Zero.

"Out of the bike lanes, into the streets," cyclists declare riding down Jay Street, talking with car drivers parked in bike lanes. Many are unaware of the danger posed by their actions. Throughout the ride, cyclists thank us for what we are doing. Others talk about doing something again if the city fails to cope with the problem.

Of course, this was not the first bike lane liberation ride for all of us. Ten years earlier, we had started these rides when the city was first laying out its bike lane program. Back in 2005, the city was a year into the crackdown on Critical Mass group rides that took place the last Friday of every month. Part of the purpose of the bike lane liberation rides was organizing a fun and meaningful group ride after Critical Mass became overly policed. Over the years, we create a mythology and storyline of the bike lanes, using the streets as places for theater, graffiti, agitprop, and public performance. Sometimes we borrow from the Surrealists and Situationists on our rides, remapping the fading bike lanes of the city with chalk, in our twenty-first-century model of *detournement*. I find myself quoting Herbert Marcuse as we pedal, suggesting there has to be more to urban life than a means of necessity. Our wanderings throughout the city, beyond work, have to mean something (Shepard, 2011). We had to be able to get there.

Pedestrians and cyclists are killed every thirty-six hours in New York City; 265 lives were lost to traffic violence in 2014, more than in comparable locales such as Amsterdam, where only six cyclists are killed a year, on average; conversely twenty-eight cyclists were killed by cars in New York in 2019 (Fitzsimmons, 2020; Orange, 2013). Groups such as Right of Way and Families for Safe Streets have pointed to a more urgent cycling activism. While cyclists view the bike lanes as public spaces, offering the sorts of eyes on the streets that Jane Jacobs applauded, the NYPD seems to follow Robert Moses' playbook, clogging the bike lanes with cars, emblems of an outmoded model of urbanism framed around automobiles, rather than nonpolluting transportation and connectivity.

This was most certainly the case on our third bike lane ride in November 2015. A group of us met on Jay Street and Myrtle Avenue. Bike lanes are filled with cars parked all along the street, as we get ready for our ride. A few of us conducted radio interviews before we started riding. "We get no respect," Dulcie laments. "It's like Rodney Dangerfield. We are doing this to save lives." She should know. On August 7, 2014, she was struck and badly injured by a car. "There have been eleven deaths since Halloween," she explains, asking us to attend the Ride of Remembrance that Sunday at noon at City Hall. The point of the action was to ignite a conversation, reminding police and others that their actions count. "It sends a message," notes Josh Bisker, another ride participant. "This is a reminder to police. We are not asking them to punish people. We are asking them to remind people to act responsibly." Riders were asking the police to set an example that laws matter and not demonstrate selective enforcement of laws they do or do not prefer. Carrying signs declaring "If You See Something, Say Something about Cars or Even Garbage Dumpsters in Bike Lanes," we ride out to the corner of Dekalb Avenue and Classon Avenue, where police park every day, along with their garbage dumpster. On arrival at the location we find, sure enough, the front of a police car stretched across the bike lane. And it is not alone. Several other police cars, as well as two garbage dumpsters, clog the bike lane. Cyclist after cyclist confirms the point, swerving away from the police car into the path of just the kind of speeding cars that hit Dulcie. Police cars have been blocking this bike lane since 2008. The police have little to say about it, except that they want their own parking spaces.

The intersection of Dekalb and Classon is also the home of the 88th Precinct. We see a few police walking inside and ask if they have a minute to talk with us. Two walk inside without acknowledging our question.

"Is this a police matter?" asks another one.

"Yes, it has to do with health and traffic laws."

She walks inside. We see several police inside the vestibule, looking out at us. After a few minutes, out walk two police who warn us not to block the egress to the building or we will be arrested. Several of us ask about police blocking the bike lane. At this point, the police begin to raise their voices, noting they really do not care. "If you block this you will be arrested!" they scream at us.

"They [the police] apparently care about obstructions but only from one point of view," notes Josh, laughing. "That was me being threatened with arrest for asking about a police matter."

Walking out, we ride up to the dumpster which has long sat on the bike lane. A few of us give it a push, to try to get the dumpster out of the lane, which we eventually do.

"If you move the dumpster, that can damage the cars," two police warn, clearly annoyed at everyone.

"Moving that Dekalb dumpster out of the bike lane with our bodies," says Josh, "[was a] great image. Everyone hates that thing being there, and months of arguments about it came down to us using our shoulders to move it. And either a cop or someone who was working at the precinct yelled, 'Fuck you, you're an asshole' at us. Unreal. Proud to be a streets #activist!"

"I had a beautiful dream a month ago," confesses Atchu! of the Occupy Revolutionary Games Working group, "having absolutely no roads for cars anymore, an amazing subway network only, and above the ground, bike lanes, trees, art-play spaces, homes, grandpa shops." Many of us have had those dreams.

As the city encounters more and more of the effects of global warming, including floods, hurricanes, diseases, and congestion, nonpolluting transportation offers hope and an image of a different, more sustainable model of urbanism. Bikes we used to play with as kids offer a means with which to transform cities, making them better spaces. Each ride helps us rethink what streets are there for. "Play mediates social practices and creates new spaces for rethinking and experiencing social life. It is intertwined with fantasy and imagination. . . . This playfulness creates not just new subject positions but also novel forms of communication and ways of experiencing the world" (Tucker, 2012, 83). In other words, unlike work, ludic social action helps us engage in nonalienating experience as we attempt to turn the hegemonic system of traffic flow, parking, cars, and fossil fuels on its head and to make way for a more sustainable urbanism.

CONCLUSION

On August 31, 2020, cars lost the right of way on Jay Street. "City transit honchos debuted their newest busway project on Jay Street on Monday, clearing the usually-busy thoroughfare of car traffic in favor of bikes and public transportation," writes Kevin Duggan (2020), of the *Brooklyn Paper*. That day, I rode through and found the space to be as congested as ever. Trucks and delivery vehicles filled the street, with no visible difference, despite the call from the city. "The Department of Transportation closed off 0.4 miles of the roadway between Livingston and Tillary streets to through-traffic for cars starting Aug. 31 between 7 am and 7 pm on weekdays, in order to speed up travel times for buses, trucks, drop-offs, and cyclists," says Duggan.

Still, the city is moving in favor of public transportation and nonpolluting transportation (Colon, 2020).

There is certainly an "all the world's a stage" quality to the naked bike rides, poetry events, and performances described in this chapter; from this lens, we really are all players, as friends become actors capable of acting up together. But to what end? Here a festive spirit of exhilarating entertainment blends with a political agenda aimed at progressive political change. The aim is to move spectators to join in the fun, to become part of the concrete action of social change (Ornstein, 1998, xiv–xv, 6–9). Each of the projects described in this chapter suggest there are ways to imagine alternatives. They repudiate while offering something else, pointing to ways of liberating the imagination in favor of affect and care. Here, humor is a resource for social movement engagement, adding vitality to the process of social change. It creates spaces for players to practice nonalienating humanity, connecting with each other, and experimenting with new ways of building community outside of reified ways living and being. Each bike ride engages a clash between social forces, with one side in favor of a social order based around automotive transportation, suburban space, and social control, conflicting with another supporting the "eyes on the streets" Jane Jacobs described, as a city open to multiple points of view (Jacobs, 1992; Mitchell, 2003). Here, everyone is invited into a dialogue about community building, favoring multiple points of view. The model is open to all to take part. And quite often police and onlookers do take part. Sometimes they disagree, engaging in a theater of domination, arresting or siding with authorities. Often they become involved in a larger dialogue.

While play certainly has its limitations, and is indeed frowned upon by many involved in contemporary organizing, for others it helps us expand social networks and participatory politics, making entry easy and fun (Chayko 2008; Shepard, 2011). In their own often modest way, games, pranks, and the social actions described herein help open up creative spaces and ways of rethinking repressive social systems and mechanisms of social control. In order to find space on a stage increasingly dominated by uniformed bodies fixated on crowd control, street theater and activist performance offers a creative, fluid alternative.

Certainly, there are other noncompetitive games to play. Witnessing the horrors of World War I, the Surrealists learned this. But can we? Can we laugh at both those in power and ourselves? With a little humor, we are all invited to change the rules of the game. Each ride or poem described here invites participants into a dialectical crash of opposites, of clashing forces. Studying the dialectics of nature, Friedrich Engels concentrated on relationships between and within these opposing constellations—"love and hate," "good and bad," and "identity and difference." He asserted that those forces that appear as opposites are less independent of each other than imagined and are actually joined within internal relations (Ollman, 1976, 55).

John Beckman (2014, xiii) suggests that an abiding spirit of fun, "so popular among Americans, can make even the scariest social differences exciting; it can bring even the bitterest adversaries into a state of feverous harmony." Such interactions transform social experience. "For conflict is the active ingredient in fun. Risk, transgression, mockery, rebellion, these are the revving motors of fun," argues Beckman (2014, xiii). Here, play reminds us of other ways of being, of creating space, and of opening conversations with difference. "At even the diciest moments in history the people's rebellion has strengthened democracy. It has allowed people to form close bonds in spite of prejudices, rivalries, and laws," argues Beckman (2014, xiv). The living theater of the city connects us all in this performance.

Just as Living Theater performances of *Paradise Now* ended with the audience in the street, the public space party Judith Malina imagined, Jane Jacobs described, and the activists here perform compels us to see that the city works best when it is created by and for everyone in a public commons. The use of playful interventions helps satirize the limits of the rational mode of politics, simultaneously offering alternatives built around community organizing, autonomous movements, affinity groups, friendship networks, civic participation, creativity, social action, and flow. In this way, ludic activity serves as a form of pleasure activism, in which social Eros becomes a way to bring about an image of a world we hope to create, full of humor, poetry, health, pleasure, and active engagement. After all, the living theater of the streets is most vital when everyone takes part in the performance.

NOTES

1. As early as June 4, 1947, Judith Malina (1984) wrote in her diary: "While I was waiting for Julian to return from his Sierra adventure last summer it was to Lola, my old schoolmate from Piscator's, in whom I confided all the earliest plans for the Living Theater, and with whom I shared the dreams of the most important work of my life, for which I am now preparing."

2. There is, indeed, a long tradition in left-wing politics that treats politics as a dour, sober consideration of interests, ends, and policy solutions. This approach is highly cognitive and calculated. It assumes political decisions should be made using cost-benefit analysis rather than emotions (Goodwin et al., 2001).

3. Some 264 bikers were arrested for participating in the Critical Mass community ride on August 27, 2004, a few days before the Republican National Convention; within the week 1,800 people were arrested. After that ride, which was the culmination of a near-decade of bike and public space activism, police shadowed every Critical Mass event, sapping the joy and spontaneity out of them at least in New York. For a while there, the Critical Mass had become a sort of Temporary Autonomous Zone (TAZ) here, subject to its own limitations. The TAZ had become a primary

image for the movement of movements. Yet, even Hakim Bey was aware of its limitations. He explained, "As soon as the TAZ is named (represented, mediated), it must vanish, it will vanish, leaving behind it an empty husk, only to spring up again somewhere else, once again invisible because indefinable in terms of the Spectacle" (Bey, 1991, 101). By 2019, 2020, the rides were back, with more and more participants screaming, "Black Lives Matter!"

4. "Each 'plateau' is an orchestration of crashing bricks extracted from a variety of disciplinary edifices," notes Brian Massumi in his foreword to *A Thousand Plateaus*. "They carry traces of their former emplacement, which give them a spin defining the arc of their vector. The vectors are meant to converge at a volatile juncture, but one that is sustained, as an open equilibrium of moving parts each with its own trajectory" (Massumi, 1987, x).

Chapter 14

Notes and Conclusion from the Global Climate March to Paris: Dystopia versus Utopia in Dialectical Urban Activism

Much of this story has been about conflicts over public space, between remembering and forgetting, repression and expression, gardens and housing, social control and ludic expression, use and exchange. It has traced an embodied model of urbanism transforming cities, one community garden, squat, bike lane, and mutual aid project at a time. Through the living theater of the city, we've considered stories of people and public spaces and their relationship to the ever-shifting landscape of the city. Through DIY activism, we can all participate. The future of cities depends on all of us taking part in a shift in the way we engage, consume, compost, travel, create homes, support health, and live. Conversely, the future of the world depends on cities finding solutions.

In this dialectic, Friederick Engels suggests, there is no "either or"; rather, a new story takes shape as a "this and" (Ollman, 1976, 56). Here, movement narratives intersect and connect, birthing new stories. Such thinking helps us consider what the collisions and interconnections of opposites that are such a part of urban life can mean about how we relate to each other and the spaces in which we live. Throughout these stories about gardens and homes, nonpolluting transportation and labor, public spaces, and the ongoing "mutual interaction" between these pieces of the body of the city, when one thing shifts, a building rises or falls, a commons becomes a restaurant, or a new garden is born, the internal relations between them are altered (Ollman, 1976, 15, 17). Everything is dependent on everything else in this ever-flowing city. Cities play a distinct role in the history of capitalism. They were the place for its birth and the capital accumulation strangling them. They are also spaces for the class struggle bearing art and housing, work, and social movements (Merrifield, 2014, 1). They might also be the spaces where we reinvent ourselves, as we move toward—hopefully toward a new model of sustainable urbanism. After all, everything is changing. Nothing is the same. We are evolving. "I don't think we should change the book yet," notes Bertell Oll-man (2016). "There has to be space for that crack in the ceiling. The hope for something, light pouring in for something else. The world is changing. Even the climate is changing—not just nature—but we need a change in interaction between ecology and human beings." Ollman and others, such as Joel Kovel (2007), suggest the enemy of nature is capitalism. The question is, what will it become as tides rise and fires rage? And how can cities sustain themselves? Are there alternative storylines? And how can the notions of dialectal activism explored here broaden our thinking? These are questions we have traced throughout these chapters. They've propelled the activism and stories of this project. As we conclude, more questions open up.

TOWARDS A COUNTER-VORTEX

Shortly before I left for the World Climate Change Conference 2015, or COP21, in December 2015 in Paris, I had a conversation with garden historian and writer Bill Weinberg, whose story is traced throughout these pages. We talked about gardens and housing and the collisions between solutions and catastrophe, utopia and dystopia, regeneration and decay seen in cities. Touring the community gardens and squats of Alphabet City, he revels in the innovation seen there. "But at the same time, you've also got these super-development luxury projects which are going on all over the city. Literally, they want to build a mile-high skyscraper in Abu Dhabi. The opposite trajectory is still going full steam ahead. And so, we're still a little bit of a counter-vortex. Generally, all of civilization is going down into this big vortex, deeper into unsustainability, just heading toward collapse into ecological and social hell, social fragmentation and collapse. And people who are creating bio-swales, we are counter-vortices, creating a little bit of a vortex going in the opposite direction, toward sustainability, toward community, toward survival, toward authentic culture. And creating a little bit of a counter-tendency to the general tendency toward collapse. And maybe instead of a collapse into social and ecological hell, we can have a *controlled collapse,* an induced implosion of the fossil fuel industry. That's what needs to happen. Rather than going full speed ahead with the hubris of building mile-high skyscrapers and super highways—which is going to lead to an *un*-induced implosion, a collapse into ecological hell and social dystopia—we need to have an induced implosion, where we can actually *intentionally* scale back the juggernaut and make things more human-scale and more sustainable, so as to avoid the collapse happening on terms other than our own, which is not going to be pretty." All over the world, people are talking about a degrowth movement.

Sitting there with Weinberg, I make the point that Homo sapiens have only been around for a short period of geological time. By most accounts, our cousins the Neanderthals died off some 40,000 ago—possibly because it appears they failed to adapt to a changing world. Walking through Spain along the Camino de Santiago, we made a trip to Atapapuerca, where they discovered human descendants from just 48,000 years ago. These relics remind us a lot came before the Homo sapiens and will probably come afterward. Nature has long had ways of coping with our limitations.

"And we've done an awful lot of damage," Weinberg points out. "People always say the Sahara used to be a forest, etc. Well yeah, but obviously the worldwide ecological destruction has gotten exponentially more dramatic just in the last 100, or 150, since the industrial revolution. And now it's just getting refined to a whole other level with biotech and cybernetics and so on. There is just no comparison to what it was. Just compare what has been happening in the last 150 years—which is really a mere blink in the evolutionary sense. It's just amazing how much we've lost in such a short period. Forests, fisheries, biodiversity, carbon in the atmosphere—it's just mind-boggling how much we've fucked things up in such a short span of time. And people still have this idea—although less and less all the time—that it's sustainable, that we can go on doing this. The World Bank just issued a statement that global extreme poverty has dropped below 10 percent for the first time. Well, maybe it has. But is it sustainable? Economic growth is based on sucking oil out of the ground and pulling minerals out of the earth and destroying forests—it's not sustainable. We are borrowing from the future."

As we talk, Weinberg and I contemplate alternative storylines for this human narrative. "You can't predict the future in terms of details with certainty, but you can predict the future in terms of general trends with a reasonable degree of accuracy," Weinberg follows. "We are already committed to climate change. The carbon in our atmosphere is not coming out. It's a question of *how much* climate change and what we are going to do about it? You can predict that climate change is going to continue. Even if we stopped using fossil fuels tomorrow, we'd still be committed to generations of climate change. That's where it's incumbent upon us to try to provide compelling examples, like bioswales, and to keep alive the history of struggles which have been waged to make those examples possible, to make the existence of these alternatives possible, and to provide some intellectual clarity as to what it's going to take to implement meaningful solutions, and to repudiate the free-market utopianism that we can keep on going with market-driven economic growth forever and get out of global poverty through endless economic growth. I can predict that's not going to work. I feel confident in that."

Weinberg's thoughts linger as I make plans to go to Paris. I thought about my younger brother's master's paper at the London School of Economics, which suggested capitalist growth is carcinogenic. They wouldn't entertain it. That was twenty-five years prior. Today such comparisons are not uncommon. Still, solutions are everywhere. It's a dialogue many would be having in Paris.

COP21

I bought tickets well before the November 13, 2015, terror attacks in Paris. They radically altered the context of the COP21 climate conference, creating a set of dueling crises, with environmental and terrorist concerns forming a sort of double helix, cataclysmic images of people fighting over resources and armed guards mining the barricades between rich and poor. It is like a scene from a postapocalyptic science-fiction movie. "This might be the situation in France during the cop 21," says Paris activist John Jordan on Facebook on November 17, 2015, responding to the news that the protests had been canceled by the French government. "Let's put all our creativity into think-ing what to do," suggests Jordan. "How to continue to resist the real state of emergency whose scale is the size of the sea, the sky and the soils. . . . The future will be one of authoritarian governments trying to deal with the front of terror on one hand and social and ecological collapse on the other, we can chose to accept their states of emergencies or show that this is a time for the opposite of war and crack downs on civil liberties, this is a time to stand for justice and for real democracy to arise." With the state taking away our free-doms to protect us, my friend and colleague Greg Smithsimon, who moved to Paris for the year, comments: "For those of you wondering, how long does it take for a government to use a state of emergency as an excuse to cancel protests that have nothing to do with emergency, wait no longer. The answer is four days."

On November 18, Naomi Klein (2015) follows with a story in *The New Yorker* suggesting, "Major shocks like the Paris attacks are awfully good at changing the subject. But what if we decided to not let it happen? What if, instead of changing the subject, we deepened the discussion of climate change and expanded the range of solutions, which are fundamental for real human security? What if, instead of being pushed aside in the name of war, climate action took center stage as the planet's best hope for peace?"

In his day, Walter Benjamin lived through a different set of crises, their abstractions reverberating with us today. In his "Theses on the Philosophy of History," Benjamin (1968, 257–58) suggests: "The tradition of the oppressed teaches us that the 'state of emergency' in which we live is not the exception but the rule. We must attain to a conception of history that is in keeping with this insight. Then we shall clearly realize that it is our task to bring about a real state of emergency." Towering above it all is "the angel of history," writes Benjamin, tapping into a profoundly un-Marxist secularized version of Messianic Judaism, combined with a dialectical analysis. "His face is turned toward the past. Where we perceive a chain of events, he sees one catastrophe which keeps piling wreckage upon wreckage and hurls it in front of his feet. The angel would like to stay, awaken the dead, and make whole what has been smashed. But a storm is blowing from paradise; it has got caught in his wings." Violence is everywhere, so the angel can no longer get close. "The storm irresistibly piles him into the future to which his neck is turned, while the pile of wreckage grows skyward. This storm is what we call progress" (257–58). The storm blows from paradise. Does progress blow us away?

Flying into Paris, it feels like I am arriving at this pile of wreckage, looking like anything but progress. Armed guards and police are everywhere. Makeshift memorials are up all over for people who were killed in November. People just stand looking at the images of the bicycle locked outside whose rider never returned from the Bataclan or a photo of a friend's face accompanied by a long-burned-out candle. At the memorial at Republique, someone has wheat pasted a photo of two lovers kissing in black and white. Like the famous street photography, this is a familiar image here; it is printed all over the city. Everyone hopes Paris can be a place where we can make love, not war. As I arrive, doors are being kicked in, with arrests under the auspices of the state of emergency. Even George Bush did not ban protest after 9/11 (although he did arrest those who did so at his events). Yet, this is the case in Paris, where all protests had been banned, opening a striking set of contrasts between those calling for the world to cope with the climate crisis and those reeling from the terrorist bombings. More and more of us see these dueling crises as part of one glaring threat to a shifting global ecology and its spiraling unintended consequences, including floods, tsunamis, migration crises, pandemics, and escalating tensions between people and their natural homes. There is no planet B, note climate activists. While science-fiction movies offer plotlines for us colonizing other planets, most of us would rather stay here and make it work ourselves for our children's children. That's why we came to Paris.

Walking through the streets, I find myself thinking of Benjamin, just as I had to begin the story. Keenly aware of the violence and contradictions of his era, Walter Benjamin remained fixated with the high and low culture of his Paris. He is said to have wanted to leave the decadence and exploitation of the city and be converted, just not today (Berman, 1982, 146). The pulse of the city thrives in just such a jazz-like urban dialectic, a contrast between the tragic and comic elements of life. The most ludic of dialecticians, he suggested we recognize the game-like dimensions of living. This play takes place within a tragicomic stage, offering a useful intermediating space between what is real and what is fantasy, between liberation and repression, possibility and pain (Marcuse, 1955). "The class struggle," writes Benjamin (1968, 255), "manifest themselves in this struggle as courage, humor, cunning, and fortitude." He irreverently calls into question official versions of victories and successes, the emergencies of the past, present, and future. In the same way, activists in Paris are trying to highlight these tragicomic dynamics. This is the story of a few of my experiences in Paris, dancing with the present as "true pictures of the past flit by" (Benjamin, 1968, 255).

Sitting in jail a few weeks prior with members of the Professional Staff Congress, my union, I was killing time talking about Paris. Someone says that several union labor activists were going and I should hook up with them. In between emails, Sean Sweeney, director of International Program for Labor, Climate and Environment, invited me to an event taking place during the COP21. "You are on a special guest list for tomorrow's night's event with Jeremy Corbyn and Naomi Klein, at Salle Olympe de Gouges."

After watching the first week of COP21 from New York, cheering for activists who fought the state of emergency decree from the French government prohibiting public assembly, I arrive on Sunday. The scenes of Paris look like Seattle, tear gas and riot police clashing with those in the streets asking the world to take notice. There seem to be a lot of terrorist attacks whenever we plan to get together for big movement escalating events. It happened in September 2001 with the International Monetary Fund (IMF) protests planned in DC, which were canceled. And it was happening now. Activists had been on the streets all week. Others had been preemptively arrested and held for the duration of the conference.

"The Manifestation is a right," notes my host's amiable son when I arrive in Paris, looking out at the Pompidou where my friends were staying. After greetings with the family and getting settled, Greg and I head out to the Festival of Alternatives at Marie de Marteuil.

Full of images of energy bikes and organic farming, the festival is terrific. The first person we run into is Andrew Boyd, our longtime friend from movements past and future in NYC. He is busy talking about the Climate Ribbon, a piece of visual art used to engage audiences about what they might lose as a result of climate change. I had seen it the year before at the end of the People's Climate March. Simple and interactive, people are drawn to it. On my ribbon, I post a message about the Brooklyn tides ebbing to and from our waterfront home. Greg, my Brooklyn neighbor, mentioned our kids and the homes we've created along the waterfront.

We stumble into Reverend Donna Schaper from Judson Memorial Church, who is busy taking in interfaith events throughout the city. "The cops were rough on Saturday," she says. I hear her preach every other Sunday. Standing there, she notes, "Here at COP21 there is a youthful spirit . . . a palpable sense of hope. . . . Whether the subject is a green bond for large cities or riding a bicycle so that you can charge your cell phone or blend your free smoothie, the spirit has that vibe, that playful spirit of early hope. . . . Beautiful, edible oyster mushrooms. . . . I'm not going all the way to hope . . . But I am feeling resilient."

On Monday, Greg and I stroll out to catch the Naomi Klein talk: "Now Is Not the Time for Small Steps: *Solutions to the Climate Crisis and the Role of Trade Unions.*" I have always had an ambivalent relationship with labor, especially after the movement repeatedly benefits from the efforts of anarchists in Seattle and Occupy, who help it gain traction, before inevitably disavowing the radicals who put wind back in their sails, even if for a moment. The pattern repeats and repeats itself.

"Labor is full of zombies," adds a man standing behind me at the talk. "But they are the only real chance, the real possibility we have for a change in class consciousness. But they are full of fuddy duddies, with no alternate thinking to Blairism," he pontificates.

Over the last few years, I have worked fighting the politics of austerity on the one hand and in support of a robust urban ecology on the other. In Paris, I come to see both movements as interconnected, with trade unions and environmental activists endeavoring to support a vibrant public commons for all.

Then British labor leader Jeremy Corbyn strikes a qualitatively different chord, linking labor and environmental issues in his address to the crowd, outlining the need for a qualitative expansion of ownership of the means of production of energy, with renewables and solar, creating jobs, rethinking energy policy, and expanding a conversation about what we can and cannot do. "Humankind is capable of amazing things, if we find solidarity with the earth, connect with each other, and expand our imagination."

What will the future look like if we connect all these pieces? If we continue at our current pace of increasing temperatures up by seven degrees, we will certainly be looking at more wars and violence, floods and hurricanes, and droughts and floods. After the disasters, who helps? asks Corbyn—the public sector, nurses, social workers, firemen, and so on. The time to cut the public sector is not now. The room roars in applause. If we watch climate change grow, we will see more fights, floods, war, droughts, leaving waves of refugees. Let's deal with these issues. Don't blame the victims. Defend forests that provide carbon cover. Chico Mendez fought to save forests and humanity itself. Let's learn from his fight for humanity. What do we want the world to look like, he wonders, a place with biodiversity and equality? This is a place with equality, where people can breathe clean air and drink clean water, a world of peace and security. Governments have a duty to preserve our common good. Move beyond blame to solutions. So, how do we get this world? Through a just transition to work. Inequality is a wrong waste of our resources. Be inclusive of the working class. Democratize energy ownership within our sustainable limits, so our kids' kids have a world to grow up and thrive in.

He ends with a quote by Arundhati Roy: "Another world is not only possible, she is on her way. On a quiet day, I can hear her breathing."

Naomi Klein follows outlining what is at stake. What is the role of the trade union movement in the climate movement, she wonders? Without seeing the final language, she argues the COP21 deal will lead us to a three degree Celsius rise in temperatures, not less than two degrees. We need 1.5 degrees to survive, not three or four. We are already living in the era of dangerous warming. We are living it. The deal that will pass will steamroll over redlines, expanding the threat to the planet. On December 12, activists will be on the streets peacefully protesting, challenging the ban on protests. Liberty means more than football and markets. It means a diversity of approaches. The right to protest is vital to all wins past and present. As we join them, we must say yes to what our world can look like. It can be more than a life of climate chaos, racism, and austerity. We need to think big, stepping beyond our crisis of imagination. We need to imagine a post-carbon economy, she declares, referring to the "Leap Manifesto," a document drafted by climate activists including herself calling for Canada to divest from fossil fuels. The climate crisis hit at a time of neoliberal economics. We saw the implications when Hurricane Katrina hit New Orleans. Because of neglect, the levees could not hold, reflecting the crumbling infrastructure of disinvestment in cities. The storm highlighted a "we cannot" sense of tolerated incompetence among those in government, more than willing to walk away from problems as people starve and suffer. Shock doctrine followed; homes were torn down to make way for new redevelopment, displacing bodies and families who'd been there for generations. This is how our system copes with storms and climate chaos, explains Klein. Hence, the slogan system change and not climate change. We need public sector workers in place who are trained and ready to deal with problems. Yet, for them to be there, we need to fight the ill logic of austerity. So, when we talk about coping with climate change, we also have to be countering narratives of austerity. This means fighting the IMF. It means challenging the incoherent logic of scarcity.

The alternative is renewables. Fight to see the connections, pleads Klein. Invest in infrastructure. Expand the non-carbon economy. These are social workers and nurses. This is health care. These are public sector workers. This is a healthy workforce. This is a post-carbon future. Here, we care for the earth and each other. Leave it in the ground. Stop the extraction of oil. Cut corporate welfare. Transition is inevitable, justice is not, Klein acknowledges. We are going to have to fight for this better world. We need energy justice. The climate movement needs to beat back the carbon infrastructure. Build a new economy, instead of protecting the old one. Try something new. Now is not the time for small steps. It's time for bold steps to leap forward.

The room gives Klein a rousing applause.

I have always been weary of the rhetoric of "leaps" and "revolution." The Chinese Great Leap Forward in the 1950s left millions dead. In our ecosocial transition, I don't want to miss a crop cycle. In this revolution, I hope no one loses a head.

Several of the speakers on the panel suggest using language around a just transition, not a great leap forward. Trade unions need to be a part of the just transition. The public sector has to be a part of that just transition. We need government to act. Austerity is a sham. If the earth was a bank, we would have saved it by now, a labor activist concludes.

An organizer representing nurses in New York stands up to talk about the campaign to ban fracking in their state. There, nurses went out and educated their workers about the health impacts of fracking, joining movements and mobilizing a half a million people to participate in the People's Climate March. Listening to her talk, I had a flashback to action after action of banner drops and rallies against fracking. For years, we fought fracking, going to rallies and organizing environmental awareness bike tours, zaps, and actions, as the campaign to ban fracking expanded. Looking at the win from December 2014, the message was clear: we have to imagine a new, more sustainable future for New York, as an urban ecology that moves beyond quarterly profit reports and short-term gains. This is a civil society movement expanding solidarity, nature defending itself. Activists repeat this refrain all week long.

During the question and answer session, Klein and several others talk about the need for a new kind of thinking shifting from an expansion to a regeneration point of view. Moving from monoculture to support for biodiversity has to be an opportunity, not a threat. And trade unions have to be a part of this thinking. The fight for a sustainable world has to be an opening for new thinking about organizing, work, and development.

Is it possible to avoid catastrophe? It is not easy to know. No one can predict. A dialectic of utopian versus dystopian images of the future pervade conversations here. Many see these as last days; others imagine a different kind of relationship between humans and the earth. Klein and company offer a compelling counter-narrative. After all, conversations about the apocalypse are as old as history; people have been predicting it at least since Thucydides. Today these anxieties are built into the very marketing of disaster capitalism, explains Klein. "One shouldn't underestimate the craving for apocalypse," note the Invisible Committee (2015, 35) in their tome *To Our Friends*, "the lust for Armageddon that permeates the epoch." It's been "totally absorbed by capital" (Invisible Committee, 2015, 36). In Paris, cultural capital was contested terrain.

TUESDAY—FOSSIL FUEL OUT OF CULTURE

The days in Paris are amazing, with late-night conversations and stories and discussions. On Tuesday, I head out for prop making with my friends from Not An Alternative, Liberate Tate, and BP or Not BP, walking through the rain to the meeting spot across town. There, people were busy making umbrellas for the big action at the Louvre the next day.

"The police are putting up barriers every day," notes Jason.

The morning is an encounter with generations of protest cultures. There is a nervous energy of collaborating with new people or people who do not know who you are. Certain voices are defensive, some are more open. But we hang out, milling around the dark meeting space, a hundred of us looking for a way to contribute the best way we can.

Beka and Chris call for a short meeting around 1:30. So, we all circle up, introduce ourselves, and start a conversation about ways to get fossil fuel money—oil sponsorship—out of cultural institutions. Chris from BP or Not BP points out the gallery at the Louvre is sponsored by Total, an oil company. Activists from around the world are in the room. We talk about roles people can take. The scenario is to get close to the pyramid and open umbrellas that say, "Fossil Fuels out of Culture," in front of the Louvre and have the picture blasted out to the world. It's a simple action. There are multiple roles we can all take, including tweeting out photos, scouting, choreography, or actually carrying an umbrella. I love the action plan and our message. The bills we plan to drop in the museum remind: "Dear Louvre, When Total sponsors you, you sponsor Total. Don't sponsor climate chaos." To pull off the action, we have to get the right shot. If we can't get inside one of the two lines of barricades, we are going to have to go outside to get the shot. But we have to get it.

The activists will meet at 9:30 am the next day, take the subway to Tuileries Metro, come in through the garden, not the arch, and meet. The team includes twenty-one umbrellas, eight ushers to clear the space, two stage directors, and Chris to call for the umbrellas to open up to reveal our message. But will we get in to get to the pyramid? I volunteer to be a stage director. Several of us go out to the Louvre to plan. There is really no bad shot at the Louvre. But we'd like to get past the first line of barricades just outside the security check. Ideally, everyone will enter around 11 am for the noon action. Yet, there is no consensus about a plan. Finishing scouting, I go stroll through the epic city, taking in the moody views in the rain.

At 7 pm, I make my way to a session called "Oil Out of Culture," at Les Laboratoires D'Aubervillliers with several of the groups who had been planning the action all morning.

Mel Evans and Gavin Grindon describe the successful Liberate Tate campaign to force the Tate museum on the Thames to turn away from fossil fuel sponsorship. Through a series of guerilla actions, this group turned the grand entrance of the museum into a living theater for performance and questions about sponsorship, mission, and purpose. On one occasion, activists stayed all night, setting up a compost loo in the museum. On another, they poured molasses on the floor, imitating the BP oil spill and highlighting the messy relationship between its sponsors and climate chaos. Just exactly how much money is the Tate getting from big oil? The group asked for a firm number. After all, oil sponsorship of culture helps add a boost of badly needed positive public relations for companies that have been polluting coastlines from Alaska to the Gulf Coast.

"If we can resist this, we can write a new future for ourselves," says Mel, the author of *Artwash: Big Oil in the Arts*.

In their own ways, each of these groups challenges the commodification of ideas and culture, positing that exchange must control art and ideas.

Chris from BP or Not BP describes the campaign to transform the British Museum into a space for theater, with performances that compelled reactions, art pushing policy changes, bridging the divide between the museum's sponsors and its obligation to the public. Recalling the financial and ecological crisis, these activists hope for a different kind of public commons.

Beka from Not an Alternative describes her group's history over the last decade in Brooklyn. The group has worked with other groups, including Picture the Homeless, to highlight the high number of vacant buildings in juxtaposition to issues of homelessness in New York City. There are more vacancies than homeless people, the group reminds the world. Yet the city refuses to accrue an accurate count. Still, gentrification rages, displacing people all over Brooklyn. The group works to ask questions about science museum donors, such as the Koch brothers, who deny climate change, working with scientists to urge museums to cut ties with climate deniers. Each of these groups supports a growing call for cultural institutions to divest from fossil fuels, while taking these institutions back from private interests. They see museums as public spaces for ideas.

"Museums tell us what it means to be human," says Beka. From the refugees to floods to rising tides, museums can and should help us come to grips with what it means to live in an era of climate change. They are here to create a space to contemplate collective action.

"Museums are liminal spaces," says Mel.

"We are unpacking bundles of history, unraveling sponsors with ties to colonialism," Chris follows. Museums are mutable, living entities. By March of 2016, BP would announce it was ending its twenty-six-year sponsorship of the Tate. The Louvre would be the following day. Or so we hoped.

WEDNESDAY—DIRECT ACTION FROM THE LOUVRE
TO NOTRE DAME

It's rainy when I leave in the morning for the big action, making it to the meeting space by 9:30. The center is buzzing with energy. People are rehearsing and singing, zipping in and out, taking calls, conspiring, and planning what to do if and when they got through security into the museum. The plan is to meet under the arch at 11 am and trickle beyond the barricades by 11:30, one or two at a time.

After a few rehearsals, we all make our way to the subway. I ride with Chihiro, a filmmaker from the Netherlands. Police cars are lined up around the museum. Men holding guns and dressed in riot gear. I walk past the barricades.

For the next hour, I'd text the other scouts who gradually trickled in. By noon, everyone was at the museum but the umbrella crew. Photographers and media are everywhere. I see friends from New York and Germany and Paris—everyone but the umbrella crew. The security is now lined up by the barricades, inspecting all bags.

"Yates was turned away," says Mark from New York. "They saw a divestment flyer in his bag and sent him away."

"Where are the umbrellas?" I ask Sumo, the other scout. "It's hard to coordinate with a big group." Adrenaline is pouring out of my ears.

Figure 14.1.   The angels of history outside the Louvre.

Source: Photo by Benjamin Shepard.

"I just got a text from Chris saying let's go with Plan B," notes Sumo. "Tell everyone. Plan B."

I wander through the crowd telling people. A policeman with a huge gun walks up to me and I zip away, telling more people as we zip out of the barricade. Many of the police follow the group of us leaving. As we go, a group of angels appear at the barricades. It's all getting weird. The crowd moves at them. Looking at them, I'm thinking of Benjamin's "angel of history" looking backward. I see one of the umbrellas just outside the barricade.

The clash between chaos and choreography can be both jarring and invigorating, exhilarating and exhausting, in these moments. I recall the IMF World Bank Meeting in 2000, the last time I took such a role, with kids in masks running to and fro, spray painting cars, and blocking police, as we tried to stay on plan for the day. I eventually gave up. No need to contain such abundance. "You gotta embrace the energy," counseled Brother Ron in that moment fifteen years prior.

Back at the Louvre, we all walk back to see the umbrellas in place.

"I guess we were their diversion," says Beka.

"Ben, you look really terrible," notes my buddy Marc, pointing out the sweat pouring off my head. It's always good to have friends around to point out when you are looking purple.

The demo works. Everyone is happy.

Wandering around among friends, I run into Chihiro, who I took the metro with to the action. I asked her about the experience. "Before getting to the pyramid there were bag inspections . . . a rush of adrenaline getting through . . . most people made it through and we could do our action in PLAN A mode." The sun is shining and we have a whole day to go. Everyone is milling around trying to figure what to do next. Some are going to have a nap or hit the general assembly later on.

"There's an action at Le Bourget!" notes a young woman from Germany. The day of actions would continue from the Louvre to the Bourget to Notre Dame. Marc and I wander off to lunch, chatting with Chihiro, who joins us. We chat about her movie and talk about striving for something smarter of this world, making new rebel friends everywhere we go. On the way out, I stumble into an elderly woman holding her newspaper. We start to chat. She asks where I am from.

"The USA," I explain.

"No, Americans are all closed minded, all the same, all conformists." She practically spits, looking at us. But we're smiling and she's smiling. I mention a few Americans who love Paris: Allen Ginsberg, William Burroughs, Nina Simone.

"Oh Americans . . . yeah you are either the worst or the best," she follows, mentioning that maybe there are some OK Americas, Noam Chomsky, for example. We wander over to lunch at La Palette on the other side of the river and we order lots of coffees. Gradually, we find our conversation taking on the destruction versus regeneration conversation permeating Paris. Chihiro talks about indigenous versus alienated relations to the land. Marc refers to the poetry of the apocalypse. And I order an éclair, listening to my smart friends.

"Don't be naïve about power," notes Chihiro. "Indigenous people live with the environment. This is the opposite of alien species who do not know how to live with the environment. Rather they are alienated from it."

"There are ways out of this clash of cultures," I chime in.

"The city is a space for alienation," she explains. "You don't know where your food comes from."

"They are also living breathing things," I add.

"They are living beyond their capacity," explains Chihiro. "We have to move beyond a destructive system, marked by trade. How can we reverse this?"

"By creating sustainable cities," I chime in.

We talk and walk and make our way to the metro. Chihiro tells me about her favorite trees, the Palinka in Chiapas. On the metro, we chat about the movement, about funders dropping the calls for action after the bombings, and the gap between the delegates and those on the street.

"AIDS activists would take it over, disrupting the conference," I suggest, referring to international AIDS meetings.

"The lack of infrastructure for these demos is a mess," explains Chihiro. "There is another dynamic," she explains. "Kids growing up and separating and letting go of childhood and being destructive, sometimes undermining these efforts."

"But there is a creative dynamic in the destruction," I chime in. Still, I agree with her sentiment about the generational oedipal struggle.

Finally, we arrive at Le Bourget where the meetings are taking place. For Chihiro, this is nauseating perverse climate politics. "The COP21 where money gets saved and land and locals are sacrificed," she says. "The whole civil society space at COP21 is nauseatingly designed for greenwashing . . . Getting some new ideas for appropriate popup actions: How about doing a flash mob of people throwing up . . . do a flash mob of people standing on the tables, taking their pants down, and start shitting. The message? 'Your politics is crap.'"

We walk by talk after talk, booth after booth. In the corner in the back, Chihiro points to a dimly lit poorly attended session, noting they are considering the need for 1.5 degree max climate change, instead of a policy that allows for 2 degrees. "You can see how much audience there is for these matters," she observes. "They are practically in the dark."

After an hour or so we leave.

"Enough of this Bourget," declares Chihiro. So we start to train back to the city, to the zone of action. Chihiro has heard about a flash mob at Notre Dame. We zip over there, meeting activists dressed in holiday garb, planning to stage a sing out about the extension of a new airport.

Nathalie, of the JEDI group, greets everyone taking part in our singing-mob action against the airport expansion NDDL. She passes out lyric sheets, inviting everyone to participate and sing. While certainly protest-themed, the vibe at Notre Dame is strikingly warm and holiday-like, as we make a joyful noise over the Seine.

Invigorated by the sing out, we read poems and stroll to the Zone Action Climatique (ZAC).

"Don't emphasize hope," cautions Chihiro. "It precludes action."

Still, out of this clash between hope and despair, utopia and apocalypse, we talk creative solutions. Take action, Chihiro explains. Climate change is a symptom of a larger problem of a system that extracts resources without putting anything back. Yet today the earth seems to be pushing back. New spaces are opening for alternate solutions. Much attention has been on predictions about resolutions to the crises of capitalism. Out of the crisis and great leaps from capital, we think of the calamities of Mao and Stalin, as well as economic crises in 1929 and 2008.

"We've had a blind faith in crises," declare the Invisible Committee (2015, 21), referring to Marxists, economists, and ecologists. "There are still Marxists who try to sell the current crisis as 'The Big One'" (21–22). It's the left's version of the Last Judgment.

After all, Rosa Luxemburg speculated that barbarism could emerge from capitalism. But what of ecosocial transition? It seems to be on everyone's mind. What is it going to be: barbarism or a just transition, a great leap forward of a human-scale shift, dystopia, apocalypse, or something brighter?

"Bring light into the darkness," Chihiro concludes, finishing a poem.

I read Laurence Ferlinghetti's "I am waiting." We are all waiting and pushing, wading through history's murky waters. That's why we are here. From the Louvre to Le Bourget to Notre Dame to the ZAC, this twelve-hour conversation has brought me through a rush of feelings, between the cops at the Louvre, the singers at Notre Dame, the crap at the trade show Le Bourget, and the abundant narratives of our stroll through Paris, the stories all connecting to each other. At the end of the evening, I tweet out a message from 350.org: "We Don't Have Another Lifetime To Wait. Tell the negotiators meeting in Paris: Listen to the demand for action echoing in the streets: keep fossil fuels in the ground. Transition to 100 percent renewable by 2050."

THURSDAY—PROP MAKING

Marc and I are in top spirits when we wake up. We'd been up chatting till 4 am. The next morning we zip out to some of the art spaces to make banners. On our way, we stroll by Republique, where people have constructed a make-shift memorial for the dead killed during the terrorist attacks. Greg and I had gone out earlier in the week to Bataclan. It is striking how open these spaces are even after the state of emergency. The city of New York took down the peace memorial at Union Square Park almost immediately after 9/11. With national political ambitions compelling him to tie our loss into a call for ven-geance, New York mayor Rudy Giuliani quickly put an end to the peace vigil there. The same cannot be said of Paris, where sign after sign calls for peace, love, and understanding. There are certainly calls for vengeance in the air, as early French election results on Sunday point out. But the memorials feel open, full of images of kissing bodies, paint, color, passion, and compassion. It is hard not to feel a tragicomic pulse in the energy of these resilient streets. Graffiti everywhere, with ideas filling the streets, Marc and I make our way to the prop-making space. A hundred people are in the room, with banners and paint, cardboard and art supplies everywhere. And there at the corner, looking at a banner, is the familiar image of David Solnit. I'd seen him every night the year before as we prepared for the People's Climate March in New York City.

He smiles and gives me a hug when I greet him, providing a welcoming orientation to the prop-making session, showing us banner materials and sug-gesting slogans, paints, and brushes. Movements thrive when they open space for us all to participate in whichever fashion we can.

Marc and I spend the afternoon working on our own banners. Looking at the slogans, I ask Nick what he thinks. The author of *The People's Art History of the United States*, he suggests we paint something declaring "I Fart in Thy General Direction" in homage to the old Monty Python gag of the French telling off King Arthur. That's just what we were talking about last night; message to the COP21: "Your politics is crap." It's in the zeitgeist. We decide to go with "Ligne Rouge, Justice Climatique/ Red Lines, Climate Justice." This is the slogan of the movement. We are drawing a red line, which you cannot cross and the world cannot cross. This is a red line, from greenwash-ing to red lines of emergency. Eventually, we start in on the next banner, joking with paint and chatting. And Nick seriously suggests, "COP21: I Fart in Your General Direction," as a protest sign. There are hundreds of signs here, many earnest. So, we follow his call. We paint our beautiful sign and go to one more meeting, stating we have to go to another meeting tomorrow at 1 at the ZAC to find out about D12. Drama and suspense is everywhere. Crusty punks are walking in and out. Big plans on the streets of Paris. Too many meetings to attend. Naomi Klein speaks to a huge crew at the ZAC as we are painting. Earlier in the day, the demonstration we were looking for the day before had actually happened. A group of some 600 activists got inside Le Bourget, zapping the meeting and reminding the delegates of our red line, that we need more than platitudes or an empty declaration of victory from the leaders. The temperature has risen by .86 degrees centigrade, and people are already dying; droughts and heat waves are already starting. It can't go any higher, activists declare, disrupting the meeting, drawing a red line through the proceedings.

As John Jordan explains, "It's also a battle over who tells the story of the outcome. Will it be governments and corporations or social movements who get to have the last word? We cannot let them declare this agreement a triumph, when in fact it will consign millions of the poorest people to death."

But what about D12? You'll find out tomorrow, they tell us.

FRIDAY—FINAL MEETING AND A FRIEND FROM NEW YORK

I sleep in, barely making it on time to the 1 pm meeting at the ZAC. On the way out of the door, I get a message from 350.org with the big plan for D12. But it is still good to be at the big meeting. There are literally thousands of people in the room, a few people speaking into mics on the stage. This is what it must have been like the night before ACT UP's "stop the church" action in 1989, I think. I've only heard of meetings this big. Humongous banners hang from the ceiling.

The red line action will take place just below the Eiffel Tower on the Avenue de la Grande Armée, with a moment of silence for victims of climate, war, and the war on the poor.

I start to walk around the side, stumbling into my old buddy Bill Talen, aka Reverend Billy, standing with Chris from BP not BP, who have collaborated together on one of the British Museum BP zaps.

The facilitator asks us to talk about what we hope will happen tomorrow and what we are worried about. We each want to create an abundant image. I sit with Billy, talking about the intersecting narratives of the week.

"Free the Disney Six," I chime in, recalling one of our favorite actions sixteen years prior. "Free the Disney Six," he follows, laughing. We talk about the story this week. There's the "the earth is going to fall apart" narrative, the dialectic of desolation versus creativity. But I think we can take a leap into abundance with biodiversity and loving each other, I chime in.

Billy follows, "In Paris, we feel the sea-change that is taking place within the souls of the activists. It is dawning on us that a revolution must take place. For the centuries that the CO2 has been rising, a middle class has been building in the imperial industrial countries. We consumers have been taught to look the other way when it comes to the violence of our businesses that our nation states press on people around the world. Now finally with climate change we can no longer do this. The other end of this colonialism, sweatshop economies, and military occupation is coming back to haunt us. Why would our governments believe that we would offer serious opposition? We never have, but we will now."

"They are banning protest, but the real threat is global warming," notes one of the facilitators. "Standing below the Arc de Triomphe, this symbol of colonialism, we will recall those lost to climate change war and the war on the poor. When you hear the thirty fog horns tomorrow, we will have a moment of silence. And then we erupt! Paris is the dance, not the end. May 2016, we shut down the fossil fuel infrastructure. It is us with our disobedient bodies that are going to do the work that they have failed to do in Le Bourget and over the last 21 years. And we are going to reappear. We'll draw our red line in the sand. At the Place de la République, massive and resolute, we'll erect a kissing wall."

"Make love, not war," I chime in with Reverend Billy. It sounds so hokey, but in a world with too much repression it's more necessary than ever.

"It's not hokey, we are too separated from each other with our gadgets," he replies.

Paris is not the end, notes my hero John Jordan, explaining the scenario, looking out at everyone. Remember, "resistance is the key to joy," he concludes, chiming back into the joy of protest narrative, which first drew me to Reclaim the Streets, ACT UP, and DIY politics.

D12 is going to be one for the ages.

D12—LIGNE ROUGE, JUSTICE CLIMATIQUE

I walk out to the Pantheon to see Reverent Billy preach in front of melting ice. The ice is part of an installation by Olafur Eliasson, who shipped in eighty-eight tons of Arctic ice from Greenland and placed it in the shape of a clock. Literally melting into the cobblestones, it demonstrated everything that is at stake in regard to climate change. Over two weeks of the conference, much of it melts away (NPR, 2015).

"Ice is an interesting thing because it's binary," explains Waleed Abdalati, of the Cooperative Institute for Research in Environmental Sciences. "People get it. You see, 'Oh, it was there and now it's not.' And you can see change. Temperature, you know what does 1 degree C mean? It's 1 degree centigrade warmer. So what does that mean? But ice, there's a very visual story that's unfolding there, whereas with temperature it kind of creeps up on us and it's hard to associate with directly" (NPR, 2015).

The ice seems to tell the story of our fragile planet in ways few of us can. The internal relations between the ice and our climate, between our activity and its shift in form, the ebb of our oceans, between islands, cities, and rising tides opened up dialogue between those who saw an apocalypse and those who see a space for a different kind of world, a problem to be solved; some favor revolution, others reform. Still with the ice disappearing in front of us and previous conceptions of the world crumbling, this dialectic of connection and separation helps forward our story as an uprising, an aufbegehren, into something new. Many in Paris see these as the last days. Certainly, there is a threat. But as Pete Seeger always reminds us, no one can predict there is no hope.

Walking through the city, I stroll past the Pompidou Center to Notre Dame, where the Indigenous People's block had started a ritual. Tom Goldtooth of the Indigenous Environmental Network is speaking. "We are the red line. We have drawn that line with our bodies against the privatization of nature, to dirty fossil fuels and to climate change. We the defenders of the world's most biologically and culturally diverse regions. We will protect our sacred lands. Our knowledge has much of the solutions to climate change that humanity seeks."

"We come here with a present for Paris. We know what happened November 13," says Casey Camp-Horinek of Ponca Nation, Oklahoma. "We Indigenous People know how it feels to have someone kill innocent ones. We offer this symbol in memory of the lives lost, and thank you for hosting us on this sacred day."

I stroll over the Seine River, looking out at the majestic city. As I arrive at the Pantheon, people are walking in slow circles around the ice. Only a few pieces are left. The rest has melted. Eventually, everyone circles up, holding hands and meditating.

"Oooommmm," we breathe. The man leading the ritual suggests that it is not a good day for the future of the human species. He invites us to sing, cry, or respond. Most are quiet, taking in the moment. Some cry out and make sounds of animals. Like many times in the week, I start to laugh. There is only so much earnestness I can take. I look back at Billy with a smile.

"Turn around man with purple cap," he whispers, referring to my hat, starting to laugh himself. I have always been more drawn to the ludic dynamic of movements, the tragicomic. A few of us start singing the old freedom song, "Oh Freedom, Oh Freedom," clapping. And the mood lightens. Soon enough, we are winding our way through a spiral dance just like we used to have in Tompkins Square Park in the East Village of New York.

And Billy starts preaching. "We've got a church here. . . . A church of stop shopping, where we're in recovery from our grandparents. . . . We enter bank lobbies and businesses supporting climate change and sing until we are kicked out. . . . We've traveled to Ferguson three times. People chant 'Hands Up! Don't Shop! Hands Up! Don't Shop!' I've adopted this costume. I'm in recovery from Fundamentalism, from the Dutch Reform church where I was brought up, the group that lay the foundation that supported Apartheid. We're dealing with the same evil here." He describes a "pursuit of healing all over Paris," referring to the trip from the Pantheon to the Eiffel Tower, past the Arc de Triomphe, the talks with radical friends . . . "The document we are talking about today does not have mysteries included. It is reduced to data, not oceans . . . Not an indigenous people story of Greenpeace. In the old days when a boat went out, they brought mystics, and threw the IChing. Now they don't and that's a mistake. We must carry the mysteries in our bodies. . . . This must be a revolution, not a revision. We have to save our souls as we sing. As you pass the arch, that might open things. I remember. In my childhood there was an arrogance of the spiritual communities," notes Billy in reference to the New Age Communities in California, who thought it was best to pray for purity rather than act. He could not stand that stance. "But I'm calling to mind the complexity. We are going to have people coming at us. Where is our IChing? I'd like to lock arms and go to the earth. I ask the earth to be with us. Humans must change. Reverse it. Stop being predators. We are from an unbroken line of ancestors. Take responsibility. Get fossil fuels out of high art. Be at Argentina and the Ave of the Grand Armée at half past eleven!"

As Billy finishes, a group starts to sing to the earth:

> People gonna rise up like the water. Gonna turn this crisis around.
> I hear the voice of my great granddaughter, calling this crisis around.
> . . . Saying shut that gas plant down.

Leaving, a few others scream, "We are part of the re evolution."

"We Are the Earth defending itself."

A few of us get a coffee after the ritual and make our way to the action. Billy and I talk about his life and activism, our adventures together through the years, Billy's mentors, and how powerful it is to be in Paris.

This was going to be another one of those magnificent moments. We could all feel it, riding the metro. Bodies flood through the city, out of the subway, just as they had with the People's Climate March the year before. A movement was growing from New York to Paris and everywhere in between.

"What do we want—climate justice," people scream, pouring into the Avenue de la Grande Armée. Bodies are everywhere I can see, like VE day, all red, drawing a line in the sand that the world cannot pass. Samba bands are playing. Tears roll down my eyes when I look at the thousands and thousands of people who have defied the protest ban. The police stand back. What can they do? They chose to let Paris be Paris, the color of red, of Eros, of abundance everywhere, creating a red line for the world not to pass. John Jordan is slam dancing with marching bands. Play fills the streets.

"The red lines suggest a new aesthetics, a new color for our movement," says Yates McKee, standing on hand. Out of the dialectic of apocalypse and utopia, a new narrative for the environmental movement is taking shape, a new garden in the beauty of these bodies. "There's a carnivalesque and a new urgency within this clash, a new vocabulary rejecting green washing in favor of red. Between the state of emergency, we are seeing new tactics and old." He describes the red lines and this tension as a "militant uniformity."

The red lines represent a stark demarcation, the minimal necessity to prevent environmental collapse. "The right to soil, the right to water, the right to a just transition," explains John Jordan.

"On the streets, we are feeling like we are a turning point," notes Bill Talen, standing on the Avenue de la Grande Armée with tens of thousands. "In terms of creative nonviolence, and whatever it takes to survive." We talk about the negotiations and those who "keep coming up with compromises that are really genocide, compromises for just a small number of people who are all making money on the deal." Looking around, Talen smiles. "It's a good moment and I'm nourished in my activism being here."

A group of red inflatable barricades tumble down the avenue, bouncing through the air into the distance. Paris is, after all, the city that invented the barricade. Up through the air, these inflatables seemed to carry that history and transcend it, to be of it and outside it, ebbing through the interplay between history and crisis, melting ice and rising temperatures, migrating bodies and shifting economies. A samba band is playing. People are jumping up and down, slam dancing to the music. Beats tumble with the barricades, between streets of bodies moving and shaking to the marching bands performing Bello Ciao. Inflatable barricades bound down the Avenue de la Grande Armée, their ludic irreverence pushing back against the French State of Emergency. "Goodbye my beautiful, goodbye my beautiful, goodbye my beautiful, goodbye." We dance through steps to the right and left, looking at the present, at capitalism, stepping back with a glance toward barricades ripped from these streets from revolutions past with a long abstraction of struggles for equality, solidarity, and fraternity, back to the future and then to the present, seeds of a sustainable future growing from our uprising. Now we were moving. The sprouts of a better world are everywhere (Ollman, 2016).

A group of kids start chanting, "A ati, anti capitalista," bouncing up and down, dancing to the popular anti-capitalist chant.

"We are unstoppable, another work is possible," the crowd roars.

"Does anyone want to save the planet?" note a group of radical clowns.

"Leave it in the earth," says one sign, referring to fossil fuels.

"No More CO2lonialism," reads another sign. "Protect Mother Earth" and "Grand Parents Against Global Warming." Another: "You can't save the earth while bombing her."

A man with a beard and a sign declares, "Crossing Red Lines Requires Consent," and unfolds David Solnit's epic "IT'S UP TO US" kilometer-long red and white banner. Hundreds of us hold it.

"Pedal Power, Not Dirty Power," declare cyclists. Pointing to human-powered solutions and body power, hundreds join the magnificent bike bloc.

A woman draws a red line down her face and stands in front of a sign with the words "1.5 or chaos."

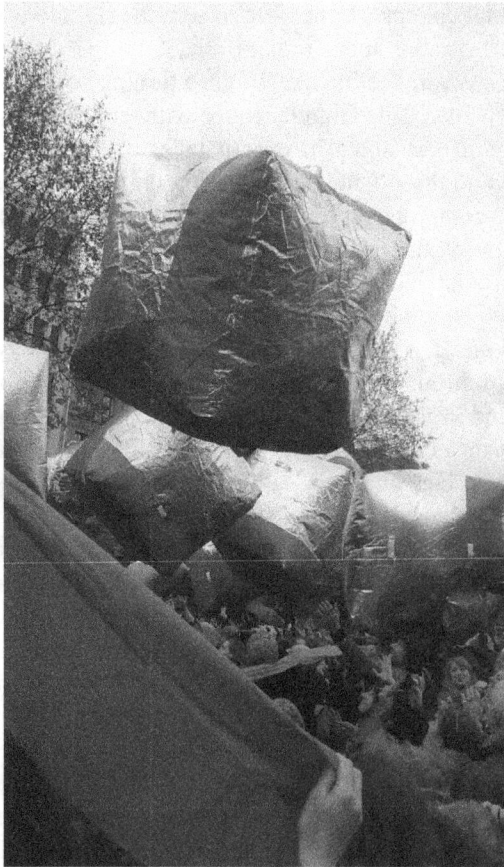

Figure 14.2. Barricades bouncing down the Avenue.

Source: Photo by Benjamin Shepard.

Figure 14.3.   D12 Ligne Rouge, Justice Climatique, red lines for justice.

Source: Photo by Nicolas Lambert/Climate Prints.

"We want a future and its none of your business," reads another sign. "Are you having fun yet," David Solnit greets me, smiling, unfolding the epic red lines banner.

"The ecology that desperately needs repair is that of planetary governance itself. And that is precisely where artist-activists are directing their energies," notes T. J. Demos (2015).

A man dressed in a mermaid outfit carries a sign: "Mermaids for Climate Justice."

A young woman with her hair pulled back and dressed in a black suit is walking up and kissing everyone, leaving traces from her red lipstick on our cheeks, red lines for justice from our hearts to the streets, part of the kissing wall. We run into friends everywhere along the route.

"We are too separated from each other," says Billy, supporting the gesture. Paris is about care, to save the world. The day is a testament to the art and abundance of an ever-flowing social movement, social Eros expanding around us, creating a repairable counter-narrative by movements of people in the streets, not the delegates inside the conference.

"We're not drowning. We're not going anywhere," scream the crowd. "99 percent stand for climate!"

"Whose planet, our planet?"

Making our way to the Eiffel Tower, we find ourselves walking with the Rhythms of Resistance, a pink block, playing drums, many with faces covered, dancing, sprinting against cars, into traffic. We all run along, into the streets with them, in exuberance, into the toward what feels like a celebration of a different kind of freedom, the Eiffel Tower in the distance.

"We want system change, not climate change," people scream. "No war! No warming!"

"Touts ensemble, Touts ensemble. Oui! Oui! Oui!"

More and more people join us, stepping from the sidewalk to the streets as we make our way to the Eiffel Tower. At the tower some formed a kissing wall. Others sit in the street hoping, praying, and longing for something better of this world.

That afternoon, the details of the COP21 are released, with world leaders agreeing to keep warming below 1.5, but probably closer to 3.7 degrees Celsius. As the activists had predicted, this is nothing close to adequate. But activists had made their point, taking control of the conversation instead of waiting for delegates to decide. They have already pushed the conversation far beyond Copenhagen. Through direct action, a global movement lay the groundwork for another story, a narrative extending beyond fossil fuels to a different kind of future. It is a story heard around the world. We can both condemn the limits of the COP21 and point to the framework as a tool for organizers to push forward. It will be up to people to hold governments accountable while turning the tide.

"It's the most propulsive earth activist street demo I've ever been blessed to march in, and the only time I was with earth-lovers where they had the energy that could compare with Black Lives Matter," says Billy. In New York, a red lines action is taking place at the same time in Times Square. "In New York City, the militarized police have it in mind to eradicate activism that they do not agree with, whether it is the homeless, earth activists, or the memorial for cop-murdered citizens. And yet the First Amendment is persistent. It is not forgotten. Activism founded this country," Reverend Billy continues. "The First Amendment was remembered by a great mix of activists at Times Square on Saturday, on the same day that the COP21 climate talks concluded and Paris protesters—including a certain televangelist-with-non-patriarchal-god—were marching from the Arc de Triomphe to the Eiffel Tower. In Times Square, singers from the Stop Shopping Church joined folks in surrounding the institution that pours more CO_2 into the air than any other: The Pentagon."

Despite all the problems, Paris moved things forward, one step up, two back. As my friend Peewee Nyob points out, I'm an apocalyptic optimist. Sure, the deal had its limitations, to state things mildly. We'd like to have something much better. No doubt 3.5 Celsius warming will usher in rising tides and chaos. As George Appenzeller suggests, "A reduction to 1.5 degrees Celsius will require reaching zero emissions over the next 30 years and negative emissions thereafter. By the time we reach between 1.5 and 2 degrees Celsius increase in temperature, some damage will be complete. . . . The Paris agreement is probably the best that can be obtained, but it is too little too late." Still, a counter-narrative took shape as people flooded the streets, defied the protest ban, found agency, and outlined what had to be done in the future. We pushed forward with a framework offering a break with fossil fuels in much the same way the 1964 surgeon general's report on smoking and health changed a generation's mind about cigarettes. With red lines drawn from our hearts to the streets, full of art and social Eros, D12 was a wonderful culmination. In the months and years to come, activists would have to work to make it a reality.

People have lots and lots of opinions about the deal. But as Naomi Klein tweeted after the agreement, this gives the world something to work with. No accord would have been far worse. On the streets of Paris, direct action and disobedience had the day, beating back the state of emergency. And, for this, we should celebrate. John Jordan pointed out on Facebook: "Fucking hell getting this all done was hard work but watching this makes tears come to my eyes and it all becomes worth it . . . Thank you all those comrades who stuck to it through thick and thin . . . We pushed the French govt into a corner with our defiance, we forced them not to repress us and despite their state of emergency we took to the streets with dignified disobedience . . . next stop is shutting down the fossil fuel industry with our bodies. . . . Alternatiba asked for permission to do their dumb human chain under the Eiffel tower and govt said no and put them in a boring militarized sheep pen at the end of the champ de mars. Redlines never asked permission and the joyfully wild unauthorized march that left the arc de triomphe ended up bang under the Eiffel tower . . . that's the power of disobedience for you . . . As Alice Walker says RESISTANCE IS THE SECRET OF JOY."

At 2:31 pm, May Boeve of 350.org tweeted out a message:

Today is a historic day: as tens of thousands of people filled the streets of Paris, politicians finalized a major new global climate agreement. The deal in Paris includes an agreement to limit global warming to below 2 degrees Celsius, with an aim of 1.5 degrees, and achieve climate "neutrality" that will require phasing out fossil fuels soon after mid-century. That's not what we hoped for, but it's still a deal that sends a signal that it's time to keep fossil fuels in the ground, and for investors to cut their ties with coal, oil and gas by divesting. This deal represents important progress—but progress alone is not our goal. Our goal is a just and livable planet.

Flying home from Paris, two of the people sitting by me were watching movies, one *The Matrix* and the other *South Pacific*. Humans are a virus, suggests Agent Smith in *The Matrix*:

> I'd like to share a revelation that I've had during my time here. It came to me when I tried to classify your species and I realized that you're not actually mammals. Every mammal on this planet instinctively develops a natural equilibrium with the surrounding environment but you humans do not. You move to an area and you multiply and multiply until every natural resource is consumed and the only way you can survive is to spread to another area. There is another organism on this planet that follows the same pattern. Do you know what it is? A virus. Human beings are a disease, a cancer of this planet.

To my right, the women are singing "I'm Gonna Wash That Man Right Out of My Hair" in *South Pacific*. Looking at both images, I think of the earth, of Mother Nature scrubbing her head, full of gnats drilling and poking, fighting, launching bombs, cutting forests, picking her hair. Half asleep, I'm thinking maybe the rising tides are like that shampoo in *South Pacific*. These humans, we've only been here for a short time; these ants crawling on the planet's face constitute a small bit of the planet's history. But we've created lots of trouble in our cities full of stories.

I hear it has been hot in New York. By the end of the year, we find out that 2015 eclipsed the year before as the hottest year on record by a long shot. Over the next few years, things would get weirder as the absurd became real. A subsequent U.S. president would pull out of the COP21, followed by the next who would try to get us back in. Around the world, activists pushed to stop fossil fuel infrastructure and pipelines on the ground, blocking trains carrying petroleum products and construction projects for fracked gas. Students walked out of classes. Environmentalists glued themselves to trains and stripped in at parliament, filling cities around the world with disobedient bodies, pushing against time to force politicians to address the problem as heat waves and floods, melting ice caps, and migration crises only intensified. By 2018, the United Nations' scientific panel on climate change issued a dire report warning that without fundamental societal changes, earth will feel climate change's full brunt in the next twenty-two years. Greta Thunberg demanded politicians act as though their houses were on fire. Cities from London to New York declared climate emergencies. Yet much of the damage was done. With the earth's biodiversity threatened, natural defenses that had kept viruses away lost ground; humans became more vulnerable. Outbreaks and pandemics raged; cities faced crisis after crisis.

From a rotting jail cell Antonio Gramsci (1971) reminds us: "The old world is dying, and the new world struggles to be born; now is the time of monsters." How do we dream of a better world? How do we tell a more livable story of our planet and then create it? Doing so, we inevitably find ourselves in a clash. Every action creates a reaction. Our carnival is their disorderly conduct. The dialectic is everywhere, in every opening and closing, a yin and a yang in each moment, even the endings for the old B movie. That's what Paris was about. It is what dialectical activism teaches us.

Sitting on that flight back from Paris, my mind wandered back to a scene in a movie theater as a kid, toward the end of *The Rocky Horror Picture Show*, the final words: "And crawling on the planet's face. Some insects called the human race. Lost in time. And lost in space. And meaning." We danced and sang and loved that movie. There was always a sequel to the B movie growing up. Will there be another one for us?

***

Back in Brooklyn, Billy and I'd continue that conversation from Paris. "What people don't see is that the same knee that was on George Floyd's neck will be on all of ours," says Billy, on a walk in GreenWood Cemetery, five years later, referring to both climate chaos and the policeman who kneeled on the neck of Floyd for eight minutes, the twin crises of police brutality and COVID-19, creating their own storm. The ways COVID-19 impacted New York and regular people coped, fostering mutual aid networks and solidarity, dispatches about this double helix, between brutality and gestures of care—these constitute the final narrative of this volume.

Chapter 15

Afterword: From Pandemic to Solidarity, Mutual AID from Plague Days to Autonomous Zones

In March 2020, the country became engulfed in a pandemic requiring people to look out for each other. The weeks and months to come were characterized by official denial from the federal government and by gestures of care and connection among impacted communities. Mutual aid expanded in countless directions, bundles of stories of movements growing through waves of support, narratives dovetailing, ideas flowing through stories of fear and connection, inequalities exposed, with movements growing as people reached out to each other. "The result is friendships, deep care and support," says Marina Sitrin (2020).

A sustainable urbanism requires mutual aid.

The following considers manifestations of mutual aid and support born as a pandemic raged. After the death of George Floyd, who was recovering from "SARS-CoV-2, the virus that causes COVID-19," at the hands of a Minneapolis police officer, a social movement around social inequality and Black lives led to weeks of protests (Neuman, 2020). The experience of the pandemic (which also created mutual aid and support) laid the groundwork for a transformational social movement. Case examples include emergency responses and food delivery with New Alternatives for LGBT Youth, jail support and activism in the Black Lives Matter Movement in Brooklyn, and food and mutual aid in the City Hall Autonomous Zone.

Epidemics expose a great deal about who we are. They always have. Old orders die. New ideas take shape. Mirrors shatter.

"There is something deep here connected to what is the real truth about who we really are, not what we are told about ourselves," says social movement scholar Marina Sitrin (2020). "Yes, we are afraid. Yes, we feel pain and vulnerability, and what we do with that, again and again, throughout history and now more than ever, is to reach out to one another and find ways to care for each other."

In March 2020 the world went into quarantine. One night in the midst of it, I found myself watching Akira Kurosawa's *Seven Samurai*, his 1954 film about war-torn sixteenth-century Japan. Its real subject, of course, is modern anxieties about old ways of living under attack. "This is the nature of war," says one of the samurai. "By protecting others, you save yourself. If you only think of yourself, you'll only destroy yourself." While our president might not understand the point, many others do seem to know that we benefit by extending care, a safety net catching people, helping us see that we need each other. Our health depends on it. Yet, protecting others is never simple.

The days since the COVID-19 pandemic began have witnessed countless forms of support, as activists and neighbors, healthcare workers and service providers, the healthy and the sick connect, breaking isolation. Wave after wave of people, including high school kids, preachers, bikers, queers, rise and resisters, and homeless folks cooking and sharing resources, cheering and screaming. As we march, each of us share stories, offering more supplies, our destinies entwined, our liberation tied to each other's survival. Greeting those on the way back from City Hall, across the Brooklyn Bridge, or riding, or marching, solidarity expands as we walk together, New Yorkers in a Critical Mass against racism and inequality. It is hard to separate protests over Black Lives, the pandemic, and the marches for the dead. They all overlap, each intersecting with the next.

It is OK to feel. At certain points everyone has felt fearful, says Sitrin. "Be vulnerable or open, protective or protecting, we can and are doing all of these things, and . . . that makes this moment both horrific and transformative in a deeply hopeful way."

Veterans of the AIDS crisis see resemblances in the nonresponse approaches to COVID and AIDS, looking at the patterns of a global pandemic and the social responses. AIDS activist Cleve Jones reminds us:

> AIDS came they said don't worry it only kills gays.
> 30 million heterosexuals and their children died.
> But don't worry Covid-19 only kills old people.

We'd have to take care of each other or die, many of us thought, recognizing the old lines from the poem "September 1, 1939" by Auden (1940).

Over time the struggle shifts from a global health pandemic to a struggle for lives, particularly Black and brown lives disproportionately impacted by COVID (CDC, 2020). The map of COVID in New York very much mirrors maps of poverty in the city. "Many of the neighborhoods with the highest number of cases per capita were areas with the lowest median incomes and largest average household size," notes *The New York Times* (2020). The actual impact of COVID moves in divergent directions, revealing a stark reality as the pandemic flows into the existing lines of inequality.

As long as some are sick, everyone is vulnerable. Our destinies as intertwined into a single garment of history, as MLK used to say. Some even carry the slogan on signs at Black Lives Matter actions. In countless circles, people start looking out for each other. Without support from the federal government, many see a need for mutual aid (Peterman, 2020; Solnit, 2020). Mutual aid, as anarchists have noted for over a century, manifests as intertwined survival and development across species (Cleaver, 1993). As a relational tendency, it offers a solution and a practice in building interconnections ripe with the potential for expansion. Mutual aid also offers us a lens through which we can address questions about interdependence that Martin Buber (1984) recognized, seeing others as neighbors, as people to understand.

ON MUTUAL AID

Social movements overlap, with common themes between reactions to lack of government help tackling COVID-19 and other contemporary protest movements against systematic racism and similar forms of bigotry. We see the co-occurrence and evolution of movements that are derived from seemingly distinct tragedies and social ills. Such a patterned manifestation *could* be coincidental, but there are some common threads that indicate that there is a deeper relation and/or that the responses are rooted in a common ethos (ethos here as in an ethical system). That ethos? Mutual aid. What comes to bear is a yearning for solidarity, an impulse toward cooperation and support. Certainly, one could propose mutual aid is response to a fragmentary, dislocated global economic system, or anomie (Spade, 2020).

"The great majority of people in ordinary disasters behave in ways that are anything but selfish," posits Rebecca Solnit (2020), looking back on her experience with Common Ground Collective after Hurricane Katrina. Quite often, she says, what we witness is "a lot of creative and generous altruism and brilliant grassroots organizing. With the global pandemic, these empathic urges and actions are wider and deeper and more consequential than ever." To put it simply, people want to support each other. Take the infusion of cycling and environmental activists into the Black Lives Matter movement. "This is your fight too," Street Riders chant on their weekly rides in support of the Black Lives Matter protests, imploring people from across the five boroughs of New York City to respond to their call for human rights, for people across ethnicities to look out for each other. "See others as yourself," declares a sign on another bike. The response is striking, with thousands joining the weekly rides. Between COVID-19 and the subsequent waves of Black Lives Matter protests, doctors and nurses applaud anti-racist activists; a flourishing of donations for protective equipment changes hands; community projects take shape; a free food refrigerator is placed down the street from my house; and harm reductionists journey throughout the city on outreach. These are just a few of any number of practical forms of support as regular people reach out to each other in reciprocal exchange (Spade, 2020).

"A dozen years ago, the term 'mutual aid' was, as far as I can tell, used mostly by anarchists and scholars," says Solnit (2020). The concept has long been a part of social movements. First developed and explored by the anarchist prince Kropotkin (1987 [1902]), he suggests: "There is in Nature *the law of Mutual Aid,* which, for the success of the struggle for life, and especially for the progressive evolution of the species, is far more important than the law of mutual contest." "There is in Nature *the law of Mutual Aid,* which, for the success of the struggle for life, and especially for the progressive evolution of the species, is far more important than the law of mutual contest." For Eric Laursen (2020), the work challenged a "dog-eat-dog morality that capitalism had embraced through a misreading of Darwin's theory of evolution." David Graeber and Andrej Grubacic suggest: "Such interventions . . . reveal aspects of reality that had been largely invisible but, once revealed, seem so entirely obvious that they can never be unseen" (quoted in Laursen, 2020). It is one of the great ideas of the anti-authoritarian social movements. "In the midst of the pandemic, it is everywhere," says Solnit (2020), signs on street corners, people tabling, giving away food.

Mutual aid within the context of the COVID-19 crisis builds on the dynamics of the moment, as one crisis leads to the next, from financial to ecological to public health to environmental to questions about inequality. "In the midst of a global crisis, we must listen, learn, and build with people from around the world," notes Astra Taylor. "A crisis is a turning point." Such times can lead to economic disrepair, shock doctrine, and fascism, or possibility for something more abundant. Stories about mutual aid "teach us a great deal" (quoted in Sitrin 2020).

MUTUAL AID AND LOSS

The cases we learned of first were from our students at City University of New York, the largest urban university system in the United States, where a majority of students are people of color. And then friends of friends, a teacher, a housing advocate for people with HIV/AIDS, a high school classmate, a social worker who provided shelter for the homeless who got sick herself, a nurse who took her own life. The Centers for Disease Control

(2020) confirms: "Long-standing systemic health and social inequities have put some members of racial and ethnic minority groups at increased risk of getting COVID-19 or experiencing severe illness, regardless of age. Among some racial and ethnic minority groups, including non-Hispanic black persons, Hispanics and Latinos, and American Indians/Alaska Natives, evidence points to higher rates of hospitalization or death from COVID-19 than among non-Hispanic white persons." The health disparities revealed by COVID-19 were anything but new (SAMHSA, 2020). Neither were the losses.

Mid-April social worker Spence Halperin gets word from work:

> Today from our CEO: "With a heavy heart, I report that 53 clients have passed away and that in our staff, one subcontractor and two home health aides have passed away due to the Coronavirus."

My friend Mark Milano draws our attention to the loss of an AIDS activist. "To those who think COVID-19 is just another flu: my fellow long-term survivor Ed Shaw just succumbed to it. After beating AIDS for 32 years, this damn virus took him. Rest in Power, Ed."

I'd known Ed for decades. Person after person we knew, dead, hundreds a day.

"I can't believe my government is not helping everyone out," says one of my students in a Zoom class.

At first the city dragged its feet about closing schools, continuing business as usual, with basketball games in the gym at my daughter's school in early March. That was until a group of parents informed the city of plans to pull their kids, supporting each other and the health of their families, regardless of official policy. Joining labor unions and worker organizations, teachers and staff protest and provide mutual aid to students and each other, as well as nurses and other "essential" workers engaged in similar acts of mutual aid and solidarity. L. A. Kauffman, one of the organizers, and I talk about the project. For years now, we've supported each other in our activism. The last time we'd seen each other in the real world, I had "just gotten out of D.C. jail yet again, after another direct action, this time one calling for 45's removal from office," writes Kauffman, who was there to offer moral support and aid after the arrest. Throughout our conversation we discuss "the challenges of collective action in the age of social distancing," the ways regular people, parents, neighbors, students, and communities help each other and look out for everyone.

In lieu of a coordinated government response, mutual aid starts to flourish. People are offering recipes and food recommendations, movie picks, book chats over Zoom, food delivery, support for rent strikes, and other forms of solidarity (Arjini, 2020; Tam, 2020).

In Brooklyn, anti-gentrification group Equality for Flatbush begins a campaign called the Brooklyn-shows-love-mutual-aid-project: "Since March 25th, we have delivered over 191 community kits of non-perishable food items and household supplies to community members living in the neighborhoods of Bed-Stuy, Brownsville, Bushwick, Canarsie, Coney Island, Crown Heights, East Flatbush, East New York, Flatbush, Fort Greene, Kensington, Marine Park, and Mill Basin. Any and all Brooklynites who need grocery/supply deliveries, medication pick-up/drop-offs, tenant/rent-strike organizing support, and other forms of material aid."

Countless community groups step in. Housing Works creates services and housing for homeless kids in a shelter for people with COVID. Volunteers such as New York writer Tim Murphy work to get kids in these shelters food and supplies, as well as get medical workers protective equipment.

Watching all this take place, the good we see from people and the neglect from the government, one of my students posts a comment from Mikhail Bulgakov's *Master and Margarita* in a reaction blog about the pandemic. "Yes, man is mortal, but that would be only half the trouble. The worst of it is that he's sometimes unexpectedly mortal—there's the trick!" Sometimes we surprise ourselves. We are wonderfully horribly made, fragile and resilient, ugly and beautiful at the same time. Over and over, students talk about patience and silver linings, the yin and yang of how we support each other. We cheer for healthcare workers at 7 pm every night, roars going up all over Brooklyn, neighbors greeting each other. People make the best of it, despite the insanity. Efforts to help can be seen in countless ways, a cat sanctuary down the street, where people feed the strays by the canal. Our city of friends expands and contracts, some hiding away, the losses pile up; the ones we adore get sick. A drag performer from my wife's high school in Staten Island dies on the couch. His boyfriend was on the way home. We toast to him. But sometimes it is too much.

Each day, I bike through the city, glad to be in the metropolis instead of the country, where many have retreated, happy to be in town during the crisis. Glynnis MacNicol (2016) notes: "It is, of course, not a holiday, nor is the city nearing the end of a long night. The witchy New York hour between yesterday and today is now the New York of all day, every day. A nightmarish bizarro world set to the soundtrack of sirens. Everything is still here, but off . . . Now food delivery people are on the front lines, risking their health to keep us fed, and the restaurant sector that has long been the lifeblood of New York alive." We see a lot here. When I get a flat tire on the Brooklyn Bridge, a man stops to help. Sitting on our stoop, Ed offers us PPE and a story. We give him greens from the garden, mutual aid expanding by the day.

More notices of people getting sick, my work colleague Victor Ayala writes: "Those who know me understand my silence and distance . . . today

I want to share a very emotional and touching moment. My friend and colleague of 30 plus years called me from her ICU bed to say goodbye. In between breaths we expressed our love for one another and encouraged Hope and Prayers. She reminded me to hold on to our memories and love we shared while traveling to conferences and the many lunches and profound discussions about religion and higher education. Call ended with I love you . . . I will continue to hope and pray for her and yes hold onto our memories, love and respect for one another."

For many in the AIDS world, this is nothing new. "We are fighting for our lives once again," notes Greg Gonzalves. "Activism was a response to mourning, but also a way to obscure grief," he follows. "We need to take care of each other, ourselves as we continue the fight." And take care of each other we do.

My friend Michel Coconis is one of many involved. "My mutual aid activities have included (or so I believe)" volunteering, dropping "off food and diapers, putting masks together with our local Emergency Management, driving folks to the store or shopping for them, and reading newspapers and magazines to ppl who cannot get them from the library." Still, Coconis cautions, "I'm actually not sure which of these is technically mutual aid . . . I have been to one drive-by rally on releasing ppl from Ohio's prisons and jails." There is a fine line between mutual aid and charity, with which many are still grappling. The definitional demarcation between charity and mutual aid is important. Other cases are positive and meet needs but may not be mutual aid.

Jessica Rosenberg of Long Island University notes, "I am thinking about my daughter-in-law, a medical social worker in a Staten Island Hospital. Each day, she helps grieving families who have loved ones dying of covid—19. She provides the missing link between the hospital structure and loved ones who are desperate for information. She consoles and comforts. She helps patients get ready to leave the hospital and ensures that they have the essential resources they need. She fights for patients being prematurely discharged and who are not ready to leave the hospital. She is an advocate. Because of the dangers of her work environment, she contracted coronavirus." The degree of risk is real.

Nancy Kusmaul says: "The University of Iowa School of Social Work and Mercedes Bern-Klug . . . are running bi-weekly support groups for practicing nursing home social workers." Groupworkers have used Kropotkin's *mutual aid* since the dawn of that tradition, because groupwork requires developing and building mutually supportive relations.

"My partners and I created a 'Bergen County COVID Support Group' on Facebook and conducted live talks on multiple issues to help our community get through these difficult times," adds Suzanne Badawi, MSW, LCSW, of Ramapo College of New Jersey.

Others look to those left behind. Throughout April and May, I take part in #FreeThemAllFridays car and bike caravans. "As COVID-19 spreads across the country, immigrants continue to be locked up in ICE detention without adequate medical or sanitary facilities. The undocumented community is shut out of state relief even as they provide the essential labor that keeps New York running." Cyclists join "to say ENOUGH IS ENOUGH. We demand that Governor Cuomo use his emergency powers to order the release of all ICE detainees locked up in NY State to safeguard human life and public health. We also stand in solidarity with all prisoners and call for their freedom amid COVID-19."

Increasingly, we turn to movement work, addressing the gaps in the safety net, the inequality exposed by the crisis, via policy advocacy, helping to fight unemployment, supporting coworkers, running clinical trials, housing homeless people in hotels through community fundraising, looking at health disparities, bridging the gap from direct action and direct services, trying to be creative problem solvers, and collaborating with researchers and community providers.

NEW ALTERNATIVES

New Alternatives is a Manhattan-based group providing services for LGBT homeless youth, a group that disproportionately experience homelessness. Queer youth make up nearly 40 percent of the city's homeless youth but only 7 percent of the youth population. New Alternatives helps them to transition out of the shelter system with education, life skills training, and basic needs like food and hygiene, Sunday meals, groups, and case management. Like many organizations, they shut their doors with the New York Pause, ending Sunday meals. Over time, the group's director, Kate Barnhart, grew more and more concerned about those with compromised immune systems, who faced increased health risks. Darrell Wimbush, a security guard at their space inside a midtown church located on West 40th Street, started to have the same concerns, hearing more and more clients worry about the coronavirus and their own isolation. In response, he worked with Barnhart to create a drop-off program for those unable to take the trains to come pick up meals (Simon, 2020). Countless volunteers, including myself, joined the effort, getting out of our homes, doing something. Every day we connect we feel better. Each of us gains a sense of community building, supporting the city and those inside it, doing our parts. The program is a vital example of mutual aid.

My seventeen-year-old daughter and I volunteer to drop off food and bring supplies one afternoon a week from April through June. Some weeks we take food to the Bronx, others to the Lower East Side, often both. Sometimes, we drop off in the Far Rockaways, witnessing the ways the city has changed. "I'd rather be taking food out than sitting at home," says the seventeen-year-old, helping navigate the pickups, coordinating with the clients. The drop-offs reveal something extraordinary about our city—the sprawling gaps in needs and experience, passing homeless people on the street, new street murals, candles, chalk, photos, and makeshift memorials outside of buildings. This is a sight we see repeated over and over again, street memorials for the dead. "Those are his kids," says an onlooker, chatting on the sidewalk as we leave, referring to the memorial, many more bearing witness, or helping those who remain cope.

Jewdi Clech of the NYC Disorder of Sisters describes getting involved with coordinating the meal drop-offs. "When COVID hit NYC, I got sick the first week and thought, 'Gee, I wish there was some way I could help people even though we are all home.' Then I got the call." Clench would spend the next three months "diligently calling, texting and communicating with the LGBTQ youth folx through New Alternatives to check in with them and help arrange food delivery." For many, such as Clench, providing material support actually supports their mental health. Completing those three months, he felt compelled to thank Darnell, Kate, drivers such as myself, and the other volunteers. "I know it wasn't easy . . . we cannot thank you enough for the opportunity, it made me happy to be a part of the community and find a way to participate . . . Thank you to all of the drivers who tolerated my last minute messages, spreadsheets, complicated instructions, calls, check-ins, last minute requests, and bullying behavior to see if you'd yet again be willing to venture out, but braved COVID and curfews to get food to people who needed it. Roughly 350 meals per week, for the past twelve weeks have been distributed—that's more than 4000 meals!"

Certainly, we were not the only group out providing aid during the peak weeks of the pandemic. Harm reduction groups across the city reached out to those in need. Tamara Oyola Santiago, Alexis Del Rio, and Nelson Gonzalez brought survival supplies to drug users in upper Manhattan and the Bronx via their organization Bronx Móvil. Santiago recalls: "One late night, we were doing outreach outside a shelter on 182nd Street, and a participant looked at us and said, 'Harm reduction on the streets—love is love.' That made our night. Also, we started getting boxes of beautiful cloth masks sewn by hand—we have no idea who's sending them." Another night, a man got out of his car and approached them. Santiago said, "Do you use drugs? Because I have syringes." The man replied, "Why do you have to do that?" One of the participants in the program jumped in adding, "This stuff saves lives and prevents HIV and hepatitis C." Santiago did not have to say a word. "The mutual-aid networks that have arisen are beautiful. The Church of St. Francis of Assisi in Herald Square gave us an average of 100 meal bags every time we went out" (quoted in Murphy, 2020).

The last Tuesday in May, we make our way from Brooklyn to Times Square, up to 99th Street, down to the Lower East Side, and out to Rockaway Beach. Homeless people wait outside at West 40th Street, many in the street. People are hungry. Seemingly invisible, many more have no place to stay or get away from the virus. On our way up to Times Square, a man is asleep in the street by a corner. People step over, ignoring him on their way. All over the city, homeless people have little to nowhere to shelter themselves from COVID. Homeless people can't shelter in place, they can't "stay home." It's a message activists repeat again and again.

The next day, the last Wednesday in May, I attend a rally at City Hall organized by the #HomelessCantStayHome campaign. Walking there, the first person I see is Kate Barnhart of New Alternatives. "85 deaths in NY shelters is unacceptable," says Barnhart, wearing a mask on her first time out in weeks since she's been coordinating care and running her organization from her home. "They are directly a result of the negligence of de Blasio. It is essential the homeless population be given a chance to shelter in hotels rather than crowded shelters with higher rates of infection."

At City Hall, homeless New Yorkers and advocates set up dozens of symbolic "body bags" and gravestones before the mayor's press briefing. Holding signs that read "COVID + DHS = DEATH" and "Mayor de Blasio: there is blood on your hands," protestors gather to mourn the lives of seventy-eight New Yorkers who have died (almost certainly an undercount) as a result of the mayor's failure to guarantee homeless people the right to safely socially distance in hotel rooms and permanent housing.

"Stop the sweeps, give homeless people a place to sleep," says Lynn Lewis of Picture the Homeless. For years now, her organization has pushed the city to count the number of housing units that exist in New York, challenging the scarcity narrative driving real estate speculation.

"We need housing not empty luxury buildings for speculation," reads a sign held by Fran, a member of the Stop Shopping Choir.

"Homeless people are dying," says Donald, of Families for Freedom.

The action is also in memoriam and honor of Nikita Price, a Picture the Homeless member since 2006 and organizer for more than a decade. Nikita tragically passed away shortly before the action. Until his final days, Nikita was organizing for the safety and survival of homeless people in New York City and against police violence.

Standing in front of a row of dozens of body bags in front of City Hall, police behind him, Christoph explains, "I'm here for all the voices, all the people who cannot be here, cannot be heard. How many lives will be lost over the cost of a hotel room? We're lives that matter. We count. We matter." In the weeks to come, this point become more and more prophetic.

A WOUND FROM ONE PANDEMIC TO THE NEXT

The next day, May 28, I attend a funeral for Larry Kramer, the founder of the AIDS Coalition to Unleash Power. All week, the world swirled with action. Word about a policeman in Minneapolis, who kneeled on unarmed George Floyd's neck for eight minutes and forty-six seconds as he begged for life, was making national news. Watching the video of Floyd, face on the concrete, saying "I can't breathe" before dying, tears pour down my face, a flood of images of everyone who had died lately, mostly from communities of color. And then the sense of shame, frustration, déjà vu. Here we are again. Rodney King and Eric Garner, whose last words were "I can't breathe" in Staten Island. And then Larry Kramer, a white man who started ACT UP and GMHC. He sounded the alarm that this would impact everyone. Kramer reminded us that there was a place for anger. We could use that anger. We could channel that anger. The feelings about the horror could be translated into action. This wasn't the stuff of adolescent misbehavior. We could ACT UP. We could and should disobey, especially in the face of the horror, when Black people are killed by cops, when Abner is tortured, when Patrick is shot, when George is killed, when your friends are getting sick and no one is doing anything about it.

It's all the same thing, homophobia and racism, Jay Walker, of Rise and Resist, says, speaking at Kramer's memorial. Over the next few months, he takes part in subsequent street actions calling for the city to defund the police. I'd run into him almost daily at protests, activists responding to the deaths of Black and brown people at the hands of the police as well as the pandemic. Walker (2020) writes, "First, the inaction in response to Ahmaud Arbery's murder, then the police execution of Breonna Taylor, then a white woman calling the police on birdwatcher Chris Cooper in the Central Park Ramble, and the one-two gut punches of the death of legendary activist Larry Kramer, less than a year after he had delivered an impassioned speech after our inaugural 2019 Queer Liberation March, and the murder of George Floyd by Minneapolis police. Our members and organizers took to the streets in protest."

We all know the 400 years of horror that never seems to recede. Day after day rallies for Black Lives, moving from one borough to the next, bike rides, street rallies, speak-outs, over bridges, across highways, through traffic, across town. At each rally people support each other, share food, supplies, and aid.

Throughout the summer, thousands join the weekly Justice Rides, reclaiming public space in a world where Black bodies, immigrant bodies, where women, those who look different are suspect and subject to scrutiny and quite often violence. Each ride offers solidarity and support against the violence of racism and sexism, as well as automobiles. Standing in the shadow of the Verrazano Narrows Bridge, Orlando, one of the organizers, speaks before a ride. "Thank you!!!!" he screams. "There is no place in the world I'd rather be than riding with you. I am doing this for my friend Peter who was killed by the police. Each ride gives me strength. Thank you for coming down here. Just know it's not unnoticed. We're all in it together. Let's keep it going. It ain't going to stop."

CITY HALL AUTONOMOUS ZONE

During drop-off days for New Alternatives, we make our way past the rallies in the Rockaways on the beach in Queens, across Manhattan, and at City Hall. There activists began an occupation, dubbed Occupy City Hall or City Hall Autonomous Zone, in late June. They are calling for the city to reduce the police budget by one billion dollars and reinvest that money in the needs of communities of color. Food and supplies pour in from all over town. When there is more than needed, they send it to New Alternatives. Social movements such as the Black Panthers and Occupy have long looked to models of food exchange as a form of movement building. The practice became ever more important as more and more people faced food insecurity, job losses, with deepening poverty and precarity. With tables for food and communications and art, the City Hall Autonomous Zone is very much an exercise in mutual aid.

The City Hall Autonomous Zone builds on the model from Seattle. Bridgette Read (2020) describes the scene: "On June 9, an area of around six blocks in downtown Seattle became known as CHAZ, the Capitol Hill Autonomous Zone." CHAZ came to be after clashes between police and protesters—before the police recognized the area as a makeshift temporary autonomous zone for the movement. Without law enforcement, community stepped in; people provided support, dubbing it the Capitol Hill Organized Protest. The police announced a "decreasing footprint" around the East Precinct "as an exercise in trust and deescalation." In lieu of law enforcement, community members organized protests, arts, and community events. A spirit of mutual aid took shape—free food, a medical center, a garden, and a giant Black Lives Matter mural (Read, 2020).

Each day I drop by New York's autonomous zone. I run into different friends taking part and adding support. Strolling by, my friend Stacy tells me about Seattle and the ways both spaces are experimenting with mutual aid in their own ways, with more gardens in Seattle, a lot more organization in New York, images of beauty in both. From the very beginning committees form around composting, sanitation, a library, gathering donations for meals and supplies, including clothing.

A central call of Occupy City Hall was to defund the police. As activists sleep outside, the #HomelessCantStayHome coalition makes significant breakthroughs in budget negotiations. The inside and the outside work in tandem. "The municipal budget negotiations were disastrous from the per-spective of justice and building working class power," notes Craig Hughes, a social worker with the Urban Justice Center. Still, he points out that while most council members side with police and supported the council speaker's sham police-centered budget there were some unexpected wins based off of years of organizing and efforts to reshape the policing narrative put forth by successive administrations, much of which was led by homeless folks them-selves and all of which was grounded in the perspective that cops are never the answer to homelessness. For example, the Subway Diversion program is formally ended. That is a major win in this context. Not only had nonprofits like Human. NYC organized against it effectively, but it is actually the tes-timonies of people who experienced it that provided its most damning and effective indictments. In fact, the sole city council hearing on the matter was interrupted by people who have experience with homelessness making clear what a farce it was through a skit that saw these activists removed by council security. The NYPD's "Homeless Outreach Unit" is disbanded, which is a significant win in creating distance from homeless people and the cops and decentering policing from "homeless outreach." And the NYPD is removed from overseeing security operations at shelters. In a budget with few wins, these were some tangibly useful outcomes. The question of how to harness power to meet need is ever present in mutual aid, including in distinctions between "charity" and "solidarity," between "reform" and "transformation" or "revolution."

QUEER LIBERATION MARCH AND JAIL SUPPORT

As negotiations continue inside and activists sleep outside City Hall, New Yorkers celebrate pride weekend. The official pride parades were canceled as a result of COVID, yet local parades continue. Bikes zip and to and fro around the zone the night of the yearly Drag March. After a month of pro-tests, no uptick in COVID cases had emerged among the groups of activists in attendance, almost universally wearing masks and staying in public. The Queer Liberation March would take place on the last Sunday in June.

Little did anyone expect it to be another example of the need for police reform, yet that is exactly what happened. That last Sunday in June, activists in the occupation join the Queer Liberation March for Black Lives and against Police Brutality, solidarity expanding. From Foley Square to Washington Square, some 50,000 people peaceably march together, converging at Washington Square Park. There, Jay Walker (2020), Bill Cashman, and others see police "indiscriminately throwing innocent, non-violent Pride March attendees to the ground."

Alexis Danzig and Jamie Bauer, of Rise and Resist, try to de-escalate the scene and provide jail support for those who were arrested. The two activists describe the ways jail support functions as a form of mutual aid: "I learned everything I know about jail support during ACT UP," says Alexis Danzig. "Jail support matters because the through-line of direct action is solidarity to build skilled, resistant community. We plan actions together, in person; we listen carefully and democratically to each other to create strong, engaging, disruptive protest; we take care of each other during arrests and while in jail; and we ensure that there is on-site community—jail support—for each person arrested at an action we plan, as they are released. People are tired and sometimes disoriented after being arrested and processed; jail support is there to receive people and attend to their immediate needs, feed them and help them get home or to medical attention. Jail support connects people to the community of legal support—and solidarity continues through any court appearances. Sunday night after QLM the jail support community that's been active took over from us. They kept in touch with Reclaim Pride until everyone was released. It's a pleasure to work with responsible people from different communities, we share many similar ethics."

Jamie Bauer follows, "There are two different forms of support—one for organized civil disobedience with an expectation of arrests—and one for a situation where the police arrest without warning and all of a sudden there are unexpected arrests of people. Alexis and I are more used to the first situation. There is a great structure that's been set up for the second. The first keeps track of who's arrested, who needs to be contacted, medical concerns, etc. We keep track of who got out, charges, etc. It's a little easier because we know who we are looking for. Sunday was different because there was a lot of conflicting information and we didn't know who, and why. But either way, the NYPD knows we are out there waiting for people and we believe that helps make sure they don't get roughed up again or lost in the system."

Alexis recalls a new chant. "'Who keeps us safe(r)? We keep us safe(r)!' This is the sweet-spot where we of the ACT UP generation really overlap with the new kids. I love that chant."

AMNESIA AND MUTUAL AID AND AN
ENCHANTED CITY

The crisis has exposed the best and the worst of our city. A doctor who works down the street tells us he's lost half his patients with COVID-19, sometimes fifty a day. It is nothing to be proud of he says during the nightly cheers for healthcare workers. "This crisis has laid bare the routine processes of structural violence" the poor endure, notes social worker Jesse Bernstein (2020). "The politics of disposability—the triage of who must be prioritized for survival and whose survival is up for debate or relegation—are in full display."

There's an adage in New Orleans; people care for each other when storms hit. It's a feeling of magic. Those are the times when we remember what is most important, that we are all in it together. We need each other. Unfortunately, those moments pass and we separate. It's better to stick together. Yet that fellow feeling dims as people get back to business. AIDS activists saw the same sentiment take place with AIDS treatment. Peter Staley writes: "I know many are saying COVID will change things forever, creating a new normal. But I'm reminded of the post-plague years in the U.S. (starting in 1996), when the LGBT community pivoted away from AIDS before you could blink, almost as if it had never happened.[1] The collective pain can create its own kind of backlash, where a 'return to normal' floods in quickly to help everyone forget (for a while). Sadly, I'm pretty sure a year after we get a vaccine, we'll go right back to burning up the planet."

Sixty thousand Americans died in the Vietnam War in some twenty years, while some 260,000 died of COVID-19 in the first year in the United States, 1.41 million worldwide. And people are fighting about what it means. The amnesia express wants us to forget. But reminders are everywhere.

"Be good to everyone, LOVE," declares a mural painted on a boarded-up shop window in the Bowery in Lower Manhattan. The boarded-up walls of downtown are full of such displays. The streets look like art galleries, thanks to the creative flourishing of regular people. The implicit message: we should remember what it means to offer support. Each day, the papers carry more and more obits, stories of police abuse, and ever-spiralizing crises. We still catch glimpses, the feeling of magic when people connect, providing food and care. It's a place where colors fly off spray-paint cans; poetry grows of chance encounters among strangers conjuring an alchemy of ideas, approaches to care, support, and even joy. This is a place where we play in the rain or imagine other worlds; rituals invoke spirits, the dead dance with the living, and the faeries lead us into a blurry world in between. Here pieces of green find inspiration in the cracks in the sidewalk, crawling up from unknown worlds, eternal returns of the repressed. Cycling through these streets, one

Figures 15.1, 15.2, 15.3, 15.4. Scenes from the City Hall Autonomous Zone, Queer Liberation March for *Black Lives* and against police brutality, and cyclists on the Williamsburg Bridge, Summer 2020.

Source: Photos by Benjamin Shepard.

occasionally stumbles into a rally or a march, or garden, someone offering a hand, or occupied space, disappearing and reappearing in a critical mass. We find the homeless sleeping and more people marching, in deep appreciation of our collective humanity. All the while Thanatos, who lurks nearby leaving bodies in his wake, is held at bay, survivors consoled by mutual aid. Exploring these gestures of care, one witnesses a secret history of a distinct urban practice led by regular people, organizers and dreamers, faerie magic and a creative clash between a new colossus and Moloch (Dann, 2020). A sustainable urbanism requires mutual aid. At a time of plague, when the poor are left to make do, layoffs are rising, and a cavalcade of bodies are marching for something better, gestures of mutual aid are a reminder: we can reimagine the city.

NOTE

1. Although certainly many AIDS activists translated their actions into efforts to address the global pandemic. ACT UP inspired the Treatment Action Campaign (see Shepard, 2002).

References

Aaron, B. (2015). DMV Revoked License of Driver Who Killed Allison Liao for Just 30 Days. *Streetsblog.* Accessed January 30 from http://www.streetsblog.org/2015/01/30/dmv-revoked-license-of-driver-who-killed-allison-liao-for-just-30-days/.

Adorno, T. (1973). *Negative Dialectics.* New York: Bloomsbury Academic.

Adorno, T., Benjamin, Walter, Block, Ernst, Brecht, Bertolt, and Lukács, Georg. (1977). *Aesthetics and Politics: The Key Texts of the Classic Debate within German Marxism.* New York: Verso.

Arjini, Nawal. (2020). Defending One Brooklyn Brownstone Is Just the Beginning. Accessed July 13 from https://www.thenation.com/article/politics/crown-heights-eviction-defense/.

Altman, D. (1972). *Homosexual Oppression and Liberation.* Sidney: Angus and Robertson.

Amster, R., DeLeon, A., Fernandez, L., Nocella II, A. J., and Shannon, D. (2009). Introduction. In *Contemporary Anarchist Studies*, pp. 1–8. New York: Routledge.

Anderson, L. (2015). The Dark Side of Purple. *The Villager.* December 31, 2015. http://thevillager.com/2015/12/31/the-dark-side-of-purple/.

Anderson, L. (2016a). All Purple's Daughters. *The Villager.* January 21, 2016.

Anderson, L. (2016b). Purple: Paragon or Pariah? *The Villager.* January 28, 2016.

Anarcho. (2001). Anarchism and Freedom. Accessed July 28, 2009, from http://www.struggle.ws/anarchism/writers/anarcho/talks/anarANDfreedom.html.

Aronowitz, S. (1981). *The Crisis in Historical Materialism.* New York: Praeger.

Aronowitz, S. (2003). *How Class Works: Power and Social Movement.* New Haven: Yale University Press.

Aronowitz, S. (2014–2015). Class Notes from the Institute for the Radical Imagination.

Auden, W. H. (1940). "September 1, 1939" from *Another Time.* New York: Random House.

Bader, E. J. (2005). Ambulatory's Many Obstacles. *Brooklyn Rail.* May. https://brooklynrail.org/2005/5/local.

Bauer, J. (2020). Correspondence with the author.

Bulgakov, M. (1994). *Master and Margarita*. New York: Grove Press.

Bakunin, M. (1842/2002). The Reaction in Germany. In Sam Dolgoff (ed.), *Bakunin on Anarchism*. Montreal: Black Rose Books.

Barnosky, A., et al. (2012). Approaching a State Shift in the Earth's Atmosphere. *Nature*. Accessed April 12, 2021, from http://web.stanford.edu/group/hadlylab/_pdfs/Barnoskyetal2012.pdf.

Baudrillard, J. (1981/1994). *Simulacrum and Simulation*. Ann Arbor, MI: Éditions Galilée (French) and University of Michigan Press.

Beckman, J. (2014). *American Fun: Four Centuries of Joyous Revolt*. New York: Pantheon Books.

Benjamin, W. (1968). Theses on the Philosophy of History. In Hannah Arendt (ed. and intro.), *Illuminations*, pp. 253–64. New York: HBJ.

Benjamin, W., and Asja, L. (1978). Naples. In *Reflections*, pp. 163–73. New York: Harcourt Brace.

Berkowitz, R. (2003). *Staying Alive: The Invention of Safer Sex*. New York: Basic Books.

Berman, M. (1982). *All That Is Solid Melts into Air*. New York: Penguin.

Bernstein, J. (2020). Losing Kathy. Accessed from https://hardcrackers.com/losing-kathy-slow-violence-social-service-work-new-york-city/.

Berry, D. (2004). "Workers of the World, Embrace!" Daniel Guérin, the Labour Movement and Homosexuality. *Left History* 9(2): 11–43.

Bey, H. (1991). *T.A.Z.: The Temporary Autonomous Zone, Ontological Anarchy, Poetic Terrorism*. Brooklyn, NY: Autonomedia.

Big Bang Party. (2007). Artgasm for Radical Queers. Accessed December 24, 2010, from http://www.bigbangparty.org/party.html.

Bike Bloc Mission Statement. (2014). http://peoplesclimate.org/bikebloc/; https://www.facebook.com/Bikeblocpeoplesclimate. Accessed September 17, 2014.

Bioremediation Ball. (2014). The Beneficial MudBall Ball: Garden Celebration of Bioremediation. June 1. Accessed January 30 from http://www.meetup.com/nycpermaculture/events/175864922/.

Birch, E. (2012). Case Studies Study Research and Its Application to Urban Planning. In *The Oxford Handbook of Urban Planning*. Accessed January 30 from http://www.oxfordhandbooks.com/view/10.1093/oxfordhb/9780195374995.001.0001/oxfordhb-9780195374995-e-14.

Blotcher, J. (1999). Anarchy, Inc. On Its 30th Anniversary, Activists Reflect on the Short-Lived Revolution That Was Gay Liberation Front. *New York Blade News*. June 4.

Bogad, L. M. (2005). *Guerilla Electoral Theater: Radical Ridicule and Social Movements*. New York: Routledge.

Bordowitz, G. (2002). Oral History with the ACT UP Oral History Project. Accessed December 26, 2010, from http://www.actuporalhistory.org/interviews/interviews_01.html#bordowitz.

Borja-Villel, M., Valazquez, T., and Bringas, T. D. (2014). Foreword. *Playgrounds, Reinventing the Square*. Museo National Centro De Arte. Reina Sophia. Siruela. Madrid.

Bronfenbrenner, U. (1979). *The Ecology of Human Development*. Cambridge, MA: Harvard University Press.

Brown, A. M. (2004). I Hate Politics: Confessions of a Pleasure Activist. In A. M. Brown and W. U. Wimsatt (eds.), *How to Get Stupid White Men Out of Office:*

The Anti-Politics, Unboring Guide to Power, pp. 18–27. Brooklyn, NY: Soft Skull Press.

Brown, A. M. (2009). Interview with Adrienne Maree Brown: Voices of Climate Justice. *Race, Poverty and Environment: A Journal for Social and Environmental Justice* 16(2). Retrieved July 13, 2011, from http://urbanhabitat.org/cj/brown.

Brown, G. (2007). Mutinous Eruptions: Autonomous Spaces of Radical Queer Activism. *Environment and Planning* (39): 2685–98.

Buber, M. (1984). *I and Thou*. Trans. Ronald Gregor-Smith. New York: Scribner.

Buck-Morris, S. (1977). *The Origins of Negative Dialectics: Theodor Adorno, Walter Benjamin, and the Frankfurt Institute*. New York: Free Press.

Butters, S. (1983). The Logic of Inquiry of Participant Observation. In S. Hall and T. Jefferson (eds.), *Resistance through Rituals: Youth Subcultures in Post-War Britain*, pp. 253–73. London: Hutchinson University Library.

Calder, R. (2013). $40,000 Booby Prize: Breast Gal Tops NYPD in Suit. *New York Post*. October 30, 2013, pp. 1, 7.

Carlsson, C. (2008). *Nowtopia*. Oakland, CA: AK Press.

Carneiro, R. (2000). The Transition from Quantity to Quality: A Neglected Causal Mechanism in Accounting for Social Evolution. *Proceedings of the National Academy of the Sciences of the United States of America*. 10.1073/pnas. 240462397.

Cauvin, H. (1998). Activists Bugged by City Land Auction. *Daily News*. July 2.

Cavalieri, W. (2010). E-mail correspondence with the author. December.

Caygil, H., Coles, A., and Klimowski, A. (1998). *Introducing Walter Benjamin*. London: Icon Books.

Centers for Disease Control. (2020). COVID-19 in Racial and Ethnic Minority Groups. June 25. Accessed https://www.cdc.gov/coronavirus/2019-ncov/need-extra-precautions/racial-ethnic-minorities.html.

Chateavert, M. (2014). *Sex Workers Unite! A History of the Movement from Stonewall to Slutwalk*. Boston, MA: Beacon Press.

Chayko, M. (2008). *Portable Communities: The Social Dynamics of Online and Mobile Connectedness*. New York: State University Press of New York.

Church Ladies Song Book. (2005). Accessed December 1, 2005, from http://www.churchladies.org/.

City Council, New York. (2014). The Right of Way for Pedestrians and Cyclists. Accessed January 30 from http://legistar.council.nyc.gov/LegislationDetail. aspx?ID=1688022&GUID=5BE864B6-D4CE-434F-88CF-D720F543B6AC& Options=&Search=.

Cleaver, H. (1993). Kropotkin, Self-Valorization, and the Crisis of Marxism. *Anarchist Studies*. https://la.utexas.edu/users/hcleaver/kropotkin.html.

Clench, J. (2020). Facebook post.

Coates, J. (2003). *Ecology and Social Work*. Halifax: Fernwood Books.

Colon, D. (2020). Good News: The Jay Street Busway Starts on Aug 31. *Streetsblog*. August 26. Accessed from https://nyc.streetsblog.org/2020/08/25/good-news-the-jay-street-busway-starts-on-aug-31/.

Conquergood, D. (2002). Performance Studies, Interventions and Radical Research. *The Drama Review* 46(2): T174.

Critchley, S. (2002). *On Humour*. London: Routledge.

Crimethinc. (2017). Fighting for Our Lives: An Anarchist Primer. Accessed from https://crimethinc.com/2017/11/28/fighting-for-our-lives-an-anarchist-primer.

Crimp, D. (2002). *Melancholia and Moralism*. Boston, MA: MIT Press.

Crow, S. (2014). *Black Flags and Windmills*. Oakland, CA: PM Press.

Dann, K. (2020). *Enchanted New York: A Journey along Broadway through Manhattan's Magical Past*. New York: NYU Press.

Danzig, A. (2020). Correspondence with the author.

Davis, M. (1990). *City of Quartz*. New York: Verso.

Davenport, C., et al. (2015). Greenland Is Melting Away. *The New York Times*. 27 October. https://www.nytimes.com/interactive/2015/10/27/world/greenland-is-melting-away.html.

David. (2015). Rentboy Was Closed Because the Government Thinks I Need to Be Saved. *The Guardian*. 7 September. www.guardian.com.

Day, Richard. (2005). *Gramsci Is Dead*. London: Pluto Press.

Dehkan, A. (2015). Seven Gardens to Be Destroyed by HPD. 31 December. http://nyccgc.org/2015/12/seven-gardens-to-be-destroyed-by-hpd/.

Deleuze, G., and Guattiari, F. (1983). *Anti Oedipus: Capitalism and Schizophrenia*. Minneapolis: University of Minnesota Press.

Demos, T. J. (2015). Playful Protestors Use Art to Highlight the Inadequacy of the Paris Climate Talks. *Truthout.org*. https://truthout.org/articles/playful-protesters-use-art-to-draw-attention-to-inadequacy-of-paris-climate-talks/.

Douglas, G. (2015). Bike Lanes and Other Acts of Civic Improvement through Civil-Disobedience. Accessed November 15 from https://www.architectmagazine.com/design/guerrilla-bike-lanes-and-other-acts-of-civic-improvement-through-civil-disobedience_o.

DuBrul, S A. (2013). *Maps to the Other Side: Adventures of a Bipolar Cartographer*. New York: Microcosm.

Duggan, K. (2020). City Launches Busway on Jay Street. *Brooklyn Paper*. September 1. https://www.brooklynpaper.com/jay-street-busway-launch/.

Duggan, L. (2004). *The Twilight of Equality*. Boston, MA: Beacon Press.

Duncombe, S. (1997). *Notes from the Underground. Zines and the Politics of Underground Culture*. New York: Verso.

Duncombe, S. (2002). Introduction. In S. Duncombe (ed.), *Cultural Resistance: A Reader*, pp. 1–15. New York: Verso.

Duncombe, S. (2007). *Dream*. New York: New Press.

Eco, U. (1976/1886). *Travels in Hyperreality*. New York: Harvest HBJ.

Ehrenreich, B. (2007). *Dancing in the Streets*. New York: Metropolitan Books.

Eiland, H., and Jennings, M. (2014). *Walter Benjamin: A Critical Life*. Cambridge: Harvard University Press.

Einstein, A. (2013). How I See the World. Accessed January 2 from http://www.knowledgeoftoday.org/2013/01/albert-einstein-how-i-see-world.html.

Eizenberg, E. (2013). *From the Ground Up: Community Gardens in New York City and the Politics of Spatial Transformation*. Burlington: Ashgate.

Ellis, C., and Bochner, A.P. (2000). Autoethnography, Personal Narrative, Reflexivity: Researcher as Subject. In N. Denzin and Y. Lincoln (eds.), *The Handbook of Qualitative Research*, 2nd ed., pp. 733–68. Thousand Oaks, CA: Sage.

Engels, F. (1877). Anti-Dühring. https://www.marxists.org/archive/marx/works/1877/anti-duhring/introduction.htm#022.

Engels, F. (1886). Ludwig Feuerbach and the End of German Philosophy. https://www.marxists.org/archive/marx/works/1886/ludwig-feuerbach/.

Escoffier, J. (n.d.). Herbert Marcuse. Encyclopedia of LGBTQ Culture. Accessed July 30, 2009, from http://www.glbtqarchive.com/ssh/marcuse_h_S.pdf.

Feinberg, D. (1994). *Queer and Loathing: Rants and Raves of a Raging AIDS Activist*. New York: Viking Press.

Ferguson, S. (1999). A Brief History of Grassroots Gardening in NYC. In Peter Lamborn Wilson and Bill Weinberg (eds.), *Avant Gardening*. New York: Autonomedia.

Ferguson, S. (2015). Gardens Now Seen as Key Part of Future Storm Defense Plan. *The Villager*. Accessed November 5 from http://thevillager.com/2015/11/05/gardens-now-seen-as-key-part-of-future-storm-defense-plan/.

Fifth Estate unsigned editorial. (2008). Party Like It's 1929. *Fifth Estate* 43(3): 3.

Figueroa, R. (n.d.). Friends of Brook Park. Retrieved February 27, 2012, from http://www.benjaminheimshepard.com/.

Firestone, S. (1970). *The Dialectic of Sex*. New York: Farrar, Strauss, and Giroux.

Fitch, R. (1993). *The Assassination of New York*. New York: Verso.

Fitzsimmons, E. (2020). More Pedestrians and Cyclists are Dying in N.Y.C. Drivers Are Often to Blame. Drivers—Careless, Distracted, Going Too Fast—Are Usually Responsible for the Growing Death Toll. *The New York Times*. March 10. https://www.nytimes.com/2020/03/10/nyregion/nyc-deaths-pedestrian-cycling.html.

Foster, J. B. (2000). *Marx's Ecology: Materialism and Nature*. New York: Monthly Review Press.

Foster, J. B. (2015). Marx and Ecology: Common Threads and a Great Transition. *Monthly Review*. December. http://monthlyreview.org/2015/12/01/marxism-and-ecology/.

Fraser, S. (2012). The Hollowing Out of America. *The Nation*. Accessed December 3 from http://www.thenation.com/article/hollowing-out-america/.

Freeman, J. (1972). Tyranny of Structurelessness. Pamphlet by the Anarchist Workers Association. Accessed June 1, 2009, from http://www.christiebooks.com/PDFs/The%20Tyranny%20of%20Structurelessness.pdf.

Freire, P. (1970). *Pedagogy of the Oppressed*. New York: Continuum International.

Frey, N. L. (1998). *Pilgrim Tales: On and Off the Road to Santiago: Journeys along an Ancient Way in Modern Spain*. Berkeley: University of California Press.

Fried, B. (2013). The Origins of Holland's "Stop Murdering Children" Street Safety Movement. February 20. *Streetsblog*. Accessed January 30 from http://streetsblog.net/2013/02/20/the-origins-of-hollands-stop-murdering-children-street-safety-movement/.

Friends of the Church of Stop Shopping. (2014). Petitioning District Attorney Cyrus Vance Jr. Reverend Billy Faces One Year in Jail, Asks for Petition Signatures. Accessed December 8, 2014, from https:// www.change.org/p/reverend-billy-faces-one-year-in-jail-asks-for-petition-signatures.

Furness, Z. (2010). *One Less Car*. Philadelphia, PA: Temple University Press.

Gamson, J. (2005). *The Fabulous Sylvester*. New York: Henry Holt and Company.

Gilloch, G. (2002). *Walter Benjamin: Critical Constellations*. London: Polity Press.

Goldman, E. (1916). Birth Control. *The Emma Goldman Papers*. Accessed January 29, 2008, from edu/Goldman/Curricula/WomensRights/letter.html.

Goldman, E. (1923/2001). Letter to Dr. Hirschfeld. In C. Bull (ed.), *Come Out Fighting*, pp. 3–6. New York: Nation Books.

Goldman, E. (1931). *Living My Life*. http://theanarchistlibrary.org/library/emma-goldman-living-my-life.

Goldman, E. (1969). *Anarchism and Other Essays*. New York: Dover.

Goldstein, R. (2002). *The Attack Queers*. New York: Verso.

Gonzalves, G. (2020). Facebook post.

Goodwin, J.; Jasper, J.; and Polletta, F. (2001). *Passionate Politics: Emotions and Social Movements*. Minneapolis: University of Minnesota Press.

Gordan, D. (2015). Guerrilla Bike Lanes and Other Acts of Civil Improvement through Civil Disobedience. Accessed from http://www.spontaneousinterventions.org/reading/guerrilla-bike-lanes-and-other-acts-of-civic-improvement-through-civil-disobedience.

Graeber, D. (2004a). The New Anarchists. In Tom Mertes (ed.), *Movement of Movements: Is Another World Really Possible?*, pp. 202–15. New York: Verso.

Graeber, D. (2004b). *Fragments of an Anarchist Anthropology*. Chicago, IL: Prickly Paradigm Press.

Gramsci, A. (1971). *Selections from the Prison Notebooks*. New York International Publishers.

Grant, M. (2013). *Playing the Whore: The Work of Sex Work*. New York: Verso.

Green, N. (1979). The Purple People. *New York Magazine*. August 27, 1979, pp. 64–72.

Grindstaff, M. (1998). Bioremediation of Chlorinated Solvent Contaminated Groundwater Prepared for U.S. EPA Technology Innovation Office. Accessed January 30 from https://clu-in.org/download/studentpapers/meganfin.pdf.

Grove, D. (2007, March 11). Harm Reduction [audio podcast]. Retrieved from http://theoccasionalfag.com/index.php?post_id=191044#.

Guerin, D. (1970). *Anarchism*. New York: Monthly Review Press.

Guerrilla Gardening. (2015). Seed Bombs: A Guide to Their Various Forms and Functions. http://www.guerrillagardening.org/ggseedbombs.html.

Gusfield, J. R. (1986). *The Symbolic Crusade*. Champaign: University of Illinois Press.

Hall, D. (2003). *Queer Theories*. New York: Palgrave Macmillan.

Halperin, D. M. (1995). *Saint-Foucault*. New York: Oxford University Press.

Halperin, S. (2020). Facebook post.

Hammett, J., and Hammett, K. (2007). *The Suburbanization of New York*. Princeton, NJ: Princeton Architectural Press.

Haraway, D. (1991). A Cyborg Manifesto: Science, Technology, and Socialist-Feminism in the Late Twentieth Century. In *Simians, Cyborgs and Women: The Reinvention of Nature*, pp. 149–181. New York: Routledge.

Harpignies, J. P. (2009). 1969 episode. Correspondence with the author. 22 May.

Harstock, N. (1998). *The Feminist Standpoint Revisited and Other Essays*. Boulder, CO: Westview Press.

Harvey, D. (2005). *A History of Neoliberalism*. New York: Oxford University Press.

Harvey, D. (2013). *Rebel Cities*. New York: Verso.

Heckert, J. (2006). The Anarchy of Queer: Rethinking Poststructuralist Possibilities and the Politics of Sexuality. http://www.anarchist-studies-network.org.uk/documents/The_Anarchy_of_Queer.pdf.

Hegeman, R. (2009). Kan. Abortion Doc Killed in Church; Suspect Held. Accessed April 15, 2021, from https://siouxcityjournal.com/news/kan-abortion-doc-killed-in-church-suspect-held/article_440e7ff3-3725-5a34-bd20-30a22f8b05c0.html.

Hembrow, D. (2011). Stop Child Murder. January 10. http://www.aviewfromthecyclepath.com/2011/01/stop-child-murder.html.

Hertzberg, H. (2003). Northern Light. *The New Yorker*. July 7. p. 24.

Hessle, S. (2014). *Environmental Change and Sustainable Social Development: Social Work-Social Development Volume II*. Surrey: Ashgate.

Heywood, C. (1989). *Touching Our Strength*. San Francisco, CA: Harper Perennial.

Highleyman, L. (1988/1995). An Introduction to Anarchism. Accessed May 24, 2009, from http://www.black-rose.com/articles-liz/intro-@.html.

Holleman, H. (2015). Method in Ecological Marxism: Science and the Struggle for Change. *Monthly Review*. October. http://monthlyreview.org/2015/10/01/ method-in-ecological-marxism/.

Hollibaugh, A. (2000). *My Dangerous Desires*. Durham, NC: Duke University Press.

Holt, J. (2008). *Stop Me If You've Heard This One Before*. New York: W.W. Norton.

Holt, M., and Treloar, C. (2008). Pleasure and Drugs. *International Journal of Drug Policy* 19: 349–52.

Holtzman, B., Hughes, C., and Van Meter, K. (2004). Do It Yourself . . . and the Movement beyond Capitalism. *Radical Society* 31(1): 7–20.

Horton, D. (2006). Environmentalism and the Bicycle. *Environmental Politics* 15(1): 41–58.

Howard, S. (2006). Interview with the author.

Huizinga, J. (1950 [1938]). *Homo Ludens: A Study of the Play Element in Culture*. Boston, MA: Beacon.

Humm, A. (2009). Police Charged with False Arrests of Gay Men at Adult Video Stores. *The Gotham Gazette*. February 2.

Invisible Committee. (2015). *To Our Friends*. Boston, MA: MIT Press.

Irwin, W. (2002). *The Matrix and Philosophy: Welcome to the Desert of the Real*. Chicago, IL: Open Court.

Jacobs, J. (1961/1992). *The Death and Life of Great American Cities*. New York: Vantage.

Johnson, C. (2008). Liberty, Equality, Solidarity: Toward a Dialectical Anarchism. In Roderick T. Long and Tibor R. Machan (eds.), *Anarchism/Minarchism*. London: Routledge.

Jones, C. (2020). Facebook post.

Juris, J. (2007). Practicing Militant Ethnography. In S. Shukaitis and D. Graeber (eds.), *Constituent Imagination: Militant Investigations/Collective Theorization in the Global Justice Movement*, pp. 164–78. Oakland, CA: AK Press.

Kattalia, K. (2011). A Threat to Local Gardens. *The New York Times*. Retrieved April 27, 2011, from http://eastvillage.thelocal.nytimes.com/2011/04/27/athreat-to-local-gardens/.

Kauffman, L. A. (2004). A Short, Personal History of the Global Justice Movement. In E. Yuen, D. Burton-Rose, and G. Katsiaficas (eds.), *Confronting Capitalism: Dispatches from a Global Movement*, pp. 275–88. New York: Soft Skull Press.

Kauffman, L. A. (2014). Interview with the author. November.

Kauffman, L. A. (2020). Facebook post.

Kearney, S. (2014). "The Community Garden as a Tool for Community Empowerment: A Study of Community Gardens in Hampden County" (2009). Master's Theses 1896—February 2014. Accessed 30 January from Paper 361. http://scholarworks.umass.edu/theses/361.

Kennedy, K. E. P., Grov, C., and Parsons, J. T. (2010). Ecstasy and Sex among Young Heterosexual Women: A Qualitative Analysis of Sensuality, Sexual Effects, and Sexual Risk Taking. *International Journal of Sexual Health* 22(3): 155–66.

Kimmelman, M. (2013). In Istanbul's Heart, Leader's Obsession, Perhaps Achilles' Heel. *New York Times*. June 7.

Kirsch, Max H. (2000). *Queer Theory and Social Change*. New York: Routledge.

Kissack, T. (2008). *Free Comrades: Anarchism and Homosexuality in the United States, 1895–1917*. Oakland, CA: AK Press.

Klein, N. (2002). *Fences and Windows*. Debate. New York: Picador.

Klein, N. (2015). Why a Climate Deal Is the Best Hope for Peace. *The New Yorker*. November 18. http://www.newyorker.com/news/news-desk/why-a-climate-deal-is-the-best-hope-for-peace?intcid=mod-latest.

Knight, L. (2006). Garbage and Democracy. *Journal of Community Practice* 14(3): 7–27.

Koehnlein, B. (2015). Subject: [Bk-list] Remembering Murray Bookchin. Date: December 2, 2015. To: Bk-list <bk-list@lists.mayfirst.org>.

Komanoff, C. (2012). The Bicycle Uprising. *Streetsblog*. http://www.komanoff.net/bicycle/Bicycle_Uprising.pdf.

Komanoff, C., and Members of Right of Way. (1999). *Killed by Automobile: Death in the Streets in New York City 1994–1997*. Accessed April 15, 2021, from http://www.komanoff.net/cars_I/KBA_entire_2015.pdf.

Kovel, J. (2007). *The Enemy of Nature: The End of Capitalism or the End of the World*. New York: Zed Books.

Kropotkin, P. (1987 [1902]). Mutual Aid: A Factor of Evolution. https://www.marxists.org/reference/archive/kropotkin-peter/1902/mutual-aid/introduction.htm.

Kurosawa, A. (Director). (1954). *Shichinin no samurai [Seven samurai; motion picture]*. Japan: Toho.

Lamborn Wilson, P., and Weinberg, B. (eds.). (1999). *Avant Gardening: Ecological Struggle in the City and the World*. Brooklyn: Autonomedia.

Laqueur, Thomas. (2003). *Solitary Sex*. New York: MIT Press/Zone Books.

Laursen, Eric. (2020). Remembering David Graeber., https://indypendent.org/2020/09/remembering-david-graeber-scholar-troublemaker-friend/.

Lefebvre, H. (1996). *Writings on Cities*, E. Kofman and E. Lebas (trans. and eds.). Oxford: Basil Blackwell.

Lefebvre, H. (2014). *Critique of Everyday Life: The One-Volume Edition*. New York: Verso.

Lenin, V. (1976). *Collected Works*, 4th ed., vol. 38. Moscow: Progress Publishers, pp. 247–68. Accessed from https://www.marxists.org/archive/lenin/works/1915/cons-lect/ch02.htm.

Linebaugh, P. (2014). *Stop Thief! The Commons, Enclosures and Resistance*. Oakland, CA: PM Press.

Logan, J. R., and Molotch, H. L. (1987). *Urban Fortunes: The Political Economy of Place*. Berkeley: University of California Press.

Lopez, G. (2014). What I Meant to Say. https://verdantcities.wordpress.com/2014/09/08/what-i-meant-to-say/.

Lukács, G. (1968). *History and Class Consciousness: Studies in Marxist Dialectics*. Boston, MA: MIT Press.

Lukács, G. (1975). *The Young Hegel: Studies in the Relations between Dialectics and Economics*. Boston, MA: MIT Press.

Luxemburg, R. (1915). The Junius Pamphlet: The Crisis of German Social Democracy. https://www.marxists.org/archive/luxemburg/1915/junius/.

MacNicol, Glynnis. (2016). The New York You Once Knew Is Gone. The One You Loved Remains. *The New York Times*. April 16.

Maffesoli, M. (1993). *The Shadow of Dionysus: A Contribution to the Sociology of Orgy*. Albany: State University of New York Press.

Maffesoli, M. (1996). *The Time of the Tribes: The Decline of Individualism in Mass Society*. Thousand Oaks, CA: Sage Press.

Malina, J. (1984). *The Diaries of Judith Malina, 1947–57*. New York: Grove Press.

Marcuse, H. (1955). *Eros and Civilization*. Boston, MA: Beacon Press.

Marcuse, H. (1941/1960). *Reason and Revolution: Hegel and the Rise of Social Theory*. Boston, MA: Beacon Press.

Marcuse, H. (1973). On the Philosophical Foundation of the Concept of Labor in Economics. *Télos* (16): 9–37.

Martin, J. (1973). *The Dialectical Imagination*. New York: Little Brown.

Marx, K. (1844). Economic and Philosophical Manuscripts. Accessed from https://www.marxists.org/archive/marx/works/1844/manuscripts/preface.htm.

Marx, K. (1845). Theses on Feuerbach. https://www.marxists.org/archive/marx/works/1845/theses/theses.htm.

Marx, K. (1848). The Manifesto of the Communist Party. https://www.marxists.org/archive/marx/works/1848/communist-manifesto/index.htm.

Marx, K. (1973). *Grundrisse: Foundations of the Critique of Political Economy*. New York: Penguin Classics.

Marx, K., and Engels, F. (1846/1970). *The German Ideology*. New York: International Publishers.

Massumi, B. (1987). Foreword to *A Thousand Plateaus: Capitalism and Schizophrenia*. Minneapolis: University of Minnesota Press.

Mattilda aka Matt Bernstein Sycamore. (2004). Gay Shame. In Matt Bernstein Sycamore (ed.), *That's Revolting*. Brooklyn, NY: Soft Skull Press.

Mayor Bloomberg's townhouse. *New York Daily News*. Retrieved July 15, 2011, from http://www.nydailynews.com/ny_local/2010/07/29/2010–0729_cyclists_advocacy_group_times_up_plans_to_protest_outside_mayor_bloombergs_townh.html.

McAdam, D. (1996). The Framing Function of Movement Tactics. In Doug McAdam, John McCarthy, and Mayer Zald (Eds.), *Comparative Perspectives on Social Movements*, pp. 338–56. Cambridge: Cambridge University Press.

McKay, G. (ed.). (1998). *DiY Culture: Party and Protest in Nineties Britain*. London: Verso.

McKay, G. (2011). *Radical Gardening: Politics, Idealism, and Rebellion in the Garden*. London: Frances Lincoln.

McKinley, J. (1997). Neighborhood Report: East Village Fax Attack Puts Garden Defender in Legal Paper Jam. *The New York Times*. November 23. http://www.nytimes.com/1997/11/23/nyregion/neighborhood-report-east-village-fax-attack-puts-garden-defender-legal-paper-jam.html.

McKinley, J. (1998). Adam Purple's Last Stand. *The New York Times*. February 22, 1998. "The City," Section 14, pp. 1, 10.

McLaughlin, P. (2002). *Mikhail Bakunin: The Philosophical Basis of His Anarchism*. New York: Algora.

McLemee, S. (2009). Fifty Years after Stonewall. *Inside Higher Ed.* 25 June. Accessed June 26, 2009, from http://www.insidehighered.com/views/mclemee/mclemee247.

McWilliams, N. (2004). *Psychoanalytic Psychotherapy: A Practitioner's Guide*. New York: Guilford Press.

Merrifield, A. (2002a). *Metromarxism: A Marxist Tale of the City*. New York: Routledge.

Merrifield, A. (2002b). *Dialectical Urbanism*. New York: Monthly Review Press.

Merrifield, A. (2014). *The New Urban Question*. London: Pluto Press.

Meyers, C. (2015). Personal correspondence with the author.

Milano, M. (2020). Facebook post.

Mitchell, D. (2003). *Right to the City: Social Justice and the Fight for Public Space*. New York: Guilford Press.

More Gardens! (2002). *How to Save Your Community Garden!* By the More Gardens Coalition. Zine.

Morreall, J. (1987). *The Philosophy of Laughter and Humor*. New York: State University Press of New York.

Morreall, J. (2012). Philosophy of Humor. *Stanford Encyclopedia of Philosophy*. http://plato.stanford.edu/entries/humor/#Inc.

Morse, C. (2015). Ecology or Catastrophe: The Life of Murray Bookchin. *Institute for Anarchist Studies*. November 23. https://anarchiststudies.org/2015/11/23/ecology-or-catastrophe-the-life-of-murray-bookchin-by-janet-biehl-review-by-chuck-morse/.

Moynihan, C. (2010a). New Rules Worry Community Garden Advocates. *The New York Times*. July 6. Retrieved July 15, 2011, from http://cityroom.blogs.nytimes.com/2010/07/06/impending-rules-worry-some-community-gardeners/?emc=eta1. ENVIRONMENTAL.

Moynihan, C. (2010b). The Bulldozers Are Coming: Garden Crusaders Hop on Their Bikes. *The New York Times*. August 1. Retrieved July 15, 2011, from http://www.nytimes.com/2010/08/02/nyregion/02gardens.html?_r=1&ref=nyregion.

Murphy, T. (2020). This Trio Took Care of the Bronx's Homeless Drug Users Through the Worst Months of COVID-19. *The Body*. August 26. https://www.thebody.com/

article/bronx-movil-homeless-drug-users-covid-19?fbclid=IwAR0aaDtnZCpkrka EG5HDSZ90EOqHnyiBXveEMX8E_73wuou6I3LQ3DssKeI.

Myerhoff, B., and Ruby, J. (1982/1992). A Crack in the Mirror: Reflective Perspectives Anthropology. In *Remembered Lives: The Work of Ritual, Storytelling, and Growing Older*, pp. 307–40. Ann Arbor: University of Michigan Press.

Negri, A. (1991). *Marx beyond Marx: Lessons on the Grundrisse*. Brooklyn, NY: Autonomedia.

Nettle, C. (2014). *Community Gardening as Social Action*. New York: Routledge.

Neuman, S. (2020). Medical Examiner's Autopsy Reveals George Floyd Had Positive Test for Coronavirus. *NPR*. June 4. https://www.npr.org/sections/live-updates-protests-for-racial-justice/2020/06/04/869278494/medical-examiners-autopsy-reveals-george-floyd-had-positive-test-for-coronavirus.

The New York Times. (2020). New York City Coronavirus Map and Case Count. Updated July 7. https://www.nytimes.com/interactive/2020/nyregion/new-york-city-coronavirus-cases.html.

The New York Times Editorial. (2010). Keeping the Gardens Green. *The New York Times*. August 2. Retrieved July 15, 2011, from http://www.nytimes.com/2010/08/03/opinion/03tue4.html.

NHS. (2014). Cycling Safety Special Report. http://www.nhs.uk/news/2014/02February/Pages/Cycling-safety-a-special-report.aspx#danger.

Nicolaus, M. (1973). Foreword and translation. *Grundrisse*. By Karl Marx. New York: Penguin Books.

Notes From Nowhere (eds). (2003). *We Are Everywhere*. London: Verso.

Nova, J. (2009). Correspondence with the author. May 31.

NPR. (2015). Here and Now. Rapidly Melting ICE. September 12, 2015.

NYCCGC. (2015). NYC-Gardens Coalition Announcing Gardens Rising. October 29.

Nye, B. (2011). The Climate Reality Project. https://www.climaterealityproject.org/climate-101.

Nyong'o, Tavia. (2008). Do You Want Queer Theory (Or Do You Want the Truth)? Intersections of Punk and Queer in the '70s. *Radical History Review* (100): 103–20.

O'Kelly, Kathleen. (1993a). Review: Everything You Ever Wanted to Know about Anarchism. *Workers Solidarity*, no. 38. Accessed January 1, 2002, from http://surf.to/anarchism.

O'Kelly, Kathleen. (1993b). New Law Aids Pimps and Protection Rackets. *Workers Solidarity*, no. 40. Accessed January 1, 2002, from http://surf.to/anarchism.

Ollman, B. (1976). *Alienation: Marx's Conception of Man in Capitalist Society*, 2nd ed. Cambridge: Cambridge University Press.

Ollman, B. (2003). *Dance of the Dialectic: Steps in Marx's Method*. Urbana: University of Illinois Press.

Ollman, B. (2016). Seven Essential Steps in Marx's Dialectical Method. *The Marxist Education Project*. January 13.

Orange, R. (2013). How Safe Are the World's Cities for Cyclists? *The Guardian*. November 20. http://www.theguardian.com/lifeandstyle/2013/nov/20/how-safe-are-worlds-cities-for-cyclists.

Ornstein, C. (1998). *Festive Revolutions*. Oxford: University Press of Mississippi.

Osborne, D. (2009). Bloomberg's Home Targeted in False Arrests Protest. *Gay City News*. February 14.

Pace, Natalie. (2015). Who's Got the Power? We've Got the Power! October 15, 2015. http://www.huffingtonpost.com/natalie-pace/whos-got-the-power-weve-g_b_8297920.html.

Paisner, Allison. (2015). Five Reasons Why You Should be Promoting Urban Agriculture in Your City. May 9. www.publicceo.com/2015/05/five-reasons-you-should-be-promoting-urban-agriculture-in-your-city/.

Pensky, Max. (2001). *Melancholy Dialectics: Walter Benjamin and the Play of Mourning*. Amherst: University of Massachusetts Press.

Peterman, Anne. (2020). Mutual Aid Disaster Relief One Minute Video. https://globaljusticeecology.org/mutual-aid-disaster-relief-one-minute-video/.

Phenix, L. M., and Selver, V. (1985). *You Got to Move*. Cumberland Mountain Educational Cooperative.

Powers et al. (2013). Social Work Education in the Era of Global Environmental Crisis. *Council on Social Work Education Global Social Work—The World Is Here*. November 2. Dallas, TX.

Purple, A. (2006). Adam Purple Interviewed by Amy Brost—StoryCorps Oral History Project. November 22. http://classic.harveywang.com/podcast.html.

Pyles, L., and Adam, G. (eds.). (2016). *Holistic Engagement: Transformative Social Work Education in the 21st Century*. New York: Oxford University Press.

Ralson, W. (2020). Oslo Got Pedestrian and Cyclist Deaths Down to Zero. Here's How. November 18. https://www.wired.co.uk/article/oslo-pedestrianisation.

Raya, R., and Rubin, V. (2006). Safety, Growth, and Equity: Parks and Open Space. *Policy Link*. Retrieved July 14, 2011, from http://www.scribd.com/doc/34475582/Safety-Growth-And-Equity-Parks-and-Open-Space-Introduction.

Read, B. (2020). What's Going on in the CHOP, the Seattle Occupied Protest Zone? https://www.thecut.com/2020/07/whats-going-on-in-chaz-the-seattle-autonomous-zone.html.

Reich, W. (1980). *The Mass Psychology of Fascism*. New York: Farrer, Strauss and Giroux.

RHA. (2008). Presentation at New York Anarchist Bookfair. Judson Memorial Church, New York.

Rhodes, C. (2014). Mycoremediation (Bioremediation with Fungi)—Growing Mushrooms to Clean the Earth. A Mini-Review. *Chemical Speciation & Bioavailability*. Accessed January 30 from https://www.tandfonline.com/doi/abs/10.3184/0954229 14X14047407349335.

Rilke, R. M. (1934). *Letters to a Young Poet*. New York: Norton.

Ritchie, N. (2008). Principles of Engagement: The Anarchist Influence on Queer Youth Cultures. In S. Driver (ed.), *Queer Youth Cultures*, pp. 261–78. Albany, NY: SUNY Press.

Rogue, J., and Shannon, D. (2008). Call for Papers: "Queering Anarchism." Accessed August 18, 2009, from http://www.goodreads.com/story/show/22002.Queering_Anarchism.

Rubin, G. (1975). The Traffic of Women: Notes on the Political Economy of Sex. In R. Reiter (ed.), *Toward an Anthropology of Women*, pp. 157–210. New York: Monthly Review Press.

Russell, T. (2010). *A Renegade History of the United States*. New York: Free Press.

SAMHSA. (2020). Double Jeopardy: COVID-19 and Behavioral Health Disparities for Black and Latino Communities in the U.S. https://www.samhsa.gov/sites/default/files/covid19-behavioral-health-disparities-black-latino-communities.pdf.

Sanders, B. (1996). *Sudden Glory: Laughter as Subversive History*. Boston, MA: Beacon.

Savitri, D., and Talen, B. (2011). *The Reverend Billy Project: From Rehearsal Hall to the Super Mall with the Church of Life after Shopping*. Ann Arbor: University of Michigan Press.

Sawyer, E. (2002). An ACT UP Founder "Act's Up" for Africa's Access to AIDS. In Benjamin Shepard and Ron Hayduk (eds.), *From ACT UP to the WTO: Urban Protest and Community Building in the Era of Globalization*, pp. 89–90. New York: Verso Press.

Sayer, D. (2013). *Prague: Capital of the 20th Century*. Princeton, NJ: Princeton University Press.

Schaper, D. (2007). *Grassroots Gardening*. New York: Nation Books.

Schaper, D. (2015). COP21 and the resilience of skateboarders. Eco Catholic. Accessed December 5, from https://www.ncronline.org/blogs/earthbeat/eco-catholic/cop21-and-resilience-skateboarders.

Schechner, R. (2002). *Performance Studies: An Introduction*. New York: Routledge.

Schreiber (2020). Paul Schreiber <paulschreiber@gmail.com> transaltbrooklyn@googlegroups.com.

[TABK] Wired UK: Oslo Got Pedestrian and Cyclist Deaths Down to Zero. Here's How. November 24.

Sears, D. (1977). *The Sex Radicals*. Lawrence: Regents Press of Kansas.

Sedgwick, E. (1990). *Epistemology of the Closet*. Berkeley: University of California Press.

Seeger, P. (2001). *The Songs of Pete Seeger, Vol. 2*. West Chester, PA: Appleseed Records.

SFLA. (2007). Students for Life—How to Organize a Vigil at an Abortion Clinic. Accessed May 26, 2009, from http://www.studentsforlife.org/index.php/resources/organize-an-event/organizeavigilatanabortionclinic/.

Shepard, B. (1997). *White Nights and Ascending Shadows: An Oral History of the San Francisco AIDS Epidemic*. London: Cassell Press.

Shepard, B. (2002). Introductory Notes on the Trail from ACT UP to the WTO. In B. Shepard and R. Hayduk (eds.), *From ACT UP to the WTO: Urban Protest and Community Building in the Era of Globalization*, pp. 11–20. New York: Verso.

Shepard, B. (2009). *Queer Political Performance and Protest: Play, Pleasure and Social Movement*. New York: Routledge.

Shepard, B. (2011). *Play, Creativity and Social Movements: If I Can't Dance It's Not My Revolution*. New York: Routledge.

Shepard, B. (2013). From Flooded Neighborhoods to Sustainable Urbanism. *Socialism and Democracy* 27(2): 42–46.

Shepard, B. (2013–2015). Right of Way Field notes. In possession of this author.

Shepard, B. (2014). *Community Projects as Social Activism: From Direct Action to Direct Services*. Thousand Oaks: Sage.

Shepard, B., and Hayduk, R (eds). (2002). *From ACT UP to the WTO: Urban Protest and Community Building in the Era of Globalization*. New York: Verso.

Shepard, B., and Smithsimon, G. (2011). *The Beach Beneath the Streets: Contesting New York's Public Spaces*. New York: SUNY Press.

Shepard, B., Totten, V., and Homans, M. (2012). The Human Services Response to Social Problems—How, Who, and Why. Plenary Address National Organization of Human Services Conference. Milwaukee, WI.

Shively, C. (1974/2001). Indiscriminate Promiscuity as an Act of Revolution. In C. Bull (ed.), *Come Out Fighting*. New York: Nation Books.

Shukaitis, S. (2009). *Imaginal Machines*, pp. 13–14. Brooklyn: Autonomedia.

Shukaitis, S., and Graeber, D. (2007). *Constituent Imagination: Research + Resistance in the Global Justice Movement*. Oakland, CA: AK Press.

Showden, C., and Majic, S. M. (eds.). (2014). *Negotiating Sex Work: Unintended Consequences of Policy and Activism*, p. 336. Minneapolis: University of Minnesota Press.

Simon, S. (2020). Security Guard Cooks Meals for Homeless LGBTQ Young People. June 26. https://www.ny1.com/nyc/all-boroughs/news/2020/06/26/security-guard-cooks-meals-for-homeless-lgbtq-young-people.

Singh, N. P. (2004). *Black Is a Country*. Cambridge: Harvard University Press.

Sites, W. (2002). *Remaking New York*. Minneapolis: University of Minnesota Press.

Sitrin, M. (2020). *Introduction. To Pandemic Solidarity: Mutual Aid during the Covid-19 Crisis*. Sitrin, M., and Colectiva, S. (eds.) London: Pluto Press.

Sledge, M. (2014). Occupy Protesters Arrested for Satirizing Police Repression Reach $22,000 Settlement. *Huffpost Politics*. June 24. http://www.huffingtonpost.com/2014/06/24/occupy-protest-settlement_n_5527486.html.

Smith, D. (1998). "Queer Theory" Is Entering the Mainstream. *The New York Times*. January 17.

Smith, N. (1996). *The New Urban Frontier: Gentrification and the Revanchist City*. New York: Routledge.

Snow, D., and Trom, D. (2002). The Case Study of Social Movements. In B. Klandermans and S. Staggenborg (eds.), *Methods of Social Movement Research*. Minneapolis: University of Minnesota Press.

Soja, E. W. (1996). *Thirdspace: Journeys to Los Angeles and Other Real-and-Imagined Places*, p. 33, footnote 8. Malden, MA: Blackwell.

Solnit, D. (ed.). (2004). *Globalize Liberation*. San Francisco, CA: City Lights Press.

Solnit, R. (2010). *A Paradise Built in Hell*. New York: Penguin.

Solnit, R. (2020). The Way We Get through This Together: The Rise of Mutual Aid under Coronavirus. May 14. https://www.theguardian.com/world/2020/may/14/mutual-aid-coronavirus-pandemic-rebecca-solnit.

Spade, D. (2020). *Mutual Aid: Building Solidarity during This Crisis (and the Next)*. New York: Verso.

Spencer, A. (2005). *DIY: The Rise of Low-Fi Culture*. London: Marion Boyars.

Springer, E. (1991). Effective AIDS Prevention with Active Drug Users: The Harm Reduction Model. In M. Shernoff (ed.), *Counseling Chemically Dependent People with HIV/AIDS*, pp. 141–58. Binghamton, NY: Haworth Press.

Sproule, R. (2015). How Gardening Can be the Bomb. http://www.sherwoodpar-knews.com/2015/04/30/how-gardening-can-be-the-bomb.

Staley, Peter. (2020). Facebook post.

Stephan, K. (2013–2015). Press Statements and Testimony. http://www.rightofway.org/campaigns.

Stevens, J. (2005). Somatic Mind. *New Left Review*. 33. https://newleftreview.org/II/33/jacob-stevens-somatic-mind.

Sunshine, S. (2015). Interview with the author. October.

Tam, Paulina. (2020). In South Brooklyn, Volunteers Step in to Help Low-Income Residents Struggling during Pandemic. *ABC News*. May 25. https://abcnews.go.com/Health/south-brooklyn-volunteers-step-low-income-residents-struggling/story?id=70862506.

Tatchell, P. (1989). Freud and the Liberation of Human Desire. http://www.peter-tatchell.net/lgbt_rights/psychiatry/freud.htm.

Teal, D. (1971/1995). *The Gay Militants*. New York: St. Martin's Press.

Tedlock, B. (1991). From Participant Observation to Observation of Participation: The Emergence of Narrative Ethnography. *Journal of Anthropological Research* 47: 69–94.

Tent, P. (2004). *Midnight at the Palace*. Los Angeles, CA: Alyson Books.

Thorpe, D. (2014). The 12 Rules for Sustainable Urbanism. http://www.sustainab-lecitiescollective.com/david-thorpe/239556/12-rules-sustainable-urbanism.

Time's Up! (2010). Time's Up! Statement on the New Garden Rules. Retrieved July 17, 2011, from http://www.times-up.org.

Trahar, S. (2009). Beyond the Story Itself: Narrative Inquiry and Autoethnography in Intercultural Research in Higher Education. *Forum: Qualitative Social Research* 10(1). Accessed September 30, 2014, http://www.qualitative-research.net/index.php/fqs/article/view/1218/2653.

Transportation Alternatives. (2014). The Fight for a 25 Mile Per Hour Speed Limit. Accessed January 30 from http://www.transalt.org/issues/speeding/fight-for-a-25-mph-speed-limit.

Trotsky, L. (1924). Literature and Revolution. http://home.igc.org/~itobr/education/literature_&_revolution.pdf.

Tucker, K. H. (2012). *Workers of the World, Enjoy!* Philadelphia, PA: Temple University Press.

Vélez, A. (2004). Interview of Andrew Vélez. ACT UP Oral History Project. February 26, 2004.

Vitale, A. (2008). *City of Disorder*. New York: NYU Press.

Wagner, G. (2015). *Climate Shock: The Economic Consequences of a Hotter Planet*. Princeton, NJ: Princeton University Press.

Walker, J. (2020). 51 Years after Stonewall, New York's Queer Liberation March Faces Police Violence. *The Nation*. July 3. https://www.thenation.com/article/society/queer-liberation-march-police-violence/.

Warner, M. (1993). Introduction. In M. Warner (ed.), *Fear of a Queer Planet*, pp. vii–xxxi. Minneapolis: University of Minnesota Press.

Warner, M. (1999). *The Trouble with Normal*. New York: Free Press.

Weber, M. (2002). *The Protestant Ethic and the Spirit of Capitalism: And Other Writings*. Ed. Peter Baehr. Trans. Gordon C. Wells. New York: Penguin Classics.

Weichselbaum, S. (2010). Cyclists' Advocacy Group Time's Up! Plans to Protest Outside. July 29. *New York Daily News*.

Welsh, I. (1993/1996). *Trainspotting*. New York: W.W. Norton.

WeWantYou. (2009). Message to rha@lists.riseup.net Parade w/out a permit recap. June 22.

Wilson, P. L., and Weinberg, B. (eds.). (1999). *Avant Gardening: Ecological Struggle in the City and the World*. Brooklyn, NY: Autonomedia.

WNBR. (2010–2014). Notes on the New York City World Naked Bike Ride. Possession of the author.

Woodside, S. (2001). *Every Joke Is a Tiny Revolution*. Self-published manuscript.

Yin, R. K. (1994). *Case Study Research*, 2nd ed. Thousand Oaks, CA: Sage.

Zapf, M. K. (2009). *Social Work and the Environment: Understanding People and Place*. Toronto: Canadian Scholars' Press.

Zastrow, C. (2004). *Introduction to Social Work and Social Welfare*, 8th ed.. Belmont, TN: Brooks/Cole.

Ziff, A. (2012). Plant Sex and Why Diversity Matters. *Huffington Post*. September 27, 2012. http://www.huffingtonpost.com/amy-ziff/gmo-seeds_b_1910921.html.

Žižek, S. (2002). *Welcome to the Desert of the Real*. New York: Verso.

Zukin, S. (2004). *Point of Purchase: How Shopping Changed American Culture*. New York: Routledge.

Index

www.ingramcontent.com/pod-product-compliance
Lightning Source LLC
Chambersburg PA
CBHW050633280326
41932CB00015B/2627